READING MEMORY AND IDENTITY IN THE TEXTS OF MEDIEVAL EUROPEAN HOLY WOMEN

Edited by

Margaret Cotter-Lynch and Brad Herzog

READING MEMORY AND IDENTITY IN THE TEXTS OF MEDIEVAL EUROPEAN HOLY WOMEN
Copyright © Margaret Cotter-Lynch and Brad Herzog, 2012.

First published in 2012 by
PALGRAVE MACMILLAN®
in the United States—a division of St. Martin's Press LLC,
175 Fifth Avenue, New York, NY 10010.

Where this book is distributed in the UK, Europe and the rest of the world,
this is by Palgrave Macmillan, a division of Macmillan Publishers Limited,
registered in England, company number 785998, of Houndmills,
Basingstoke, Hampshire RG21 6XS.

Palgrave Macmillan is the global academic imprint of the above companies
and has companies and representatives throughout the world.

Palgrave® and Macmillan® are registered trademarks in the United States,
the United Kingdom, Europe and other countries.

ISBN: 978–0–230–61986–9

Library of Congress Cataloging-in-Publication Data

Reading memory and identity in the texts of medieval European holy
women / edited by Margaret Cotter-Lynch and Brad Herzog.
p. cm.—(New Middle Ages)
Includes bibliographical references.
ISBN 978–0–230–61986–9
1. Literature, Medieval—Women authors—History and criticism.
2. Literature, Medieval—Religious aspects—History and criticism.
3. Memory in literature. 4. Women and literature—History—Middle
Ages, 500–1500. I. Cotter-Lynch, Margaret, 1974- II. Herzog, Brad.

PN682.W6R37 2011
809'.89287—dc23   2011039088

A catalogue record of the book is available from the British Library.

Design by Newgen Imaging Systems (P) Ltd., Chennai, India.

First edition: April 2012

10 9 8 7 6 5 4 3 2 1

Printed in the United States of America.

For LaRee, Deverl, and Ginger
Mary-Alice, Jim, and Sean

CONTENTS

PREFACE

Cheryl Glenn

Sent from the Power,
I have come
to those who reflect upon me,
and I have been found
among those who seek me.
Look upon me,
you who meditate,
and hearers, hear.
Whoever is waiting for me,
take me into yourselves.
Do not drive me
out of your voice,
or out of your ears.
Observe. Do not forget who I am.
　　　　—from "The Thunder: Perfect Mind," Gnostic Gospel[1]

"Whatever you do, don't waste your time writing about someone like, um, um, Margery Kempe. *She* was crazy."

Such was the advice my medieval professor gave me when I was in graduate school, strategizing ways to combine my interests in rhetoric, feminism, and early modern literature. Stanley Kahrl was excited by the prospect of a graduate student exploring medieval literature through a feminist lens, insisting that I read and cite Riane Eisler's *Chalice and the Blade*.[2] When I protested, before relenting, his enthusiasm sputtered a bit. It took him a while to realize that *my* feminist tendencies might not automatically lead to *his* choice of subject selection. Nevertheless, he kept his skepticism in check as I conducted trial runs with my feminist readings of various genres and figures, from fabliaux to revelations, from the fierce Grendel's mother to the submissive Griselda.

My feminist-scholar adventures included rereading the fabliaux (the anonymous "Dame Sirith" and Geoffrey Chaucer's "The Reeve's Tale" and "The Merchant's Tale"); the romance and the lai (*Sir Gawain and the Green Knight*, Chrétien de Troyes's "Knight of the Cart," and Chaucer's "Franklin's Tale"); Marian literature (the *N-Town Cycle* of Corpus Christi plays); religious literature (the *Pearl*, *Ancrenne Wisse*, the Katherine Group of writings); medieval mysticism (Julian of Norwich's *Revelations of Divine Love*, *The Book of Margery Kempe*, Hildegard von Bingen's *Scivias* [*Know the Ways*] and *Liber divinorum operum simplicis hominis* [*The Book of Divine Works*]); and veiled women's various interventions into religious, literary, and cultural affairs (Heloise's *Problemata*, Dhuoda's letters [*Liber Manualis*], Hrotsvitha's dramas, and Christine de Pisan's *City of Ladies* and *Book of Three Virtues*).

My graduate-school exploration into the various communities of women populating the medieval territory has sustained me intellectually over the past 20-something years, probably because that journey itself was my destination. As I started reading the texts listed in the previous paragraph, there was relatively little scholarship available to guide me, and most of what was available had been published much earlier, before 1980. Thus, I stopped at any settlement that looked promising, "promising" serving as my rationale for subject selection. Now, thinking back on the early solid recovery work that aided my exploration—work by scholars such as W. Butler-Bowden,[3] Edmund Colledge and James Walsh,[4] Louise Collis,[5] Peter Dronke,[6] Mary Erler and Maryanne Kowaleski,[7] Sharon Farmer,[8] Dorothy Gardiner,[9] Frances and Joseph Gies,[10] Etienne Gilson,[11] Sister Mary Pia Heinrich,[12] P. Molinari,[13] and Katharina Wilson[14] (to name a few and omit too many)—I feel indebted. Although most of this scholarship was neither ostensibly feminist nor rhetorical, it provided me the foothold I needed when I began to recuperate medieval women's contributions to rhetorical theory and performance.

Ironically—or maybe not—most of my medieval publications have centered on Margery Kempe and her Julian-of-Norwich inspiration, text-based literacy practices, autobiography, rhetorical techniques, social influence, religious stratagems, and (what might be labeled) protofeminism. Margery was unusual, to be sure; after all, she has left us with the earliest extant autobiography in English. And she was dramatic, too, to the point of being flamboyant. But crazy? I don't know. I don't know that it matters.

Even though Professor Kahrl has been gone for nearly 20 years, I would like to think that despite his warnings to me about women such as Kempe, he would have been energized and amused by my scholarship as well as in awe of how feminist theory could actually open up medieval studies in such relevant and compelling ways. Then he would deny that he had ever admonished me to stay away from Margery (or that *The Chalice and the Blade* was a must-read). I am smiling as I think back on my studies with him.

What I know for sure is that he would be delighted with this edited collection, astonished that there was so very much still to be known about so very many medieval religious women.

> "A New Enterprise"
> Wisdom is
> sweeter than honey,
> brings more joy
> than wine,
> illumines
> more than the sun,
> is more precious
> than jewels.
> She causes
> the ears to hear
> and the heart to comprehend.
>
> —Makeda, Queen of Sheba[15]

When Margaret Cotter-Lynch and Brad Herzog approached me about their idea for these essays, I was delighted by the thought of such an enterprise. Who would have thought—even 20 years ago—that anyone would pull together such a valuable collection? *Reading Memory and Identity in the Texts of Medieval European Holy Women* invites us to reevaluate the identity of medieval nuns, saints, abbesses, scholars, cenobites, and mystics—women whose lives have for too long been assessed as only marginally important to the shaping of medieval culture writ large. Crucial contributors to that culture were the male authors (Chaucer, Geoffrey of Monmouth, William Langland, Richard Rolle, John Gower, Sir Thomas Malory), who fashioned literature that reflected medieval culture's values, practices, and identities. The unknown authors of influential works such as *Sir Gawain*, *The Bestiary*, *Pearl*, *The Travels of Sir John Mandeville*, and the Corpus Christi plays might be anonymous, but they were *surely* male. Women authors (save for Marie de France) were unimaginable. Little wonder, then, that the lives and works of medieval holy women have been under-researched and undervalued—that is, until most recently.

Reading Memory and Identity joins the exciting new enterprise of writing medieval holy women into our intellectual history, an enterprise surely facilitated by Mary Carruthers's landmark *Book of Memory: A Study of Memory in Medieval Culture*[16] and the more recent *Craft of*

Thought: Meditation, Rhetoric, and the Making of Images, 400–1200.[17] Other
recent work central to this scholarly venture is Rosamond McKitterick's
History and Memory in the Carolingian World,[18] Eric Jager's *The Book of
the Heart,*[19] Allan Mitchell's *Ethics and Exemplary Narrative in Chaucer and
Gower,*[20] and Elisabeth Van Houts's *Memory and Gender in Medieval Europe
900–1200.*[21] The editors tell me that my work on Margery Kempe's
"popular literacy" was also important to their vision,[22] given that popular
literacy was predicated on the art of memory, to wit, of listening, remembering, and saying (rather than reading and writing). Thus, the vision of
these editors moves beyond the triangulation of memory, imagination,
and imitation in many of the aforementioned studies to investigate how
medieval memorial arts—from widely circulating stories of saints' lives
to widely quoted scripture—framed and made possible rhetorically savvy
discursive representations of female holy identity.

In addition to providing readers keen insights and convincing examples
of the ways medieval memorial arts underpinned constructions of identity, Cotter-Lynch and Herzog also—and just as importantly—challenge
traditional patriarchal notions of *who* and *what* "counts." For instance,
who qualifies as an author during the medieval period? Does someone
who relies on an amanuensis? Someone who relies on images and oral
recitation to deliver a text? How about an anonymous author? Might such
an author ever be female? How does the level of what twenty-first-century readers consider to be formal education influence the answer? And
what about the issue of audience? Does a female-only audience even matter? After all, if the audience is composed solely of women, does it have
any measure of agency? Or is it merely a passive receptacle of instruction,
regardless of whether the rhetor is male or female?

Besides interrogating the criteria for author and audience (vis-à-vis the
texts in this collection), the editors also confront established principles of
what qualifies as an intellectual endeavor, a rhetorical endeavor, a rhetorical practice. Might poetry, translation, hagiography, a miracle collection, iconographic and discursive representations of visions, love lyrics,
and autobiographies be eligible? What about a religious work of imaginative literature or an alleged historical account? Or does their eligibility
depend upon their having been already vetted by a body of scholarship
already devoted to that particular composition, genre, or author? Does
eligibility as religious intellectual endeavor depend upon whether the
author is male or female, well-educated or (by modern standards) illiterate, aristocratic, or religious? And even if the endeavor meets (or doesn't
meet) the criteria rendering it intellectual, what does it take for that religious composition to be considered a rhetorical practice or rhetorical
performance? Is that eligibility also tethered to the quantity of previous

scholarly attention given to the performance or practice or to the sex and status of the author? Finally, the editors compel readers to consider the material conditions necessary for the production and circulation of identity expectations and constraints for medieval holy women as well as the conditions necessary for accepting, repudiating, or modifying a prescribed identity, whether that identity is one of gender, class, religious status, or education. Thus, Cotter-Lynch and Herzog tantalize readers with big questions that merit the considered research and writing that all of these essays work in concert to provide.

> Sophia!
> you of the whirling wings,
> circling encompassing
> energy of God:
> you quicken the world in your clasp.
> One wing soars in heaven
> one wing sweeps the earth
> and the third flies all around us.
> Praise to Sophia!
> Let all the earth praise her!
>
> —Hildegard of Bingen[23]

The nine chronologically arranged chapters composing this collection provide a kaleidoscopic view of medieval holy women, with each chapter offering a distinctive constellation of shared elements: women, religion, memory, texts, visuals, and identity. Mutually supporting, these chapters enrich one another as they simultaneously explain how a medieval woman's identity was shaped by culturally constructed expectations and how her own intellectual, religious, social, and literary contributions emphasized and deemphasized specific qualities of that identity.

As I said earlier in this introduction, Professor Kahrl believed that Margery Kempe was crazy, undoubtedly deterred from taking her seriously by the fact that her holy revelations began postpartum, perhaps during postpartum depression. Female scholars, such as Hope Phyllis Weissman and myself, however, have taken Margery seriously from the start. As Weissman argues, "To diagnose Margery's case as 'hysteria' need not be to trivialize her significance or reduce her *Book*'s value as cultural testimony."[24] The same strength of argument (she didn't autograph the manuscript; she used an amanuensis; she was a minor figure; she had no followers; she was postpartum) has been used to exclude most of the medieval holy women in this collection from our sustained scholarly attention for too long. With this collection, these women are gaining the audience they have long deserved. We readers, too, now have access to long-silenced voices, those of medieval holy women. For that, we have the editors, Margaret Cotter-Lynch and Brad Herzog, to thank.

Notes

1. Jane Hirschfield, trans. and ed., "The Thunder: Perfect Mind," in *Women in Praise of the Sacred: 43 Centuries of Spiritual Poetry by Women* (New York: HarperPerennial, 1995), 30–33.
2. Riane Eisler, *The Chalice and the Blade* (San Francisco: Harper, 1987).
3. Margery Kempe, *The Book of Margery Kempe*, ed. W. Butler-Bowden (London: Oxford University Press, 1940).
4. Julian of Norwich, *A Book of Showings to the Anchoress Julian of Norwich*, eds. Edmund Colledge and James Walsh, 2 vols., Studies and Texts 35 (Toronto: Pontifical Institute of Mediaeval Studies, 1978).
5. Louise Collis, *Memoirs of a Medieval Woman: The Life and Times of Margery Kempe* (1964; repr., New York: Colophon-Harper, 1983).
6. Peter Dronke, *Abelard and Heloise in Medieval Testimonies* (Glasgow: n.p., 1976); Dronke, *Women Writers of the Middle Ages: A Critical Study of Texts from Perpetua to Marguerite Porete* (Cambridge: Cambridge University Press, 1984).
7. Mary Erler and Maryanne Kowaleski, eds., *Women and Power in the Middle Ages* (Athens: University of Georgia Press, 1988).
8. Sharon Farmer, "Persuasive Voices: Clerical Images of Medieval Wives," *Speculum* 6, nos. 1–3 (1986): 517–43.
9. Dorothy Gardiner, *English Girlhood at School: A Study of Women's Education through Twelve Centuries* (London: Oxford University Press, 1929).
10. Frances Gies and Joseph Gies, *Women in the Middle Ages* (New York: Perennial-Harper, 1978).
11. Etienne Gilson, *Heloise and Abelard*, trans. L. K. Stook (Ann Arbor: University of Michigan Press, 1960).
12. Sister Mary Pia Heinrich, *The Canonesses and Education in the Early Middle Ages* (PhD diss., Catholic University of America, 1924).
13. P. Molinari, *Julian of Norwich, the Teachings of the Fourteenth-Century Mystic* (London: Chapman, 1985).
14. Katharina M. Wilson, ed., *Medieval Women Writers* (Athens: University of Georgia Press, 1984).
15. Jane Hirschfield, ed., "Makeda, Queen of Sheba," in Hirschfield, *Women in Praise of the Sacred*, 13.
16. Mary J. Carruthers, *The Book of Memory: A Study of Memory in Medieval Culture*, 2nd ed., Cambridge Studies in Medieval Literature 70 (Cambridge: Cambridge University Press, 2008).
17. Mary J. Carruthers, *The Craft of Thought: Meditation, Rhetoric, and the Making of Images, 400–1200*, Cambridge Studies in Medieval Literature 34 (Cambridge: Cambridge University Press, 2000).

18. Rosamond McKitterick, *History and Memory in the Carolingian World* (Cambridge: Cambridge University Press, 2004).
19. Eric Jager, *The Book of the Heart* (Chicago: University of Chicago Press, 2000).
20. Allan Mitchell, *Ethics and Exemplary Narrative in Chaucer and Gower* (New York: Palgrave Macmillan, 2009).
21. Elizabeth Van Houts, *Memory and Gender in Medieval Europe 900–1200* (Toronto: University of Toronto Press, 1999).
22. Cheryl Glenn, "Author, Audience, and Autobiography: Rhetorical Technique in *The Book of Margery Kempe*," *College English* 53 (September 1992): 540–53; Glenn, "Medieval Literacy outside the Academy: Popular Practice and Individual Technique," *College Composition and Communication* 44 (December 1993): 497–508; Glenn, "Re-examining *The Book of Margery Kempe*: A Rhetoric of Autobiography," in *Reclaiming Rhetorica*, ed. Andrea Lunsford (Pittsburgh: University of Pittsburgh Press, 1995), 53–72; Glenn, *Rhetoric Retold: Regendering the Tradition from Antiquity through the Renaissance* (Carbondale: Southern Illinois University Press, 1997).
23. Hildegard of Bingen, "Antiphon for Divine Wisdom," in *Women in Praise of the Sacred*, ed. Jane Hirschfield (New York: HarperPerennial, 1995), 67.
24. Hope P. Weissman, "Margery Kempe in Jerusalem: *Hysteria compassio* in the Late Middle Ages," in *Acts of Interpretation: The Text in Its Contexts, 700–1600: Essays on Medieval and Renaissance Literature*, eds. Mary J. Carruthers and Elizabeth D. Kirk (Norman, OK: Pilgrim, 1982), 202.

ACKNOWLEDGMENTS

A project such as this does not reach fruition without the help of many people. We wish to thank our families for their patience and support, without which we would not have completed this volume.

We also express thanks to our contributors for their research, hard work, willingness to revise, and incisive critiques. We had the privilege of collaborating with a group of remarkable scholars to create a more expansive and insightful collection of essays than any of us could have produced alone.

We would like to acknowledge Saginaw Valley State University and the Organized Research Fund at Southeastern Oklahoma State University for financial support in the early stages of this project.

Finally, we are especially grateful to our series editor, Bonnie Wheeler, and to Palgrave Macmillan for their encouragement, insights, and help in preparing this volume for publication.

CONTRIBUTORS

Claire Barbetti received her PhD from Duquesne University. In 1998 she cofounded the interdisciplinary journal *Janus Head* and worked as coeditor for five years. A working poet, she has published her work in *Cimarron Review*, *How2*, and *The Drunken Boat*, among others. Palgrave Macmillan published her book-length study on medieval visions and ekphrasis, *Ekphrastic Medieval Visions: A New Discussion in Interarts Theory* in the New Middle Ages Series in 2011.

Margaret Cotter-Lynch is an associate professor in the Department of English, Humanities, and Languages at Southeastern Oklahoma State University. Her research focuses on the representation of gender in early medieval hagiography. Her current book project is entitled *Mother, Gladiator, Saint: The Transformations of St. Perpetua across the Middle Ages*.

Cheryl Glenn is Liberal Arts Research Professor of English and Women's Studies at the Pennsylvania State University. Her scholarly work focuses on histories of women's rhetorics and writing practices, inclusionary rhetorical practices and theories, and contexts and processes for the teaching of writing. Her scholarly publications include *Rhetoric Retold: Regendering the Tradition from Antiquity through the Renaissance*; *Unspoken: A Rhetoric of Silence*; *Silence and Listening as Rhetorical Arts*; *Rhetorical Education in America*; *The St. Martin's Guide to Teaching Writing*; *The Writer's Harbrace Handbook*; *Making Sense: A Real-World Rhetorical Reader*; *The Harbrace Guide for College Writers*; and numerous articles, chapters, and essays. She and J. Michael Hogan coedit "Rhetoric and Democratic Deliberation," a Pennsylvania State University Press series. With Shirley Wilson Logan, she coedits the Southern Illinois University Press series Studies in Rhetorics and Feminisms. Glenn's rhetorical scholarship has earned her three fellowships from the National Endowment for the Humanities (NEH) and book awards from Choice and from the Society for the Study of Early Modern Women.

Elissa Hansen is currently writing her doctoral dissertation on ideas about time in fourteenth-century English contemplative literature at the University of Minnesota, where she holds the university's Doctoral Dissertation Fellowship (2011–2012). Her research interests include vision-ary and contemplative spirituality, religious identity and community for-mation, and intersections between literature and natural philosophy.

Brad Herzog is an associate professor of English at Saginaw Valley State University in Michigan. His publications and recent national and inter-national conference presentations address the role of memory arts in the composition of Julian of Norwich's *Showings* and *The Book of Margery Kempe*.

Ella Johnson is an assistant professor of Systematic Theology at St. Bernard's School of Theology and Ministry in Rochester, New York. Her research and publications focus on theology and anthropology in the writings of medieval women monastics.

Catherine Keene recently completed her PhD at Central European University in Budapest. She is currently preparing her dissertation, a biography of Saint Margaret, Queen of the Scots, for publication.

Ana Maria Machado is a professor of Portuguese Medieval Literature at the University of Coimbra and a member of the Centre of Portuguese Literature. She has published several articles on Portuguese and Latin hagiographies, and she is preparing an edition of the Portuguese *Flos Sanctorum* (1513).

Helene Scheck is an associate professor of English at the State University of New York at Albany. She is the author of *Reform and Resistance: Forms of Female Subjectivity in Early Medieval Ecclesiastical Culture* and coeditor of *Intertexts: Studies in Anglo-Saxon Culture Presented to Paul E. Szarmach* and *Rhetorics of Plague, Early and Late*. Her current work focuses on women's intellectual culture in the early Middle Ages.

Barbara Zimbalist is a PhD candidate at the University of California–Davis, where she is completing a dissertation titled "Talking with God: Christ's Speech in Medieval Women's Visionary Texts." She has recently held fellowships through the Bancroft Library, the Fulbright Commission, and the Belgian American Educational Foundation. In addition to an essay on early modern prose romance, she has published on Middle English devotional literature and works on the intersection of women's visionary texts, lyric poetry, and devotional prose in England and the Low Countries.

INTRODUCTION

Margaret Cotter-Lynch and Brad Herzog

If you have seen the mosaics of Antioch, you know of their intricate beauty: the majesty of the Striding Lion, the brilliance of Oceanus. Elaborate borders and detailed figures are fashioned from collected fragments of rock and glass. Like mosaics formed of pebbles and glass, medieval memory networks were constructed with readily available materials—cultural commonplaces, tropes, examples, scriptures, and authorities. For the western European Middle Ages, memory networks informed the production of texts, communities, and personal identities. While each text, person, and community was distinct, the materials used to construct them were picked up from the past. Combined together, these inherited fragments of memory were reconfigured to the purposes of particular people, places, and cultures, even as the pieces themselves remained individually discernable. Thus, each new creation was concretely built with shards of the past, selected and reorganized yet still recognizable to all who shared the common cultural traditions of Western medieval Christianity.

The centrality of memory networks to the production of medieval identities informs every chapter in this collection. The texts discussed range geographically and chronologically from the court of Charlemagne to Margery Kempe's England. All the chapters, however, argue that an examination of the gender-specific ways in which memory networks were constructed can help us to better understand medieval texts. Medieval memory has been the focus of numerous studies over the past two decades, since the 1990 publication of the first edition of Mary Carruthers's *The Book of Memory* instigated the modern scholarly reevaluation of the ways in which the concept of memory is culturally contingent and the ways in which a medieval Christian understanding of the nature and uses of memory might help us to better read the texts of far-removed cultures. In *The Book of Memory* and *The Craft of Thought*, Carruthers eloquently explains that, for western European religious culture in the Middle Ages, memory arts were integral to reading, meditation, composition, and character formation. The process of "memorative composition" is revealed through the etymological overlap of the words "invention" and "inventory," as it is through the double sense of the word "recollection."[1] The formation of memory inventories through reading, meditation, and experience was itself a rhetorical process, as "memories are not tossed into storage at random, they 'are put in' their 'places' there, 'colored' in ways that are partly personal, partly emotional, partly rational, and mostly cultural."[2] Reading was central to the construction of memory inventories; these memory inventories then provided the basis for compositions: texts, prayers, and lived identities were all formed through "memorative composition." Rhetoric thus informed two stages of medieval composition. First, memory inventories were formed and categorized according to rhetorical principles. Second, texts and identities were both invented rhetorically, through the deployment of memory inventories.[3]

Identity and character were thus understood as rhetorical inventions employing the arts of memory. As Carruthers points out, from the perspective of medieval memory arts, you are what you read. You are only considered to have read what you remember, by incorporating the "res" of what you read into your individual memory inventory. Your memory stores are then the material basis of your ethical actions. By extension, reading and memory constitute individual and collective identities, for individuals shape their identities through ethical actions as expressions of memory—and communities fashion collective identities through common attitudes and ideas reflected in shared memory structures. A careful consideration of medieval memory can thus lead us to a better understanding of both writing and reading: how texts were produced and the uses they served in identity formation.[4]

This collection examines how women were remembered in medieval texts and how this commemoration shaped individual and communal identities. We extend Carruthers's claims by illustrating how conceptions of gender informed and were informed by memory networks. The texts examined here show how the textual applications of memory arts defined ideas about gender identity for the individuals and communities that read them. The chapters in this book—by interrogating how women, in particular, were remembered in medieval texts—offer new perspectives on gender formulations in the medieval Christian West through attention to the textual interplay between reading, memory, and identity.

In the range of memorial texts here discussed, a few broad categories emerge for thinking about gender and memory in medieval religious texts. In the first section of this introduction, we will discuss the active, rather than passive, nature of remembering and the construction of memory inventories. Next, we will examine how individual identities were shaped through the formation and application of memory inventories. Third, we will show how communities were formed and defined through shared memory networks. Finally, we will look at cases of the gender-specific application of the memory arts, as exemplified in the chapters in this collection.

Active Memory

To remember is always an active choice, not a passive state. Every act of remembering involves a conscious or subconscious decision about *what* is worth remembering and *how* it is worth categorizing within one's memory stores. These decisions are necessarily informed not only by personal choice but also by cultural context: what one has been taught as worth remembering and how one has been taught to structure one's understanding of the world. Conversely, examining what we forget can help us to better understand what, why, and how we remember. As Carruthers explains, "Communal forgetting" was effected in medieval communities "not through some variety of amnesia, but by applying carefully the mnemotechnical principles of blocking one pattern of memories by another through 'crowding' or overlay, and by intentional mnemonic replacement."[5] For example, the Christians in Rome used the technique of "overlay" to appropriate significant pagan sites and procession routes. In the seventh century, they dedicated the Pantheon as a Christian church, and they appropriated the route and date of the Roman procession of Robigalia for the "Christian procession of the Great Liturgy."[6] By overlaying pagan sites, routes, and festivals with their own memory networks, Christians drew on the symbolic and cultural power of these underlying sites while blocking much of their pagan meaning and appropriating them for Christian purposes.[7] A similar dynamic worked in the reading and reinterpreting of texts, as a classical poem such as Virgil's Fourth Eclogue was reinterpreted and remembered according to a Christian hermeneutic.[8]

Utility, rather than accuracy, was generally privileged as the basis for making these mnemonic decisions for the Christian Middle Ages. In their chapters, both Margaret Cotter-Lynch and Claire Barbetti build upon Carruthers's assertion that "the matters memory presents are used to persuade and motivate, to create emotion and stir the will. And the 'accuracy' or 'authenticity' of these memories—their simulation of an actual past—is of far less importance . . . than their use to motivate the present and to affect the future."[9] This emphasis upon utility rather than accuracy in turn makes memory malleable—as a culture's needs change, so the memories it keeps will change to fulfill current uses. As Patrick

Geary explains in *Phantoms of Remembrance*, "A society that explicitly found its identity, its norms, and its values from the inheritance of the past, that venerated tradition and drew its religious and political ideologies from precedent, was nevertheless actively engaged in producing that tradition through a complex process of transmission, suppression, and re-creation."[10]

As an example of this dynamic, Barbara Zimbalist's chapter discusses how the relationship between author and audience is privileged over the specificity of the hagiographic subject in Clemence of Barking's *Life of St. Catherine*. Clemence's concern is less with Catherine herself—the accurate, or not, commemoration of the early Christian martyr—than with the uses Catherine's story could serve for her twelfth-century audience. Similarly, Claire Barbetti says of Hildegard von Bingen's *Scivias*, "What matters is not whether what is reported is real, but, as Carruthers suggests, how the case of these images resonate with a social narrative."[11] According to Ana Maria Machado, in her chapter on the Portuguese reception of the *Vitae Patrum*, it is the remembered images of women, as distinct from real women, that pose the primary danger to the desert monks. This emphasis upon mental images demonstrates the preoccupation with the uses of memory within hagiographic texts.

All of the chapters in this volume interrogate the ways in which particular events, ideas, and texts were remembered and forgotten by particular authors in particular compositions. These authors, in writing about holy women, at once adopt (and sometimes omit) previous tradition and refashion it by adjusting the structures of memory networks for individuals and communities, thus shaping their identities.

Memory and Individual Identity

Whereas Quintilian asserted the virtuosity of virtue (the rhetorical efficaciousness of "the good man speaking well"), medieval authorities inverted the relationship. For them, the rhetorical art of memory, applied in meditation, served as a means to reach the end of fashioning a virtuous character. This personal approach to memory work and character building corresponds to the tropological and anagogical levels of reading: the act of "digestive meditation" constitutes "the ethical activity of making one's reading one's own."[12] Medieval scholars and religious used reading and meditation to construct memory networks that had moral and ethical value. For medieval authorities, the activity of shaping a memory network was the "activity" of shaping a "character" or "temperament."[13]

Describing how the classical era's canon of memory transformed into medieval memory arts, Frances Yates explains that medieval authorities reinterpreted the *Rhetorica ad Herennium* and Cicero's *De inventione*, shifting the use of memory arts from civic discourse in the classical era to private meditation, moral edification, and religious education in the Middle Ages.[14] While affirming this basic shift in focus and purpose, Mary Carruthers contends that religious men and women in the Middle Ages developed their own craft of memory arts, or *sancta memoria*, which functioned as a form of rhetorical invention for devotional texts, exercises, and individual character.[15] Medieval memory arts also incorporated diverse aspects of reading and interpretation. As a result, Carruthers argues, reading, memory, rhetorical invention, and identity were intimately intertwined for medieval authors and audiences.

Helene Scheck and Elissa Hansen, in their contributions to this collection, assert that female authors demonstrate gender-specific reading and writing practices. These practices participate in the process of identity formation that Carruthers describes. As Carruthers states, "One's first relationship with a text is not to encounter another mind (or subdue it, as one suspects sometimes) or to understand it on its own terms, but to use it as a source of communally experienced wisdom for one's own life, gained by memorizing from it however much and in whatever fashion one is able or willing to do."[16] Reading here is an essentially personal experience, integral to the process of identity formation. One's reading experience— what one takes from a text—is necessarily determined by the identity of the reader. Simultaneously, the reading helps to further shape that identity: "And this memorized chorus of voices, this ever-present florilegium built up plank by plank continuously through one's lifetime, formed not only one's opinions but one's moral character as well. Character indeed results from one's experiences, but that includes the experiences of others, often epitomized in ethical commonplaces, and made one's own by constant recollection."[17]

The formation of both one's memory network and one's identity is inherently rhetorical; reading and remembering a text necessarily involves a transformation of both the individual and the text:

> We read rhetorically, memory makes our reading into our own ethical equipment ("stamps our character") and we express that character in situations that are also rhetorical in nature, in the expressive gestures and performances which we construct from our remembered experience, and which, in turn, are intended to impress and give value to others' memories of a particular occasion.[18]

As an example, Ella Johnson's chapter demonstrates how Gertrud of Helfta rhetorically deploys recalled tropes in her *Exercitia spiritualia* in order to incorporate women into a religious context shared with men, thereby stretching conventional conceptions of appropriate female behavior. Since Gertrud believed that traditional gender roles, expectations, and behaviors interfered with women's progress toward God, she constructed spiritual exercises that encouraged readers to reject restrictive conventions regarding gender. Moreover, Gertrud employed memory inventories in her exercises to "invent a new way of being female," a way that consisted in calling "women to be Christians first."[19]

Like Johnson, all of the authors in this collection, explicitly or implicitly, address questions of how reading and memory might—or might not—function differently for medieval women than for medieval men. For instance, do women assimilate (read remember) texts differently than men? If we follow Carruthers's argument that one's reading is shaped by one's experiences, then women's reading must have differed from men's, since lived experiences differ by gender. If the shapes of shared memories, and the structures of memory inventories, are deeply influenced by culture, then we can expect women to be remembered differently than men, as the categories according to which memories are inventoried function differently for different genders. If, as Carruthers asserts, memory is deployed into ethical action, again we should expect a difference, as the arenas of expected and acceptable action were circumscribed differently for men and women. Finally, as medieval memory arts function on the cusp of, and to some degree mediate, the separation between the public and private spheres, we should again expect a difference between men and women in the deployment of memory arts, as men and women were expected to relate differently to the public and private spheres. Women such as Gertrud of Helfta, Hildegard of Bingen, Clemence of Barking, Julian of Norwich, and Margery Kempe deployed gender-inflected memory networks to compose texts, claim authority, and appeal to audiences of women and men. Male authors likewise deployed gender-inflected memory networks in the textual commemoration of women such as Perpetua, Margaret of Scotland, and Sara in order to shape individual and communal identities around shared understandings of gender categories.

Memory and Community

Carruthers emphasizes the shaping of character as a process of private meditation through the deployment of memory arts while simultaneously demonstrating the ways in which authors used similar applications of memory arts to construct characters and shape identities in written texts. In this collection, we examine how men and women authorized their texts by encouraging their public readership to locate the texts' female characters, subjects, or personas within strategic memory networks.

Medieval memory arts supported public discourse as well as private meditations. As Catherine Cubitt has noted, "Remembering is an inherently social activity."[20] As Claire Barbetti, Margaret Cotter-Lynch, Brad Herzog, and Catherine Keene demonstrate in their chapters, the structures imposed upon memory can define a community. Individuals can be initiated into a community by acquiring a defined memory base, whereas individuals themselves can be identified as community members by adopting, recognizing, or demonstrating salient features of the community's memory structures. For example, capital criminals in medieval England could escape hanging for a less painful death if they could recite a verse from the Bible, thus situating themselves within a particular memory network as members of the clerical class who were "immune from hanging by legal custom."[21]

Medieval Christian communities, in particular, were defined by their remembrance of a shared religious heritage. The liturgy, as the center of all medieval Christian religious practice, is at its essence memorial, as discussed in Ella Johnson's chapter, "In mei memoriam facietis" (do this in memory of me). Barbara Zimbalist draws on Karl Uitti's work to argue that "hagiography's ultimate function is to link the narrator, the subject, and the reader together as a Christian community through a shared participation in the memorialization of the Christian saint."[22] Similarly, Claire Barbetti writes, concerning Hildegard, "The verbal translation of a vision is not merely a mimetic activity; it uses the tools of the memory arts to place elements in such a way as to engender a culturally agreed upon meaning."[23] These chapters all contend that the construction of shared memory networks, and thus of community, is a primary function of the texts they examine. These shared networks are in part constituted according to particular conceptions of gender.

Medieval religious communities were deeply identified by their memorial functions. The daily activities of professional religious were defined by commemoration: the liturgy, the veneration of the saints, praying for the dead, reading, meditation, and the copying of texts. Indeed, the essence of the holy life—*imitatio Christi*—consisted in modeling one's own identity on the remembered Christ. Medieval religious authors self-consciously placed themselves, their texts, and their audiences within specific memory networks in order to shape the understanding of the text and the identities of both author and audience. Illustrating this point, Brad Herzog notes that Margery Kempe creatively fills in the "gaps" in biblical and devotional accounts[24] by imagining herself in places of prominence—caring for the Christ child and grieving at Christ's death.[25]

Placing images (even of oneself, as Kempe does) in commonplace settings (loci or topoi) is a clear strategy of memory arts. Kempe also invites her audiences to resituate themselves within strategic memory networks. As this example shows, memory arts can serve as significant resources for rhetorical invention.

Using memory arts for composition (including invention), medieval authors established their authority through calling upon and rearranging their audience's memory stores. As Margaret Cotter-Lynch describes in her chapter, an author's "message, then, comes not from introducing new material, but rather from selecting, juxtaposing, and arranging information and images already at the readers' disposal" in their memory stores.[26] Carruthers writes, "Such adaptive freedom is enabled by complete familiarity with the text, the shared memory of it on the part of both audience and author, and hence a delight both in recognizing the familiar words and in the skill with which they have been adapted to a new context."[27] Memory is a collective project in communities, which define both their purposes and their identities through shared memory networks.

Commemorating Women and Constructing Texts

The chapters collected in this volume all examine the interconnected ways in which gender, identity, and memory function in medieval texts about holy women. While they address a wide variety of texts, temporally and stylistically, composed by both men and women for a variety of audiences, all of the chapters examine the common concerns of female authority and individual and community identities in texts that commemorate women.

Helene Scheck's chapter begins the discussion by asking what commemorating Dido, the Virgin Mary, and the women attached to court alongside Charlemagne might tell us about women's literary production in ninth-century Francia. Specifically, Scheck suggests that, for the canonical Carolingian text *Karolus Magnus et Leo Papa*, "Anonymous" might well have been a woman. The fragmentary text purports to remember Charlemagne and in particular the 799 visit of Pope Leo to the king at Paderborn and the court of Aachen. The poem, which survives only in a fragment, has long been regarded as anonymous and anomalous within the body of surviving literature of the period. Scheck argues that this anomaly—including the emphasis upon remembering women in the text—may suggest female authorship and indeed a stronger role than has previously been assumed for women in the literary milieu at Aachen.

A second Carolingian poem commemorating women, "In Natale Sanctarum Feminarum," serves as the subject of the second chapter in the collection. In "Mnemonic Sanctity and the Ladder of Reading," Margaret Cotter-Lynch provides a reading of Notker's poem that demonstrates the shaping of individual and communal identities through the deployment of memory arts. Notker refashions his audience's memory of the martyr Perpetua in order to establish a shared community around a particular understanding of the category of "holy women."

Catherine Keene similarly examines the commemoration of a female saint employed to shape communal identity in her examination of the miracle collection of Saint Margaret of Scotland. Intrigued by the unusually high concentration of dreams and visions within this miracle collection, Keene determines that the authors of the text consciously enlisted both local literary and Roman Catholic ecclesiastical traditions in presenting Saint Margaret as a unifying figure, at once native and Catholic, supporting the dynastic claims of her descendants.

Hildegard of Bingen offers us an opportunity to examine the uses of commemoration for establishing community, identity, and authority in a text written by an identifiable woman. In her study of Hildegard's *Scivias*, Claire Barbetti argues that the twelfth-century abbess used the techniques of ekphrasis to bridge the divide between the public and private spheres for both her audience and herself, simultaneously carving out a societal space for her voice as an authoritative woman.

Clemence of Barking's twelfth-century version of the *Life of St. Catherine* provides Barbara Zimbalist the opportunity to examine how a female author writing about a female subject for a female audience constructs the process of remembering. Zimbalist shows how Clemence structures her text in order to rhetorically interpolate her readers into an ethical system. By thus engaging her audience's memory networks, Clemence produces a story that functions as moral instruction.

Ana Maria Machado, in her chapter, examines how women were remembered in medieval Portuguese translations of the *Vitae patrum*. By tracing which women get named as individuals, versus which women are represented only as images or types, Machado demonstrates the preoccupation of Portuguese translators with the dangers of remembered images of women, as distinct from the praised actions of real, identifiable women. Machado also examines how Portuguese translators helped readers of the *Vitae patrum* recall memories of evangelists who were repentant sinners in ways that created new gender identities.

Whereas the *Vitae patrum* illustrates gender-specific formulations of memory networks, Gertrud of Helfta's *Exercitia spiritualia* deploys widely accepted memorial tropes from the Bible and liturgy in order to include both women and men in a common formulation of religious experience. In her chapter, Ella Johnson argues that Gertrud implicitly challenges assumptions about gender specificity by explicitly conflating gender markers in her descriptions of meditative and spiritual activities.

The fourteenth-century mystic and theologian Julian of Norwich clearly constructed her *Revelations of Divine Love* by placing descriptions of her remembered visions within the shared mnemonic structures of the medieval Church. In her chapter, Elissa Hansen demonstrates how Julian rhetorically deploys the memory and imitation of the Virgin Mary to construct a space in which the recluse could assert her authority and relevance without directly threatening ecclesiastical hierarchy.

Finally, Brad Herzog describes how Margery Kempe self-consciously models her narrative on virgin martyr's legends in order to situate herself within a saintly category for her audience. In describing at length her own commemoration and imitation of well-recognized holy women, Margery simultaneously shapes her identity through her devotional practices, and—by invoking remembered commonplaces from virgin martyrs' tales—invites her audience to identify themselves as her "converts."

All of the chapters in this volume interrogate the complex interrelationship of reading, memory, and identity as they examine the ways in which medieval holy women remembered and were remembered in texts. Reconstructing male-authored texts in memory, female authors produced space for their own public authority, even as male authors used the same textual tradition and memory arts to delineate women's possibilities for acceptable action. Both male and female authors recombined textual shards into unique mosaics, restructuring memory networks in order to define individual and communal identities in relation to gender.

Notes

1. Mary J. Carruthers, *The Book of Memory: A Study of Memory in Medieval Culture*, 2nd ed., Cambridge Studies in Medieval Literature 70 (Cambridge: Cambridge University Press, 2008), 240–41.
2. Mary J. Carruthers, *The Craft of Thought: Meditation, Rhetoric, and the Making of Images, 400–1200*, Cambridge Studies in Medieval Literature 34 (Cambridge: Cambridge University Press, 2000), 15.
3. Carruthers, *Book of Memory*, 12.
4. As Patrick Geary has explained, even though most medieval people were illiterate, books were still central to the culture. Patrick Geary, *Phantoms of Remembrance: Memory and Oblivion at the End of the First Millenium* (Princeton, NJ: Princeton University Press, 1994), 135. In this volume, we understand "reading" to be contact with and consumption of texts, whether that consumption takes place visually (by physically looking at words on a page) or aurally (by listening to a text read or repeated).
5. Carruthers, *Craft of Thought*, 54.

6. Ibid., 56.
7. Ibid., 56–57.
8. For an introduction to the rich medieval tradition of reading the Fourth Eclogue as a prophecy of Christ's birth, see Stephen Benko, "Virgil's Fourth Eclogue in Christian Interpretation," *Aufstieg und Niedergang der römischen Welt*, 2nd ser., 31, no. 1 (1980): 646–705.
9. Carruthers, *Craft of Thought*, 67.
10. Geary, *Phantoms of Remembrance*, 51.
11. Claire Barbetti, "Secret Designs/Public Shapes: Ekphrastic Tensions in Hildegard's *Scivias*," chapter 4 in this volume.
12. Carruthers, *Book of Memory*, 205–6.
13. Carruthers, *Craft of Thought*, 21.
14. Frances A. Yates, *The Art of Memory* (Chicago: University of Chicago Press, 1966), 53, 60–61, 76–77.
15. Carruthers, *Craft of Thought*, 10–24.
16. Carruthers, *Book of Memory*, 202.
17. Ibid., 222.
18. Ibid., 226.
19. Ella Johnson, "'In mei memoriam facietis': Remembering Ritual and Refiguring 'Woman' in Gertrud the Great of Helfta's *Exercitia spiritualia*," chapter 7 of this volume.
20. Catherine Cubitt, "Memory and Narrative in the Cult of Early Anglo-Saxon Saints," in *The Uses of the Past in the Early Middle Ages*, ed. Yitzhak Hen and Matthew Innes (Cambridge: Cambridge University Press, 2000), 31.
21. Carruthers, *Craft of Thought*, 44.
22. Karl D. Uitti, *Story, Myth, and Celebration in Old French Narrative Poetry, 1050–1200* (Princeton, NJ: Princeton University Press, 1973), 26, quoted in Barbara Zimbalist, "Imitating the Imagined: Clemence of Barking's *Life of St. Catherine*," chapter 5 in this volume.
23. Claire Barbetti, "Secret Designs/Public Shapes: Ekphrastic Tensions in Hildegard's *Scivias*," chapter 4 in this volume.
24. Denise L. Despres, "The Meditative Art of Scriptural Interpolation in *The Book of Margery Kempe*," *Downside Review* 106 (October 1988): 258 [253–263].
25. Margery Kempe, *The Book of Margery Kempe: A New Translation, Contexts, Criticism*, trans. and ed. Lynn Staley (New York: Norton, 2001), 15, 16, 50.
26. Margaret Cotter-Lynch, "Mnemonic Sanctity and the Ladder of Reading: Notker's 'In Natale Sanctarum Feminarum,'" chapter 2 of this volume.
27. Carruthers, *Book of Memory*, 116.

CHAPTER 1

NUNS ON PARADE: MEMORIALIZING WOMEN IN *KAROLUS MAGNUS ET LEO PAPA*

Helene Scheck

Karolus Magnus et Leo Papa in its entirety (such as we have it) celebrates Charlemagne as father of the expanding Frankish realm, soon to be the new seat of the empire, and protector of both realm and Church. Among other things, it provides a literary record of Pope Leo's famous visit to Paderborn in 799, recounting the unfortunate blinding and mutilation of the pontiff and Charlemagne's swift and sure response to that incident. Although many scholars focus primarily on the poem's presentation of that event, the modern title is inaccurate in its suggestive emphasis. As Dieter Schaller has demonstrated, the poem that survives is a fragment of a larger whole that recounted Charlemagne's ascendency.[1] The poet refers to two previous books or sections, which do not appear in this manuscript; the section of the poem that does remain trails off after 536 lines, clearly unfinished. It would seem that the first two sections offer background on Charlemagne's rise and that the poem would reach its culmination in the coronation of Charlemagne. It is, therefore, a poem of interest to historians. Its use of classical sources, themes, and forms makes it interesting to literary historians as well. The poem, which I will call *Karolus Magnus* for simplicity's sake, is even more attractive to the scholarly imagination because of its eccentricity: it is anomalous in genre and its mix of generic elements, its use of sources, and also its somewhat unusual selection of images. The poem's singularity, perhaps most apparent in a pageant scene showcasing the women of Charlemagne's family, suggests a talented, erudite writer based at court but nonetheless outside of the poets' circle and begs the question, therefore, of female authorship. I begin with an analysis of that scene as a way to reopen the question of authorship and propose the possibility of female author-ship along with several likely candidates; along the way I engage larger questions about the processes of memory and memorialization in relation to female learning and women's participation in cultural production in Carolingian Francia.

Women at the Center

Epic in scope, the poem has as its main subject Charlemagne. And yet, describing the royal pageantry at Aachen, the poem positions Charlemagne's queen and daughters prominently at the center rather than on the margins, assertively positioning themselves rather than pas-sively providing the backdrop in front of which the men march. The presentation of Charlemagne's queen, Liutgard, begins the procession of women on a strong note. After a glowing portrait of Charlemagne as the wise and generous king admiring the contours of his bustling new royal city of Aachen, the poet moves to a portrait of Queen Liutgard that dif-fers from all other contemporary accounts of her.

As Charlemagne's consort, Liutgard is an important personage, of course. Alcuin corresponds with her and clearly respects her position and her person. In an early letter, he encourages good habits and invites her to turn to him for the care of her soul while Charlemagne is in Saxony.[2] She may well have looked to him for spiritual guidance and with questions relating to faith and the scriptures. In one letter addressed to Charlemagne, Alcuin answers spiritual questions that had been posed by a woman he describes as "mea filia, famulavestra fidelissima" (my daughter, your most faithful handmaiden), which most likely describes Liutgard.[3] Alcuin also seems to be trying to cultivate connections for her, presumably on the basis of her stature, whether she is recognized officially as queen or not, presenting gifts on her behalf to Paulinus of Aquileia and to Æthelburga, abbess of Flaedenbyrg and daughter of Offa, king of the Mercians.[4] In both cases he asks that they pray for her; in the second case, however, he asks that Æthelburga enter Liutgard's name into her book along with the names of the sisters, saying that "Honorabilis tibi est amicitia illius et utilis" (honorable is her friendship to you—and useful).[5] And yet Janet Nelson notes, "The woman who replaced [Fastrada] as Charlemagne's bedfellow [i.e., Liutgard] was significantly never referred to by Alcuin as 'queen,' and seems never to have played a prominent public role."[6] If Alcuin does not officially recognize her as queen, he does at least acknowledge her political importance. Still, Liutgard seldom shines. Theodulf of Orleans praises Liutgard's beauty as well as her zeal for learning in his poem on the court, though his presentation infantilizes her, positioning her among Charlemagne's children rather than at his side as queen and their stepmother.[7] It may be that she is a young bride, but her rank should override that biological reality. Einhard refers to her only in passing as he recounts Charlemagne's marital history.[8] She bore him no children, so for Einhard there was really nothing else to say. That view corroborates Nelson's remark about Liutgard's lack of public presence.

In contrast to these contemporary portraits, *Karolus Magnus* depicts Liutgard as a queen fully possessed of title and respect due a woman of her rank: "Hinc thalamo cunctata diu regina superbo/Procedit, multa circum comitante caterva,/Liutgardis Karoli pulcherrima nomine coniux" (Hence from her stately quarters, lingering long, the queen proceeds, surrounded by a great following, Liutgard, beautiful wife of Charles).[9] Like the legendary Dido upon whom this portrait was likely modeled, Liutgard is a queen who fully embraces her stature. Dressed in purple garments and richly adorned in jewels with a crown matching that of Charlemagne, which the poet describes in careful detail, she carries herself like a leader: "Magnanimos inter proceres regina superbo/Gaudet equo, et iuvenum circum manus emicat ardens" (The queen rejoices on her proud horse among grand noblemen, with a company of fiery young men springing forth about her).[10] She apparently enjoys riding a horse that matches her own temperament; interestingly this detail echoes the description of Virgil's Ascanius on a hunt.

Charlemagne's daughters also take the spotlight, if only for a moment, following after two of their brothers. Significantly, of the sons, only Charles and Pippin appear in this processional; Louis is conspicuously absent.[11] Whereas the poet's description of Pippin is lengthy, the description of Charles, though positive, is slight, occupying barely 4 lines in comparison to Pippin's 12 and Gisla's 14; indeed, each daughter, even Rhodhaid, the daughter of a concubine, is given more than that. Charlemagne's eldest daughter, Rodtrud, leads, accompanied by a choir of nuns. If the poet were striving for historical veracity, surely her aunt Gisla, abbess of Chelles until her death in 810, would have led the nuns of Chelles, not Rodtrud, especially since Rodtrud never served as abbess.[12] That Gisla does not figure at all in the poem is curious. After all, she frequented her brother's court and attended his imperial coronation in Rome, so surely would have been present at a public celebration such as this, particularly one that drew out Charlemagne's daughters from their cloistered lives. Indeed, she appears in at least two other court poems. It may be that in this immediate context, the appearance of Gisla might distract from the poet's vision of Charlemagne as *pater optimus*. By positioning Charlemagne's daughter rather than sister here as leader representing the wealthy and powerful royal monastic community of Chelles in this ceremonial family portrait, the poet simultaneously underscores Charlemagne's role, literally, as paterfamilias and the authority conferred on his daughter.

Showcasing not just Rodtrud but all of Charlemagne's daughters in this fashion, the poet constructs a world in which women as well as men share in dynastic power. Bertha comes next with her female companions, young noblewomen living at court. Like most of the other women, she appears on horseback and, more than either of her brothers, is the image of her father: "Voce, virili animo, habitu vultuque corusco,/Os, mores, oculos imitantia pectora patris/Fert" (In voice, manly spirit, character and flashing countenance, mouth, demeanor, eyes, she resembles the heart of her father).[13] This presentation may be one of the reasons her lover Angilbert was considered a candidate for authorship, though his treatment of her in the court poem we know he wrote does not come close to this presentation.[14] The poet here displays an active, virile, vivacious, and morally upright woman, heir to her father's grace and charisma, in contrast to Angilbert's "excellent maiden."

Bertha in turn is followed by Charlemagne's daughter Gisla, probably abbess or prioress of Notre Dame de Soissons, who leads her nuns through the streets as if on parade: "Gisala post istas sequitur candore coruscans;/Virgineo comitata choro, micat aura proles./Tecta melocineo fulgescit femina amictu,/Mollia purpureis rutilant velamina filis,/Vox, facies, crines radianti luce coruscant" (Gisla follows after them, flashing brightly; accompanied by her choir of virgins, the golden progeny glitters. The woman shines in the fabric, soft purple garments gleaming from the threads, voice, face, hair glittering in the light, flash).[15] More regal than monastic here, though certainly appearing before the public in both capacities, she and her nuns, like Rodtrud before her, create quite a spectacle.

Some of Charlemagne's daughters appear on horseback, as if ready for the hunt, and all sport rich, royal attire, dominated by the colors of purple and gold accented with rare gems. The attention to the female members of the royal family, particularly as it exceeds that paid to the men, seems unusual and suggests at least a poet less invested in the typical gender hierarchy; the active stance of these women and the unusual context in which they are placed argues for female authorship. As Peter Godman notes, "The description...of the imperial family and its entourage is not only the fullest of its kind in Latin poetry since the work of Venantius Fortunatus two centuries earlier; it also incorporates the most elaborate encomium on the women of the Carolingian house yet written by a contemporary author."[16] But the descriptions are as revealing as the poetic eccentricity Godman notes. That is, it is not just the number of lines devoted to the women of Charlemagne's family, which is substantial in itself, but the character of those descriptions. In that segment of the poem, the women do not stand by passively; although they are well dressed and well decorated to indicate their royal status, they do not serve as pure ornamentation (as in other court panegyrics). Here the poet borrows plentifully from Venantius Fortunatus's *De virginitate* to extend Marian majesty to the royal women, as Godman demonstrates; Mary's heavenly rule provides an ideal model for terrestrial queenship. Throughout this section, the poet also makes use of Virgil's epic to fortify the presentation of royal women as leaders in their own right, as in the earlier example of Liutgard.

No other Carolingian author, before or since, allows women such potency.[17] Theodulf's poem on the court poses the most striking contrast, treating Charlemagne's daughters very quickly and making them appear static and passive.[18] Angilbert's poem "To Charlemagne and His Entourage" celebrates the intellectual abilities of Rodtruda, but her portrait stands alone and is not nearly as extensive.[19] Rodtruda's sister Bertha, Angilbert's mistress, also appears with the wish that she may enjoy his poetry, and Charlemagne's sister, Gisla, though a woman famed for her intellect, figures in Angilbert's poem in the most unimaginative way as any monastic woman might.[20] In all, Angilbert displays greater interest in two of Charlemagne's daughters and acknowledges some active, critical capacity. Alcuin, likewise, nods to one intellectually curious young woman, probably Charlemagne's daughter Gisla, encouraging her interest in astronomy.[21]

Otherwise, women do not figure in Alcuin's poem on the court at all. Even these sympathetic accounts do not come close to *Karolus Magnus* in displaying women as part of the Carolingian machine. Even later, if Ermoldus Nigellus accords the empress Judith the "limelight," as Godman avers, it is short-lived and in the service of a political statement.[22]

In the *Karolus Magnus*, the young women appear active as well as beautiful and bedecked with splendid clothing and jewelry. They do not adorn the court but figure as part of the ruling elite displayed before Aachen in anticipation of the hunt. Whether on horseback or leading a choir of nuns, the women in their spiritual and secular roles participate in this typically male activity. As Godman points out, there is no evidence that women would have participated in the hunt at this time. He cautions, rightly, that the poem ought not to be taken as a reflection of historical reality. But rather than serving simply as a device to heighten the splendor of Charlemagne, as Godman argues, the placement and posturing of these women in the context of the ceremonial gathering preceding the hunt at Aachen function symbolically to locate these women in the framework of

Carolingian power. Were the intent merely to highlight Charlemagne's power, surely the poet would have paid due attention to all three heirs as well; and the women would likely not have appeared on horseback but somewhere on the margins of a male-centered hunting processional as spectators. The inclusion of all daughters born before 800 while one son, Louis, does not appear is curious and a point to which I shall return later. For now, I would like to consider the question of authorship.

The Question of Authorship

The poem appears in one manuscript from the monastery of Saint Gall (Zurich, Stadtbliothek MS C78), dating to the late ninth century, but most scholars agree that the poem was composed in the first half of the ninth century, probably in the first decade.[23] Because of its fragmentary nature, it is difficult to ascertain much about the author or the circumstances under which the poem was written, though there is room for a good deal of speculation. Given the level of the poet's sophistication in grammar, style, and handling of classical materials, the poet would have been well educated. Based on its use of some rare classical texts and its subject matter, it was probably written by someone who had access to the library at Aachen.[24] It is also possible that the poet had been educated at court and retained mentally the range of classical texts indicated in the poem. Its subject matter suggests that the author spent time at court at any rate, had an interest in promoting Charlemagne's legacy, and maintained connections with court life. In more than a century since scholars have taken up the question of authorship, several candidates have been suggested: Alcuin, Angilbert, Einhard, Hibernicus Exul, Modoin, Theodulf of Orleans, and, assuming a much later date of composition, Walafrid Strabo. Though the writings of all have some sort of stylistic parallels in the poem, most are weakly connected on stylistic grounds and have been more or less eliminated.[25]

Overreliance on stylistic analysis limits the pool unnecessarily, since it can only take into account known texts. Given the likelihood of loss—indeed, this poem barely survived—that method seems needlessly to rule out possibilities of authorship. Surely the handful of known poets did not write all the poems that survive, and the survivals themselves must represent only a portion of the texts actually produced during the period. As a means of discerning authorship, therefore, stylistic analysis is a helpful tool, but it is neither fully objective nor exhaustive in the sense that all extant poems and letters have been compared to this poem—there is a process of selection in the first place that singles out the most likely candidates for comparison. But other parallels may be found in less likely sources, and those sources may still lurk, unedited, in the archives or may be lost to us entirely. As John Contreni notes, 60 known male authors exist from the last quarter of the eighth through the end of the ninth century; many works have not survived and many remain unattributed.[26] We cannot imagine that these authors wrote it all; nor ought we to imagine that all authors were male. We have fairly strong, if finally inconclusive, evidence that women were involved in textual dissemination and even composed or supervised the writing of several chronicles and saints' lives. A poem celebrating a historical moment seems not to stretch beyond reason: Hrotsvit of Gandersheim would write an epic celebrating Otto's feats in the middle of the next century.

Interestingly, female authorship has not even been considered. And yet women as well as men of the court would have been equally well acquainted with Charlemagne's trip to Paderborn, Pope Leo's visit there, and, certainly, the court at Aachen, which is most carefully described to impart local and courtly flavor. Even if women did not participate in the royal hunt, they could imagine it just as easily as any court scholar who also likely never participated in such events. Moreover, noblewomen of the Carolingian period were well educated and productive as scribes and hagiographers as well as chroniclers in their various communities. Scholars are finding that women may have written more than tradition has acknowledged. Bernhard Bischoff has famously demonstrated the importance of female scriptoria based on the example of the monastery at Chelles, which opened up further investigation into women as writers, not just copyists.[27] Rosamond McKitterick and Janet Nelson have both made compelling cases for female authorship and patronage of chronicles.[28] Based on these and other arguments, John Contreni has called for more open-minded assessment of anonymous texts, rather than the traditional assumption that, unless explicitly indicated, texts were written by men.[29] Some women were lauded for their intellectual abilities: Alcuin calls Charlemagne's sister, Gisla, "mathematica" and "femina verbi potens," for example, and Angilbert praises Charlemagne's daughter Rodtruda's poetic sensibility.

In the absence of known female authors, though, it is difficult to determine female authorship on the basis of either style or content. We know that women were educated, were trained and experienced as scribes of the highest caliber, and displayed an interest in literature. But what might they have written? Can we conceive of women as poets? A little more than a century later, Hrotsvit of Gandersheim wrote epic and narrative poetry in addition to her dramatic works, so we might extend back from her example. Within a century of this poem, for example, Dhuoda would produce a moral guide for her son. We know, too, that the empress Judith had a keen appreciation for the literary arts. In the eighth century, Leoba and other women of the Boniface circle were trained in poetry, as were their male counterparts, and they did compose verses to share with their correspondents. That women might have executed more polished, lengthy poetic works than survive in the Boniface correspondence does not stretch plausibility. But if so, how can we know when we encounter a poem by a woman? Women who would be writing—that is, women with the ability and means to do so—may have had the same sort of background and experience as their male counterparts. Similar training, a similar court environment, similar motivations and interests may produce a degree of gender neutrality in style and content, in which case any argument for female authorship would be difficult indeed.

But even if the education, scholarly resources, intellectual environment, political and social interests were all the same, the question of gender as perceived socially, lived personally, and relating to perceptions of being remains. Even without benefit of twentieth-century discussions on the question of what it is to read as a woman, can we say that women would have read—and written—exactly as men, given the same scholarly preparation and environment? The process of immasculation that Elaine Showalter identified for the twentieth-century female reader must have operated in the ninth century as well and perhaps even more virulently. But would it have been the only process? Would there have been no resistance without Elaine Showalter or Judith Fetterley or Adrienne Rich to point out the dilemma of women estranged from their own experiences championing or identifying with "universal" values that foreground their own devaluation? Without even considering notions of resistance, since there really is no way to ascertain such impulses, we can only speculate as to how women may have internalized the texts they read and studied.

The question is not just about intellectual abilities and access to texts, therefore, but approaches to and assimilation of texts in the process of learning and how those texts might be filtered through or organized by personal experience. Like the mosaics of Antioch with which this volume opens, memory and identity are both composed of readily available materials in the public domain. Reading and memory become intensely personal as we, builders of our own life edifices, construct "expressive gestures and performances...from our remembered experience."[30] As Cotter-Lynch and Herzog explain in the sections "Active Memory" and "Memory and Individual Identity" in the introduction to this volume, the type of texts learned help to map the mental landscape, as do individual attitude, intention, character, and gender.[31] Several chapters in the volume demonstrate how women, too, might participate actively in an

ethics of reading, even while assimilating texts that come almost completely from the memories and experiences of men, scripted by men for
masculinist ends. Clemence of Barking reinvents hagiographical texts,
infused with new material, through her complex use of the *oratio recta*;
Hildegard of Bingen's ekphrastic recollections of her visions retool the
conventions of *fin amor*. Julian of Norwich's *imitatio Mariae* reinterprets
this standard trope to new literary ends. Gertrud of Helfta crafts formal exercises to free women from the constraints of perceived notions of
femininity, and Margery Kempe uses both authorized and unauthorized
texts, introducing "a personal voice into her public religious drama," to
create her own space for worship, subverting the very authorities that
authorized them while resisting the label of heretic.[32]

In the case of Carolingian Francia, even if men and women learned
together in the same setting from the same instructor(s) and with the
same materials, the texts would not signify the same way for women as for
men, given differences of socialization and points of identification within
the texts. How would the compendium of classical and Christian texts
available to the intellectual elite at the court of Charlemagne accord with
and map onto lived female experience? And how might a woman reas-
semble those texts in her own creation? Would that quintessential medieval school text, Virgil's *Aeneid*, be read, assimilated, and re-presented
the same way by a woman as by a man? Would aspects of leadership be
praised, admired, and categorized the same way? With which characters
might a woman identify? We would do well to remember that individuals
are gendered beings; if experience and identity formation are contingent
on gender, ethics of reading must be as well.

When trying to assign authorship in an era when we know women
participated in intellectual culture, particularly when considering the
authorship of a poem that bears little resemblance to anything else produced in its own time, we would do well to keep in mind that the process of memory, the very shaping of the mental landscape, is not purely
rational and objective but is a rhetorical process experientially informed,
emotionally charged, and culturally contingent.[33] It is safe to say that,
since women were socialized differently from early childhood and would
have experienced the world differently on that basis, they would also
have processed their texts and lessons differently, even if learning and
reading alongside their male counterparts. And as remembering subjects,
they may well have produced different or "eccentric" compositions. In
the remainder of this chapter, I argue that *Karolus Magnus* may be one
place where we can see fairly clear marks of female reception and perception of classical and Christian texts available to the intellectual elite of the
day, a rhetorical expression of one woman's mental landscape.

The poem is certainly eccentric—in style, in focus, and, according to Godman, in its peculiar use of Venantius Fortunatus's *De virginitate*, which, as he notes, remains unexplained by catalogers of the poem's sources.[34] Though an odd choice for an epic celebrating secular power, Venantius's poem provides a particularly useful model for linking earthly rule to divine, an important aspect of Carolingian political thought, given that "the hierarchy of heaven, presided over by the Virgin Mary, in Venantius's poem stands behind the hierarchy of the court, with Charlemagne at its head, in *Karolus Magnus et Leo Papa*."[35] Taking Godman's point further, I propose that superimposing Charlemagne over the Blessed Virgin produces a double effect, not only making earthly power divine but broadening the typically masculine power structure to include women. This is not the Blessed Virgin of the later Middle Ages with whom Mother Julian identifies, suffused with humility and compassion;[36] this is the Queen of Heaven who, though perceived as an intercessor in this early period, was more regal than maternal and therefore also a symbol of power, as evidenced by contemporary texts and iconography.[37] That Venantius's poem was more likely to be read—and studied—by women means that it also was more likely to be retained in their mental archives for future use, suggesting at least the possibility of female authorship, which may explain this peculiar use of source material for a secular epic.[38]

For Godman, the use of Venantius's poem on virginity makes sense in practical terms. According to Godman, a poet wishing to praise a court in which women figure prominently would find Venantius's poem particularly useful, since it provides a rare model for female pageantry. This rationale seems inadequate if that were the only purpose behind the poet's choice of source. Certainly the poet could have described (and embellished) courtly gatherings without models, as other court poets do. If the object was to trump prior versions, it is also not clear why a model would be necessary. Moreover, it does not explain why the poet would wish to expand on the presentation of women at the hunt, which this poet does. Indeed, Godman worries that the poem's literary devices may be credited with too much historical veracity, as an unrefracted glimpse into Charles's court at Aachen on the eve of his coronation, and the status of women in that context. He cautions, therefore, that while the presence of women is important, one ought not "to seek realism from it":

> Its author's imagination had been engaged by symbolic parallels between the earthly and heavenly hierarchies; his object was to provide an idealized image of imperial power. To search for cynegetic detail in his work, or to attempt to find analogues for it in nonliterary sources (where the attendance of women at the boar hunt is seldom, if ever, recorded), is therefore

futile for predictable and positive reasons. Neither in the annals nor even in earlier poetic encomia on Charlemagne's court are the true analogues of this hunting scene to be found.[39]

Certainly historical veracity is not the point. As Janet Nelson cautions, "Beware! This is poetry. Genre takes its toll on historicity, even if this poem was written soon after the events it describes."[40] The idyllic scene surely did not replicate any historical moment but stylized a ritual procession for literary and political effect. Since he does not even consider the possibility of female authorship, Godman can only explain the prominence of women as a vague fact in Carolingian history and as a simple literary device in the poem. For him, the use of the device is motivated by the poet's competitive spirit, not by any real admiration for the women, as the poet "concentrates on the appearance of the imperial ladies, arrayed with an opulence surpassing the grandeur of Theodulf's earlier description, as a means of evoking *splendor imperii*."[41]

Reading the women as ornament when they have been so carefully displayed as active misses an opportunity for deeper analysis of the relation of the poem to women (which admittedly is not a concern for Godman). The poem celebrates not just the future emperor but his family as well, his queen and daughters along with two of his sons. Since the image of Charlemagne as paterfamilias extends beyond the literal parameters of his own family to the realm at large and, indeed, to the Christian empire he would soon rule, it sends a larger message about how the poet views the nature of the realm and its citizens. It also reads women into the scene of empire where they, too, are leaders—Rodtrud and Gisla as abbesses or at least prioresses, Bertha with her own entourage.[42] Rhodhaid, Theodrada, and Hildtrud also are surrounded by their retinues. That women are commissioning and also likely creating chronicles in this period, such as the *Annales mettenses priores* produced under the supervision of Gisla at Chelles,[43] suggests that they had an interest in the presentation of the rulers and assumed an active role in the formulation of dynastic identity. The paternal flavor may seem to modern readers to characterize male authorship, but it is certainly not beyond the scope of female authorship, principles, or taste, particularly if the author was a member of Charlemagne's family.

Venantius's *De virginitate* is not the only instance in which the poet imagines Charlemagne's power through a female exemplar. The poet draws heavily on Virgil's *Aeneid* to trace Charlemagne's trajectory from the building of Aachen to imperial eminence. One might expect that the poet would model the Frankish ruler on Aeneas; one would not, however, expect Virgil's Dido to lend color and dimension to Charlemagne's majesty. Indeed, Godman notes that the poet freely adapts book 4 of Virgil's *Aeneid* to draw out Charlemagne's court procession. Charlemagne's retinue mirrors Dido's, as do other, ornamental details. Most interesting, a golden fillet adorning Charlemagne's hair is, as Godman notes, "transferred" from Dido to Charlemagne. That choice seems eccentric at best for the period and unlikely for a male author. Other poets find in the character of Aeneas a suitable model for Charlemagne, who is to establish, after all, a new Rome just as Aeneas established a new Troy; although describing Charlemagne as a new Aeneas, this poet is also able to recognize the viability of Dido as a model of regal power. That artistic choice seems more readily born out of female consciousness than male, where a focus on Dido's power rather than her pathos seems unlikely. A woman studying the *Aeneid* would be more likely to identify with the figure of Dido and would probably be more open to Dido as regal model. Even if it was only subconsciously, Virgil's description of Dido's crown may have struck a young girl studying the *Aeneid* and found a place in her memory for later retrieval, whereas a male student may have identified with Aeneas or other male leaders, fixating on details of their presentation as marks of power. I am not suggesting this is a willfully subversive move but that it can be explained as an organic part of a woman's learning process deeply rooted in her consciousness or character. The combination of Venantius's *De virginitate* with Virgil's *Aeneid*, along with other classical and Christian sources, may exemplify a uniquely female assimilation of source materials to read and express a view of leadership and power from a feminine perspective.

Candidates for Authorship

Some must wonder how a woman of that period could possibly have written a poem that exceeded the talents of even Angilbert, whom Alcuin fondly named "Homer." This is pure conjecture, of course, but a trail worth pursuing, if only speculatively. Such a thing might have happened not in spite of the period but because of it since, during Charlemagne's reign, certain privileged women of the court may have had a unique opportunity to join the poets' circle—or at least hover on the periphery. Thus I argue that eccentricities in genre, style, and adaptation of sources as well as the poem's attention to women in the sources and inclusion of women in a genre that traditionally excludes them suggest that the poet was a woman, probably of Charlemagne's family. There are several strong possibilities: Charlemagne's sister, Gisla, who was a powerful person in her own right, as abbess of four important royal monasteries (Chelles, Soissons, Jouarre, and Faremoutiers); his cousins, Gundrada or

Theodrada, both educated at court and both later abbesses of royal communities; his daughters, all of whom would have been well educated at the palace school; and finally, a woman writing under the supervision or at the request of any of these women.

One candidate for authorship is Charlemagne's cousin Gundrada, who lived at court as a virgin devoted to God. Paschasius Radbertus celebrates her virginity, though not her learning.[44] Educated at court, Gundrada studied under Alcuin, perhaps together with Angilbert and/or Modoin. Alcuin notes her knowledge of grammar in a letter accompanying a copy of his treatise against adoptionism.[45] And in his dedicatory letter for *De ratione animae*, he lauds her wisdom as well. Given her relationship with Alcuin and her characterization elsewhere, I would like to suggest that her time at court offered greater potential for development than just testing and strengthening her sexual willpower. Gundrada remained at court until Louis the Pious succeeded his father and "purged" the court, sending her to the monastery of Ste. Croix, Poitiers. Had she been motivated primarily by piety, she would have taken orders far sooner at one of the prominent dynastic monasteries appropriate to her family and rank. She chose to stay at court, however, though she did not seem to take part in court life the way other women did.

Intellectual life at court may well have been the main attraction for her. There she had access to the palace school and library and could also have participated in the circulation of letters among the scholars at court. Certainly Alcuin wrote to her and presumably had received a number of letters from her, though none survive. If she did study under Alcuin at the same time Modoin and Angilbert did, that would account for stylistic and thematic similarities as well as exposure to the same classical sources. Gundrada also apparently taught at court until she was sent to preside over the community of Ste. Croix at Poitiers upon Louis's accession in 814.[46] Like male scholars at court, Gundrada had access to Charlemagne's famous library, as we know from the letter accompanying *De ratione animae*, in which Alcuin tells her to check whether various other treatises on the soul may be in that collection.[47] The male scholars would also have had such access, of course. But court scholars by and large, as McKitterick points out, are "also the men of affairs who ran the kingdom."[48] I would therefore like to introduce the (possibly radical) notion that, because she would not have been preparing for public service as such male peers as Modoin, Angilbert, Candidus, and Fredegisus would have been, Gundrada would have had greater leisure to pursue, even indulge in, her own studies. She is, in short, an independent scholar of means with high intellectual capacity. Not only may she have had greater opportunity to compose an extended piece, she would almost certainly have had a unique perspective from which to rethink classical, Christian, and court models available to her. Given that the poem represents not only the first epic of the Carolingian era but also an unusual reworking of the source materials—classical and Christian—a female author such as Gundrada, well educated but with a different range of experiences and interests, makes sense. Because no writing of hers survives, we can only speculate, but there is no reason to believe she could not have pulled it off.

Another strong possibility for authorship is Charlemagne's sister, Gisla. Though she never married, Gisla participated in building the Carolingian dynasty through other means. As she was abbess of Chelles and (in name at least) Soissons, Jouarre, and Faremoutiers, Brie, Gisla's domains were not inconsequential. Scriptoria existed at most, if not all, of these foundations where some of the most exquisite manuscripts of the period were produced.[49] She also made a substantial donation to the royal monastery of Saint Denis.[50] The relic collection at Chelles was among the largest of its day, attesting not only to Gisla's spiritual inclinations but also to her status, not to mention her keen political savvy. Relics attract pilgrims; they also demonstrate otherworldly support of worldly ventures. They are just the thing to legitimate and sanction the ruling family.[51] Gisla seems also to have enjoyed a public role: not only did she visit her brother at court and receive visits from him and others, including Alcuin of York; she also accompanied him on the journey to Rome where Charles was coronated emperor on Christmas of the year 800. In fact, she relates the details of the event to Alcuin, who apparently could not accompany the emperor.[52] It is likely that she traveled to Paderborn to witness the meeting of her brother and Pope Leo as well.

In terms of interest and ability, there is no reason to believe Gisla could not have written such a poem, though no poem known to have been written by her (or any other woman of the Carolingian court) exists. Gisla's correspondence with Alcuin reveals a thirsty intellect and a commanding spirit. In one surviving letter to him, she and her niece Rodtrud plead ignorance in not being able to make their way through Augustine's commentary on the gospel of John and urge Alcuin to complete his treatise so that they may learn the complexities of that gospel from him.[53] In doing so, John Contreni points out, they are expressing frustrations to be expected of all but the most learned in tackling what must have been an extremely obscure text riddled with references to a very foreign land and cultural context.[54]

Gisla also seems to have had an interest in history or at least in chronicling her family's rise to power. As noted earlier, Janet Nelson argues that the *Annales mettenses priores* was written at Chelles under her supervision. The production of this chronicle and possibly others—in addition to Gisla's relic collection, her support of Saint Denis, and the church she built dedicated to Saint Mary—all speak to an active interest in promoting the family dynasty with her brother at the center of it. It is certainly possible that the poem was commissioned by her; it is also possible that she herself wrote the poem. That Alcuin calls her "femina verbi potens" suggests poetic and rhetorical skill in addition to the many other talents she clearly possessed.

In addition to motive, she had the means: Gisla certainly would have had access to the tremendous variety of source texts associated with the poem through the court library and also through the multitude of texts that coursed through the scriptoria under her supervision. We know one of Bede's texts came to her through Alcuin for copying.[55] Given her clear devotion to intellectual pursuits, it is not unreasonable to expect that she may also have committed those texts to her own mental library. The absence of Gisla from the poem is noteworthy, given her appearance in two other court panegyrics and her active involvement in court affairs and events, which we can glean not only from the poems but also from Alcuin's letters and chronicle evidence. The fact that she herself is not mentioned in the poem when she frequented court at Aachen and was likely there in attendance at Paderborn may support authorship rather than patronage. If she had commissioned the poem, the author would almost certainly have felt compelled to depict her within it and would have been right to do so. Were she the author, however, modesty may have prevented her. I will pick up this question again a bit later.

Other possibilities also exist, such as Charlemagne's daughter Rodtrud, who resided at Chelles with her aunt and likely served as prioress when Gisla was ill. Clearly she would have had the very best education, including lessons in Greek from Paul the Deacon as she prepared for marriage to the heir to the Byzantine throne.[56] She may, therefore, have been intimately familiar with another of the poem's chief sources and a model for Charlemagne, Corippus's *In laudem Iustini Augusti minoris*.[57] As mentioned earlier, Angilbert calls her "mentis clarissima virgo";[58] Alcuin, too, praises her for her intellect, together with her aunt Gisla. In addition, Rodtrud would have had access to the court library as well as to all texts that came through the lively scriptorium at Chelles. As with Gisla, if Rodtrud were the author or patron, the poem would have to be dated before 810, the year of her death.

Gundrada's sister, Theodrada, who became abbess of Notre Dame de Soissons in 810, is another possibility. Theodrada was involved in promoting the Anianian reforms instituted under Louis the Pious after 816 and ensuring observance of the Benedictine rule in the recently founded Saxon women's monasteries from her new base at Herford. Because of her role in spreading Anianian reform and also because of her relationship to Adalhard, she enjoyed a strong relationship with Corbie, an important training monastery with a productive scriptorium. In order for her to achieve this sort of status, it seems to me she must have been a well-educated woman and one fully invested in the Carolingian imperium. Like her sister, she would have been educated at the palace school.

Another viable candidate, though perhaps not as interesting since we could not assign a name to her, is one of the nuns at Chelles or Soissons under the abbacy of any of the royal women. That the poet spends a considerable amount of time on the description of the young Gisla with her choir of virgins, for example, speaks in favor of her patronage while serving as abbess of Soissons. At any rate, the poem certainly could have been written at Chelles or Soissons and by a nun.

So which of these is the best candidate? Of course, a definitive argument for a particular female author is nigh impossible with the paucity of material evidence available to us. But I will puzzle it out nonetheless to open up larger considerations of gender and authorship. Too often possibilities for understanding women's scholarly contributions are foreclosed because of the limitations of sources and methodology. This is an opportunity to think about women not just performing the labor of copying but engaging in creative, intellectual activity and to think about the women themselves—something scholars seldom do because there is so little to work with. The easiest solution may be to attribute the poem vaguely to some woman residing at the royal monasteries of Chelles or Soissons. Greater specificity is possible, though.

Although all of these women had the capacity, the material support, and presumably the will to write such an epic, Gundrada stands out as the one with greatest opportunity and perhaps greatest motive. Though her sister, Theodrada, would certainly have been well educated, she came to monastic devotion after a marriage and with a daughter. Her education, therefore, probably did not reach the level of Gisla's, Rodtruda's, or Gundrada's, nor would she have had ready access to the palace library. Moreover, the course of her life would not have provided her the leisure to study and write available to her sister or those such as Rodtrud who had long lived in a monastic setting. Rodtrud is an enticing possibility, but given the portrayal of Rodtrud in the poem, perhaps patronage is more likely than authorship, though the bounds of propriety in that circumstance are unclear. Moreover, the absence of Louis also seems inconsistent with Rodtrud, since she named her only son after him and he named a daughter after her, suggesting a favorable relationship between the two. Her younger sister Gisla remains a possibility; the fact that the poet dwells at greater length on depicting her than on the other siblings is suggestive but probably more indicative of patronage than authorship. Charlemagne's sister, Gisla, is among the strongest candidates, given her clear sense of dynastic mission. The poem would certainly match her character, as far as we can ascertain it through the murkiness of centuries and dearth of material. The omission of Louis would be odd, though not impossible, since she seems to have favored Charles, not Louis, for succession.[59] But then the sparse four lines devoted to Charles are puzzling.

Gundrada presents the most compelling case for authorship, not least because that would also allow for greater flexibility in dating the poem, which would in turn help resolve two questions in its presentation of family members. Though most scholars now believe the poem was written shortly after Charlemagne's coronation in 800, there is really no good reason to do so aside from the subject of the poem. It makes sense that the epic was composed in celebration of Charlemagne's coronation as emperor, but that does not mean it had to have been composed on the spot or even a few years out. It is also possible to imagine a different political impulse for the composition of an epic celebrating Charlemagne's triumph. We might envision Gundrada as a "remembering subject," hearkening back to the peak of Charlemagne's career after his death when she lost her standing at court. Though she, too, might have participated in cultivating the dynastic imagination with a celebratory poem following imperial coronation, I would argue that she would have been especially motivated to compose such a poem after Louis's accession to the throne and her removal from the palace.

The later date may also explain two conspicuous absences from the poem, those of Charlemagne's sister and his son Louis. The fact that Gisla does not appear in a poem depicting so fully female leadership makes more sense if the poem is dated after her death in or before 810.[60] Still, her absence may also simply be a matter of excluding all but Charlemagne's immediate family. Louis's absence is not so easily explained, particularly with a later date, when his accession to the throne became imminent. For his absence during the segment relating to Pope Leo, it may be that the author chose to follow one chronicle that notes Louis's deployment elsewhere in the realm when the pope arrived in Paderborn. But Charles was not there either, in the poem and according to the Royal Frankish Annals, and yet as *primogenitus* he is first among Charlemagne's children in the ceremonial processional at Aachen. The whereabouts of Louis during Charlemagne's Saxon campaign of 799 do not account for Louis's absence from the ceremonial gathering at Aachen when all of his sisters and brothers are in attendance. Since that event is fully fictional, any omission of one of Charlemagne's children is telling, particularly the omission of a son and potential heir to the throne when the poet manages

to include even the youngest daughters and even the daughter of a concubine. The poem strives, after all, to show Charlemagne as *pater optimus*,
whatever the historical realities.

Admittedly we know very little about Gundrada, and no trace of her
writing survives for stylistic comparison. It is nevertheless easy to imagine that as poet she might well hearken back nostalgically to the promise
of Charlemagne's rule in a utopian vision where he is the best father—
literally and metaphorically; where he cultivates learning and himself
is most learned; where he ensures justice to all; where he defends the
Church and promotes its teachings; where she was supported in his court.
She may also look to the future by adumbrating the potential offered by
Charles and Pippin as heirs to the throne even as she erases Louis from the
picture, which is what this poem effectively does. Louis's absence from
the portion of the poem that survives is significant, since both events
described in the fragment signal political status. The ceremonial preparation for the hunt at Aachen following the poetic account of the building of that "new Rome" depicts the members of the royal family as a
way to pay homage and also to display the most important personages of
that burgeoning dynasty. Given the poet's other liberties, the omission of
Louis here is telling.

Louis is also absent from the account of the historic meeting of
Charlemagne and Pope Leo at Paderborn. At Paderborn, Pippin is sent
to retrieve the ailing Leo; Charles and Louis are nowhere in sight. The
Royal Frankish Annals note that Charles was sent to fight the Slavs and
was expected back shortly; no mention is made of Louis, but his biography suggests he, like Charles, may have been otherwise engaged.[61] As
the third son, he would not have been chosen for the embassy anyway;
the interesting point is that the poet spends so much time on the embassy
itself. As Nelson notes, the encounter had the effect of enhancing not
just Charlemagne's profile but Pippin's as well. Significantly, this episode mirrors Charlemagne's own journey when just a child to escort
Pope Zachary in a symbolic gesture orchestrated by his father to signify
his status as heir to the Frankish throne.[62] If a later date for this poem is
accepted, the poet's inclusion of Pippin's embassy—taken together with
the relatively lengthy description of him in the earlier encomium of
Charlemagne's children—may be politically charged, projecting retro-
spectively a different outcome in the transmission of imperial power by
setting Pippin in the limelight, thereby reminding the reader that it was
he who was selected for this symbolic mission, not Louis, and making all
the more conspicuous Louis's total absence from the poem.[63]

The poem may be read, then, as a later development of the court
panegyric conjuring up for its readers the glory of the past in relation to

the present reality. That is, it may be as much critique as praise or critique through praise of what has been lost.[64] The complete omission of Louis in its encomium of Charlemagne's family preceding his symbolic hunt cannot possibly be an oversight when even Charlemagne's illegitimate daughter Rhodhaid appears in the ranks. Charles and Pippin are given the same sort of attention each of the daughters enjoys, though ironically neither one lives to continue their father's legacy. As Margaret Cotter-Lynch reminds us in her study of Notker's recasting of Perpetua's story, forgetting is as important as remembering.[65] Of course, Louis cannot really be erased from the contemporary scene over which he rules. Carruthers has shown that obliteration is rarely effective.[66] Here, the absence created draws attention to itself. From this perspective, the poem functions as an indictment of Louis, which only makes sense if the poem was written after Louis's accession—or at least after the death of Charles in 811 when his ascension to the throne seemed clear.[67] Not unlike other poetic statements, this poem may have offered a nostalgic vision of Charlemagne's promise—and Pippin's as the once favored heir—as a way to express dissatisfaction with the present emperor in response to a perceived affront. Imagining Charlemagne's last queen, Liutgard, and his daughters as leaders and significant personages of the royal family redrafts the court scene and advocates for a greater public profile for women in an age increasingly suspicious of female power, particularly under the reign of Louis the Pious. Memorializing and publicizing monastic alongside secular power by showcasing nuns on parade with their worldly siblings may add another dimension as the great age of the double monastery is coming to a close and monastic women experience heightened restrictions on their activities within and without the cloister. The poem is, perhaps, a bittersweet remembrance of the possibilities—however limited by our standards—offered women during the reign of Charlemagne and a provocative reinvention of public memory.

Who better than Gundrada to write such a poem? A student of Alcuin, she arguably had the training and the means, with access to Charlemagne's illustrious library. She may well have read or at least heard the celebratory poems circulating at court and may also have benefited from Modoin's early attempts at exploiting Virgilian classicism and improved upon them. Since no writing by her survives, we cannot guess as to her talent, but we cannot discount that possibility simply because she is a woman. As a woman scholar living at court and yet apart as a virgin devoted to God, Gundrada was in a peculiar position and may well have used it to her advantage. That may explain the eccentricity of style and use of sources "in provocative contrast or innovative combination" and enable what Godman calls "a literary independence denied to any of [the poet's] peers."[68] Finally, as one of Louis's disenfranchised cousins, and one who was not given an active role in his monastic reform movement, she also had motivation for writing him out of the triumphal narrative of Charlemagne's ascendancy.

Even if my argument for Gundrada's authorship fails to convince, the poem resonates powerfully as a testament to women, drafting Charlemagne's power through two iconic women—Dido and the Virgin Mary—while displaying strong and active women as part of Charlemagne's imperial entourage. If the poem were eccentric in a mediocre way, or in a way that displayed poor education or weak talent, scholars would not hesitate to ascribe it to a woman. That the poem is noted for its sophisticated use of classical and Christian sources as well as its cleverness and grammatical acuity should not preclude the possibility of female authorship but should rather make us think further on it and the other artful anonymous poems of its time. Hrotsvit of Gandersheim would do something similar in her epic of Otto the Great a century and a half later. Even as she showcased powerful female figures alongside the iconic emperor, she self-consciously acknowledged writing in a form typically reserved for male authors, and yet that did not stop her from doing so. Why can't we imagine that a formidable female talent preceded her?

Notes

1. Dieter Schaller, "Das Aachener Epos für Karl den Kaiser," in *Frühmittelalterliche Studien* 10 (1976): 134–68.
2. Alcuin, Letter 50, in *Epistolae*, ed. Ernst Dümmler, MGH, Epistolae 4, Epistolae Karolini Aevi 2 (1895; repr., Munich: MGH, 1994).
3. Ibid., Letter 149.
4. Ibid., Letters 96 and 102.
5. Ibid., Letter 102.
6. Janet Nelson, "Charlemagne—Pater Optimus?" in *Courts, Elites, and Gendered Power in the Early Middle Ages* (Aldershot, UK: Ashgate, 2007), ch. XV, p. 279.
7. For a more detailed discussion of Theodulf's treatment of Liutgard, see Helene Scheck, *Reform and Resistance: Formations of Female Subjectivity in Early Medieval Ecclesiastical Culture* (Albany, NY: SUNY Press, 2008), 35–36. Theodulf's poem appears as "On the Court" in *Poetry of the Carolingian Renaissance*, ed. and trans. Peter Godman (Norman: University of Oklahoma Press, 1985); the relevant passage can be found on pages 154–55.
8. Einhard, *Einhardi Vita Karoli Magni*, ed. O. Holder-Egger, MGH. Scriptores rerum Germanicarum in usum scholarum (Hanover, Germany: Hahn, 1911), 22. The most recent translation is provided in *Two Lives of Charlemagne*, trans. and ed. David Ganz (New York: Penguin, 2008), 31.

9. Lines 182–84. This and all subsequent quotations are from *Karolus Magnus et Leo Papa*, ed. Ernst Dümmler, MGH Poetae Latini Aevi Carolini 1 (1881; repr., Zurich: Weidmann, 1964), 366–79.

10. Lines 193–94.

11. The poem presents all children alive in 800 *except* Louis. See Karl Ferdinand Werner, "Die Nachkommen Karls des Grossen," in *Karl der Grosse: Lebenswerk und Nachleben*, vol. 4, ed. Wolfgang Braunfels (Düsseldorf: Verlag Schwann, 1967), 403–79, at 442–43.

12. Though Rodtrud probably would have succeeded Gisla as abbess, she died in the same year; she may have served as prioress during Gisla's illnesses, though. See the Royal Frankish Annals, s.a. 810.

13. Lines 221–23.

14. Angilbert, "To Charlemagne and His Entourage," in *Poetry of the Carolingian Renaissance*, ed. and trans. Peter Godman (Norman: University of Oklahoma Press, 1985), 114–15, lines 47–49. For some discussion of the representation of women in this poem, see Scheck, *Reform and Resistance*, 39–40.

15. Lines 229–33.

16. Peter Godman, "The Poetic Hunt," in *Charlemagne's Heir: New Perspectives on the Reign of Louis the Pious (814–840)*, ed. Peter Godman and Roger Collins (Oxford: Clarendon Press, 1990), 578.

17. Nevertheless, in "Charlemagne's Daughters," Anton Scharer reads women in Carolingian poetry, including *Karolus Magnus* and the other poems mentioned here, to enrich our understanding of women at Charlemagne's court and to further Janet Nelson's view that Charlemagne's daughters played a significant political role. His essay appears in *Early Medieval Studies in Memory of Patrick Wormald*, ed. Stephen Baxter, Catherine E. Karkov, Janet L. Nelson, and David Pelteret (Farnham, UK: Ashgate, 2009), 269–82.

18. See Scheck, *Reform and Resistance*, 34–37.

19. Godman, *Poetry of the Carolingian Renaissance*, 114–15, lines 43–46.

20. Angilbert, "To Charlemagne and His Entourage," lines 38–41.

21. Ibid., lines 41–44. I follow Dümmler in identifying Gisla as referent.

22. Godman, "Poetic Hunt," 565–89, esp. 575–86.

23. A date of 799 has also been proposed, with the view that the poem had been written for the occasion of the pope's visit to Paderborn as a sort of welcome gesture, or immediately following that auspicious event. Schaller has made a convincing case for a post-coronation date, tied in to his argument that the poem was written in celebration or commemoration of that event. Subsequent scholars seem to have adopted that view. More recently, in "Moduin's 'Eclogues' and the 'Paderborn Epic'" (*Mittellateinisches Jahrbuch* 16 [1981]: 43–53), Roger P. H. Green has argued that the poem was written after Modoin's *Eclogues* and benefited from the poetics displayed therein. Since the *Eclogues* date roughly to the first decade of the ninth century, that would put *Karolus Magnus* somewhat after the year 800. Peter Godman strikes a middle road, pointing out that

the two poems may be roughly contemporary, with the authors perhaps sharing their work. Later dates have also been suggested.

24. On the Aachen library, see Bernhard Bischoff, "The Court Library of Charlemagne," in *Manuscripts and Libraries in the Age of Charlemagne*, trans. and ed. Michael Gorman (Cambridge: Cambridge University Press, 1994), 56–75. Originally published as "Die Hofbibliothek Karls des Großen," in *Karl der Große: Lebenswerk und Nachleben, II: Das geistige Leben* (Düsseldorf: Schwann, 1965), 42–62. Most scholars assume, as Bischoff does, that *Karolus Magnus* was composed at court because of the wealth of source materials it draws on. Though an accurate reconstruction of Charlemagne's library is impossible, the evidence we do have suggests a library surpassing all others in western Europe at the time.

25. The most stridently championed have been Angilbert, Einhard, and Modoin. At this time, Einhard and Modoin appear to be the frontrunners. See especially Schaller's argument for Einhard's authorship in "Das Aachener Epos für Karl den Kaiser" and Green's argument for the primacy of Modoin's Eclogues in "Moduin's 'Eclogues' and the 'Paderborn Epic.'" Francesco Stella argues for Modoin, recognizing that the question remains unresolved: "Autore e attribuzioni del 'Karolus Magnus et Leo Papa,'" in *Am Vorabend der Kaiser Krönung: Das Epos "Karolus Magnus et Leo Papa" und der Papstbesuch in Paderborn 799*, eds. Peter Godman et al. (Berlin: Akademie Verlag, 2002), 19–33. Although Angilbert was close to the family, a proficient and well-received poet (for which reason, presumably, Alcuin nicknames him Homer), the poem does not fit with his work. And if Manitius, who first ascribed authorship to him, is correct in his assessment, the poem exceeds Angilbert's grammatical and prosodic abilities ("die größere grammatische und prosodische Schulung in dem Epos sprichtgegen Angilberts Autorschaft," cited in Stella, "Autore e attribuzioni," 21). For Einhard, we have little basis for stylistic comparison. In fact, the impulse behind the recommendation for his authorship seems to derive simply from the desire to identify some poem with him, since at least one of his contemporaries makes reference to his poetic talents. Clearly that is not enough. Schaller makes the point, rightly, that Einhard's abilities and inclinations ought not to be judged by the prose works of his late years when he is writing as an old man under a different regime; still, it seems unlikely that he would display such interest in the women of court at one point and then later, when discussing Charlemagne's family specifically, not give them due attention. Though certainly Einhard may have wanted to celebrate the imperial coronation, the execution does not fit fully with his own sensibilities: that is, whereas Einhard seems to care little about and for the women of Charlemagne's family, and may even resent the degree of autonomy accorded them, the poem's author certainly pays attention to it and even flaunts it in places. Einhard likely would have treated the princes differently as well.

More recently, in his very useful survey of the question of authorship, Francesco Stella settles finally on Modoin, though he admits the question is not firmly resolved; he is simply the strongest possibility for Stella. Modoin was a student of Alcuin and a well-regarded poet, and the stylistic parallels still make a compelling case. The many echoes of Modoin's eclogues in *Karolus Magnus*, combined with Modoin's profile, are alluring: he was in the right place at the right time, and he had the skill to execute such a composition.

Because of the poem's eccentricities and thematic as well as generic inconsistencies with Modoin's eclogues, however, the case for his authorship remains ultimately unconvincing. I share the skepticism of Christine Ratkowitsch, who argues that the stylistic parallels can be explained in other ways. Arguments for authorship based exclusively on stylistic analysis seem to be finally inconclusive—certainly one would not base a plagiarism case solely on such evidence. The echoes may explain influence rather than authorship, though it is difficult to determine which direction the influence runs. Green has argued that Modoin's eclogues came first and that the *Karolus Magnus* poet improved upon the rhetorical structures therein. Alternatively, both may have been influenced by another, now obscure source. The two authors may have even shared one another's work, as Godman suggests.

26. John Contreni, "The Carolingian Renaissance: Education and Literary Culture," in vol. 2 of *The New Cambridge Medieval History*, ed. Rosamond McKitterick (Cambridge: Cambridge University Press, 1995), 719 [709–57].

27. Bernhard Bischoff, "Die Kölner Nonnenhandschriften und das Skriptorium von Chelles," in *Mittelalterliche Studien: Ausgewählte Aufsätze zur Schriftkunde und Literaturgeschichte* (Stuttgart: Anton Hiersemann, 1966), 1:16–34.

28. See especially Janet Nelson, "Gender and Genre in Women Historians of the Early Middle Ages," in *The Frankish World: 750–900* (London: Hambledon, 1996), 183–97; Rosamond McKitterick, "Women and Literacy in the Early Middle Ages," in *Books, Scribes and Learning in the Frankish Kingdoms, 6th–9th Centuries* (Aldershot, UK: Ashgate, 1994), XIII, and, more recently, *History and Memory in the Carolingian World* (Cambridge: Cambridge University Press, 2004), esp. 9–13 and 125.

29. Contreni, "Carolingian Renaissance," 709–57 and elsewhere.

30. Mary J. Carruthers, *The Book of Memory: A Study of Memory in Medieval Culture*, 2nd ed., Cambridge Studies in Medieval Literature 70 (Cambridge: Cambridge University Press, 2008), 226 and 21. See also the section "Memory and Identity" in the introduction to this volume.

31. Carruthers explains, "As the composer, acting like a master builder or *architectus*, fits his tropes onto the foundation stones of a text, he must smooth, scrape, chip off, and in other ways adapt and 'translate' the *dicta et facta memorabilia* he is using as his materials. So the edifice of one's life (so to speak), although created from stories available to all citizens, is also a fully personal creation, an expression (and creation) of one's character." *The Craft of Thought: Meditation, Rhetoric, and the Making of Images,*

400–1200, Cambridge Studies in Medieval Literature 34 (Cambridge: Cambridge University Press, 1998), 21. As the other chapters in this volume demonstrate, gender plays a role in this process of learning, assimilation of texts, and mapping consciousness. Through the example of Perpetua, for instance, Margaret Cotter-Lynch shows how Notker of Saint Gall exploits and reconfigures common hagiographical texts and images to shape textual community through his deft handling of memory arts, remembering as well as forgetting. Similarly, Ana Maria Machado surveys how the Portuguese redactors of the *Vitae patrum* reshape representations of women in recollecting those ancient stories.

32. Brad Herzog, "Portrait of a Holy Life: Mnemonic Inventiveness in *The Book of Margery Kempe*," chapter 9 in this volume.

33. See Carruthers, *Craft of Thought*, 15; Cotter-Lynch and Herzog describe the complexities of this process in the section "Active Memory" in the introduction to this volume.

34. Godman, "Poetic Hunt," 578.

35. Ibid., 579.

36. See Elissa Hansen's "Making a Place: *Imitatio Mariae* in Julian of Norwich's Self-Construction," chapter 8 in this volume.

37. Hilda Graef, *Mary: A History of Doctrine and Devotion*, vol. 1, *From the Beginnings to the Eve of the Reformation* (New York: Sheed and Ward, 1963), esp. 101–81.

38. This is not to say that men did not read and value the poem. According to Michael Lapidge, Venantius's entire corpus was available at the monastery at York from which Alcuin hailed. Moreover, De virginitate is the only one of Venantius's poems certainly known to Bede, suggesting that it may have circulated separately in eighth-century Northumbria. Michael Lapidge, *Anglo-Latin Literature, 600–899*, 2 vols. (London: Hambledon Press, 1996), 1.404–407.

39. Godman, "Poetic Hunt," 579.

40. Nelson, "Charlemagne—Pater Optimus?," ch. XV, p. 270.

41. Godman, "Poetic Hunt," 581.

42. For nuanced readings of the status and role of Charlemagne's daughters at court, see Janet Nelson, "Women at the Court of Charlemagne: A Case of Monstrous Regiment?" in *Medieval Queenship*, ed. John Carmi Parsons (London: St. Martin's, 1993), 43–61; and Scharer, "Charlemagne's Daughters."

43. On this example, see especially Nelson, "Gender and Genre"; McKitterick, "Women and Literacy"; and McKitterick, "Politics and History," in *History and Memory in the Carolingian World* 125 [120–32]. Although Yitzhak Hen notes that the evidence is far from conclusive, he too acknowledges that as a strong possibility: "The Annals of Metz and the Merovingian Past," in *The Uses of the Past in the Early Middle Ages*, eds. Yitzhak Hen and Matthew Innes (Cambridge: Cambridge University Press, 2000), 175–90.

44. "Quibus inhaerebat ex latere sexu, soror Gundrada nomine, dispar, sed virtutibus procul dubio compar, fratribus assiduitate praesens, si quidem virgo familiarior regi, nobilium nobilissima, quae inter venereos palatii ardores et iuvenum venustates, etiam inter mulcentia deliciarum et inter omnia libidinis blandimenta, sola meruit (ut credimus) reportare pudicitiae palmam, et potuit (ut dicitur) carnis spurcitias inlaeso calle transire" (To these [her siblings] the sister Gundrada clung fast, in constant attendance on her brothers, [unequal] in sex, but [beyond a doubt equal] in virtues. Although the virgin, most noble of nobles, was friendly to the king, and although she dwelled amid the wanton heats of the palace and charms of the youths, even amid caresses of delights and blandishments of passion, yet she alone was worthy to bring back the palm of modesty. She was able to cross over foulness of the flesh by an unharmed path). Paschasius Radbertus, *Vita Sancti Adalhardi*, MGH, SS 2, edited by George H. Pertz (Hanover, Germany: Hahn, 1829), 527; translated as "The Life of Saint Adalhard," in *Charlemagne's Cousins: Contemporary Lives of Adalard and Wala*, trans. Allen Cabaniss (Syracuse, NY: Syracuse University Press, 1967), 47. My clarifications and emendations are indicated by brackets.

45. I follow Dümmler here in assigning that letter to Gundrada; Ganz believes it was addressed to Gisla, but doesn't explain why.

46. In his *De ratione animae*, which he dedicated to her, Alcuin makes reference to her "*scholasticis.*" In "Alcuin, *De ratione animae*: A Text with Introduction, Critical Apparatus, and Translation," ed. James Curry (PhD diss., Cornell, 1966), p. 62, line 21.

47. Alcuin, *Epistolae*, letter 309.

48. McKitterick, *Books, Scribes and Learning*, 165.

49. See especially Bernhard Bischoff, "Die Kölner Nonnenhandschriften und das Skriptorium von Chelles"; Rosamond McKitterick, "Nuns' Scriptoria in England and Francia in the Eighth Century," in *Books, Scribes and Learning*, VII.1–35.

50. Janet Nelson, "Perceptions du Pouvoir chez les Historiennes du Haut Moyen Age," in *Les Femmes au Moyen Age*, ed. M. Rouche (Maubeuge, France: Maulde et Renou-Sambre, 1990), 77–87, and "Gender and Genre."

51. Jean-Pierre Laporte, *Le trésor des saints de Chelles* (Chelles, France: Société archéologique et historique de Chelles, 1988), esp. 49–160.

52. Her letter does not survive, but his response to her does. See Alcuin, *Epistolae*, letter 214, esp. 358, lines 24–27.

53. Ibid., letter 196.

54. Contreni, "Carolingian Renaissance," 717–18.

55. Alcuin, *Epistolae*, letters 88 and 216.

56. That marriage never did come to fruition, though she was being cultivated to the role of empress.

57. On the poet's use of Corippus, see Christina Ratkowitsch's impressive study, *Karolus Magnus—alter Aeneas, alter Martinus, alter Iustinus:*

Zu Intention und Datierung des "Aachener Karlsepos" (Vienna: Verlag der Österreichischen Akademie der Wissenschaften, 1997).

58. Angilbert, "To Charlemagne and His Entourage," 143.

59. Nelson, "Charlemagne—Pater Optimus?," ch. XV, p. 279, points out that the *Annales mettenses priores*, likely written at Chelles under Gisla's supervision, calls Charles "*primogenitus*" and that he is also listed first in Gisla's charter to Saint Denis in 799.

60. On the difficulty of determining the date of Gisla's death, see Nelson, *Frankish World*, 194n75. Rodtrud and Pippin both died in 810; their appearance in the poem is easily explained, regardless of date, since they are Charlemagne's children, which makes Louis's absence all the more conspicuous if the poem is dated after 810.

61. Nelson, "Charlemagne—Pater Optimus?," ch. XV, p. 279–80.

62. Ibid., 279.

63. The question of succession was not clear-cut, even when Charles and Pippin were alive. It is possible that the emphasis on Pippin's embassy may suggest that the poem was composed after Charles's death when Pippin would have been the clear successor, but in that case one would expect more flourish in the earlier encomium. In any case, I speak here of poetic desire, not Charlemagne's own inclinations.

64. On the priority of utility over accuracy, see "Active Memory" in the introduction, along with chapters by Cotter-Lynch and Barbetti in this volume.

65. "Mnemonic Sanctity and the Ladder of Reading: Notker's 'In Natale Sanctarum Feminarum,'" chapter 2 in this volume.

66. Carruthers, *Craft of Thought*, 46.

67. Traditionally the poem is dated to between 800 and 814, Charlemagne's years as emperor. Although it is certainly possible that the poem may have been written to celebrate the emperor during his lifetime, there is no basis to rule out a later date of composition. If the poem were written between 811 and 814, one would expect Louis to be highlighted in it somehow. On dating, see Schaller, "Das Aachener Epos," 148–59, and Peter Godman, introduction to *Poetry of the Carolingian Renaissance*, 22–24.

68. Godman, "Poetic Hunt," 585.

CHAPTER 2

MNEMONIC SANCTITY AND THE LADDER OF READING: NOTKER'S "IN NATALE SANCTARUM FEMINARUM"

Margaret Cotter-Lynch

In the late ninth century, the monk and schoolmaster Notker of Saint Gall composed a hymn for the Church's festival commemorating holy women. "In Natale Sanctarum Feminarum," or "For the Festival of Holy Women," provides a case study in how a text could deploy the memory arts to shape both individual and institutional identities around specific conceptions of gender. A liturgical poem intended for a monastic audience, this sequence demonstrates the memorial function of hagiography and its role in the construction of both individual and communal monastic identities. Notker represents Saint Perpetua in his hymn through carefully selected images from her *Passio*, which he then contextualizes among images of Mary and Eve. Through his hymn, Notker instructs his audience in how to read, remember, and understand Perpetua's text. One effect of this mnemonic instruction is to suppress the possibility of the nuanced reading of gender that Perpetua's *Passio* invites. Notker's text instead structures the audience's memory around binary gender categories, in which women's sanctity and paths to holiness are clearly differentiated from those of men. This conception of gender difference, in turn, is constitutive of community membership, as Notker interpolates his audience into a community defined (in part) by its shared memory and understanding of holy women.

Notker's hymn is mnemonic on several levels and thus reveals a sophisticated engagement with the craft of memory in medieval monastic culture. Notker Balbulus, or Notker the Stammerer, composed his *Liber Ymnorum* between 881 and 887. "In Natale Sanctarum Feminarum" is one of the hymns contained in this book; specifically, it is a sequence, a particular form of hymn just becoming popular in Notker's time, designed as a mnemonic aid for remembering the sequence of notes attached to the final "a" of the "Alleluia" sung before the Gospel during mass.[1] Notker's poem thus participates in a self-consciously mnemonic genre. The words were composed as aids in remembering a sequence of musical notes during the liturgy. As a defined part of mass, the sequence also participates in the innately memorial function of the liturgy as a whole.[2] This mnemonic function is highlighted through the structural location of the sequence in the mass: it is the prelude to the Gospel reading, in which the life of Christ is repeated and remembered for the audience.

In addition, for ninth-century Saint Gall, reading and writing themselves were considered mnemonic devices, as language was primarily understood as an oral (and aural) act. Letters written on a page were signs of vocal sounds, which in turn represented meaning. Historically, Notker and Saint Gall in the ninth century were poised at the beginning of a transition from understanding language as a predominantly oral phenomenon to understanding writing as directly significant of meaning (and the concomitant shift from oral to silent reading practices).[3] For Notker, the words on the page were still mnemonic devices for linguistic sounds. This is all the more true in the case of song lyrics, which were in turn mnemonics for musical notes.

Thirdly, the physical layout of the words of the poem on the page is mnemonic, as the visual structure of the poem imitates the shape of a ladder, thus reflecting the first word of the hymn (*scalam*) and at the same time the mnemonic structure underlying the sequence as a whole. As a Benedictine, Notker knew Benedict's use of the image of Jacob's ladder as a mnemonic aid in the seventh chapter of the Benedictine Rule, and thus Notker participates in the ladder's subsequent adoption as a common mnemonic image in medieval monastic literature.[4] For Benedict, the image of Jacob's ladder provides a visual structure within the monk's memory, in which the literal steps of the ladder each correspond to figurative steps on the road to humility and thus to unity with God. Notker's hymn follows a parallel thematic trajectory—overcoming sin to reach holiness—again through the visual image of the ladder, here reflected in the layout of the words on the page.

Notker's "In Natale Sanctarum Feminarum" is thus mnemonic at its inception, musically, semantically, and visually. These aspects of the hymn demonstrate Notker's deep participation in what Mary Carruthers terms the "memory arts," or a highly structured system of mnemonic techniques that suffused the way medieval monastics read, thought, and lived.[5] The mnemonic structures that inform the text's organization and composition likewise inform the text's reception. The words of Notker's hymn and the images they evoke are meant as mnemonic triggers for the audience, eliciting the memory of other texts. Notker's poem functions as a series of pointers to texts, stories, and symbols already present in the reader's/listener's memory. Notker's text then orders and prioritizes these remembered texts, with the goal of shaping both what the readers remember and how they remember it. Notker's sequence, in short, is about how you (should) remember what you read.[6] In the opening lines of the poem, Notker recalls two dreams recounted by Saint Perpetua in her third-century *Passio*. He then continues on to recall biblical images in constructing his narrative of Everywoman's ascension to God. Notker's sequence is thus an exercise in textual memory for his audience, calling up a series of texts, images, and references from his listeners' memory stores in order to succinctly tell a story, while simultaneously reordering those memory stores to construct his narrative. By examining which images are included versus excluded, we can see how Notker uses memory to construct gender in the minds of his audience and, by extension, how he transforms both individual and institutional identities.

In order to better understand the memorial process by which Notker constructs his audience's identities, I will first examine how the words of Notker's hymn use and transform memory stores, then move on to explore the implications of this transformation for the composition of identity. We will begin by looking Notker's poem in detail:[7]

> Scalam ad caelos subrectam,
> tormentis cinctam—

Cuius ima draco servare cautus invigilat iugiter,	Ne quis eius vel primum gradum possit insaucius scandere,
Cuius ascensus extracto Aethiops gladio vetat exitium minitans,	Cuius supremis innixus iuvenis splendidus ramum aureolum retinet—
Hanc ergo scalam ita Christi amor feminis fecit perviam, ut dracone conculcato et Aethiopis gladio transito	Per omne genus tormentorum caeli apicem queant capere et de manu confortantis regis auream lauream sumere.
Quid tibi profecit profane serpens,	Cum virgo pepererit incarnatum

quondam unam
decepisse mulierem

Qui praedam tibi tulit et
armilla maxillam forat,

Nunc ergo temet virgines
vincere cernis, invide,

Et viduarum
maritis fidem
nunc ingemis integram,

Feminas nunc vides in bello
contra te acto duces existere

Quin et tua vasa
meretrices dominus emundat

Pro his nunc beneficiis
in commune dominum
nos glorificemus
et peccatores et iusti,

dei patris
unicum dominum Jesum?

Ut egressus Evae natis
fiat, quos tenere cupis.

Et maritatas parere
filios deo placitos,

Qui creatori
fidem negare
persuaseras virgini.

Quae filios suos instigant
fortiter tua tormenta vincere.

Et haec sibi templum
dignatur efficere purgatum.

Qui et stantes corroborat
et prolapsis dexteram
porrigit, ut saltem
post facinora surgamus.

A ladder stretched up to heaven,
surrounded by torments—

The bottom of which the careful dragon
watches over to guard perpetually

Lest anyone be able to climb
even the first step unscathed,

The ascents of which Aethiops
forbids, with drawn sword
threatening death,

On the top of which
the splendid youth, leaning,
holds the golden branch—

Therefore the love of Christ thus makes

Through all sorts of
torments they
might be able to attain the
top of

this ladder accessible to women,

heaven and take the golden
laurel

so that by trampling the dragon

from the hand of the
comforting king.

and passing by the sword of Aethiops

What benefit for you,
unholy serpent,
to have once
deceived one women

When a virgin bore
incarnate
of God the Father
the only Lord Jesus?

Who took away the reward from you
and pierces your jaw with a hook,

So that a way out would be made
for the children of Eve whom
you desire to hold?

Therefore now, envious one,
you see virgins defeat you,

And married women yield
sons pleasing to God,

And now you mourn
the pure faithfulness
of widows to their husbands,

You who persuaded
a virgin to deny
faith to her creator.

Now you see women come forth
as leaders in the war against you,

They who urge their sons
strongly to conquer your
torments.

And God cleanses even
prostitutes, your vessels,

And deigns to make of them
a temple purified for himself.

Now for these benefits,

Who both strengthens the
standing
and reaches out his right hand
to the fallen, so that at least
we may rise after our crimes.

in common both
sinners and just men
let us glorify the Lord,

The opening of the poem recalls the story of the saints Perpetua and Felicitas. The two women, along with a group of fellow Christians of both genders, were martyred in Carthage in 203 AD. Their tale is preserved in a text partially written by Perpetua herself while they were in prison, the *Passio Perpetuae*.[8] In the autobiographical portion of the *Passio*, Perpetua recounts four divinely inspired dreams that she experiences during her time in prison. In the first seven stanzas of his sequence, Notker conflates images from two of these dreams to construct a metaphor of the ascent to heaven. In Perpetua's first dream, she sees a ladder extending to heaven. A dragon guards the bottom, and the sides of the ladder are studded with swords and knives, positioned to cut anyone who turns, stumbles, or otherwise strays from a straight path up. Perpetua is initially frightened but is encouraged by her companion Saturus at the top of the ladder. She then steps on the dragon's head and ascends. At the top, she meets a kindly shepherd who gives her cheese to eat; Perpetua awakens with the taste of cheese still in her mouth. In the fourth dream related in the *Passio* (the middle two, concerning the salvation of Perpetua's deceased brother Dinocrates, are not a factor in the hymn), Perpetua looks down to see that her body has become male; she then battles an Egyptian gladiator in the arena where she is to be martyred. She defeats the Egyptian in combat and is awarded a branch with a golden apple by the trainer. Perpetua, in the self-authored portion of her *Passio*, glosses the Egyptian as a representation of the devil.

In Notker's hymn, we see a number of these elements conflated into a single vision of the ascent to heaven for all women, who are here placed in the position of Perpetua. The Egyptian gladiator is now an Ethiopian gladiator, added to the dragon and other unspecified "torments" (presumably including knives and swords) that make the ladder to heaven forbidding. We find a youth bestowing a golden branch to Perpetua at the top of the ladder, thus replacing Perpetua's reward of cheese from the shepherd in her first dream with the golden branch awarded for gladiatorial victory in her fourth dream. Allegorically, Perpetua's two dreams are largely analogous and dependent upon classical and biblical imagery, allowing Notker's message to be understood by those who might not be directly familiar with Perpetua's *Passio*.[9] The "splendid youth" at the top of the ladder and the "golden branch" awarded to Perpetua recall Apollo and Virgil's *Aeneid*. The ladder, as already noted, recalls Jacob's ladder, while Perpetua's stepping on the head of the dragon recalls the commonplace of Mary stepping on the head of the serpent that deceived Eve. Notker's conflation here provides his audience with an easily understandable message: original sin (if we read the dragon as the serpent), the devil (as represented by the gladiator), and other "torments" impede one's progress to heaven. Perpetua and all women are capable of overcoming these obstacles in order to reach heaven and their celestial reward.

As Notker continues, he turns from Perpetua's *Passio* to direct biblical references to further frame his narrative of women's ascent to heaven. His sequence recalls the stories of Eve and Mary while directly addressing the devil, here represented by the serpent. Notker traces the ascent of womankind toward redemption from the Old to the New Testaments, predictably figuring Mary as the antidote to Eve. Progress toward sanctity is thus figured in terms of a progression between two opposed terms: Mary redeems the sin of Eve as the New Testament supplants the Old. In both cases, we have a pair of opposites (Mary and Eve; New and Old Testaments); in both cases—and, in fact, throughout Notker's poem—the journey toward sanctity is figured as a vector from a spiritually inferior point toward a spiritually superior one. The ladder form, which defines both Perpetua's dream and Notker's poem, represents this vector visually: poised at the bottom of the ladder, the one who would become holy must journey toward the top.

As the poem progresses, a further parallel is drawn back to the images from Perpetua's *Passio*, given that Notker could expect his audience to recall the commonplace of Mary stepping on the head of the serpent just as Perpetua stepped on the head of the dragon. Here, again, Notker's poem depends upon the memories of his readers for its meaning; with a few phrases, he can evoke the messages of Genesis, Job, and the New Testament without explaining the details. Notker's aim here is not to describe to his readers how a serpent once deceived a woman nor to explicate that by piercing the serpent's jaw with a hook Christ forces him into submission and equates the serpent with Leviathon as a being that can only be defeated with the help of God.[10] Notker assumes that the details of these stories are already well known by his audience. Instead, he selects and recalls images and references out of his reader's memorial stores in order to structure these remembrances to convey his desired meaning. Notker's message, then, comes not from introducing new material but rather from selecting, juxtaposing, and arranging information already at his readers' disposal.

The rest of the poem then makes explicit the ways in which all women can and should strive to identify with holy women such as Perpetua as characterized by Notker. With Eve and Mary evoked as two poles, predictably, women should seek to overcome Eve to become like Mary. All classes of women, as identified by sexual status, are then interpolated into this system. Notker's identification of women as either virgins, mothers of sons, faithful widows, or prostitutes (who are hopefully "purified") describes all women in terms of their sexual relationships to men (or lack thereof). Notker thus fixes all women—including, by implication, Perpetua—within a clearly categorized and hierarchized system. Notker's poem constructs a mnemonic system for the memories it evokes by assigning values to these memories and by fitting the images he references within a system of distinctions: Mary redeems Eve; Christ subdues the devil; good overcomes evil; women, by their relationships to men, come to participate in salvation. Although the overt message of the hymn "For the Festival of Holy Women" is that women can become good, "male" and "female" are still posited as opposed poles. Women achieve redemption through faithfulness to their husbands, encouraging their sons, and/or through God's agency. Women are clearly different from men, weaker and more prone to sin; the lesson of the last two stanzas of the poem is that if *even women*, through the grace of God, can be redeemed, so can sinful men.

In the final two stanzas, this hierarchical view of gender and salvation is enacted in the poem itself as Notker widens the subject of his poem to include both men and women. Notker turns from directly addressing the devil in the earlier stanzas to including his readers of both genders in an "us." The first-person plural of "*glorificemus*" is further identified by the masculine plural substantive adjectives "*peccatores*" and "*iusti*." Here, as in other romance languages, the masculine plural denotes either a group of all men or a group that includes both men and women. Either way, the poem shifts from discussing women in particular to directly addressing men as well. The implicit message is, thus, if even women can overcome seemingly insurmountable obstacles to reach heaven, so can sinful men. Notker's poem here works by simile, not by identification: just as women can overcome their history and nature to become holy (often by means of men, as when they "urge their sons strongly to conquer [Satan's] torments"), so men can move from the category of "*peccatores*" to the category of "*iusti.*" The holy women's usefulness as a didactic model to repentant male sinners is predicated upon their innate difference from men. The hymn clearly indicates that holiness, and the means to it, is fundamentally different for men and for women; the hope for male readers indicated in the last two stanzas assumes that redemption is categorically easier for men than for women.

This gloss of the hymn, of course, relies heavily upon tropes that would have been familiar to Notker's audience, whether that audience was strictly monks at Saint Gall, a wider audience of male and female religious, or a congregation that included lay churchgoers of both genders. My argument here is that Notker's choice to recall the *Passio Perpetuae* serves to integrate the third-century text into a conventional, institutionally sanctioned, binary conception of gender at radical odds with a close reading of the early text. Many scholars have noted the seeming incongruity of Noker's use of Perpetua's *Passio* here. As Peter Godman notes in the introduction to his anthology *Poetry of the Carolingian Renaissance*, "Drawing on the *Passio Perpetuae*, [Notker] consciously writes its antithesis."[11] Perpetua's *Passio* includes the self-authored prison journal of a 22-year-old nursing mother who leads a group of male and female martyrs and has a dream in which she inhabits the body of a man; such a text does not easily fit into clear ninth-century ecclesiastically authorized gender categories.[12] In fact, I would argue that the third-century text radically undermines conceptual models predicated upon clear gender difference and strongly resists the type of reading imposed upon it by Notker and others (including Saint Augustine).[13] Perpetua's own accounts of her visions, like Hildegard of Bingen's visionary descriptions discussed by Claire Barbetti, can be read as the deployment of oneiric images to authorize her own text, direct its reading, and legitimize her public role. In contrast, in Notker's hymn, we see an early example of the hagiographic dynamic discussed by Catherine Keene regarding the *Miracles of St. Margaret*: just as Keene claims that the monks of Dunfermline Abbey carefully selected the contents of Margaret's miracle collection in order to situate the story and its audience within a particular political and geographic orientation, here Notker selects images from Perpetua's passion that allow him to integrate Perpetua's story and his hymn's audience within a particular theological understanding of gender.

Two primary points of contrast thus emerge between Perpetua's *Passio* and Notker's sequence. For Notker, feminine sanctity is characterized by clear gender difference and a concomitant difference in the routes to holiness for men and women: women are defined by their sexual relationship to men and access sanctity by means of that relationship.[14] However, both of these assumptions clearly differentiate Notker's poem from Perpetua's own text. Clear gender distinctions are questioned in the *Passio* on several levels. Perpetua, as a young woman, seems to be the leader of a group of both male and female Christians arrested and condemned to martyrdom. Her sexual status, as the nursing mother of an infant, is shown to be erased by her status as a Christian and a martyr; she gives up her son, who is miraculously weaned, in order to face her sentence.[15] A striking aspect of Perpetua's *Passio* is precisely her refusal to be defined through her relationships to men. Although Perpetua is the apparent leader of both male and female Christians imprisoned for their faith, traditional family relationships are presented as unimportant to her status as a Christian. Firstly, she repeatedly disobeys and repudiates her father to maintain her faith. Secondly, there is strikingly no mention at all of the father of Perpetua's baby; most readers have assumed that she was married, yet there is absolutely no mention at all of a spouse in the original text. Indeed, this absence is so striking that later redactors felt a need to add in a husband for her; a husband first appears in the (presumably) fourth-century anonymous *Acta*, and he becomes a fixture in many later versions of her story.[16] Finally, in direct contradiction to Notker's description, Perpetua does not "urge [her] son strongly to conquer [the devil's] torments." Rather, she abandons her infant son in order to face and conquer torments herself. Notker's poem thus integrates Perpetua into the very gender-based hierarchy that her own *Passio* resists. For Notker, women are identified by sexual status and their relationships to men; he fails to mention that Perpetua refuses to identify herself by either. Both in the ways Notker frames Perpetua's story and in the details of her *Passio* that he chooses to omit, Notker writes Saint Perpetua into his audience's memories according to a structure that aligns with his own ideas of the relationship between gender and holiness, and thus he overwrites the gender implications of Perpetua's original text.

Perpetua's *Passio* is perhaps most famous among modern scholars for the dream in which Perpetua is often said to "become male," thus undermining the very concept of rigid gender identification. A brief look at Perpetua's fourth dream as recounted in the third-century Latin text illustrates this point. In Perpetua's vision, she is escorted from prison by the deacon Pomponius, who leads her to the amphitheater where she knows she is to be martyred. Once there, Pomponius reassures her and departs, leaving her in the middle of the arena, watched by the crowd. Then she tells us,

> And because I knew that I was condemned to the beasts, I marveled that there were no beasts let loose on me. And there came out an Egyptian, foul of look, with his attendants to fight against me. And to me also there came goodly young men to be my attendants and supporters. And I was stripped and *was changed into a man* [*facta sum masculus*]. And my supporters began to rub me down with oil, as they are wont to do before a combat; and I saw the Egyptian opposite rolling in the sand. And there came forth a man wondrously tall so that he rose above the top of the amphitheater, clad in a purple robe without a girdle with two stripes, one on either side, running down the middle of the breast, and wearing shoes curiously wrought made of gold and silver; carrying a wand, like a trainer, and a green bough on which were golden apples. And he asked for silence, and said: "This Egyptian, if he prevail over *her*, shall kill *her* with a sword; and, if *she* prevail over him, *she* shall receive this bough."

The two then fight, and Perpetua defeats the Egyptian, at which point she continues:

> And I came forward to the trainer, and received the bough. And he kissed me, and said to me: "Peace be with thee, *my daughter.*" And I began to go in triumph to the Gate of Life.[17]

This vision is often talked about, by Saint Augustine as well as late twentieth- and early twenty-first-century feminist critics, as the one in which Perpetua "becomes a man."[18] I argue elsewhere that this passage instead actually dismantles conventional gender dichotomies, to mark Perpetua as *at once* male and female.[19] I further see this refusal of clear binaries as characteristic of Perpetua's narrative as a whole.[20] Whether we read Perpetua here as "becoming male" or as erasing the male/female dichotomy by being both genders at once, however, it is clear that Perpetua's *Passio* denies the strict gender boundaries that are central to Notker's system. Notker completely elides this aspect of Perpetua's fourth dream while simultaneously repurposing images from that same dream to support his binary hierarchical version of gender difference. Thus, numerous "difficulties" of Perpetua's text are similarly elided by Notker in the process of making Perpetua emblematic of Everywoman. This is done through Notker's superimposition of an alternative mnemonic system over his readers' memories of the third-century saint. Notker's poem thus provides us a potent example of what Mary Carruthers calls "overlay" and "communal forgetting."[21]

The timing of the composition of Notker's hymn is relevant here. During his reign as emperor of the Carolingian Empire from 814 to 840, Louis the Pious enacted a range of ecclesiastical reforms. Notable among these was a regularization—read restriction—of the roles available to women in the church. Double monasteries—in which both men and women were cloistered and which often had abbesses presiding over both male and female religious—were abolished. As Helene Scheck has discussed, independent, unmarried women such as Gundrada were forced to take religious orders under Louis. Claustration of female religious was much more strictly enforced, ending the practice of nuns providing community services such as education and health care, which were now more exclusively the prerogative of men. Writing in the immediate aftermath of this more strict definition of women's roles, Notker reflects the new, narrower understanding of the paths of holiness appropriate to religious women. Notker thus deploys the memory arts in the defense (or construction) of something relatively new, that is, an understanding of gender introduced and enforced by the ninth-century ecclesiastic reforms. This aspect of Notker's poem exemplifies the emphasis upon utility rather than accuracy in medieval memory: "The matters memory presents are used to persuade and motivate, to create emotion and stir the will. And the 'accuracy' or 'authenticity' of these memories—their simulation of an actual past—is of far less importance (indeed is hardly an issue at all) than their use to motivate the present and to affect the future."[22] Notker uses memory arts to assert a particularly ninth-century system of gender. Perpetua is written into this system; by extension, the women of Notker's audience are as well.[23]

My goal here is to make two points: the first is that the comprehensibility of Notker's hymn depends upon triggering the memories of the audience. Images and ideas are invoked but not fully explained; the poem simply points to specific memories presumed already present in the minds of the audience. Secondly, this triggering actively constructs the individual and collective identities of the audience. These identities are formed through the structure the hymn imposes upon memory. Notker's hymn tells its audience what to remember—and what to forget. It tells them in what context to remember specific texts, images, and incidents and forges connections between these memorial elements in specific ways. The memorial structure that Notker provides, then, is also an institutional structure within which individuals place themselves as members of a community. By shaping his audience's memory, Notker shapes the ways they think; these thought patterns then influence both individual understandings of identity and community membership and also the behaviors that demonstrate those individual and communal identities.

Mary Carruthers's concept of "ethical reading" underlies Notker's assumptions about his hymn's audience.[24] Understanding the sequence is predicated upon familiarity with the images it evokes; this familiarity is expected to come from the audience's memorial stores, built up through ethical reading. If one's identity is shaped by what one reads, it makes a very big difference how one understands what one reads. Notker, in his hymn, is recalling specific texts to his audience's mind and also telling his audience what to do with them: Notker is, in effect, suggesting that these are the texts that are important, this is how they are connected, and this is how they apply to you, personally. This is how you should remember them. Following Notker's suggestions will then shape how an individual understands and acts in the world; Notker's text is attempting to shape its reader's identities.

Here, however, we run into trouble reconstructing the probable reaction to—or, more specifically, familiarity with—the *Passio Perpetuae* on the part of Notker's audience. The earliest extant manuscript of the Latin *Passio* is from ninth-century Saint Gall (St. Gall MS 577), and Notker was quite obviously familiar with the text. However, references to Perpetua in early medieval literature are notoriously scarce; the text did not seem to be part of the standard canon of monastic reading, and thus it is difficult to claim that much of Notker's audience would have been conversant with the text.[25] In this situation, however, I argue that we can read Notker's use of Perpetua's visions in two different yet complimentary ways, depending upon the reader/hearer's ability to access the particulars of Perpetua's story in his/her memorial stores. First, for those listeners (presumably well-read monks and perhaps nuns) who were familiar with Perpetua's story, Notker's sequence places the details of the *Passio* within a specific memorial structure in order to control the way the text was remembered by his audience. In contrast, for those listeners who were sufficiently literate to understand Notker's Latin and the biblical references, but perhaps not well-read enough to have immediate memorial access to Perpetua's dreams, Notker's text, surprisingly enough, has a very similar effect. The images of these dreams, and Perpetua herself, are simultaneously introduced and categorized through Notker's deployment of the oneiric images within his hymn. Perpetua's text and dreams themselves rely heavily upon classical and biblical imagery for their allegorical interpretation; a moderately educated ninth-century listener—upon a first encounter with images of a dragon, a ladder to heaven, and a battle with an African gladiator culminating in the award of a laurel crown—could easily interpret these images as representing spiritual victory over the devil and ascension to heaven. Whether his audience was immediately familiar with the details of Perpetua's text itself or simply well-read enough to deftly understand its images, Notker's hymn carefully circumscribes a desired interpretation of Perpetua's text: the images selected by Notker are the ones worth remembering, and Perpetua herself should be understood within a larger context of biblical and contemporary women, with whom she (it is claimed) has much in common. Whether his readers already knew of Perpetua or not, Notker provides the mnemonic structure within which this saint and her dreams should be remembered and categorized.

Carruthers's claims regarding the textual basis of individual identity also have repercussions for collective identity. Here Catherine Cubitt's work becomes useful. In her essay "Memory and Narrative in the Cult of Early Anglo-Saxon Saints," Cubitt examines several hagiographies from Anglo-Saxon England to explain the ways in which particular narrative strategies were employed in these stories to shape the collective identity of a monastic audience in specific ways.[26] Cubitt, building upon recent scholarship in psychology and sociology, cites two primary aspects of the way memory works. First, "memories are put together from fragmented sources, often in a simplified form, according to pre-existing patterns."[27] Notker takes fragments of former texts, chosen to emphasize simplicity, and puts them into a specific pattern. His text thus performs a necessary mnemonic function for his readers. Secondly, "remembering is an inherently social activity";[28] these memorial patterns are shared by communities such that remembering within a given pattern can be constitutive of community membership. These two aspects of memory are clearly deployed in Notker's text. The ladder-shaped hymn provides—or imposes—the pattern within which selected biblical and hagiographic images of women are to be remembered. The imposition of this structure upon one's memory then places the reader within a religious community defined by a shared understanding of gender identity.[29]

Since memory is active, however, we must remember to look at both what is remembered and what is forgotten. Carruthers's concept of "communal forgetting" is echoed by Cubitt: "Forgetting is as important as remembering: what is collectively discarded may be as significant as what is remembered."[30] For those who are familiar with Perpetua's text, the most striking element of Notker's hymn is not the images he includes but the images and details he leaves out. We get the African gladiator but not Perpetua's own ambiguous gender as she fights him in the arena. Notker does not mention Perpetua's family or the fact that she defied her father and relinquished her infant son in order to undergo martyrdom. We are entirely deprived of the voice of the self-possessed leader of a group of persecuted Christians who authored her own account of her imprisonment and of the divinely inspired dreams she experienced while awaiting her death. As Cubitt notes, "The structure of memory often reflects the hierarchy of power."[31] Here, Notker gets to speak and remember; Perpetua does not. Notker, in his hymn, triggers his audience to remember those aspects of Perpetua's story that comfortably fit into the institutionally sanctioned gender hierarchy of his time and elides all aspects of Perpetua's story that could call that hierarchy into question.[32]

Notker, then, in this hymn, at once re-adopts a potentially subversive text into a dominant discourse while simultaneously instructing his audience to identify themselves by and through the reading structure he provides. Through a variety of mnemonic techniques, Notker strives to reorganize his audiences' memorial stores in order to enforce conventional gender categories upon a text that can be read to undermine those very categories. In so doing, Notker interpolates his audience into not only a mnemonic but also an ethical system. In shaping how his audience reads and remembers, Notker simultaneously shapes their individual and communal identities in a way that reinforces hierarchical gender structures. Notker's hymn thus serves as an exemplary case of the ways in which medieval memorial arts were deployed within a single text in order to shape and define both individual and communal identity around a shared conception of gender.

Notes

1. For a thorough study of the sequence form, see Richard L. Crocker, *The Early Medieval Sequence* (Berkeley: University of California Press, 1977) and *Studies in Medieval Music Theory and the Early Sequence* (Brookfield, VT: Variorum, 1997).

2. Ella Johnson discusses the memorial function of the liturgy in chapter 7 of the present volume. Mary Carruthers points out that liturgy and scripture constituted the two most primary loci of memory for medieval religious: Mary J. Carruthers, *The Craft of Thought: Meditation, Rhetoric, and the Making of Images, 400–1200*, Cambridge Studies in Medieval Literature 34 (Cambridge: Cambridge University Press, 2000), 61. Janet Coleman discusses the role of liturgy and liturgical time in structuring the collective memories of monastic communities in Janet Coleman, *Ancient and Medieval Memories: Studies in the Reconstruction of the Past* (Cambridge: Cambridge University Press, 1992), 131–32. For Coleman, monks' memories as fashioned by liturgy constitute their identities, as the collective memory shaped by liturgy supplanted individual memories from monks' previous lives outside of the cloister. Catherine

Cubitt amends this assertion in Catherine Cubitt, "Monastic Memory and Identity in Early Anglo-Saxon England," in *Social Identity in Early Medieval Britain*, ed. William O. Frazer and Andrew Tyrell (New York: Leicester University Press, 2000), 253–76. Although Cubitt claims that the mnemonic forces shaping monks' memories and thus identities were more varied than Coleman accounts for, the underlying mnemonic function of liturgy remains.

3. This transition was slow and by no means strictly linear; it has its roots in late antiquity, with Isidore of Seville and Saint Ambrose, and reaches full acceptance in the twelfth century, when we see a standardization of abbreviational practices around semantics rather than phonics. For a full examination of this topic, see Vivien Law, *Grammar and Grammarians in the Early Middle Ages*, Longman Linguistics Library (New York: Longman, 1997), and Anna A. Grotans, *Reading in Medieval St. Gall*, Cambridge Studies in Palaeography and Codicology 13 (Cambridge: Cambridge University Press, 2006).

4. Benedict and David Oswald Hunter Blair, *The Rule of St. Benedict* (Fort Augustus, Scotland: Abbey Press, 1906), 41, and Mary J. Carruthers, *The Book of Memory: A Study of Memory in Medieval Culture*, 2nd ed., Cambridge Studies in Medieval Literature 70 (Cambridge: Cambridge University Press, 2008). Carruthers devotes considerable attention to the literal and figurative image of the ladder as utilized by Hugh of Saint Victor (300–302 and 448–449) and also draws a connection to the work of Richard of Bury (200). Benedict's use of the Jacob's ladder, among other mnemonic devices, is discussed on page 31.

5. Carruthers, *Book of Memory*.

6. I reiterate here the definition of reading proposed in the introduction: "In this volume, we understand 'reading' to be contact with and consumption of texts, whether that consumption takes place visually (by physically looking at words on a page) or aurally (by listening to a text read or repeated)." In the case of Notker's hymn, I would include as readers those who heard the sequence sung, provided they were sufficiently fluent in Latin to understand the words.

7. Latin text in Wolfram von den Steinen, ed., *Notkeri Poetae Liber Ymnorum* (Bern: Francke Verlag, 1960), 88. English translation my own.

8. The ancient text contains sections attributed to three separate authors: Perpetua herself, recounting her time in prison and the dreams she experienced while she was there; Saturus, one of her fellow martyrs, who writes an account of his own dream while in prison; and an anonymous redactor, who writes an introduction to the two autobiographical sections and also provides an eyewitness account of the martyrs' deaths at the end of the text. The best and most recent Latin edition is Jacqueline Amat, ed., *Passion de Perpétue et de Félicité suivi des Actes*, vol. 417, Sources Chrétiennes (Paris: Éditions du Cerf, 1996). The standard English translation is in Herbert Musurillo, *The Acts of the Christian Martyrs*, Oxford Early Christian Texts (Oxford: Clarendon Press, 1972).

Musurillo works from Shewring's edition of the text: W. H. Shewring, *The Passion of Ss. Perpetua and Felicity Mm; a New Edition and Translation of the Latin Text Together with the Sermons of S. Augustine upon These Saints* (London: Sheed and Ward, 1931). Musurillo's translation is reprinted in Elizabeth Alvilda Petroff, *Medieval Women's Visionary Literature* (New York: Oxford University Press, 1986), 70–77. Peter Dronke provides his own translation of the autobiographical portion of the text in Peter Dronke, *Women Writers of the Middle Ages: A Critical Study of Texts from Perpetua to Marguerite Porete* (Cambridge: Cambridge University Press, 1984), 2–4.

9. Even these readers, however, would be depending upon their memories of other texts (classical and biblical) to decipher Notker's hymn. This possibility will be discussed in further detail later.

10. Cf. Job 41:1–2: "Can you draw out Leviathon with a fishhook, or press down its tongue with a cord? Can you put a rope in its nose, or pierce its jaw with a hook?"

11. Peter Godman, ed., *Poetry of the Carolingian Renaissance* (Norman: University of Oklahoma Press, 1985), 67.

12. In removing all traces of Perpetua's own voice, Notker engages here in the opposite dynamic from that discussed by Barbara Zimbalist regarding Clemence of Barking's *Life of St. Catherine*. Whereas, Zimbalist argues, Clemence authorizes feminine speech by attributing large portions of the narrative to Catherine's own voice, Notker entirely erases the first-person voice from Perpetua's narrative, instead incorporating her into a list of canonical women who are talked *about*. See Barbara Zimbalist's study in chapter 5 of this volume.

13. See Joyce E. Salisbury, *Perpetua's Passion: The Death and Memory of a Young Roman Woman* (New York: Routledge, 1997). The last chapter of this book considers attempts by Saint Augustine and other late antique redactors to revise or control the gendered implications of Perpetua's text. The texts of the two Augustine sermons on Saint Perpetua known prior to 2007 are available in Shewring, *Passion of Ss. Perpetua and Felicity Mm*. A "new" sermon by Saint Augustine about Saint Perpetua was discovered in a manuscript at the University of Erfurt, Germany in March 2008; the text of this sermon can be found in Isabella Schiller, Dorothea Weber, and Clemens Weidmann, "Sechs Neue Augustinuspredigten Teil 1 Mit Edition Dreier Sermones," *Weiner Studien* 121 (2008): 227–84.

14. This is, of course, true for virgins dedicated to Christ, as well—as the very formulation "virgins dedicated to Christ" points to a woman's sexual status (as virgin) and relationship to a male figure (Christ).

15. Perpetua's nursing of her infant son is given significant emphasis in the early text, as it is the source of both her father's public protest in court that her son will die without her and the site of the first miracle recounted in the text, when the boy is miraculously weaned without any discomfort for either mother or son. Notker's omission of this aspect of the text, in combination with the substitution of the laurel wreath for the cheese as the

reward at the top of the ladder, erases any milk symbolism in Perpetua's story. See Claire Barbetti's chapter 4 of this volume for further discussion of the symbolism of cheese/milk imagery in the medieval church.

16. The text of the *Acta* is in Amat, *Passion de Perpétue*. Although Amat dates the *Acta* to no earlier than the fifth century, the sermon by Saint Augustine on Saint Perpetua discovered in 2008 appears to cite the *Acta* verbatim; as a result, it seems necessary to push the date of the *Acta* back to the fourth century. See Jan N. Bremmer and Marco Formisano, eds., *Perpetua's Passions: Multidisciplinary Approaches to the Passio Perpetuae et Felicitatis* (New York: Oxford University Press, 2012), especially the introduction and chapters 1 and 16.

17. Petroff, *Medieval Women's Visionary Literature*, 73. Originally published in Musurillo, *Acts of the Christian Martyrs*. Emphasis mine.

18. For example, Peter Dronke writes, "She is stripped of her womanly clothes, and becomes masculine...Perpetua wants to strip herself of all that is weak, or womanish, in her nature" (*Women Writers of the Middle Ages*, 14). Similarly, Joyce Salisbury asserts, "Certainly there is no more vivid image of personal change than Perpetua's dream image in which she is transformed into a man" (*Perpetua's Passion*, 108).

19. The trope of holy women becoming manly is, of course, common in hagiography, as discussed by Ana Maria Machado in her work on the *Vitae patrum* in chapter 6 of this volume. However, I claim that Perpetua's own representation of gender aligns more closely with the strategies of Gertrude of Helfta as discussed by Ella Johnson in chapter 7 of this volume. In this case, gender is refigured in such a way that it is no longer a binary opposition; rather, Christians can and do participate simultaneously in both masculine and feminine attributes.

20. This argument is developed fully in my upcoming book, *Mother, Gladiator, Saint: The Transformations of St. Perpetua across the Middle Ages*.

21. Carruthers, *Craft of Thought*, 54. The concepts of "overlay" and "communal forgetting" are more fully addressed in the "Active Memory" section of the introduction to this volume.

22. Ibid., 67. This same quote is discussed in the "Active Memory" section of the introduction to this volume and by Claire Barbetti in chapter 4.

23. In this way, we might see Notker's hymn as the antithesis of *Karolus Magnus and Leo Papa*, as "In Natale Sanctarum Feminarum" (re)orders its audience's memory according to an ecclesiastical community as imagined by Louis the Pious.

24. See the section "Memory and Individual Identity" of the introduction to this volume for a detailed discussion of Carruthers's concept of ethical reading and its role in individual identity formation.

25. Godman comments on this fact: "An unidentified allusion to the *Passio Perpetuae* is hardly comparable to a borrowing from the Bible or from a well-known classical author which might be understood by a cultivated clerical audience in a setting far removed from its original context. Perpetua's account of her martyrdom, given its limited diffusion in the

Carolingian period, required an identification which Notker does not supply" (*Poetry of the Carolingian Renaissance*, 66).

26. Brad Herzog discusses the formation of religious, and specifically monastic, communities around the cults of Saints Katherine and Margaret in later centuries in chapter 9 in the present volume.

27. Catherine Cubitt, "Memory and Narrative in the Cult of Early Anglo-Saxon Saints," in *The Uses of the Past in the Early Middle Ages*, ed. Yitzhak Hen and Matthew Innes (Cambridge: Cambridge University Press, 2000), 31.

28. Cubitt, "Memory and Narrative," 31.

29. As discussed in the introduction to this volume, Patrick J. Geary describes the formation of communal memory in the century after Notker: "A society that explicitly found its identity, its norms, and its values from the inheritance of the past, that venerated tradition and drew its religious and political ideologies from precedent, was nevertheless actively engaged in producing that tradition through a complex process of transmission, suppression, and re-creation." This, I would argue, is exactly what Notker is doing. Geary, *Phantoms of Remembrance: Memory and Oblivion at the End of the First Millenium* (Princeton, NJ: Princeton University Press, 1994), 8. My claims here regarding Notker are very similar to those made by Claire Barbetti regarding Hildegard von Bingen in chapter 4.

30. See the section "Active Memory" in the introduction to this volume. Carruthers, *Craft of Thought*, 54; Cubitt, "Memory and Narrative," 44.

31. Cubitt, "Memory and Narrative," 61.

32. As discussed in the introduction to this volume, Carruthers recounts a parallel case of institutionally enforced mnemonic overlay with the battle over the tomb of Saint Babylas in Daphne. Carruthers, *Craft of Thought*, 46–54.

CHAPTER 3

ENVISIONING A SAINT: VISIONS IN THE MIRACLES OF SAINT MARGARET OF SCOTLAND

Catherine Keene

Miracle collections reflect two groups' perspectives: those receiving and those recording the miracles. Thus, they offer insight into the processes of collective remembrance. Memory is inherently collective, as outlined in the introduction, involving communal decisions regarding the inclusion or omission of points of remembering. In miracle collections, supplicants receive supernatural aid in a way that is socially recognized and valued. Those recording the miraculous events then sift through these accounts, selecting which to document and determining how to relate them. The result is a coded map of memories that, as Aviad Kleinberg notes, forgets the saint of reality in order to create an image of the saint that is comfortably recognizable to those constructing her memory.[1] The historical Margaret of Scotland (d. 1093) is hardly represented in her miracle collection. Daughter of the royal Anglo-Saxon house, wife of King Malcolm III of Scotland, and mother to three kings of Scotland and a queen of England, she is portrayed primarily as the supernatural protector of both her dynasty and the abbey housing her shrine.[2] The saint identifies herself in the many visions included in her miracle collection not as a wife, mother, sister, or even saint but as the queen of her people: "*Ego sum Margarita, Scotorum regina.*" The number of visions of the saint and the frequency with which she introduces herself are unusual and, upon closer examination, provide clues to the collective mnemonic preferences of the community constructing her memory. This chapter suggests that such a manner of remembrance was characteristic of the cults centered on the Anglo-Scottish border, in contrast to their Continental counterparts. Furthermore, Margaret's self-identification in so many of the visions can be interpreted as a means of authentication, an attempt to bridge the gap between the Church's cautionary approach to supernatural encounters on the one hand and the monarchy's need to perpetuate the orthodoxy of Margaret's memory on the other. Thus, the memory of Margaret resolved possible tension between the local predilection for visions and the monarchy's need for a papally endorsed dynast. This is accomplished in part by portraying Margaret in terms that highlight her position as royal protectrix rather than her gender. Throughout, the emphasis of this study is on placing Margaret's cult in a historical context, demonstrating how the memory arts were employed to further specific royal and ecclesiastical goals.

Visions in the Miracle Collection

Margaret's miracle collection was probably composed in the mid-thirteenth century in support of the papal inquiry that resulted in her canonization in 1249.[3] It is unusual in that Margaret frequently appears in visions in which she introduces herself. The compilation describes 46 events within 42 chapters involving 44 persons. Of these 46 events, 27 (or 59 percent) include a vision of Margaret.[4] This percentage seems particularly high in view of the Roman Church's cautious approach to the spiritual reliability of visions. Stephen Kruger traces the perception of dreams and visions from such classical authors as Macrobius and Calcidius to patristic authorities including Augustine and Gregory the Great and then to medieval philosophers such as Albertus Magnus, Pascalis Romanus, and others. He stresses that throughout the centuries a consistent emphasis was placed on the "middleness" or the "doubleness" of dreams.[5] Augustine, for example, established a hierarchy of perception, from *visio corporalis* (ordinary sight) to *visio spiritualis* (spiritual sight) and finally *visio intellectualis* (intuitive, abstract, intellectual insight). Spiritual visions were inherently the least reliable, capable of being divine or demonic, paranormal or supernatural.[6] Following Macrobius and Augustine, the twelfth-century thinker Pascalis Romanus outlined three causes for dreams: the first is related to physical causes, the second is an "angelic revelation" (*angelicam revelationem*), and the third intermediate type of dream could be either physically or divinely inspired.[7] The authenticity of dreams and visions, therefore, existed within a hierarchy with most occupying the middle, most dubious ground.[8] Thus, Gregory the Great was prompted to warn against diabolically inspired dreams; Isidore of Seville cautions that even true dreams could be illusory; Hildegard of Bingen advises that the morality of the dreamer determines the quality of the dream; and John of Salisbury emphasizes the ambiguity of dreams.[9]

The relatively low percentage of visions in miracle collections that were roughly contemporary with Margaret's perhaps reflects the Church's historically cautious approach to supernatural encounters. In the case of those countries most proximate to the location of Margaret's cult, France and England, the percentage of visionary experiences found in miracle accounts typically hovered below 15 percent. Pierre-André Sigal notes that in a study of a total of 2,050 posthumous healing miracles collected from 76 hagiographies and 166 miracle accounts from eleventh- and twelfth-century France, only 255, or 12 percent, involved a vision of the saint.[10]

This analysis is limited to healing miracles, which might skew the results, but the number remains consistently low when viewing the entire miracle collection of individual cults. For example, Sigal's study included the miracles of Saint Foy, which were recorded in four books written in the middle of the eleventh century. Of the 123 miracles, 32 percent involved a vision of the saint, a figure significantly higher than the composite average of 12 percent but still much lower than the percentage recorded in Margaret's collection.[11] The miracles of Thomas Becket, begun in mid-1172 by William of Canterbury, include 161 miracles of which only 14 percent (or 22) described a visionary experience, a number that roughly approximates the 12 percent recorded in France.[12]

Outside England and France, miracle collections retained a similarly low number of visions. For Saint Elizabeth of Hungary, the miracles recorded in 1232 and 1235 comprised 129 miracles, only 6 of which involved a vision of the saint, less than 5 percent.[13] Although Saint Stanislaus, bishop of Cracow, was martyred in 1079, his cult flourished in the thirteenth century with the elevation of his relics in 1243.[14] Two investigations into his miracles, in 1250 and again in 1252, resulted in his canonization in 1253. Here is an example of a saint whose holy career roughly parallels that of Margaret's: they both lived in the second half of the eleventh century and were canonized in the middle of the thirteenth century. Despite these surface similarities, however, only 6 out of Saint Stanislaus's 52 documented miracles described a vision of the saint—just 11 percent.[15]

Although Margaret's cult did not conform to the practices of the time, it certainly accorded with the practices of the place for both male and female saints. A comparably high percentage of visions is found in the miracle accounts of Saint Æbbe, who was, like Margaret, a woman of the Anglo-Saxon nobility, specifically a sister of Oswiu, king of Northumbria in the seventh century.[16] Her cult was located, like Margaret's, in what was southern Scotland, centered on the priory of Coldingham, near the original site of Æbbe's monastery on land granted to the monks of Durham in 1107 by King Edgar, the son of Saint Margaret.[17] The miracle collection was written in the second half of the twelfth century, perhaps by Reginald of Durham.[18] Of the 43 recorded miracles, 24 (or 56 percent) involved a vision of the saint, a number that approximates the 59 percent of miracles in Margaret's collection that involved a vision.[19] Reginald of Durham also compiled a collection of miracles performed by the saintly hermit Godric of Finchale, a majority of which are visions.[20] Godric (d. 1170) was an English merchant who often traded with Saint Andrews in Scotland, stopping at Lindisfarne along the way and meditating on the eremitic example of Saint Cuthbert. Before long, he abandoned his mercantile pursuits and became a hermit in the marshes of Finchale near Durham.[21]

Perhaps this emphasis on visions is a faint reflection of a Celtic past that still lingered in northern England and southern Scotland, using the technique of "overlay" discussed in the introduction to appropriate past means of remembering to create new memory networks.[22] The pervasive Irish influence on insular religious practices has been well documented.[23] With such cultural cross-pollination, it would be unusual for some Celtic perceptions of the supernatural not to have been absorbed. Lisa Bitel asserts, for example, that in the Celtic (as well as the Anglo-Saxon and the Norse) cultures, the otherworld had the ability to inform, advise, and guide.[24] It carried great authority, which was ignored at great risk. She suggests that Christian missionaries used this emphasis on dreams and their interpretation as another means by which they could cement their authority in the newly converted territories on the periphery of Europe. Joseph Falaky Nagy goes one step further and documents how the Celtic Christian tradition co-opted the pagan otherworld by incorporating it directly into its own narratives.[25] According to his trifold model, the Christian saint acted as a mediator between the pagan myths and legends of the otherworld and his or her Christian audience. Furthermore, in determining the similarity in biographical details of Celtic pagan heroes and saints, Dorothy Ann Bray notes that, like his or her pagan predecessor, the saint-hero is typically situated as a mediator between the immortal divine and mortal man.[26] In this way, the pagan hero is positioned much like the Christian saint but with an emphasis in the story on visual interaction. Frequently, mythic characters were called from the pagan Great Beyond to relate their stories directly to the saint, who then reiterated them for a Christian audience. According to these interpretations, the saint was acting as an authenticating agent, retelling the cherished tales of Cú Chulainn, for example, to a receptive audience within an appropriately Christian narrative. Such a strategy made the story immediately recognizable to the audience while at the same time ensuring its orthodoxy.

Numerous anecdotal parallels between classic Celtic tales and Margaret's miracle accounts suggest a correlation between the Celtic tradition of otherworldly communications and the specific way in which Margaret was remembered. For example, *The Dream of Óengus* is an Old Irish mythological tale written in the twelfth century but derived from earlier oral accounts. In the story, the hero is seduced in his nightly dreams by a beautiful woman from the otherworld who transforms into a swan in alternate years. The hero eventually joins her, living in the otherworld as a shape-shifting birdman.[27] In another story, the warrior Nera strays outside his lord's hall one night and encounters not only a beautiful woman, whom he marries, but also a talking corpse. The next year, when Nera returns to his lord's hall to warn of an attack by a band of otherworldly warriors, he finds that no time has elapsed. In the end, Nera joins his wife in the otherworld.[28] In both these stories, contact with the mysterious Great Beyond in dreams is both sinister and consequential; you might find yourself transformed physically and trapped forever in the netherworld.

Margaret's miracle collection relates a noticeably analogous tale. A young girl and her mother are out when they hear the complaint of a young child. The mother orders the girl to find the child, but the girl objects. Finally she is overruled.

> She ran quickly to the place where the voice had been heard and, while her mother watched, she lifted up a boy who was just like her brother, who had died a little time before. He said to her, "Sister, give me a kiss." She refused, saying "I know that you are my brother, but because you have gone the way of all flesh, I am not allowed to kiss you." As they argued, he grabbed the girl's throat with his left hand and pushed her between the shoulders with his right, knocking her down and then leaving.

Like Nera, the girl finds herself confronted with a talking corpse, and being familiar with such tales, she knows that the encounter does not bode well. The mother's reaction confirms the girl's fears:

> When the mother perceived all this, the bowels of maternal compassion were moved within her for her daughter, she was almost out of her mind with pain within and great anxiety, and she ran to her, weeping and wailing, and found her possessed by a demon, prostrate on the ground and close to death, lacking speech or sensation. Then she began to grieve and to sorrow, tearing her hair, ripping her clothes and like a roaring lioness

she called out in tears to her servant, "Come, my servants, come and see if there is sorrow like my sorrow."

The mother perceives that contact with the talking corpse has caused her daughter to be possessed by a demon. The girl is "close to death," or close to departing for the otherworld, and the mother grieves as though her daughter is already dead. After being taken home, the unfortunate girl cries out, "'I see this house full of men and women, boys and girls.' She adds, 'Behold how beautiful that queen is, how fair of face, how lovely in appearance, how sweet the song of those leading the choir' and many other things of this kind."

In a second parallel with the Irish tales, the girl is being seduced by a beautiful woman, in this case described as a queen. In desperation, the parents take the girl to Dunfermline and place her "before the altar of St Margaret, the queen." The next day, Margaret appears to the girl in a dream and instructs her to go to her tomb ("the place where my bones rested"). Once at the tomb, Margaret again appears to the girl in a dream, "taking her head in her hands and placing a finger in her throat, then, as she withdrew her finger, the girl said, 'Most holy mother, I give you deep thanks for the mercy you have shown me. I feel that I have recovered my senses and the power of speech. If you would be willing to touch the place where I was struck by the demon, I know that I would be completely restored to health.'" Margaret, of course, heals the girl, who then expresses her gratitude by becoming a nun. This lengthy and involved miracle narrative contains details that would have been recognizable to an audience familiar with Celtic tales of the otherworld: talking corpses and beautiful women who threaten to spirit the young girl away. The supernatural hero, Margaret, then appears in a dream-vision, twice, to cure the girl of her multiple afflictions and return her to the world of the sensate living.[29] The important distinction being made here is between the demonic and the miraculous, ignoring issues of gender. This miracle account seems to emphasize the necessity of discernment by contrasting two visions that are on the surface remarkably similar—both featuring beautiful queens—but that differ markedly in their inspiration.

The border between Scotland and England seems to have been a particularly fertile nexus for a shared Anglo-Celtic tradition.[30] Thus, for example, Aelred of Reivaulx and Jocelin of Furness—although both Cistercians in northern England—wrote lives of Scottish saints (Ninian and Kentigern, respectively) dedicated to Scottish bishops (an anonymous bishop of Whithorn and Jocelin, bishop of Glasgow (1174–1199), respectively).[31] Aelred had strong ties to the Scottish court, having served in the royal household of Margaret's youngest son, King David I, before

taking his vows in 1134. His abiding affection for the monarch is obvious in his eulogy, *De Sancto David Rege Scottorum*, written about 1153.[32]
The association between Jocelin of Furness and the Scottish court is evidenced by his decision to compose a Life of Saint Waltheof, the stepson
of the same King David through his wife's first marriage. Like Aelred,
Waltheof grew up at the court of King David, and it is likely that the two
knew each other.

The connections were particularly strong between Durham Cathedral,
the cultural and intellectual center of the Scots-English border, and
the descendants of Margaret. Although governed by a series of Anglo-
Norman bishops and professing obedience to the archbishopric of York,
Durham claimed the Scottish royal family as one of its primary benefac-
tors.[33] Malcolm and Margaret entered into a contractual understanding
in which the monks at Durham would undertake the spiritual care of
the king and queen and their dynasty both in this life and the next.[34]
Cementing this pact, Malcolm was present at the laying of the foundation
of the new cathedral in 1093.[35] Malcolm's son from his first marriage,
Duncan, followed by Malcolm and Margaret's son Edgar, each renewed
the pact through gifts of land, intending to secure the support of the
Durham community and the divine assistance of Saint Cuthbert in their
successive bids to secure the Scottish throne.[36] In one particular charter,
Edgar tellingly refers to Cuthbert as "my lord."[37] In 1104, before becoming king, Alexander was given the unique honor of being the only secular representative present at the inspection of Saint Cuthbert's tomb.[38]
As king, he further bound the servants of Saint Cuthbert to Scotland
by selecting the prior of Durham, Turgot—who was also, incidentally,
Margaret's hagiographer—to be the bishop of Saint Andrews.[39]

In addition, a cross-border affiliation between those memorializing the
saints of Durham and those preserving the memory of Saint Margaret at
Dunfermline is suggested by similarities in their respective hagiographic
traditions. Saint Cuthbert, the patron saint of Durham, seventh-century
hermit (d. 687), and Celtic bishop of Lindisfarne, was prominently featured by Symeon, a monk at Durham and a prolific chronicler. He reports
that in the late ninth century, the precious Lindisfarne Gospels were lost
in a storm at sea while the community of Lindisfarne, fleeing Viking
invasions, was ill-advisedly and unsuccessfully attempting to move the
saint's body to the safety of Ireland. The saint informed his monks of the
location of the lost manuscript, which was, of course, undamaged.[40] This
miraculous story bears striking parallels to the single miracle recorded in
Margaret's hagiography, the loss and retrieval of her Gospel Book, suggesting contact between the cult of Saint Cuthbert centered in Durham
and that of Saint Margaret centered in Dunfermline.[41] Additionally,

the hagiographic tradition at Durham was exemplified by Reginald of Durham, whom we have already met as the author of the similarly vision-rich miracles of Saints Æbbe (probably) and Godric (certainly). He also compiled a collection of miracles performed by Durham's patron saint, recasting enthralling stories about his contact with the weird and wonderful supernatural.[42] Durham and Dunfermline, the English cathedral and the Scottish royal abbey, shared a unique cultural and hagiographic tradition, a key component of which was a predilection for visual encounters with the supernatural.

The number of visions in Margaret's miracle collection, in addition to their distinctive nature, reveals the mnemonic inclinations of the audience receiving and repeating these accounts. Claire Barbetti states, "The verbal translation of a vision is not merely a mimetic activity; it uses tools of the memory arts to place elements in such a way as to engender a culturally agreed-upon meaning."[43] Although Barbetti is speaking specifically regarding the manner in which Hildegard of Bingen opted to record her own visions, the same observation can be made with respect to how authors selected particular accounts for inclusion in miracle collections. The text recording the vision—the miracle collection—is the carefully filtered result of critical communal selection. By determining which visions to include and which to leave out, by selecting those that furthered the saint's cult and ignoring those that did not, by repeating those that were well received and ignoring those that were not, the compiler(s) of the miracle collection, a monk or monks at Dunfermline Abbey, provide insight into the nature of the community that both sought and acknowledged supernatural assistance from the saint. Margaret's miracle collection appears, therefore, to have been written for a regional audience that was familiar with, and receptive to, a tradition of portentous dreams. By selecting miracle accounts replete with descriptive dreams and visions, the monks at Dunfermline Abbey elected to situate the memory of Margaret firmly within a specific, well-defined hagiographic tradition that straddled the English and Scottish border. Like the miracle accounts of Saints Cuthbert, Godric, and Æbbe, and in direct contrast to the majority of cults in England and on the Continent, Margaret's miracle collection is accented with visions. Those reporting, recording, and receiving these accounts of divine and demonic interaction would have been uniquely attuned to their highly charged significance.

An Orthodox Dynastic Saint

The second half of this chapter describes both the Church's historically cautious approach to visions and the vested interest that the Scottish

ruling monarchy had in perpetuating an orthodox image of their ancestress. It will then outline how tension between the views of the Church
and monarchy on the one hand and a local devotion to the saint that was
so heavily weighted toward visions on the other is reconciled by taking
particular care to authenticate the visions.

Beginning in the late twelfth century and reaching its fullest articula-
tion at the Fourth Lateran Council in 1215, the Church instituted a jurid-
ical process of discernment for determining the authenticity of miracles.[44]
"The developing principles of canon law," Michael Goodich summa-
rizes, "supported the notion that evidence of the miraculous requires the
application of proper judicial procedure and the deposition of witnesses
of unimpeachable character. The aim was to achieve a single reliable
version of the events, free of contradictions and capable of withstanding
scrutiny."[45] Dreams and visions were especially problematic since by their
very nature it was difficult to find corroborating witnesses.[46] Another
complication was the fact that this rational approach collided with the
desire and the need for miraculous intervention. Supernatural approbation was, after all, an effective weapon in the ongoing fight against heresy and for the conversion of Jews. Goodich concludes that "the central
Middle Ages may be viewed as a transition period when faith in the
revelatory nature of dreams, visions and unsubstantiated cures continued
alongside the growing demand for proof supplied in accordance with the
standard rules of evidence."[47]

Scotland's ruling dynasty was keenly interested in remembering their
ancestress as a canonically orthodox saint. Sometime before 1245, King
Alexander II (1214–1249) sent a letter to the pope requesting the papal
canonization of his saintly ancestor, in support of which this miracle collection was probably compiled.[48] One of the complex and manifold motivations for this request is that Alexander was seeking, in part, to align
Scotland and the royal house with the orthodox Roman Church in con-
tradistinction to dynastic rivals who drew upon adherents to the Celtic
tradition as a source of support. Margaret's dynasty had been continually
challenged by the descendants both of Lulach, the stepson of Macbeth, and
of Duncan II, the son of Malcolm III from his first marriage. Frequently,
the resulting dynastic clashes were painted with broad strokes in terms
of a native, antifeudal faction contending with a European or Norman
feudal monarchy, a key component of which was Celtic versus Roman
practices. Such a portrait is, of course, far too simplistic, but it probably
suited the political polemics of the time and events did on occasion reflect
this view.[49] When Donald Bàn made a bid for the throne after the death
of his brother, Malcolm III, he was styled, or styled himself, as a representative of a native, Gaelic backlash against the interfering English.[50] The

hostility that Donald and his adherents showed toward Malcolm's foreign followers was motivated primarily by self-interest since it suited them politically to eliminate those who had been loyal to Malcolm and his sons by casting Donald as the true, native, Gaelic heir to the Scottish throne.[51] When his political needs changed, however, Donald found it expedient to align himself with Malcolm and Margaret's family by securing their son, Edmund, as an ally according to some ill-defined agreement to share power. The issue was not, therefore, the foreign orientation of Margaret's descendants but the dynastic struggle that was framed by it.

Anti-English factions continued to challenge Margaret's dynasty. Somerled, king of Argyll, was a perpetual thorn in the side of the Scottish monarchy through his support of his rebellious nephews (the descendants of Lulach) against King Malcolm IV, Margaret's great-grandson.[52] During the mid-twelfth century, Somerled controlled the southwestern coast of Scotland and the islands off the coast, determinedly defying Scottish royal authority.[53] In 1164, he challenged that authority by appointing a bishop strategically chosen from northern Ireland (Flaithbertach Ua-Brolchain of Derry) as the new abbot of Iona. In selecting a delegate who was oriented more toward the Celtic tradition than the Roman Church, he has been accused of essentially engaging in "an ecclesiastical equivalent of his rebellions against the Scots."[54] In another example, the affiliation between the Celtic tradition and Iona, the traditional burial place of the Gaelic kings preceding Malcolm III, was reaffirmed rather violently in 1204 when Irish clergy destroyed a Benedictine monastery that had been built there.[55]

Throughout these dynastic clashes, Margaret's descendants sought the powerful support of the papacy. In the early thirteenth century, kings of Scotland had asserted, with the overt cooperation and assistance of Rome, ecclesiastical control over Caithness, a territory in far northeast Scotland. It was ruled by the descendants of Thorfinn, whose widow (or daughter) was Malcolm III's first wife, making the Orkney dynasty kin to the descendants of King Duncan (d. 1094), Malcolm's son from that marriage. The imposition of a Scottish bishop in Caithness was deeply resented by Earl Harald of Orkney (d. 1206) as a royal intrusion on his authority. In 1201, he captured and mutilated the bishop by having his eyes stabbed and his tongue cut out.[56] King William (1165–1214) launched a military campaign to reassert his control, and Pope Innocent III demonstrated his support of the action by sending a letter demanding the punishment of the perpetrator.[57] Twenty years later, the players are different—King Alexander II of Scotland (1214–1249), Earl John of Orkney, Bishop Adam of Caithness, and Pope Honorius III—but again the bishop is attacked (this time fatally), the king retaliates, and the pope offers his written support of the king's action and authority.[58] In each of these cases, the ecclesiastical authority of the Roman Church acted to support the secular rule of Margaret's descendants.

Cultural differences were therefore even easier to identify and more effective when they could be cast in high moral terms of religious disputes. Just as the invading Normans had justified their aggression in part by alleging deviant practices in the Anglo-Saxon Church, so the differences in Scotland were defined in terms of Gaelic versus Norman culture and Celtic versus Roman religious practices. Margaret's dynasty made an early tactical move to associate itself with sanctity according to the model adopted by other fledgling monarchies struggling for control on the fringes of Europe.[59] Examples include the cults of Saints Olaf of Norway, Oswald of Northumbria, Stephen and Emeric of Hungary, Wenceslas of Bohemia, and Boris and Gleb of Kiev. In each case, the *arriviste* dynasty laid claim to legitimacy through sacral approbation. As legitimate, divinely and ecclesiastically approved rulers, they were no longer susceptible to opportunistic invasions as when, for example, Charlemagne invaded Saxony and the Normans invaded Anglo-Saxon England, both on the pretext of saving inhabitants from suspect pagan practices endorsed by previous rulers. The very real fear of such aggression is alluded to in Margaret's *Vita* when she is credited with correcting the "barbaric practices" of the native church, and this fear was likely to have remained vivid through the ensuing dynastic struggles.[60]

In fact, throughout her *Vita*, Margaret is depicted as a model of orthodox sanctity and a forceful advocate for the Roman Church. The reform of such "barbaric practices," mentioned earlier, was one of several that she championed at one ecclesiastical council in particular. As chair of this council, she also argued successfully for the dating of Easter according to the Roman custom, proper observance of the Lord's Day, reception of communion on Easter, and the prohibition of unlawful marriage practices.[61] In the miracle collection, she is referred to as "our consoler, or rather the foundation of faith in the whole region," a rather dramatic and definitive claim.[62] It seems that one of the primary purposes of King Alexander III's request for her canonization was to align himself and the Scottish royal house firmly with the Church in Rome. Margaret, being both the genetrix of the dynasty and of indisputably orthodox reputation, was ideally suited as a vehicle for solidifying this support.

In order to support the orthodoxy of her dynasty, Margaret had to be remembered in an orthodox way, and in order to be remembered popularly, she had to be remembered as a saint who appeared in visions.

Hagiographic texts needed to authenticate and validate themselves within prescriptive norms. In chapter 5 of this volume, Barbara Zimbalist considers how Clemence of Barking, a twelfth-century Anglo-Norman nun rewriting *Life of St. Catherine* in the vernacular, employed direct discourse, *oratio recta*, in imitation of Christ, in part to authenticate suspect female speech. Elissa Hansen establishes in her chapter that Julian of Norwich, working in fourteenth-century England, reconciled "her visionary experience with the institutional authority of the Church" by likening herself to the Virgin Mary. In each case, the author of the text utilized well-known hagiographic tropes, *imitatio Christi* in the former and *imitatio Mariae* in the latter, to authenticate practices toward which the Church traditionally expressed some ambivalence—female speech in the former and self-authored visions in the latter (which might also, incidentally, be construed as female speech).

Margaret's hagiographer, writing about 1100, evidently adhered to the more rational view of the miraculous:

> Let others admire the tokens of miracles which they see in others, I for my part, admire much more the works of mercy which I saw in Margaret. Miracles are common to the evil and to the good, but the works of true piety and charity belong to the good alone. The former sometimes indicate holiness, but the latter are holiness itself. Let us, I say, admire in Margaret the things which made her a saint, rather than the miracles, if she did any, which might only have indicated that she was one to men. Let us more worthily admire her as one in whom, because of her devotion to justice, piety, mercy, and love, we see rather the works of the ancient Fathers than their miracles.[63]

Although this elaborate disclaimer can, of course, be viewed as a hagiographic trope, the fact remains that Margaret is not credited with performing any miracles during her lifetime. Aside from the single account of the miraculous recovery of her Gospel Book, discussed earlier, Margaret's life is not associated with any supernatural events, and her miracle-working career would not begin until almost 100 years after her hagiography was written.

Within Margaret's miracle collection, a resolution between the predominance of visions and their inherently dubious authenticity is achieved in two ways. First, Margaret identifies herself in a significant number of the visions—26 percent—in order to authenticate their divine origin. She identifies herself most frequently as "Margaret, queen of Scots" (chapters 7, 12, 25, 39). Other times she is simply "Margaret" or "I am she" (chapters 4, 19). Once she states even more specifically, "I am Margaret whose body rests in this little dwelling," referring to the Abbey of Dunfermline (chapter 20). In this way, Margaret is acting as the interpreter between the inherently ambiguous vision and her audience, thereby establishing the authenticity of the vision. In contrast, demonic spirits remain unnamed: chapter 5 refers only to three "figures in female form." They are not even defined as women, possessing only the form of a female.

Great care is taken to specify whether the experience is a waking vision or a dream. In chapter 1, the supplicant was "close to sleep but not yet completely asleep" and awoke "as if from sleep." Margaret appears to a girl in chapter 42 "while she was awake." Sometimes Margaret herself establishes the nature of the vision, as in chapter 11 when she appears to a man and asks if he is awake. Significantly, Margaret identifies herself only in dreams, not waking visions, the single exception occurring in the final chapter, when she identifies herself in a vision that precedes a dream. The need to authenticate a dream was greater because it was deemed to be even less reliable than waking visions. The thirteenth-century scholar Albertus Magnus, following Macrobius and Augustine, outlined a hierarchy of dreams. The first type of vision is roughly comparable with Macrobius's *insomnium*, the least revelatory and most mundane dream type. At the other end of the spectrum, the waking vision of Albertus is most similar to the *oraculum*, a vision in which the divine communicates directly.[64] The compiler of Margaret's miracle collection seems to have been acutely aware of the relative assessment of dreams and waking visions. Because the latter were inherently more reliable, they did not require any further authentication, whereas the validity of dreams needed to be established, in this case through the self-identification of the saint.

Secondly, a vision of Margaret frequently resulted in the conversion or confirmation of the faith of the supplicant; the person becomes a nun or a monk or confirms his commitment to remain a monk (chapters 13, 28, 38). In one case, a man guilty of rape repents and undertakes a pilgrimage to the Holy Land (chapter 24). In chapter 11, Margaret appears to a monk tormented by demons and cures him, stating her purpose unambiguously, "I have obtained from my lord Jesus Christ, who does not want the death of a sinner but rather that he should be converted and live, that you will recover your health." The reasoning was that visions with such beneficial results could only have emanated from a benevolent source.[65]

One vision in particular illustrates the various agendas within the miracle collection by combining elements of a Celtic vision from the otherworld with an express endorsement of Margaret's dynasty in a clearly authenticated dream. In chapter 7, the king of Scotland (Alexander III) is preparing to go to war against the invading army of King Haakon of Norway.[66] One weary and ailing knight, John of Wemyss, falls asleep and dreams that he is standing outside the church of Dunfermline. He sees a beautiful lady coming out of the church, leading by her right hand a fully armored knight, with three more following behind. When the under-standably frightened knight asks who she is, she replies, "I am Margaret, queen of Scots. This knight I am leading by the hand was my husband, King Malcolm by name. The three following are my three sons, kings who lie with me in this church...I am hurrying with them to Largs, to bring victory over that tyrant who is attempting to subject my kingdom to his power." Here we have a Celtic-inspired dream-vision in which the hero returns from the otherworld to provide material aid to a supplicant. As such, it would be immediately recognizable and memorable to the audience, demonstrating and encouraging popular support for Margaret's cult. There is no doubt that it was intended to bolster support of Margaret's dynasty; she is seen leading her husband, King Malcolm, and her three sons who ruled in succession, Edgar (1097–1107), Alexander (1107–1124), and David (1124–1153). Moreover, she makes it clear that God has entrusted the kingdom of Scotland to her and her descendants forever, in perpetuity—a definite case of divine right. Margaret is therefore firmly identified as the protectrix of her dynasty through her intercession. The authenticity of the dream is confirmed first by Margaret's self-identifi-cation and then by the inclusion of two common hagiographic tropes. The knight relates it to the prior of Dunfermline, who states that "it was not the type of dream by which we are often deluded but a sign from heaven." Such clerical corroboration was deemed to be reliable because as a holy man he was invested with the ability to discern divine from demonic visions. Final confirmation comes when the events foretold by the saint come true. In this case, the knight is cured of his illness and the king of Norway is defeated and dies.

In this regard, Margaret is situated squarely within the tradition of the protective saint but with a nuanced interpretation. Saints were fre-quently cast as active defenders of their communities, beginning most notably with the Blessed Virgin as the protector of Constantinople.[67] Closer to Margaret's cult in time and space, Saint Cuthbert was respon-sible for creating a dense fog to protect Durham from the famous wrath of William the Conqueror.[68] In another instance, Cuthbert's personal antipathy caused William to be prevented by "an intolerable heat" from seeing the body of the saint, forcing him to flee the church and the city of Durham, not stopping until he had crossed the river Tees.[69] In 1164, Saint Kentigern assisted in the defeat of Somerled according to a Latin poem composed by a clerk at the cathedral of Glasgow who witnessed the conflict.[70]

A critical analysis of the twin observations of both the high number of visions in the collection and the high number of those visions in which

Margaret identifies herself allows us to advance some theories regarding the various audiences that were instrumental in crafting her memory. Both divinely and demonically inspired encounters with the supernatural permeate the miracle accounts, suggesting that the collective memory of Margaret's community preferred to view her as an interactive, involved saint, interceding forcefully on behalf of her supplicants. This predilection for supernatural encounters was specific to the geographic area that straddled the border of Scotland and England and might have been the result of a lingering Celtic heritage. At the same time, Margaret's descendants were very keen to utilize her orthodox sanctity to bolster papal support for the legitimacy of their rule. Any tension between the unusually high number of visions and the canonically approved memory of the saint is resolved by authenticating the miracle, thereby minimizing the ambiguous, middle nature of the encounter with the supernatural. The way in which Margaret was remembered and her identity invented established her both as an effective intercessor on behalf of her supplicants and as a legitimizing agent for her dynasty.

By memorializing their holy subjects through the invention of an identity, miracle collections therefore convey a great deal about the people *by whom* and the society *in which* they were constructed. A comparative and contextual analysis of how a saint was envisioned in her miracle collection thus reveals the rich repository of remembered hagiographic traditions reflecting the various agendas of both those interested in shaping how she was remembered and the communities that gave rise to these remembrances.

Notes

1. Aviad M. Kleinberg, *Prophets in Their Own Country: Living Saints and the Making of Sainthood in the Later Middle Ages* (Chicago: Chicago University Press, 1992), 148.

2. *The Life of St Margaret* was written probably by Turgot, the prior of Durham (1093–1109) and bishop of Saint Andrews (1109–1115), in the decade after her death in 1093. It exists in three manuscript versions: British Library Cotton Tiberius Diii, composed at the end of the twelfth century; British Library Cotton Tiberius Eiii, rescinded in the first quarter of the fourteenth century; and a version that exists in the same manuscript as the miracle collection, Madrid, Biblioteca Real II 2097 fos. 1v–17v, which I have translated in the appendix to my PhD dissertation, "Saint Margaret, Queen of the Scots: Her Life and Memory" (Central European University, 2010). A printed version similar to the Cotton Tiberius Diii manuscript derived from a now lost manuscript at the Cistercian abbey of Vaucelles in northern France is found in *Acta Sanctorum*, vol. 1 for

June 10 (Brussels and Antwerp: Societé des Bollandistes, 1966) and translated by W. M. Metcalfe in *Ancient Lives of Scottish Saints, Part Two* (1895;
repr., Felinfach, UK: Llanerch Publishers, 1998), 45–69. For a biography
of Margaret, see my dissertation and G. W. S. Barrow, "Margaret [St
Margaret] (d. 1093)," in *Oxford Dictionary of National Biography* (Oxford:
Oxford University Press, 2004), 632–33.

3. The dating of the miracle collection is problematic. Robert Bartlett con-
jectures "that the collection was assembled before 1249 and that the chapters demonstrably later than that date are interpolations" but ultimately
concedes that "there is no entirely plausible explanation." The collection
was almost certainly written by an anonymous monk at Dunfermline
Abbey, located in about the middle of Scotland on the northern side of
the Firth of Forth, where Margaret's relics were enshrined and most of
the miracles naturally (or supernaturally) occurred. The manuscript itself
was compiled during the reign of James III (1460–1488) and is currently
housed in Madrid at the Biblioteca del Palacio Real. Robert Bartlett,
introduction to *The Miracles of St Æbbe of Coldingham and St Margaret of
Scotland*, ed. and trans. Robert Bartlett (Oxford: Clarendon Press, 2003),
xxxvi–xxxvii. For more on the cult of Saint Margaret, see Robert Folz,
Les saintes reines du moyen âge en occident, Vie–VIIIe siècles (Brussels: Société
des Bollandistes, 1992), 93–104; Roberto Paciocco, *Canonizzazioni e culto
dei santi nella christianitas (1198–1302)* (Assisi: Porziuncola, 2006), 295–
310; and my dissertation.

4. Visions or dreams of Margaret occur in chapters 1, 2, 4, 5, 7, 11, 12, 13
(twice), 15, 17, 18, 19, 20, 24, 25, 26, 27, 30, 35, 36, 37, 38, 39, 40, 42
(twice). Also observed by Bartlett in introduction to *Miracles*, l–li.

5. Steven F. Kruger, *Dreaming in the Middle Ages* (1992; repr., Cambridge:
Cambridge University Press, 2005).

6. Barbara Newman, "What Did It Mean to Say 'I Saw'? The Clash between
Theory and Practice in Medieval Visionary Culture," *Speculum* 80, no. 1
(January 2005): 6–7 [1–43].

7. Kruger, *Dreaming*, 72.

8. Ibid., 74–78.

9. St. Gregory the Great, *Dialogues* 4.50, ed. Adalbert de Vogüé, Sources
Chrétiennes, 251, 260, 265 (Paris: Les Editions du Cerf, 1978–80); Isidore
of Seville, *Sententiae*, in *Patrologia latina*, ed. J.-P. Migne, vol. 83 (Paris:
Migne, 1844–45), pp. 537–738, 3.6; Hildegard of Bingen, *Causae et curae*,
ed. Paulus Kaiser (Leipzig: Teubner, 1903), 83, 143; John of Salisbury,
Policraticus 2.17, ed. Clemens C. I. Webb (Oxford: Clarendon Press,
1909).

10. Pierre-André Sigal, *L'homme et le miracle dans La France médiévale, XIe–XIIe
siècle* (Paris: Les Editions du Cerf, 1985), 134.

11. Pamela Sheingorn, trans., *The Book of Sainte Foy* (Philadelphia: University
of Pennsylvania Press, 1995).

12. Benedict of Peterborough, *Miracula S Thomae Cantuariensis*, in *Materials for
the History of Thomas Becket, Archbishop of Canterbury*, ed. J. C. Robinson

and J. B. Sheppard, 7 volumes (London: Longman, 1875–85), 2:21–181; William of Canterbury, *Miracula S Thomae Cantuariensis*, in Robinson and Sheppard, *Materials*, 1:137–546; Raymonde Foreville, "Les 'Miracula S. Thomae Cantuariensis,'" in *Actes du 97e Congrès national des sociétés savantes, Nantes, 1972, section de philolgie et d'histoire jusqu'à 1610* (Paris: Bibliothèque Nationale, 1979), 455 [443–68].

13. A. Huyskens, ed., *Quellenstudienzur Geschichte der hl. Elisabeth Landgräfin von Thüringen* (Marburg, Germany: N. G. Elwert, 1908); A. Huyskens, ed., *Der sogenannte Libellus de dictis quattor ancillarum s. Elisabeth confectus* (Munich and Kempten, Germany: Kempten Kösel, 1911); A. Huyskens, ed., "Die Schriften über die heilige Elisabeth von Thüringen," in *Die Wundergeschichten des Caesarius von Heisterbach*, ed. Alfons Hilka (Bonn: Hanstein, 1937), 3:329–90.

14. Wojciech Kętrzyński, ed., *Vita sancti Stanislai cracoviensis episcopi (Vita maior) auctore fratre Vincentio OFP*, in *Monumenta Poloniae Historica*, ed. Wojciech Kętrzyński (Lviv, Ukraine: Nakładem Academii Umiejętności w Krakowie, 1884), 4:319–438; Aleksandra Witkowska, "Miracula malopolskie Z XIII i XIV wieku: Studium zrodloznavcze" (Miracles of lesser Poland in the thirteenth and fourteenth centuries: A study of the sources), *Roczniki Humanistyczne* 2 (1971): 29–161.

15. Gábor Klaniczay, "Dreams and Visions in Medieval Miracle Accounts," in *The "Vision Thing": Studying Divine Intervention*, ed. William A. Christian Jr. and Gábor Klaniczay (Budapest: Collegium Budapest Workshop Series 18, 2009), 37–64.

16. Details regarding the historical life of Æbbe are found in the Venerable Bede, *Ecclesiastical History of the English People*, ed. Bertram Colgrave and R. A. B. Mynors (Oxford: Clarendon Press, 1969), iv:19, iv:25; Bertram Colgrave, ed., *Vita S. Cuthberti auctore anonymo*, in *Two Lives of Saint Cuthbert*, ed. Bertram Colgrave (Cambridge: Cambridge University Press, 1940), 60–139; Bede, *Vita S. Cuthberti*, in *Two Lives of Saint Cuthbert*, ed. Bertram Colgrave (Cambridge: Cambridge University Press, 1940), 142–306; Bertram Colgrave, ed., *The Life of Bishop Wilfrid by Eddius Stephanus* (Cambridge: Cambridge University Press, 1927), c:39.

17. Archibald C. Lawrie, ed., *Early Scottish Charters prior to 1153* (Glasgow: James MacLehose and Sons, 1905), nos. xv, xix–xxi, pp. 12–18. For the authenticity of the charters, see A. A. M. Duncan, "Yes, the Earliest Scottish Charters," *Scottish Historical Review* 78 (1999): 1–35.

18. The miracle collection was composed in the twelfth century and exists only in the fourteenth-century Durham compilation. Fairfax 6, fos. 164r–173v, Bodleian Library, Oxford. The text has been translated and edited by Robert Bartlett in *Miracles*, 2–67.

19. Bartlett, *Miracles*, l.

20. Benedicta Ward, *Miracles and the Medieval Mind: Theory, Record and Event 1000–1215*, rev. ed. (Philadelphia: University of Pennsylvania Press, 1987), 79. R. Finucane notes, however, that "about three dozen dreams and visions were recorded" out of the 222 healing miracles attributed to

Saint Godric, amounting to about 16 percent. Again, perhaps the discrepancy is the result of considering specifically healing miracles. R. Finucane, "The Posthumous Miracles of Godric of Finchale," *Transactions of the Architectural and Archaeological Society of Durham and Northumberland* 3 (1975): 47–50.

21. Reginald of Durham, *Libellus de Vita et Miraculis S. Godrici, Heremitae de Finchale*, ed. J. Stevenson, Miscellanea Biographica, Surtees Society, vol. 20 (London, 1847).

22. The influence of other cultures, particularly Scandinavian, is also possible, but this chapter focuses on the Celtic influence as an illustration. By analyzing origin legends, king lists, and royal genealogies, Dauvit Broun argues that until the thirteenth century, Scottish scholars most frequently identified the kingdom of the Scots with Ireland. Dauvit Broun, *The Irish Identity of the Kingdom of the Scots* (Woodbridge, UK: Boydell Press, 1999).

23. Kathleen Hughes notes that certain ninth-century Anglo-Saxon prayers are based on Irish examples, and J. E. Cross ascertains that Irish sources were the basis for information on Saints Patrick, Columba, and Fursa in the ninth-century Old English Martyrology. Penitential practices in Anglo-Saxon England were influenced by the Irish penitential literature, as pointed out by Allen Frantzen, while Charles Wright asserts a similar foundation for Old English homiletic literature. Colin Ireland has documented the Irish origin of ascetic immersion as a form of penance and prayer specifically in Northumbria, with Saint Cuthbert as the most notable example. Kathleen Hughes, "Some Aspects of Irish Influence on Early English Private Prayer," *Studia Celtica* 5 (1970): 48–61; J. E. Cross, "The Influence of Irish Texts and Traditions on the Old English Martyrology," *Proceedings of the Royal Irish Academy* 91, sec. C (1981): 173–92; Allen J. Frantzen, *The Literature of Penance in Anglo-Saxon England* (New Brunswick, NJ: Rutgers University Press, 1983); Charles D. Wright, *The Irish Tradition in Old English Literature* (Cambridge: Cambridge University Press, 1993); Colin Ireland, "Penance and Prayer in Water: An Irish Practice in Northumbrian Hagiography," *Cambrian Medieval Celtic Studies* 34 (1997): 51–66.

24. Lisa Bitel, "'In Visu Noctis': Dreams in European Hagiography and Histories, 450–900," *History of Religions* 31, no. 1 (August 1991): 39–59.

25. Joseph Falaky Nagy, "Close Encounters of the Traditional Kind in Medieval Irish Literature," in *Celtic Folklore and Christianity*, ed. Patrick Ford (Santa Barbara, CA: McNally and Loftin, 1983), 129–49.

26. Dorothy Ann Bray, "Heroic Tradition in the Lives of the Early Irish Saints: A Study in Hagio-Biographical Patterning," *Proceedings of the First North American Congress of Celtic Studies; Held at Ottawa from 36th–30th March, 1986* (1988): 261–71.

27. Francis Shaw, ed., *The Dream of Óengus: "Aislinge Óenguso"* (Dublin: Browne and Nolan, 1934); Bitel, "In Visu Noctis," 43.

28. Kuno Meyer, ed., "Echtra Nerai," *Revue celtique* 10 (1889): 212–28; Bitel, "In Visu Noctis," 44.

29. Bartlett, *Miracles*, 100–105.

30. Robert Bartlett, "Cults of Irish, Scottish and Welsh Saints," in *Britain and Ireland 900–1300: Insular Responses to Medieval European Change*, ed. Brendan Smith (Cambridge: Cambridge University Press, 1999), 83 [67–86].

31. Ibid., 81. For the life of Saint Kentigern, see A. P. Forbes, ed., *Lives of St Ninian and St Kentigern*, The Historians of Scotland 5 (Edinburgh: Edmundston and Douglas, 1874), 137–57; and W. M. Metcalfe, ed., *Pinkerton's Lives of the Scottish Saints*, 2 vols. (Paisley, UK: Alexander Gardner, 1889), 1:9–39. For Waltheof, see Jocelin of Furness, *Vita S. Waldevi*, ed. Guilelmus Cuperus, in *Acta Sanctorum*, August vol. 1 (Brussels and Antwerp: Societé des Bollandistes, 1733), 248–76; and George McFadden, "The Life of Waldef and Its Author, Jocelin of Furness," *Innes Review* 6 (1955): 5–13.

32. Aelred of Rievaulx, "Eulogium Davidis ab Ailredo," in *Vitae antiquae sanctorum qui habitaverunt in ea parte Britanniae nunc vicata Scotia vel in ejus insulis*, ed. Johannes Pinkerton (London: Johannis Nichols, 1789), 437–56. For a translation, see Aelred of Rievaulx, *Aelred of Rievaulx: The Historical Works*, trans. Jane Patricia Freeland, ed. Marsha L. Dutton (Kalamazoo, MI: Cistercian Publications, 2005), 45–70. For Aelred's biography, see Walter Daniel, *The Life of Aelred of Rievaulx and the Letter to Maurice*, ed. and trans. F. M. Powicke, intro. Marsha L. Dutton (Kalamazoo, MI: Cistercian Publications, 1994).

33. For the ties between the Scottish rulers and Durham, see G. W. S. Barrow, "The Kings of Scotland and Durham," in *Anglo-Norman Durham, 1093–1193*, ed. David Rollason, Margaret Harvey, and Michael Prestwich (Woodbridge, UK: Boydell Press, 1994), 311–23; Paul Dalton, "Scottish Influence on Durham 1066–1214," in Rollason, Harvey, and Prestwich, *Anglo-Norman Durham*, 340–52; Valerie Wall, "Malcolm III and the Cathedral," in Rollason, Harvey, and Prestwich, *Anglo-Norman Durham*, 325–37.

34. David Rollason and Lynda Rollason, eds., *The Durham "Liber Vitae": London, British Library, MS Cotton Domitian A.VII*, 3 vols. (London: British Library, 2007), 1.155–56; English translation in Barrow, "Kings of Scotland and Durham," 314.

35. Symeon of Durham, *Historia Regum*, in *Symeonis monachi Opera Omnia*, 2 vols., ed. Thomas Arnold, Rolls Series (London, 1882–85), 2:3–283.

36. The text of Duncan's sole surviving charter is available in Lawrie, *Early Scottish Charters*, no. xii. A translation is available in Gordon Donaldson, ed., *Scottish Historical Documents* (New York: Barnes and Noble, 1970), 16–17. For the authenticity of the document, see Duncan, "Yes, the Earliest Scottish Charters," 4. For Edgar's charter, 1095, see Lawrie, *Early*

Scottish Charters, no. xv; for authenticity of the documents, see Duncan, "Yes, the Earliest Scottish Charters," 16–35. Once king, Edgar continued to grant lands and property to Durham. See Lawrie, *Early Scottish Charters*, nos. xvii–xxii.

37. Lawrie, *Early Scottish Charters*, no. xix: "Sancto Cuthberto domino meo" (to my lord Saint Cuthbert).

38. "Capitula de Miraculis et Translationibus sancti Cuthberti," in Arnold, *Symeonis monachi*, 1:258.

39. A. O. Anderson and M. O. Anderson, ed., *Chronicle of Melrose from the Cottonian Manuscript, Faustina B. IX in the British Museum* (London: Percy Lund Humphries and Co., 1936), s.a. 1109. See also the excerpt of the Melrose Chronicle in *Early Sources of Scottish History, A.D. 500–1286*, ed. A. O. Anderson and M. O. Anderson, 2 vols. (1922; repr., Stamford, Lincolnshire, UK: Paul Watkins, 1990), 2:142; Symeon of Durham, *Historia Regum*, 2:204; John Dowden, *The Bishops of Scotland*, ed. Dr. J. Maitland Thomson (Glasgow: J. MacLehose, 1912), 1–2.

40. Symeon of Durham, *Historia Regum*, 1:64 and 1:67–68.

41. Turgot, "Life of Saint Margaret," ch. 25. The Gospel Book of Queen Margaret (MS Lat. Liturgy. Fol. 5, Bodleian Library, Oxford); facsimile: W. Forbes-Leith, ed., *The Gospel Book of St Margaret: A Facsimile* (Edinburgh, 1896). See also Rebecca Rushforth, *St Margaret's Gospel Book: The Favourite Book of an Eleventh-Century Queen of Scots* (Oxford: Bodleian Library, University of Oxford, 2007), and Richard Gameson, "The Gospels of Margaret of Scotland and the Literacy of an Eleventh-Century Queen," in *Women and the Book: Assessing the Visual Evidence*, ed. Jane H. M. Taylor and Lesley Smith (Toronto: University of Toronto Press, 1999), 148–71.

42. James Raine, ed., *Libellus de Ortu Sancti Cuthberti*, Miscellanea Biographica, Surtees Society 8 (London and Edinburgh, 1838), 63–87. Regarding Reginald's probable authorship, see Richard Sharpe, "Were the Irish Annals Known to a Twelfth-Century Northumbrian Writer?" *Peritia* 2 (1983): 137–39; M. H. Dodds, "The Little Book of the Birth of St Cuthbert," *Archaeologia Aeliana*, 4th ser., 6 (1929): 52–94; P. Grosjean, "The Alleged Irish Origin of St Cuthbert," in *The Relics of Saint Cuthbert*, ed. C. F. Battiscombe (Oxford: Printed for the Dean and Chapter of Durham Cathedral at the University Press, 1956), 144–54. Robert Bartlett is inclined to agree that Reginald might have been the author: Bartlett, "Cults," 73.

43. Claire Barbetti, "Secret Designs/Public Shapes: Ekphrastic Tensions in Hildegard's *Scivias*," chapter 4 in this volume.

44. See, for example, Nancy Caciola, *Discerning Spirits: Divine and Demonic Possession in the Middle Ages* (Ithaca, NY: Cornell University Press, 2003); Dyan Elliott, *Proving Woman: Female Spirituality and Inquisitional Culture in the Later Middle Ages* (Princeton, NJ: Princeton University Press, 2004); Michael Goodich, *Miracles and Wonders: The Development of the Concept of*

Miracle, 1150–1350 (Burlington, VT: Ashgate Publishing, 2007). For case studies of the inquisitorial process, see Robert Bartlett, *The Hanged Man: A Story of Miracle, Memory, and Colonialism in the Middle Ages* (Princeton, NJ: Princeton University Press, 2004); and Gábor Klaniczay, "Proving Sanctity in the Canonization Process (Saint Elizabeth and Saint Margaret of Hungary)," in *Procès de Canonisation au Moyen Âge: Aspects juridiques et religieux—Medieval Canonization Processes: Legal and Religious Aspects*, ed. Gábor Klaniczay, Collection de L'École française de Rome 340 (Rome: École française de Rome, 2004), 117–48.

45. Goodich, *Miracles and Wonders*, 117.

46. Ibid., 100–116.

47. Ibid., 118.

48. Bartlett, *Miracles*, xxxvi.

49. A far more nuanced characterization is detailed by R. Andrew McDonald in *Outlaws of Medieval Scotland: Challenges to the Canmore Kings, 1058–1266* (Phantassie, East Linton, Scotland: Tuckwell Press, 2003).

50. "The Scots chose Malcolm's brother [Donald] as king and drove out all the English who had been with King Malcolm." Dorothy Whitelock, David C. Douglas, and Susie I. Tucker, eds., *The Anglo-Saxon Chronicle, A Revised Edition* (New Brunswick, NJ: Rutgers University Press, 1961), 170.

51. For a discussion of hostility toward the English, see for example R. L. Græme Ritchie, *The Normans in Scotland* (Edinburgh: Edinburgh University Press, 1954), 61; G. W. S. Barrow, *Kingship and Unity: Scotland 1000–1306* (1981; repr., Toronto and Buffalo, NY: University of Toronto Press, 1998), 31; A. A. M. Duncan, *Scotland: The Making of the Kingdom*, vol. 1 of *The Edinburgh History of Scotland* (1975; repr., Edinburgh: Mercat Press, 2000), 125.

52. McDonald, *Outlaws of Medieval Scotland*, 77–79. Alternatively, Alexander Grant suggests that the nephews were descended from Malcolm III's kin, perhaps from Donald, the son of Malcolm III who died in 1085. In any event, the point remains the same; Somerled married into a family with dynastic claims to the throne and supported his nephews in their pursuit of that claim. Alexander Grant, "The Province of Ross and the Kingdom of Alba," in *Alba: Celtic Scotland in the Middle Ages*, ed. E. J. Cowan and R. A. McDonald (2000; repr., Edinburgh: John Donald, 2005), 108–9.

53. At its greatest, this kingdom included Lorn and Benderloch in central Argyll; Lismore, Mull, Coll, and Tiree; the peninsula of Morern and Ardnamurchan; Moidart and Knoydart; the Small Isles; Uist; and Barra, as well as Kintrye and the southernmost Hebrides, Islay, and Jura with their dependencies. Barrow, *Kingship and Unity*, 109.

54. William M. Hennessy and Bartholomew MacCarthy, eds., *Annals of Ulster* (Dublin: Printed for H. M. Stationery Office by A. Thom and Co., 1887–1901), 2:144 (1164); Anderson and Anderson, *Early Sources of Scottish History*, 2:253–54. The quote is from R. Andrew McDonald, *Kingdom of*

the Isles: Scotland's Western Seaboard c. 1100–c. 1336 (1997; repr., Edinburgh: John Donald, 2008), 205. McDonald asserts that Flaithbertach was very conservative in his outlook, resisting new orders from the Continent and seeking to reassert Irish Christianity. McDonald, *Outlaws of Medieval Scotland*, 113–14.

55. Hennessy and MacCarthy, *Annals of Ulster*, 2:240–42 (s.a. 1204); Anderson, *Early Sources of Scottish History*, 2:363.

56. Hermann Pálsson and Paul Edwards, trans., *Orkneyinga Saga: The History of the Earls of Orkney* (New York: Penguin, 1981), ch. 111.

57. Ibid., ch. 112; Barbara Crawford, "Norse Earls and Scottish Bishops in Caithness: A Clash of Cultures," in *The Viking Age in Orkney, Caithness and the North Atlantic: Select Papers from the Eleventh Viking Congress, Thurso and Kirkwall, 22 August–1 September 1989*, ed. Colleen E. Batey, Judith Jesch, and Christopher D. Morris (Edinburgh: Edinburgh University Press for Centre for Continuing Education, University of Aberdeen and Department of Archaeology, University of Glasgow, 1993), 135–36.

58. MacDonald, *Outlaws of Medieval Scotland*, 109–10; Crawford, "Norse Earls and Scottish Bishops," 136; John of Fordun, *Johannis de Fordun Chronica Gentis Scotorum*, ed. William F. Skene (Edinburgh: Edmonston and Douglas, 1871); translated as *John of Fordun's Chronicle of the Scottish Nation (1872)*, trans. Felix J. H. Skene, ed. William F. Skene (Edinburgh: Edmonston and Douglas, 1872), 1:289–90, 2:285.

59. Gábor Klaniczay has articulated how newly Christianized countries in Scandinavia, eastern and central Europe, and the freshly converted Anglo-Saxon kingdoms used the sanctity of their founding dynasties to argue for the legitimacy of their rule in *Holy Rulers and Blessed Princesses: Dynastic Cults in Medieval Central Europe*, trans. Éva Pálmai (Cambridge: Cambridge University Press, 2002), 62–113.

60. Turgot, "Life of Saint Margaret," ch. 16: "Moreover, there were some in certain parts of Scotland who were wont to celebrate Masses according to I know not what 'barbarous rite' contrary to the custom of the whole Church."

61. Ibid., ch. 14–16.

62. Bartlett, *Miracles*, 86–87.

63. Turgot, "Life of Saint Margaret," ch. 24.

64. For a comparison between Albertus Magnus and Macrobius, see Kruger, *Dreaming*, 120–21. For a similar hierarchical structure outlined by Calcidius, see Kruger, *Dreaming*, 28–29.

65. Zimbalist also notes in this volume that Saint Catherine's speech was implicitly sanctioned in that "her words convert her audience, and even move some to embrace martyrdom."

66. Alexander III asserted his right to rule the Western Isles, leading to armed conflict with King Haakon IV of Norway in 1263. After some inconsequential skirmishes, Haakon died in Kirkwall, Orkney. See Duncan, *Scotland*, 577–80; Barrow, *Kingship and Unity*, 117–18.

67. See, for example, Visiliki Limberis, *Divine Heiress: The Virgin Mary and the Creation of Christian Constantinople* (New York: Routledge, 1994).

68. Symeon of Durham, *Historia Regum*, 2:99–100.

69. Ibid., 2:106.

70. "Carmen de Morte Sumerledi," in Symeon of Durham, *Historia Regum*, 2:386–88; translated in T. O. Clancy, ed., *The Triumph Tree: Scotland's Earliest Poetry AD 550–1350*, trans. Gilbert Márkus (Edinburgh: Canongate Books, 1998), 212–14.

CHAPTER 4

SECRET DESIGNS/PUBLIC SHAPES:
EKPHRASTIC TENSIONS IN
HILDEGARD'S *SCIVIAS*

Claire Barbetti

The art critic Roberta Smith discusses in an interview with Sarah Thornton the process of writing reviews of museum or gallery shows that are accessible to a large public: "Art accumulates meaning through an extended collaborative act...You put into words something that everyone has seen. That click from language back into the memory bank of experience is so exquisite. It is like having your vision sparked."[1] She describes the translation of the visual to the verbal and its subsequent "fit" with memory as "so exquisite" but gives no logical reason for why this is so. Her last statement—"it is like having your vision sparked"—is vague to the point of the mystical. Yet I believe Smith's observation is an important one, if more intuited than explicated. It hints at not only the physical capacity of seeing, or the imaginative phantasm—the vividness of visuals inside our minds—but also the instant of understanding, the proverbial click and spark of sudden clarity. Her statement suggests that the visual experience alone is not sufficient for the solidification of knowledge nor the communication of meaning but that a verbal answer, which in turn accesses the memory banks (which are a great deal visual in themselves), is the collaboration required for communicative meaning. In this model, a work of art is understood not as an isolated or singular entity but as an amalgamation of varied media created in response to one another. For Smith, the descriptions and commentary of art criticism further the social contracts of meaning, of how a culture interprets both its visual experience and its visual signs.[2]

But what about putting into words something that everyone has not seen but whose constitutional elements have been seen? In other words, can verbally translating a composition of familiar elements that remains invisible to the public eye spark the same kind of "vision" over which Smith is so enthusiastic? Smith, in our contemporary art world, would not dare write a review of a dream or mystical vision as art, not unless a painting or installation piece was made to represent it. And yet to the medieval mind, such private images as dream and religious vision were considered valuable compositions in their own right and made active and available to the public. Dreams were widely cataloged and categorized, as Catherine Keene relates in her chapter in this volume. Visions translated into writing offered opportunities to expound upon scripture, to utilize with authority, and to adjust both people's experiences and their cultural narratives. Hildegard of Bingen, a German prioress of the twelfth century, was especially adept at this practice, and her visionary texts, while delving into the private nature of visions, also employ resources from her community's remembered commonplaces—biblical stories, scriptures, saintly anecdotes, and traditional images—to establish Hildegard's authority as both a woman and a messenger of God.

Hildegard of Bingen's *Scivias* is a meditative text; as a whole, it is concerned with the architecture of creation and the human soul's place within it. Its moral imperatives are often represented with spatial criteria: order, direction, progression, presence and absence from sight. As both Brad Herzog and Ella Johnson attest in their respective chapters in this collection, establishing "place" or "locational structure" is a particularly effective strategy in deploying the requisite authority to add onto/revise a culture's narrative tradition. Hildegard's text is acutely aware of space, whether inner or outer, as the stage for divine history; her text abounds with settings of the New Jerusalem, the City of God, as well as other spaces in sacred history. She also announces in the apologia to the *Scivias* that she receives her visions with the "eyes and ears of the inner self, in open places,"[3] thereby "overlaying"[4] the locale of divine spaces with the experiential spaces of private and public. The descriptions of visions from that point on latently concern the cultural division between inner life and public life represented through biblical tropes, the female body, and architectural compositions, all iconographic representations with which her audience would have been familiar. But because Hildegard's text uses art and rhetoric to build authority, especially through a mode called ekphrasis, which works largely through memory functions, a preliminary discussion of art, rhetoric, and ekphrasis is needed before I continue to examine how and through what form Hildegard's *Scivias* relays the tension between the private and public.

Hildegard's translation and recomposition of the cultural icons featured in her visions evade historically authoritative explication; they function instead as a rhetoric of meditation. Barbara Zimbalist's chapter in this volume on Clemence's *Life of St. Catherine* pays special attention to the energy of the rhetorical strategy, *oratio recta*, and its ability to engage in ethical action through its effective construction of authorship. And as discussed in the introduction to this volume, the success of such rhetorical representation depends more upon its fit with a communally agreed upon image, story, history, or memory than upon accuracy or precision. Hildegard's images, through ekphrasis, are speech acts, and like Clemence's *oratio recta*, the descriptions of Hildegard's visions do not merely recount biblical scenes and history word-for-word from scriptural sources but use familiar elements from them to construct new compositions. Hildegard's visions are accompanied by extensive glosses that not only explain but also overwrite each detail of the visions. This commentary circles around her vision compositions, glossing some images explicitly but often leaving the images to pursue tangents into other biblical lore, anecdotes, new visions, and church teachings. Her organization is at times cyclical, at times alluvial; it is not linear or chronological. Although they are sectioned and numbered, her meditations do not take the form of tract but are structured through association. This associative quality—a quality drawing upon memory and vision—lends an aesthetic flavor and form to Hildegard's rhetoric.

Are Hildegard's compositions art or rhetoric? It seems they are both. Mary Carruthers, in *The Craft of Thought*, affirms that "all medieval arts were conceived and perceived essentially as rhetoric, whether they took the form of poems or paintings or buildings or music. Each work [of art] is a composition articulated within particular rhetorical situations of particular communities."[5] As rhetorical artifacts, Hildegard's descriptions of her visions allow her the opportunity to comment extensively, with a voice of authority, on powerful, collective visual images. As a particularly visual form of verbal rhetoric, Hildegard's art engages the memory and the descriptive powers of *enargeia*, a heightened use of visual detail, which is a special component of the ekphrastic mode. *Enargeia* is also a tactic of the classical rhetorical arts associated with the bid for authority. Through this strategy, Hildegard's visions participate in both the principle and practice of ekphrasis.

It is important to note from the beginning that what I discuss in this paper as ekphrastic in Hildegard's *Scivias* is the transcription of the vision and not the vision proper, which will from here on be referred to as the ekphrastic object. Nor does my study of ekphrasis in Hildegard's work extend fully to her glosses in this chapter, for they are complicated by the forms and rhetoric of commentary. Hildegard's commentary is worth examining on its own, for it mixes a number of different genres at once: drama, commentary/explication, and even ekphrastic rendering, in which she again goes into the vision and describes it and reinscribes it. The final goal of commentary (what Carruthers explains as *skopos* in the medieval monastic tradition), while utilizing some of the same cognitive functions the ekphrastic process uses, leans more heavily toward analysis rather than composition. I do not claim the two are completely separate; analysis must assume a composition prior to undertaking an analysis of it. But the glosses work differently than Hildegard's straight descriptions, which in essence become narratives of a composition of visual experience. The focus here is how ekphrasis functions in her text, and the descriptions of the visions are the primary ekphrastic material.

Ekphrasis is a layering of representation; its use is primarily concerned with the process of interpretation. The vision, however, is by no means a typical ekphrastic object: it is not material, nor is it a viewable object. The vision, in fact, has been passed over in critical studies of ekphrastic works. Although ekphrasis has commonly and narrowly been understood as a poetic genre, a representation in poetic language of a work of art, a number of critics in the last two decades have come to recognize that ekphrasis is a principle and practice—a mode—rather than a category of poetry and, as such, creates a way of reading works that utilize this mode. Poems are not the only works that can be considered ekphrastic, and the ekphrastic object—the visual representation—does not have to be a painting or sculpture. Although W. J. T. Mitchell's analysis of ekphrasis treats only ekphrastic poetry whose object is a material image (paintings, urns, shields), he also concedes that ekphrasis travels among media.[6] Mitchell furthermore notes that certain cultural tensions, or "figures of difference" within the ekphrastic art, vary from one project to the next:

> The alien visual object of verbal representation can reveal its difference from the speaker (and the reader) in all sorts of ways: the historical distance between archaic and modern (Keats's Urn); the alienation between the human and its own commodities (Stevens's Jar); the conflict between a moribund social order and the monstrous revolutionary "others" that threaten it (Shelley's Medusa).[7]

An art descriptive of art in the mind—the mystical vision—will reveal its own figures of difference. The vision is a private experience and is much more removed from the privileged public realm. Its transcription speaks to tensions percolating among the private/practical, inner/outer, the material (useful, fleshiness) and immaterial (vision).

In the case of Hildegard's ekphrastic visions, the tension between the private vision and Hildegard's public representation of it (as a woman who culturally is relegated to the private sector of society) works as a particularly strong figure of difference. There are numerous occasions in her ekphrastic visions in which the private and public are placed in the same vicinity:

> Then I saw in the secret places in the heights of Heaven two armies of heavenly spirits who shone with great brightness.[8]
>
> After this I saw an image of a woman, pale from her head to her navel and black from her navel to her feet...She had no eyes, and had put her hands in her armpits; she stood next to an altar that is before the eyes of God.[9]
>
> He was visible to me from his head to his navel, but from the waist downward he was hidden from my sight.[10]

In contrast to these bodily images, the visions in Book 2 concerning the structure of the city of God are especially striking in their architectural computations; Hildegard's language includes measurement and geometry of the structures but is equally descriptive of what the buildings house, their inside spaces:

> Then I saw inside the building a figure standing on the pavement facing this pillar, looking sometimes at it and sometimes at the people who were going to and fro in the building.[11]
>
> Then I saw in the west corner of the building a wondrous, secret and supremely strong pillar, purple black in color. It was so placed in the corner that it protruded both inside and outside the building.[12]

Here, Hildegard employs a popular trope of Christian theology, the structure of a building as a metaphor for the order of creation and for the order of the mind's spiritual knowledge, a metaphor dating back to the writings of Saint Paul. According to Carruthers, the trope of architecture "also plays an essential role in the art of memory"[13]; she quotes Gregory the Great, using the building metaphor not only as an example of coming to spiritual knowledge but also as a way to remember how one must strive to attain such knowledge.[14]

Memory arts are essential to the ekphrastic practice. Not only does Hildegard's ekphrastic vision make broad use of a trope that has been collectively remembered and passed down by and is very familiar to a popular audience in order to persuade and establish authority, but she also uses the trope in a highly specific way that throws into relief the inside/outside of things, the tucked-away things and "secret" places of the private as well as the "armies" and altars, the visible spaces of the public.

The text of Hildegard's mystical vision is particularly adroit in negotiating between realms of private and public representation. This accomplishment is recognized especially through an analysis that takes into account the aesthetic nature of the vision and its written record's status as ekphrastic. The verbal translation of a vision is not merely a mimetic activity; it uses tools of the memory arts to place elements in such a way as to engender a culturally agreed-upon meaning. Carruthers's observation about the work of memory arts recalls the kind of work ekphrasis does: "The questions raised about a work by mneme are different from those raised by mimesis. They stress cognitive uses and the instrumentality of art over questions of its 'realism.' Mneme produces an art for 'thinking about' and for 'meditating upon' and for 'gathering.'"[15] Analyzing the vision as a composition and examining how it utilizes memory, social narratives, and icons (images laden with culturally appointed meanings) catalyzes questions about compositional inclusion and exclusion, in essence, social delineations of category. The mystical vision on the one hand is unverifiable, a private creature; Hildegard's ekphrastic rendering of it on the other assumes a place for it that is undeniably public. Transcribed, the ekphrastic mystical vision can "work through" ambivalences between what is valued as reality and what is not, what is private and what belongs to the public domain. "[Ekphrasis] can," as Tamar Yacobi asserts, "serve to thicken or pinpoint meanings, to shape response, and to bring home a latent ideology."[16] The practice of ekphrasis is itself about the working through of its current cultural categories or limits and creating new limits.[17] But in order to determine specifically how medieval ekphrasis discloses its limits, it is necessary first to examine the limits that delineate art in the Western Middle Ages.

Ekphrasis and the Medieval Understanding of Art

Ekphrasis is understood, in the general but more limited sense, as a verbal depiction of visual art; based on this definition, the ekphrastic poem typically describes a painting or sculpture, and there is no lack of this kind of literature and its analysis in the Western canon. There are, however, comparatively fewer studies of ekphrastic works in Western medieval literature than in other periods of Western literature. This may seem surprising, since the Western medieval world was and is an incredibly visual world, immersed in and driven by image. Leonid Ouspensky, a notable scholar of icons, declares that "the image is necessarily inherent in the very essence of Christianity, from its inception, since Christianity is the revelation by God-Man not only of the Word of God but also of the Image of God."[18]

Certainly the theological and political furor surrounding the icono-clastic controversy of the eighth and ninth centuries points to the central position the image takes in the culture's understanding of representa-tion, of art, of the divine and its relationship with human beings.[19] That Christianity was the foundation of the Western medieval world is unde-niable, and its consanguinity with the image in a culture whose laity were largely illiterate makes sense. Patrick Geary, in his book *Phantoms of Remembrance*, underscores the fact that, though many people were unable to read, the medieval West was nevertheless a culture organized around the book; it assumed literacy as its center rather than orality.[20] The Western medieval world's reliance on visual image and visual memory is concomitant with the structure of reading and the book: both developed alongside each other, and both acted as a means to gather, attain, remem-ber, and preserve knowledge, custom, and story. The visual and verbal do not replace each other, as Carruthers explains in her recounting of the practices of monastic rhetoric:

> The emphasis upon the need for human beings to "see" their thought in their minds as organized schemata of images, or "pictures," and then to use these for further thinking, is a striking and continuous feature of medieval monastic rhetoric, with significant interest even for our own contemporary understanding of the role of images in thinking. And the monks' "mixed" use of verbal and visual media, their often synaesthetic literature and architecture, is a quality of medieval aesthetic practice that was also given a major impetus by the tools of monastic memory work.[21]

In light of Carruthers's scholarship, namely her recognition of the con-nections among vision, text, image, memory, and rhetoric, the paucity of studies of ekphrasis in the Middle Ages is disappointing.

Some scholars, however, have studied medieval ekphrasis. Jean Hagstrum's *The Sister Arts: The Tradition of Literary Pictorialism and English Poetry from Dryden to Gray* includes a chapter discussing medieval ekphrasis and the cultural assumptions that guide how medieval texts translate the visual into the verbal. Hagstrum, like every other critic before or since who has discussed ekphrasis in the Middle Ages, considers only texts in which an art object appears: for instance, the didactic reliefs in Dante's *Purgatorio*, Chaucer's allegorical portraits in *House of Fame* or the *Knight's Tale*, and similar portraits in the *Romance of the Rose*. In typical medi-eval "literary pictorialism" (Hagstrum's term), the represented images are merely copied and tired conventions; according to Hagstrum, they are generally inferior to the originals found in Homer, Ovid, Virgil, and

Statius.[22] These disingenuous verbal images, he concludes, are included
solely with the intent to co-opt the images of the classical world to feed a
Christian one. In other words, he assumes little invention, imagination,
or creativity in these ekphrastic renderings.

Hagstrum's portrait of pictorialism in the Middle Ages posits medieval
ekphrasis as a low occasion in the history of visual imagination, an inter-
ruption between classical ekphrasis and the rampant and rich ekphrasis
that begins in the Renaissance and increases geometrically in the twenti-
eth century. It is true that medieval literature typically does not describe
concrete works of art. Most of the traditional ekphrasis that appears in
medieval literature is what John Hollander terms "notional ekphrasis,"[23]
the representation of an *imagined* work of art, including such famous passages as the raiment and shield of Gawain in *Sir Gawain and the Green
Knight*, the mural of Venus in Marie de France's "Guigemar," the walls
of the amphitheater in Chaucer's *The Knight's Tale*, and Dante's moving reliefs in the *Purgatorio*. These examples all act as didactic lessons, or
reminders of virtues, morality, how one ought to behave, or how one can
come into the fullness of being. Such ekphrastic moments in these texts
are highly stylized; they are structured similarly in form and content, a
structure not far off from the mnemonic architectural structures of Paul,
Augustine, Gregory, and Boethius, among others.[24]

Despite its lack of physical, "real-time" description, the culture of the
Middle Ages was an incredibly visual one, although perhaps in a different
way than our culture understands the visual arts and aesthetics. Aesthetic
theory was by no means an institutionalized program of thought in the
Middle Ages, certainly not in the sense that it was its own discipline or
field. There are ways, however, that aesthetics were theoretically understood in the Middle Ages. Probably the most representative of medieval
aesthetic thought was Aquinas's injunction that "art imitates nature in its
operation."[25] This assertion is significant to the shape that ekphrasis takes
in the Middle Ages because it ushers art out of the realm of mimesis: art
does not imitate nature; it imitates the way that nature works, in essence
the processes of nature. Art is not about copying what is seen. Art exists
first as form in the mind of the artist and as such is a process for working
through questions of existence, which in the Middle Ages are not separate from spiritual questions. Carruthers, in *The Book of Memory*, attributes this faculty of the mind to the classical category of *memoria*.[26] The
memory, she argues, *is* the faculty of composition in the Middle Ages;
composition exists in the mind before it is formed on canvas, carved in
stone, or scripted with ink on vellum. Because it begins in the mind first
and foremost, the physical manifestation of art—both visual and verbal—
could in the Middle Ages be used as a strategy for looking inward and for

guiding readers toward how to interpret text (and the text of the world) in order to live justly. The nature of image, with its deep associations with Christ as image and human beings made in the image of God, was revelatory, for image could open a window into the innermost qualities of being. The icon, with its "inverse perspective," is a good example of this cultural tendency. Ouspensky notes that the surface of the icon does not feign depth but remains realistically flattened so that the viewer does not go into the image: "The point of departure," he claims, "lies not in the depth of the image, but in front of the image, as it were in the spectator himself."[27] Such a paradigm helps explain why it is that ekphrasis in the Middle Ages is less concerned with representing physical manifestations of art than it is with exploring the *spaces* in which the human intellect and soul are formed, and in turn inform each other, especially at the communal level.

There are many more ekphrastic works in the Middles Ages than have been previously assumed. It is particularly important to read Hildegard's visions through an ekphrastic lens because this mode dictates its own parameters that are necessarily different from other recording forms or methods; the content of the ekphrastic vision, therefore, will be different from other literary genres. Because ekphrasis entails a process of translating one composition into another, it has the distinct ability to revise; because it uses the visual faculties of the mind, it also affects how the ekphrastic object is remembered. Yacobi explains the "peculiar logic of recontextualizing" that is the domain of ekphrasis: "The visual artifact becomes in transfer an inset within a verbal frame. Thereby it comes to signify in a new way and to serve new purposes, as well as unfold on new medial axes, all of them determined by the writer's frame of communication."[28]

Hildegard's "frame of communication" is one that posits from the start its author as a woman and therefore impoverished and weak of mind and body, but nevertheless commanded to set forth in writing what she solely has seen and heard. One of the great difficulties challenging the mystic, especially a woman mystic of the Middle Ages, was establishing textual authority. Affected modesty is a topos extending back to classical antiquity; as Ernst Robert Curtius notes, "Innumerable medieval authors assert that they write by command. Histories of literature accept this as gospel truth. Yet it is usually a mere topos."[29] Even if Hildegard's *parvitas* is "mere topos," that topos accomplishes much in terms of the tradition it is set against: a largely male textual tradition and a public one in its reference to the relationship between superior and inferior (whether the emperor and his subject in antiquity or the Creator and his subject in the Middle Ages). As a woman writing in this tradition, Hildegard's meekness is even more weighted; in the social order, she is one of the lesser. By acknowledging her humble status, she can surreptitiously become the visionary in the handmaiden's guise.

Affected modesty brings about quite a bit of showmanship. Authority's ground in the mystical text is a staged setting; there is "a great deal of thought, prayer, conversation, reading, and revision" underlying the textual representation of the mystical vision, a foundation that cannot be presented "lest it weaken the writer's fragile claim to inspiration and authority."[30] There is often a collapse of time in the presentation of visions, and Hildegard's visions are no exception. Although she acknowledges that she has experienced visions from the age of five, she nonetheless effectually hides the interpretive moment in between God's voice and her writing. God speaks to her in the text: "O human, who receives these things meant to manifest what is hidden not in the disquiet of deception but in the purity of simplicity, write, therefore, the things you see and hear."[31] And later she describes her reception of the call: "And I heard the One Who sat on the throne saying to me, 'Write what you see and hear.' And from the inner knowledge of that vision, I replied, 'I beseech you, my Lord, give me understanding, that by my account I may be able to make known these mystical things.'"[32] In fact, the divine injunction appears again and again in the text, reinforcing its authority repeatedly with the effect of a divine vocal presence right at hand. Textually, hardly any time elapses between God's command to her and her reply, between the injunction to write and the fact of the writing on the page. That moment, however extensive it might have been, is recorded in two ways: as a private, reflective moment, it is briefly alluded to in the phrase "inner knowledge," and as a public moment, it is overtly acknowledged by Hildegard as taking part in history. She writes at the end of her "Declaration," "These visions took place and these words were written in the days of Henry, Archbishop of Mainz, and of Conrad, King of the Romans, and of Cuno Abbot of Disibodenberg, under Pope Eugenius."[33] The emblems of secret, hidden, inner knowledge—"inner knowledge," "vision," "mystical things"—and those of the history, artifice, and public place do not just appear as players in the grand allegory of her visions; they are intrinsic to the seeing/perceiving/writing process itself through providing the material, impetus, and occasion. Thus they appear even in Hildegard's intentional statement and apologia. The subsequent visions are implicitly concerned with how inner life and public life intermingle (and how they are meant to intermingle) and, more important, how the sharp divide between the two through her ekphrastic writing process becomes necessarily unclear.

Another important feature in the practice of ekphrasis is one touched upon by Margaret Cotter-Lynch in her chapter, "Mnemonic Sanctity and the Ladder of Reading: Notker's 'In Natale Sanctarum Feminarum'" in this volume. She notes that Notker's poem makes especial use of social narrative and further emphasizes the ties between the visual image and mnemonic structure, as the images employed in Notker's poem were carefully selected for their social currency. The use of social narrative in the translation of the visual to the verbal in the process of ekphrasis entails exercising *memoria* and reaching into the memory bank of the culture. Hildegard's text relates parti-color and minutely detailed—vibrantly visual—representations of familiar, well-trod metaphors in the social narrative for inner life and public life. Through the practice of harnessing visual images familiar to a community and part of its social narrative, the text creates a stance from which it can speak, as a text authored by a woman, with intellectual and moral authority.

Careful attention to especially the domestic imagery of Vision Four of Book 1 and the apocalyptic images of Vision Two of Book 3 will demonstrate how the text's practice of ekphrasis functions as a carrier for Hildegard's understanding and revisioning of the private/public axis. I have divided treatment of Hildegard's visions into two categories: "Inside" and "Outside." While the text under analysis in either section could be interchanged (each has private and public or "inside" and "outside" elements), the critical material apportioned to the section "Inside" treats New Historicist and deconstructive questions: how can one know the nature of lived reality by a twelfth-century female prophet as disclosed by this text and what it has left out? The section "Outside," however, gazes unabashedly at what has been left *in*; it asks what knowledge (and what kind of knowledge) the words of Hildegard's crafted structure offer to their reader.

Inside

Vision Four of Book 1 is one of the most memorable of Hildegard's visions in the *Scivias*, perhaps because of its unusual analogy of human beings to cheeses. The analogy may not be that far of a stretch, however, when one takes into consideration the symbol of milk and its broad significance concerning the physical nurturing and spiritual shaping of the human in Judeo-Christian texts from Genesis onward. Of course, Hildegard does not explain what the images of the cheeses signify until much later in her commentary on the vision. As the image stands in the vision without her explication of its allegorical meaning, it is framed by two other striking figures whose connections to the cheese image are not explicit. I will quote it at length, for it is necessary to see how it is composed as a whole:

> Then I saw a most great and serene splendor, flaming, as it were, with many eyes, with four corners pointing toward the four parts of the world, which was manifest to me in the greatest mystery to show me the secret of the Supernal Creator; and in it appeared another splendor like the dawn, containing in itself a brightness of purple lightning. And behold! I saw on the earth people carrying milk in earthen vessels and making cheeses from it; and one part was thick, and from it strong cheeses were made; and one part was thin, and from it weak cheeses were curdled; and one part was mixed with corruption, and from it bitter cheeses were formed. And I saw the image of a woman who had a perfect human form in her womb. And behold! By the secret design of the Supernal creator that form moved with vital motion, so that a fiery globe that had no human lineaments possessed the heart of that form and touched its brain and spread through all of its members.
>
> But then this human form, in this way vivified, came forth from the woman's womb and changed its color according to the movement the globe made in that form.
>
> And I saw that many whirlwinds assailed one of these globes in a body and bowed it down to the ground; but, gaining back its strength and bravely raising itself up, it resisted them boldly.[34]

To a linearly and causally trained mind, large gaps in this text appear between, first, the purple lightning and the people carrying vessels and, second, the formed cheeses and the womb of the woman. It is not out of order to read this text with causality in mind; Hildegard herself assigns it to the allegory of the cheeses later when she explains the connection between quality of semen with caliber of human being and why deformed infants are born. Compositionally, however, causality is invisible in the ekphrastic vision and is filled in only later in the text by a sometimes over-precious drama and commentary. These lacunae might be attributed to qualities of the medieval visual imagination, in which linear perspective does not govern its composition, in which background is not separated from foreground according to the framework of positive/negative space but is concomitant with it as an equal compositional element (one can see this at work in the *Très Riches Heures*, its landscapes carrying as much allegorical weight as its human figures). But it is interesting that these gaps are also part of the textual translation. The relationships among the progression of the images in this vision are invisible, leading the reader to wonder what these relationships are.

Hildegard interprets the vision as a drama of the human body and soul, a visible form and an invisible form. The idea of visibility and invisibility appears often throughout the meditation's commentary. For example, the speaker warns that doubt of invisible things is symptomatic of following the devil and the devil's attitude that knowledge be objectifiable. Much of the action happening in this dynamic vision occurs inside another shape that is then exposed or is hidden beyond vision completely. The first image, a vague "splendor," recalls apocalyptic literature with its "flaming" nature and its positioning toward the four parts of the world. The reader is guided very quickly inside this splendor to find, like a nesting doll, another splendor within. And suddenly the reader is treated to an image of humans carrying milk on their way to make cheese and an image of all the different kinds of cheeses that are made. Then suddenly the image of a woman appears, iconic in its reference to Mary, her womb transparent and the human within on display. Allegorically, the subject of the vision is clear enough to those familiar with traditional Christian images: this is the development of the soul, its possibilities, its coming-into-being, its origin, its trials. What is not clear, however, are the mixed vehicles of this analogy—the inside of a flaming splendor, the cheeses, the womb—and the relationship among them. In its abstract expression, the splendor seems to become aligned with sacredness, divinity, mystery, secret, what belongs inside, and the inner life, even though it is set facing the four corners of the world, an airy and open place to be. Then the break occurs and the new scene materializes: humans become aligned with the activity of cheese making, an activity that appears more public, certainly noumenal, in relation to the other images in this vision. At the same time, the making of cheese is done where it is dark, where molds can creep and ripen, where liquid takes on a firm existence. As it is with milk turning to cheese, so it is with the development of the human form in the womb (later Hildegard will again conflate vehicles and replace semen for milk while explaining what the cheeses signify), and yet this development is exposed, the curtain drawn back from its ordinarily private stirring. The text transposes typical and traditional perceptions and categorizations of both sacred and secular experience. Newman admits "rapid shifts from the sensual to the symbolic or typological" in Hildegard's work, as well as a "strong tendency toward synaesthesia"[35] that make reading her visions (not to mention her commentary on top of those visions) a confusing experience for readers; as there are few stable symbols (most are metonymic and highly pliable), readers have difficulty settling on any one meaning for these analogies.

It is no coincidence that these lacunae appear as the text shifts from an inner world to a public picture and back again. As a female, Hildegard is

particularly aware of the private/public delineation; she chooses to vocal-
ize her beliefs and opinions and to preach (and write) in a time when
women were condemned for speaking publicly. Her visions are filled
with imagery that is specifically female, bodily, sensual. In the womb
imagery in the previous vision, Hildegard's text does not question the
ethical considerations surrounding whether it is right or not for the female
body to be public property. Through its ekphrastic gaps, however, the
text exposes the social idea that the female organs are in fact public and
treated as public; the text ever so subtly makes possible the assertion that
it is hypocritical that women should be excluded from the public sphere.
Hildegard's visions are concerned with questions of reality and not just the
reality beyond the corruption of human flesh and mortal life according
to the text's main intention. The text also deals with reality as Hildegard
herself experiences it: her gender is deemed by her society and culture
as less intelligent, incapable of the highest reason, and excluded as much
as possible from the public sphere. Her apologies—affected modesty—
in the "Declaration" speak to this sense of inequity but interestingly
enough pave the way for the rest of the text to speak with authority as
one of the blessed, the beatitudinally "meek." She, as female, is left to the
domestic world, the inner world; and in a powerful counter-tactic, she
equates that world with the world where one can hear the voice of God
speak.

Reality then, for Hildegard's text, is of the inner world as it opens out
upon the public. Reality comes to its fruition through representation as
text, as it is broadcast through the world, taking its place in historical
time. The vision is a revelation as it is held and interpreted by the author.
Written down, it acquires new meanings—links to the prophets, Ezekiel
and Isaiah, to Jerome, to Augustine—and power. Hildegard makes these
links, implicit in the transcription of the vision, explicit in her commentary. For her, inner knowledge—the "exemplary form" in "the mind of
the artist," the conception, and the making—*must be* a public matter; the
stakes are too high merely to meditate on a secret inner knowledge that
remains so. Although the world, that stinking pit of sin, is best avoided,
the world, the public, is also where laws are decreed, sermons spoken, values created, and people tortured and put to death. The public is the place
of power; it is where things are not only accomplished but recognized.

Hildegard's textual gaps and her ekphrastic rendering of vision all
speak to severe contradictions in the hierarchical valuing of spiritual life
over everyday, physical existence, the power granted to the public sphere
over and above the domestic, and the categorization and cataloging of
women in the order of existence. The text thus points to a disconnect
between what is respectively considered public and private experience.

Hildegard never overtly makes complaint against these problems. The formal composition and method of the text, however, speak volumes about these social discrepancies.

It is crucial to understand, as Murray Krieger's lengthy studies assert, that such spatiotemporal textual gaps are connected to the gaps made by the translation of one representation to another.[36] And this particular translation is influenced by the relationship between the visual and verbal; the cultural method and social limits behind what is appointed to these domains will likely appear in these gaps. Ekphrasis is not as a rule always critical of its sociohistorical moment. It does, however, provide for the careful reader a glimpse at how humans delineate categories because its working materials are aesthetic categories: typically, the difference and similarity in method, form, and material between painting and poetry.[37] An ekphrastic revision will therefore change the settings of the delineations in any number of ways, perhaps by altering the content, emphasis, or reception of the ekphrastic object. Hildegard's text, though it floats successfully below the heresy radar, is a particularly drastic revision (though not immediately perceived) as the ekphrastic object is itself a private representation, unseen by anyone else and unverifiable. The mystical vision-text thus challenges the values assigned to the visual/verbal binary, values that assume that the ekphrastic moment always concerns material art and poetry.

The mystical vision-text also challenges the public/private binary precisely by being written down, for the vision as ekphrastic object becomes a composition, replete with elements and images from the shared cultural memory bank. In other words, the vision no longer inhabits only the private realm. Thus the represented visions of the *Scivias* float even below the radar of secular aesthetics and its categorical assumptions. Their effect, therefore, in the canon of aesthetics is extraordinarily delicate and still waiting to emerge fully.

Outside

What becomes even more curious about Hildegard's practice is its incredible detail. Her visions (and commentaries on them) read less like the spare and "minimalist" images of other mystical visions (Catherine of Sienna's de Chirico–like Christ-ladder or Julian of Norwich's single hazelnut) than fragments of biblical and classical narratives. While Hildegard's ekphrastic object is imaginary, a private, unverifiable vision, its rhetoric uses detail and motif from popular stories, placing it within a set of socially recognized narratives. Such borrowing and repetition has the effect of verifying the narrative for her. Furthermore, she is herself at

times a character in her visions, no longer merely reporting to the reader
but physically there. A portion of her commentary to the fourth vision of
Book 2 provides this striking detail:

> And I came to a tabernacle, whose interior was all of the strongest steel.
> And, going in, I did works of brightness where I had previously done
> works of darkness. And in that tabernacle I placed at the north a column
> of unpolished steel, on which I hung fans made of diverse feathers, which
> moved to and fro. And, finding manna, I ate it. At the east I built a bul-
> wark of square stones and, lighting a fire within it, drank wine mixed
> with myrrh and unfermented grape juice. At the south I built a tower of
> square stones in which I hung up red shields and placed trumpets of ivory
> in its windows. And in the middle of this tower I poured out honey and
> mixed it with other spices to make a precious unguent, from which a great
> fragrance poured forth to fill the whole tabernacle. But at the west I built
> nothing, for that side was turned to the world.[38]

As noted earlier, the classical rhetorical arts use *enargeia*, the vivid attention to visual elements, as a method for establishing authority.[39] Hildegard
employs this method expertly. "Tabernacle," "works of darkness," fans of
feathers, manna, "wine mixed with myrrh and unfermented grape juice,"
trumpets and shields, and honey and spices and fragrance: all the exotic
gestures and *objets* of the Old Testament are found here, the stuff of the
otherworld that graced and structured the daily imaginations of medieval
peoples. In other words, these elements were a constant and near part of
the social collective memory: they are markers laced with meanings, histories, and traditions that form a narrative. What matters is not whether
what is reported is *real* but, as Carruthers suggests, how the cast of these
images resonates with a social narrative:

> Because it builds entirely through the associations made in some indi-
> vidual's mind, memory work has an irreducibly personal and private or
> "secret" dimension to it. That is also why it is a moral activity, an activ-
> ity of character and what was called "temperament." At the same time,
> because most of its building materials are common to all—are in fact
> common places—memory work is also fully social and political, a truly
> civic activity. The constant balance of individual and communal, *ethos* and
> *pathos*, is adjusted and engineered with the tools of rhetoric: images and
> figures, topics and schemes. Essential among these tools are the memorial
> *res*, the building blocks of new composition.[40]

Much of the power in Hildegard's text relies upon association: the reader's proclivity to remember other stories featuring these images or even

parts of them. Fans of feathers recalls the luxuries of Solomon, as does myrrh, which also points to the gifts of the Magi to the Christ-child, to the distant, unknown, and mysterious East, and to wealth, especially as a metaphor for spiritual riches. Honey and manna reference Canaan, the promised land. "Fragrance" alerts one to the absence of corruption and alludes to the bodies of any number of martyrs for the faith; fragrance is also expensive and rare. Inhabiting this tabernacle, this complex of cultural markers, Hildegard's figure is clearly in a place of ancient kings, but it is also a place that she herself has built (and written), as she repeats, "I did," "I hung," "I placed," "I built." At the same time, it is a place she leaves open and turned to the world beyond, both within and outside of the text.

The order of creation is clearly a central concept of the *Scivias*. As already discussed, the text resists aspects of this order in its nuances—in its blurring of the line between private and public experience—but it also voices this order through the gesture of proselytizing. The introduction to this collection quoted Patrick Geary's important observation that cultural tradition is produced not from an intact "inheritance of the past" but through a continual "process of transmission, suppression, and re-creation."[41] Hildegard's text actively produces tradition through ekphrasis, which, in its translation of the visual to the verbal, goes through the actions of "transmission, suppression, and re-creation." This production of tradition is part of the work of the memorative faculties of the mind, "recollection." But such production is also a moral act, for recollecting "is also a matter of will, of being *moved*, pre-eminently *a moral activity* [my emphasis] rather than what we think of as intellectual or rational."[42] The dynamism of memorative composition, "motivation," motion, and "being moved" are basic prerequisites in this exercise, which is profoundly connected to relationships with others, to the contiguous world. Memory, because it is not isolated to the self, is thus a "moral activity."

Initiating this "motion" or "motivation," Hildegard's ekphrastic visions require "movement" from their readers. Explaining movement of the kind that Hildegard's ekphrastic visions inspire, Carruthers states, "[Medieval ekphrases] are organizations of images amongst which one moves, at least mentally, following out the *ductus* of colors and modes which its images set. The ornamentation of such a work forms its routes and pathways, as verbal ornament does that of speech and chant."[43] The dynamism of the transcribed vision exists on the level of its making, its form, and its content. So it is no coincidence that the topoi of cartographical distance and direction, and a centripetal motion outward to the world whether through sight or intention, figure prominently in many visions of the *Scivias*.[44]

Hildegard's vision features the cartographical topoi north, east, south, and west: each direction is given a coordinate in the biblical phylogeny of humankind in the text's commentaries. Taken together, the directions also represent the created world in need of the apostolic news. In the second vision of Book 3, "The Edifice of Salvation," the directions are architectural designations given to the walled building shaped like a city. Hildegard writes,

> Then I saw, within the circumference of the circle, which extended from the One seated on the throne, a great mountain, joined at its root to that immense block of stone above which were the cloud and throne with its Occupant; so that the stone was continued on to a great height and the mountain was extended down to a wide base.
>
> And on that mountain stood a four-sided building, formed in the likeness of a four-walled city; it was placed at an angle, so that one of its corners faced the East, one faced the West, one the North, and one the South. The building had one wall around it, but made of two materials: One was a shining light like the light of the sky, and the other was stones joined together. These two materials met at the east and north corners, so that the shining part of the wall went uninterruptedly from the east corner to the north corner, and the stone part went from the north corner around the west and south corners and ended in the east corner. But that part of the wall was interrupted in two places, on the west side and on the south side...
>
> And between the building and the light of the circle, which extended from the height to the abyss, at the top of the east corner there was only a palm's breadth; but at the north and west and south corners the breadth of separation between the building and the light was so great that I could not grasp its extent.[45]

The architectural and mathematical detail recalls the directions given to Noah in Genesis. The image participates in the architectural topos of Paul, as I noted earlier. This is the text's representation of heaven as it orders the rest of creation; it borrows from the Bible, both Old and New Testaments, to represent the nature of divine creation. Here it seems the written vision is aware of the gaps, the places where logic fails, incorporating them into the positive structures of the vision, rather than producing them as unintentional spandrels. Newman argues that Hildegard "conceives of a heaven that is supremely organic and alive yet also consummately crafted."[46] The craftedness of this building—both its material (stone) and its immaterial (light) elements—does not erupt in the face of what she cannot grasp.

It seems to me that this, the gap, above all else is what she desires to tell all four corners of the world: that the in-between of the world and the light, which is *the* City, is utterly unintelligible, something that can only be imagined and imperfectly interpreted through the senses, yet is, nevertheless, the world, the condition of material existence. To put *that* into words, into text, requires some acknowledgment that it, as Dante concedes at the end of the *Commedia*, cannot be described. Hildegard does likewise here with the last breath of this vision: "The breadth was so great...I could not grasp its extent." The ekphrastic ambition, as Murray Krieger has described it, is to make accessible what is inaccessible, render known a perceived/imagined entity that is impossible for the Other to know.[47]

Language of the visual realm, what one can sense and see, plays in this text's connecting lines: spatial qualities and positions such as "breadth," "great," "between," and "grasp," not to mention the measurements and cartographical directions. As the objects listed in the vision of the tabernacle represent kingly wealth, these qualities signify order and organization, a city where everything is in its place, whose dimensions measure just so, where what lies beyond its walls proper is subject to its reach and dominion. It is the model for the public world. Yet *within* the connecting lines are impossibilities, those expanses the text grasps and does not grasp. The relationship here between the visual image and its verbal counterpart is dictated by the limits of representation, the tension-laden desire to tell and not tell stirred up by the double illusion that the text is the vision itself and is not the vision.[48] This illusion covers up the fact that the text, however, *is* both: it is the vision in the sense of its full, relatable composition—the ekphrastic vision. And it is not, nor can it ever be, the vision proper. In other words, ekphrasis is not the ekphrastic object, but it nonetheless exists fully in its own right.

Clearly, the private is not the same as the public, but in Hildegard's vision of the world, they are not entirely separate either. In her redactive text, the private and public do not vie for hegemonic power but rather work like the rhythm of the breath at the point of turnover: private leading into the public, the public revealing the private, the one giving rise to the other at the edge of its limits. Her use of aesthetic form and in particular the mode of ekphrasis is the frame for that partnership. Roberta Smith's observation that meaning in art accumulates through a collaborative act—the observation with which I began this investigation—is amplified in Hildegard's text, whose collaborative act is twofold. First, her text mixes together the formal parameters of visual composition as dictated by *memoria* and the rhetorical devices of verbal composition. And second, she melds her experience and thought with the images, ideas, and precepts of the social narrative (in fact, her thought is necessarily predicated on the social narrative). Hildegard furthers social contracts of meaning effectively through the conversation and conjoining of these media, but her text, through ekphrasis, has also found a way to subtly shift that inherited meaning to make a space for the authority of her voice. There is no denying the white-hot spark the descriptions of these visions ignite. They are, as Smith exclaimed, "so exquisite." They are exquisite in part because their audience knew (and knows) beforehand many of the constitutive images: the light, the womb, earthen vessels, the wall of stone and the wall of light of certain dimension and certain direction. It is a thrill when we recognize, meet again, certain patterns in an unexpected place; they are old friends but contextually entirely new. The familiarity is just enough to draw an audience into a reconfigured territory. The territory—particularly charged loci in *memoria*—claimed and changed by Hildegard's text becomes, through ekphrasis, a definitive destination, its landscape possessing great potential to shift gender categories and appointment, the assignments of social sector, and the understanding of what art is and how it works.

Notes

1. Sarah Thornton, *Seven Days in the Art World* (New York: W. W. Norton, 2008), 173.
2. To add to Smith's fuzzy statement and a general incomplete grasp of what images are and what they do, W. J. T. Mitchell points out, "The simplest way to put this is to say that, in what is often characterized as an age of 'spectacle' (Guy Debord), 'surveillance' (Foucault), and all-pervasive image-making, we still do not know exactly what pictures are, what their relation to language is, how they operate on observers and on the world, how their history is to be understood, and what is to be done with or about them." *Picture Theory: Essays on Visual and Verbal Representation* (Chicago: University of Chicago Press, 1994), 13. The medieval world also argued about images; though the stakes were different and involved religious systems of belief and social structure, their understanding was as confused and complicated as ours is.
3. Hildegard of Bingen, *Scivias*, trans. Columba Hart and Jane Bishop, The Classics of Western Spirituality (New York: Paulist Press, 1990), 60. The question of the authenticity of mystical vision often concerns the line between private and public experience. Sallie B. King cites Wittgenstein in her essay on interpreting mysticism, asserting that postmodern theory obliterates this line with its avowal of cultural determinism: "Two Epistemological Models for the Interpretation of Mysticism," *Journal of the American Academy of Religion* 56, no. 2 (1988), 259 [257–79]. In some ways, Hildegard is also obliterating the constructed line between private and public experience, although only in certain circumstances and not so

completely as Wittgenstein aims. Hers is not a theoretical approach but one shaped by immediate need.

4. Mary J. Carruthers, *The Craft of Thought: Meditation, Rhetoric, and the Making of Images, 400–1200*, Cambridge Studies in Medieval Literature 34 (Cambridge: Cambridge University Press, 2000), 57.

5. Ibid., 223.

6. Mitchell, *Picture Theory*, 181.

7. Ibid., 181.

8. Hildegard, *Scivias*, 1.6, p. 139.

9. Ibid., 1.5, p. 133.

10. Ibid., 2.10, p. 473.

11. Ibid., 2.4, p. 357.

12. Ibid., 2.7, p. 411.

13. Carruthers, *Craft of Thought*, 16.

14. Ibid., 18.

15. Ibid., 3.

16. Tamar Yacobi, "The Ekphrastic Model: Forms and Functions," in *Pictures into Words: Theoretical and Descriptive Approaches to Ekphrasis*, ed. Valerie Robillard and Els Jongeneel (Amsterdam: VU University Press, 1998), 33 [21–34].

17. Carruthers, in *The Craft of Thought*, distinguishes between *Bildeinsatz* and ekphrasis in a move that attempts to place to two as sub-categories under *pictura*, a cognitive faculty connected to the process of composition through *memoria*: "Whereas ekphrasis always purports to be a meditative description of a painting, sculpture, or the façade of a building, the initi-ating compositional picture can also describe a schematized landscape in the form of a world map, or a figure like Lady Philosophy, or just about any of several *formae mentis* in common monastic use: a ladder, a tree, *rotae*, a rose-diagram. The rhetorical figures called ekphrasis and *Bildeinsatz*, in other words, are types of cognitive, dispositive topos called *pictura*, which is the more general term. The most general terms of all for this cognitive instrument would include words like *ratio* and *schema*" (200).

Yet when she speaks of the architecture of buildings in her section "An Artifact That Speaks Is Also an Orator," she argues that "the actual buildings also are, in monastic rhetoric, instances of what might be called material ekphrasis" (222). The slippage of the term denotes the confusion underlying the cognitive processes—and what to call them—involved in translating the perception of one art into the expression of another. Many studies of ekphrasis have noted that there is more at stake than the narrowest definition of ekphrasis (the definition Carruthers acknowledges) will allow. It is important that much recent work done on ekphrasis displaces the term from genre category and repositions it as a process, mode, and/or practice. In the work of such theorists/critics as W. J. T. Mitchell, James Heffernan, and Barbara Fischer, the term comes to resemble what Carruthers describes as the medieval faculty of composition; in fact, ekphrasis and *memoria* are inextricably connected to one another.

18. Leonid Ouspensky and Vladimir Lossky, *The Meaning of Icons*, trans. G. E. H. Palmer and E. Kadloubovsky (New York: St. Vladimir's Seminary Press, 1989), 25.

19. Both the tracts of iconophiles such as John Damascene and the declaration from the Council of Nicaea in 787 ensure the continuation of the tradition of the iconic image as a reminder of Christ as not only Word of God but Image of God. What becomes emphasized as crucial is the idea that the icon is a receptacle of grace and has transformative power, as scripture does. This is a fine point in understanding the cathexis in the connection between art and spirituality in the Western Middle Ages. Schönborn explains that John Damascene, as a major proponent of this idea, is more focused on what the image brings about than on similitude. See Christoph Schönborn, *God's Human Face: The Christ-Icon*, trans. Lothar Krauth (San Francisco: Ignatius Press, 1994).

20. Patrick J. Geary, *Phantoms of Remembrance: Memory and Oblivion at the End of the First Millennium* (Princeton, NJ: Princeton University Press, 1994).

21. Carruthers, *Craft of Thought*, 3.

22. Jean Hagstrum, *The Sister Arts: The Tradition of Literary Pictorialism and English Poetry from Dryden to Gray* (Chicago: University of Chicago Press, 1987), 42.

23. John Hollander, "The Poetics of Ekphrasis," *Word & Image* 4 (1988): 209–19.

24. Carruthers, *Craft of Thought*.

25. St. Thomas Aquinas, *Summa Theologica*, 2nd ed., trans. Father Laurence Shapcote of the Fathers of the English Dominican Province, Great Books of the Western World, vols. 17–18 (Chicago: Encyclopædia Britannica, 1990), 1.117.1.

26. Mary J. Carruthers, *The Book of Memory: A Study of Memory in Medieval Culture*, 2nd ed., Cambridge Studies in Medieval Literature 70 (Cambridge: Cambridge University Press, 2008).

27. Ouspensky and Lossky, *Meaning of Icons*, 41.

28. Yacobi, "Ekphrastic Model," 23.

29. Ernst R. Curtius, *European Literature and the Latin Middle Ages*, 3rd ed., trans. Willard R. Trask, Bollingen Series 36 (Princeton, NJ: Princeton University Press, 1990), 85.

30. Barbara Newman, *God and the Goddesses: Vision, Poetry, and Belief in the Middle Ages* (Philadelphia: University of Pennsylvania Press, 2003), 303.

31. Hildegard, *Scivias*, p. 60.

32. Ibid., 1.3, p. 309.

33. Ibid., p. 61.

34. Ibid., 1.4, p. 109.

35. Barbara Newman, "Poet: '*Where the Living Majesty Utters Mysteries*,'" in *Voice of the Living Light: Hildegard of Bingen and Her World*, ed.

Barbara Newman (Berkeley: University of California Press, 1998), 185 [176–92].

36. See Murray Krieger, *Ekphrasis: The Illusion of the Natural Sign* (Baltimore: Johns Hopkins University Press, 1992), for discussions of represented space and time both in the ekphrastic work and its object and in the experience of the viewer.

37. Wendy Steiner, in her enormously helpful study of socially determined aesthetic relationships between visual and verbal arts, muses, "The answer to the question posed in the introduction of 'why this game [asking how poetry and painting relate to each other in a given age] is worth the candle' is that the interartistic comparison inevitably reveals the aesthetic norms of the period during which the question is asked. To answer the question is to define or at least describe one's contemporary aesthetics, and this is the value of entering once again the history of anagogical insight—and disappointment—that characterizes the painting-literature connection." *The Colors of Rhetoric: Problems in the Relation between Modern Literature and Painting* (Chicago: University of Chicago Press, 1982), 18. I have extended Steiner's framework to reach the connection between visual and verbal arts and have hazarded to broach interpreting this relationship in an era and culture besides my own.

38. Hildegard, *Scivias*, 2.4, p. 112.

39. According to Jean Hagstrum in *The Sister Arts*, "The medieval appropriation of classical pictorialism must have been directly related to the rising and falling reputation of the pagan literary classics. It may have gone out of sight during their temporary eclipse in the early Middle Ages; it apparently became prominent again in the Carolingian and Ottonian revivals of learning in the ninth and tenth centuries and in the 'proto-renaissance' of the high Middle Ages. In these periods of classical renaissance the *Ars Poetica* of Horace was known and studied, the phrase *ut pictura poesis* commented and reflected upon. The achievement of *enargeia* in rhetorical ecphrasis and poetic icon remained an alluring literary goal" (40).

40. Carruthers, *Craft of Thought*, 21.

41. Geary, *Phantoms of Remembrance*, 8.

42. Carruthers, *Craft of Thought*, 67–68.

43. Ibid., 223.

44. Carruthers elucidates the differences in how the modern West perceives memory from the medieval understanding of memory: "The Biblical notion of remembering has tended to be dismissed, until quite recently, as 're-created memory,' scarcely different from outright lying, and of no interest in the philosophy of the mind at all. Instead, a 'storehouse' model of memory, and the idea that memory is 'of the past,' have been emphasized to such a degree that memory has been accorded only a reiterative, reduplicative role—all else is 'unreal' and thus 'untruthful.'" Western ideas of memory have been concerned at least since the Enlightenment with what philosopher Mary Warnock calls "the crucial distinction, with which we are all familiar in real life, between memory and imagination

(close though these may often be to one another)...what distinguishes memory from imagination is not some particular feature of the [mental] image but the fact that memory is, while imagination is not, concerned with the *real*" (*Craft of Thought*, 68).

45. Hildegard, *Scivias*, 3.2, p. 325.
46. Newman, "Poet," 186.
47. Krieger, *Ekphrasis*, 9.
48. Please see chapter 3, "Ekphrasis and the Other," of W. J. T. Mitchell's *Picture Theory* for an amusing and practical description of the tug-of-war psychology behind ekphrastic desire and ambition.

CHAPTER 5

IMITATING THE IMAGINED: CLEMENCE OF
BARKING'S *LIFE OF ST. CATHERINE*

Barbara Zimbalist

One of the most astonishing moments in Clemence of Barking's
Life of St. Catherine occurs in the opening lines of the text. Before
beginning her narrative of Catherine's *vita*, Clemence declares her intention to "translater la vie,/De latin respundre en rumanz/Pur ço que plus
plaise as oianz" (31–34; to translate the life, expounding it from Latin
into the vernacular, in order to please more those who hear it).[1] With this
self-assured statement, Clemence, a cloistered twelfth-century female
writer, authorizes herself as a participant in the hagiographical tradition
and proclaims herself qualified to pass critical judgment on the literary
and aesthetic merits of previous (and presumably male-authored) versions of Catherine's life. This bold strategy of self-authorization is the
hallmark of Clemence's text, suffusing the *Life*'s form, content, and, ultimately, devotional and theological implications. Many of Clemence's
modern critics have focused on her declaration of *translatio*, evaluating
and commenting on her translation and transmission of Catherine's *vita*.
Clemence, however, focuses on the contemporary readers who receive
her version of Catherine's life. The very syntax of the lines reinforces her
authorial investment: Clemence moves sequentially from the act of translating ("translater la vie") to the method of translation ("de latin respundre en rumanz"), finally finishing the statement with a new clause ("Pur
ço que plus plaise as oianz"), which emphasizes those ("oianz") engaged
with the text as readers and listeners. This sequence of increasingly specific clauses moves from the activity of translation to the contemporary
reading subject, rather than the hagiographical subject, suggesting an

authorial practice that privileges the author's devotional engagement with the living mortal reader over memorialization of the immortal holy dead. This authorial focus encapsulates the text's characterization, structure, and, ultimately, the model of devotional practice it offers to the reader. Seamlessly blending traditional rhetorical strategies of self-legitimization with multiple levels of imitative narrative, Clemence reimagines hagiography as devotional activity involving both author and audience: the author's textual imitation of her subject, figured specifically as imitative speech acts, invokes a reading practice likewise patterned on imitative identification. Catherine's *Life* is itself a text of wonders; but not least among the marvels of the text is her hagiographer's self-confident assertion that "l'estuet amender/E le tens sellunc la gent user" (41–46; it is necessary to amend it, and to become accustomed to the times according to the people).

These lines vividly display Clemence's concern with the continued presence of Catherine's life and legend in the hagiographical canon, as well as her acknowledgment that its reception varies according to audience. In response to these sometimes contradictory concerns, Clemence contributes a significant amount of narrative commentary to her source text in which she draws broad parallels among Catherine, Christ, and herself. Modeling Catherine after Christ and her own narrative persona on Catherine, Clemence uses potent imitative relationships to structure the *Life* and give it powerful theological resonance. Within the *Life*, Catherine's *vita* and *passio* are modeled on Christ's life and passion in the traditional *imitatio Christi* pattern of hagiographic narrative. In the *Life*'s narrative frame, however, Clemence models her authorial persona on Catherine. Clemence's imitation of Catherine is thus an imitation of both Catherine and—at a further remove—Catherine's model, Christ. The dialectic between these relationships establishes hagiography as a devotional exercise for the author in imitation of the hagiographic subject.

Clemence figures devotion as a textual imitation of Christ's speech acts.[2] The goal of this imitation is continued spiritual activity intended to further the author's piety, achieved through the text's production and reception—a goal that resonates in general descriptions of medieval devotional practice. As I will show, Clemence's text is aimed at achieving exactly these goals, both for herself and for her prospective readers. Clemence's self-presentation in her text demonstrates an author engaged in imitation of her subject through the process of writing, thus implying that authorial production can function as devotional imitation. In this way, the author herself becomes a model of female sanctity for her readers: a woman engaging in an activity designed to further her spiritual relationship with God and her ultimate salvation—an activity, furthermore, that had the potential to encourage and promote similarly productive spiritual activity in others. As Anne Clark Bartlett has noted, "*Imitatio*—the fashioning and reconstruction of the self in accordance with the multiple models provided by the holy family, male and female saints, aristocratic ideals, and an assortment of textualized personages—was the chief aim of virtually all forms of medieval (and particularly devotional) discourse."[3] Clemence's hagiographic text allows her to perform an imitation of Christ while simultaneously providing a model for further imitation on the part of her readers. Elsewhere in this volume, Elissa Hansen examines Julian of Norwich's rhetoric in the long text of her *Revelations*, arguing that Julian's *imitatio Mariae* supports her creation of a communally accepted identity as authorial intercessor. Hansen argues, as I will throughout this chapter, that such imitative rhetorical strategies play a crucial part in the construction of narrative identity.

Although these imitative strategies are not new, Clemence's decision to structure Catherine's speech acts as *oratio recta*—direct discourse—in imitation of Christ creates an evangelical mode of imitation at odds with women's social positions in the Middle Ages.[4] Public speech, a common occurrence within the lives of virgin martyrs like Catherine, would have been highly unusual for an enclosed twelfth-century nun.[5] As Robert Clark explains, the medieval woman writing—or, for that matter, reading or listening—"is subject in the sense of being subjectED to social constraint but also in the sense that, as a subject, she constructs herself through her participation in language and culture."[6] The textually embedded imitation of such speech within saints' lives such as Catherine's, however, provided medieval women with an opportunity for public discourse within the normative tradition of hagiography. And because, as Mary Carruthers reminds us, "writing itself was judged to be an ethical activity in monastic culture," Clemence's textual performance of this imitative speech allows her to both engage in and model devotional behavior for her readers.[7] This chapter will examine Clemence's text through some of the critical parameters discussed by Mary Carruthers in *The Book of Memory*: communal and authorial memory, the textual manifestations of these modes of memory, and the reading praxes and devotional responses they evoke.

Saint Catherine's *vita* provided abundant material for creative appropriation in medieval England. Not only was her legend widely popular, but her life enjoyed a great deal of manuscript visibility. Katherine Lewis notes that in England alone, "there are at least fourteen Middle English versions of the life of St Katherine extant, in addition to twelve Latin and three Anglo-Norman lives extant in English manuscripts."[8] As a "constructed" saint, Catherine enjoyed a reputation less rigidly fixed and more various than many of her fellow saints.[9] Numerous variations on her life—visual, literary, and homiletic, among others—all emphasize particular aspects of her legend, which often coincided with specific interests of the local members of her cult. At the same time, the high visibility of the saint and her cult resulted in universal ecclesiastical recognition and earned her a feast day in the church calendar.[10] The occasionally uneasy coexistence of the various aspects of Catherine's legend, diverse associations of patronage, and copious redactions of her *vita* make Catherine the example par excellence of the tensions that could surround a single figure in the sphere of sainthood and hagiography. For virtually any aspect of the saint's life and identity, multiple potential meanings were available; and these meanings were readily on hand in the multiple versions of Catherine's *Life* that circulated throughout the Middle Ages. As Mary Carruthers has shown, the medieval author engaged with the textual tradition not in an antagonistic manner but as a source of shared values providing moral and ethical guidance. Clemence's specific engagement with Catherine's *Life*, then, might be more fruitfully understood not as a translation exercise or a selection of one version of the legend from among many, but as a productive engagement with the discourse surrounding, and proceeding from, Saint Catherine. Such engagement, when figured as imitation, functioned as devotion.

Clemence's translation renders Latin prose as Anglo-Norman poetry and in the process reshapes Catherine's legend to fit the concerns of an Anglo-Norman readership. A previous generation of critics, and even admiring editors, tended to see Clemence's *Life* as technically clumsy or even outdated.[11] Recent scholars, however, such as Jocelyn Wogan-Browne, Duncan Robertson, and Catherine Batt, argue that the *Life*'s narrative innovation and theological complexity reveal a skillful author intimately engaged with Catherine's persona and the spiritual themes of her *Life*. This engagement instantiates Clemence's formal and stylistic understanding of hagiography and its functions, which, as Margaret Cotter-Lynch and Catherine Keene show elsewhere in this volume, was perpetually reconfiguring itself to meet the needs of both authors and audiences.

As a translation, Catherine's legend is retold in the contemporary vernacular in order to provide a spiritually authoritative exemplum for a twelfth-century audience. Susan Crane notes that in the twelfth century, Anglo-Norman "was a true vernacular...[although] in the later period Anglo-Norman became an artificially maintained language of culture, English the mother tongue."[12] Clemence's choice to translate from Latin into the vernacular highlights her concern with eleventh- and twelfth-century reception. Jocelyn Wogan-Browne has argued that Clemence's translation reveals her participation in the production of a female reading community at Barking.[13] But it is the very prologue and narratorial stances Wogan-Browne cites that, in Clemence's case, move beyond community-building hagiography. Instead, Clemence uses narrative innovation to engage with the individual reader and propose a new devotional technique.

Clemence not only adds to and elaborates on the Latin source but also edits, changes, and omits portions of the source text. The disjunctions between the Latin source text and the Anglo-Norman translation highlight vernacular politics at work in the text that problematizes traditional understandings of textual authority in both the source text and the translation. Moreover, this editorial treatment of a canonical text, rather than drawing attention to the Latin source, elides its departure from canonical authority through its very difference.[14] Clemence's insistence on difference as authorial prerogative highlights her own role in the process of translation that privileges her own authorial and editorial choices over the structure of the established source text.[15] The first lines of the *Life* epitomize this type of discursive stance: "Cil ki le bien seit e entent/ Demustrer le deit sagement,/Que par le fruit de sa bunté/Seient li alter amonesté/De bien faire e de bien voleir/Sulunc ço qu'en unt le poeir" (1–6; Those who know and understand the good ought to demonstrate it wisely, that through the fruit of its bounty others will be encouraged to know it, to do good, and to desire the good according to the power that they have). These powerful first lines establish the moral imperative that provides the impetus for the text, justifying the textual production as a "good" act and implying that the author of such a text must be someone who "knows and understands the good." The implied moral authority inherent in this description of authorial identity is realized overtly by Clemence's translation, which includes original textual additions throughout the *vita*. Since she has defined authorship as an ethical action, her own narrative additions take on the weight of ethical authority, exercised as a type of "good." This ethical action is only possible, as Mary Carruthers points out in her discussion of memory in medieval authorship, through the authorial act of retelling Catherine's story within her own narrative lens: an activity that has allowed Clemence to become, in Carruthers's formulation, the *vita*'s "new author" whose writing process has provided her with the opportunity for individual moral development. By retelling Catherine's story—and imitating Catherine's speech acts— Clemence performs a type of ethical and devotional action.

Although Clemence does not alter the conventional chronology or basic episodes of the Catherine legend, the text's digressions and interpolations of additional material focus on issues more in keeping with a twelfth-century milieu than with the late antiquity of the traditional—or, following the lead of Pierre Delooz, the "constructed"—Catherine.[16] A comparison of Clemence's text with her eleventh-century Latin source reveals that Clemence introduces close to 800 lines (out of a total of 2,700) of additional original material, expanding or embellishing significant portions of the poem in comparison with the Latin source. As Catherine Batt has shown, Clemence uses courtly and chivalric language in these additions; when Catherine is introduced, for example, we are told, "En Deu mist tute sa entente,/Sa valur sa bele juvente...En ceste joie mist sa cure/Ki ne perist par aventure/Ceste boneuree meschine,/Ki tute ert en Deu enterrine" (147–58; She placed all her intent in God, her valor, her beautiful youth...in this joy she placed her heart, which did not perish by the adventure—this lovely maiden, who was all wrapped up in God). The description of Catherine as a "boneuree meschine" and of her "bele juvente" echoes typical medieval courtly language, as does the use of "aventure" to describe the events of the narrative. This type of diction, which typifies Clemence's description of Catherine throughout the text, evokes the pervasive genre of romance and the increasing popularity of courtly love in Anglo-Norman England.[17]

Furthermore, much of Clemence's original or embellished material includes descriptions of characters' emotional states, typified by the emperor Maxence's lament over the necessity of killing his queen after her conversion or the consistent narrative description of Catherine's inner thoughts and motivations throughout the poem. Such narrative passages have prompted one critic of the text to describe it as "an elegant and accomplished re-working of its source, [which] differs from many other vernacular Lives in giving an account of its heroine's state of mind rather than her looks...and in its presentation of a pagan viewpoint as capable of rational questioning of Christianity."[18] This consistent incorporation of descriptions of inner subjectivities invites comparisons to trends in twelfth-century spirituality that emphasized the spiritual state of the individual believer.[19]

However, in her most significant transformation of Catherine's *vita*, Clemence employs the stylistically complex use of direct discourse—or *oratio recta*—in almost all of the "new" narrative material that she inserts into the life. Furthermore, she emphasizes the direct discourse already present in the *Vulgata* source, in some cases transforming into direct discourse sections of the *vita* that the *Vulgata* source presents through indirect discourse or third-person narrative.[20] This proliferation of one particular rhetorical mode allows Clemence to appropriate the classical rhetorical function of *oratio recta* for the devotional purposes of hagiography, thus engaging with the subject and audience of her text as both a narrator and devotional participant.

Medieval rhetorical theory inherited a convoluted and tenuous under-standing of *oratio recta*. As Victor Bers has shown in his work on Attic drama, classical rhetoricians considered *oratio recta* as highly mimetic.[21] It was understood as the incorporated speech of a well-known figure from the past in direct discourse. As idealized discourse representative of what the past figure would very likely have said, speeches in *oratio recta* suggested both authority and verisimilitude, and writers employed such imaginative speeches to call attention to the information thus conveyed. Henrik Specht has traced the medieval reception of *oratio recta*, show-ing that this concept of idealized or imaginary impersonation surfaces in medieval rhetorical treatises under a variety of terms, including *prosopo-poeia, conformatio, sermocinatio, fictio personae, ethopoeia,* and *adlocutio.*[22] None of these rhetorical figures correlates exactly to the classical function of *oratio recta*; the closest is probably *ethopoeia*, which Specht describes as

> a formal, introspective, and essentially non-naturalistic mono-logue...attributed to a fictional hero or heroine which interrupts the nar-rative movement in order to dwell at length on the speaker's immediate thoughts and emotions in a given situation, thus simultaneously bringing out the motives and qualities of the speaker's general character.[23]

The most significant facet of the medieval inheritance of *oratio recta* is the nature of the speaker: whereas in classical usage (particularly Greek), the report of direct discourse required a historical figure, the medieval term encompasses both historical and fictional characters. In the first century CE, Quintilian began to collapse the distinction between the histori-cal and the fictional when he defined appropriate and plausible speeches by historical and fictional characters with the term *prosopopoeia.*[24] In the sixth century, Isidore of Seville defined the classical idea of *oratio recta* using the term *ethopoeia*, which encompasses the speech of historical and fictional figures; and in the thirteenth century, John of Garland defined both *prosopopoeia* and *ethopoeia* as *conformatio*, which again includes both historical and fictional figures. As these examples show, the exact termi-nology—and even the definition of—direct speech in the characteristic voice of an imaginary or historical character remained unstable through-out the Middle Ages.

However, the rhetorical trope itself remained in popular use because it was practiced in the classical and medieval schoolroom when teach-ers gave students the task of producing a speech in the voice or manner of some well-known character in order to practice style and character-ization. What emerges from the confusing etymology of these various rhetorical tropes is the repeated emphasis on matching the represented

speech to the represented figure, whether that figure be alive, dead, historical, fictional, or mythical. The consistent emphasis in medieval rhetorical sources on the "fittingness" of the style of the represented speech
indicates a focus on the process of representation itself as the most important facet of this particular trope. The represented speech may not be a
word-for-word transcription of past speech (indeed, that speech may be
largely the stuff of myth or legend, beyond any sort of historical recording, recovery, or preservation), but if its style matched a community's
notion of the context of its original utterance, it was considered successful
representation.

This reception of *oratio recta* coincides with the general privilege that
medieval rhetoric gave to *sententia* over form; Carruthers in particular has
drawn attention to a similar privileging in the preference for memorizing *ad res* instead of word for word; she explains that, particularly in the
preaching arts, the sense was considered more essential than the form of
the text in question because it allowed "adaptive freedom...enabled by
complete familiarity with the text, the shared memory of it on the part
of both audience and author, and hence a delight both in recognizing the
familiar words and the skill with which they have been adapted to a new
context."[25] In much the same way that homilies and *sententiae* incorporated quotation and privileged the sense over the exact form, hagiography
often incorporated imitative direct discourse into the *vitae* of saints.

The direct discourse of Christ, the apostles, and the saints, to name
the most popular and obvious examples, fill the pages of the vast corpus
of medieval hagiography. Clemence enters into this tradition with gusto,
characterizing Catherine through long speeches, homiletic prayers, public debates, and even conversations with Christ—who himself speaks in
extrascriptural *oratio recta*. The effect of this imitation within hagiography is much the same as the schoolroom exercise originally intended: the
author performs an imitation of the figure by representing that figure's
speech. When Clemence imitates Catherine, who is in turn imitating
Christ, imitation functions as both the content and the form of the text.
Clemence's retelling of Catherine's life provides the model for her imitation of Catherine; but by engaging in *oratio recta*, Clemence reconfigures
the form of that imitation as a process with a great degree of flexibility and
freedom to conform to the author's own formal and devotional desires.

Throughout the *Life*, Clemence places a great deal of emphasis on
Catherine's speech by presenting it as *oratio recta* and by describing the
effect of her eloquence in great detail. Whenever she speaks, Catherine's
subject is always the divinity of Christ; her words convert her audience
and even move some to embrace martyrdom. Clemence structures the

main episodes of the *Life* around the saint's speeches. In the first episode, Catherine goes to the court of the emperor Maxence to protest his new injunction to sacrifice to pagan idols. There she speaks out publicly against his law and in favor of the true God. Her protest leads to the central event of the poem: Catherine's debate with the 50 learned philosophers and the resulting conversion, martyrdom, and miraculous bodily preservation of these clerks. Clemence devotes over 600 lines to these events, almost all of them in *oratio recta*; she also presents the 200 lines of Catherine's dialogue with Maxence in direct discourse. These events take up almost one-third of the poem. The next series of events—Catherine's first round of tortures, Christ's visit to her in the dungeon, the conversion of the queen and Porphire, and the second round of tortures—all include Catherine's evangelism and prayers, represented through *oratio recta* and dialogue. The final episodes of the poem, Catherine's last earthly trial and martyrdom, include yet more public speech and direct discourse: another public debate with Maxence, Catherine's exhortation to the community that mourns her imminent death, and a final prayer delivered homiletically before witnesses. As this brief summary shows, Clemence structures the *Life* around Catherine's speech acts. While other versions of Catherine's *vita* usually include some version of Catherine's public discourse, only Clemence's version develops a parallel relationship between Catherine's speech and that of her narrator, allowing Clemence's authorial activity to be viewed by audiences as an imitation. The recognition of Clemence's imitative self-presentation, in turn, suggests the possibility for subsequent imitation on the part of the reader, potentially casting Clemence in the role of the imitated as well as the imitator. In this way, hagiography enlarges the pool of figures that might function as models for holy imitation within holy lives: not only were the subjects of *vitae* available as models for holy imitation, but their authors might be imitated as well. Clemence's text suggests this possibility by structuring the *Life* through several imitative relationships.

In keeping with hagiographic convention, Clemence depicts Catherine's *vita* and *passio* as a close imitation of Christ's.[26] Catherine performs *imitatio Christi* when speaking publicly and praying privately; in her speeches, she publicly proclaims her faith, converts pagans to Christianity, proclaims herself an eternal intercessor, models devotional practices such as prayer and praise, and performs the ultimate *imitatio* of martyrdom. All of these speech acts imitate those in Christ's *vita* and *passio*; furthermore, these speeches are all in *oratio recta*.

Clemence emphasizes Catherine's *imitatio* by depicting Christ's appearance in approval of Catherine's public speech acts. The first instance of reciprocal divine speech occurs in the form of a divine apparition. After Catherine has been cast into the dungeon for speaking against Maxentius and refusing to admit the authority of the pagan gods, she is visited by the queen and Porphire, who have heard of her victory in the debate against the philosophers and have come to hear about Christianity. Catherine converts them with a long description of the gifts of Jesus and a description of heaven; afterward, Porphire converts 200 of his own followers based on what he has learned from Catherine. Directly after this episode, in which Catherine's direct discourse plays a central role, she receives a personal visit from Jesus:

> Li bons Deus dunc la cunforta;
> Sa bone fille la apela.
> "Bele, fait il, jo sui Jhesu
> Pur qui tu as tantz mals eu.
> Jo suit un faitre kit e fis,
> Pur qui l'estrif as epris.
> Ne t'esmaier, jo sui od tei;
> Net e falt l'aie de mei.
> Plusur par tei en mei crerrunt,
> Ki senz fin od mei meindrunt." (1851–58)

(The good Lord comforted her there; called her his good daughter. "Beautiful one, he said, I am Jesus, for whose sake you have had so many evils. I am your creator who made you and for whom you have undertaken this struggle. Do not dismay yourself, I am with you; and you will not lack help from me. Through you many will come to believe in me and will remain with me forever.")

Jesus's emphasis on Catherine's role as a speaker ("Plusur par tei en mei crerrunt") emphasizes her imitation of Christ in overtly biblical language; in addition, Clemence represents Christ's speech to Catherine in direct discourse, which parallels all of Catherine's speeches up to this point in the text. Christ's explicit description of Catherine's primary purpose as evangelism and conversion endorses her rhetorically.

When compared to the Latin source text, however, this pointed identification between Catherine and Christ reveals Clemence translating freely in order to designate the speaker as Christ. The Latin text indicates only that the Lord—"Dominus"—has "appeared" to her:

> Expletis uero diebus, apparuit ei Dominus cum multitudine angelorum, quem sequebatur innumera turba virginum. Cui Dominus: "Agnosce," inquit, "filia, agnosce auctorem tuum, pro cuius nomine laboriosi

certaminis cursum cepesti. Constans esto et ne paueas, quia ego tecum
sum nec te desero; est etenim non parua turba hominum per te nomini
meo creditura."[27]

(When the day was done, the Lord appeared to her with a multitude
of angels, which were followed by an innumerable crowd of virgins. The
Lord said to her: "Behold, daughter, recognize your creator, on behalf of
whose name you took the path of laborious combat. You will be steadfast
and should not be afraid, for I am with you, nor will I forsake you; for
indeed, through you a great multitude of men [lit. a multitude of men by
no means small] will be committed to my name.")

Clemence's specification of Christ as the speaker, rather than the more
general "Dominus," reveals a distinct authorial choice to privilege and
highlight the imitative relationship in one of the key instances of direct
discourse in the *Life*. Stylistically and thematically, this speech establishes
Catherine—and more importantly, her speech—as divinely authorized
by Christ. In addition, it shows Clemence taking an active role as a translator, shaping the discursive relationships within her text to strengthen
the imitative relationship between Catherine and Christ. Thus, Clemence
authorizes Catherine and her *Life* through a combination of imitative
structures and rhetorical choices.

While Clemence's imitation of Catherine can be traced through the
Life, it is not a literal imitation; it is a textual reconfiguration of what is
presented in the text as public speech. This departure from literal imitation illustrates the flexible form of Clemence's devotional activity.
Whereas devotion to a particular saint would traditionally have included
a variety of conventional spiritual activities such as prayers for intercession, observance on feast days, and pilgrimage to shrines or reliquaries,
Clemence practiced devotion as an author by producing a version of
Catherine's *Life*.[28] This type of devotional textual production, though
less common than more traditional forms of piety, was not new to the
twelfth century; however, Clemence's devotion takes on an extra dimension through her imitative relationship with her subject. Obviously,
twelfth-century women would not have been encouraged to participate
in the public speaking that Catherine so zealously pursues. As Jocelyn
Wogan-Browne has persuasively shown, "We should be cautious about
assuming that the representation of speech by women is a representation of women's freedom to speak, and saints are exceptional as well as
exemplary for their audiences."[29] Catherine's medieval devotees faced
the dilemma of how to imitate a holy figure whose actions conflicted
with contemporary gender expectations. In her edition of the thirteenth-
century *Stanzaic Life of Katherine*, Sherry Reames notes that public
speech acts within Catherine's legend were often adapted, downplayed,

or limited to fit the social expectations of their intended audiences, precisely because their authors feared providing models of public speech for overly impressionable female audiences.[30] In light of such editorial decisions, Clemence's version of Catherine's *Life* clearly demonstrates a pointed choice to emphasize Catherine's public speech, bookended by her own authorial discourse. In the final lines of the text, Clemence claims, "Jo ki sa vie ai translatee,/Par nun sui Clemence numee./De Berkinge sui nunain./Pur s'amur pris cest oevre en mein" (2689–92; I who have translated her life am called by the name Clemence. I am a nun of Barking, for love of which I took this work in hand). When this claim is considered in connection with Clemence's intended audience, it appears that Clemence did not hesitate to present both public speech and authorial activity as available models of devotional practice to her audience.[31] Clemence's authorial activity, imitative through the textual reproduction of Catherine's public speech, thus suggests the efficacy of flexible models of imitation and devotion for both herself and her audiences—a flexibility that in the context of hagiography suggests a freedom to determine individual devotional response on the part of the reader.[32]

Just as Clemence invokes authority for her own devotional practices, so also she emphasizes the Lord's authorization of Catherine in her hagiography. A key moment of divine sanction occurs in response to Catherine's final speech. Before she is beheaded, she publicly prays that she will become an intercessor:

> Sire, pur tuz cels te requier,
> Ki de m'aie avront mestier,
> E ki pur tei tant m'amerunt,
> Que t'aie par mei querrunt,
> Sire, dune lur bone aie
> E en lur mort e en lur vie,
> E s'il unt dulur u agoisse,
> Que par ta grace aidier lur poisse…
> Pri que a tes angeles seit livree
> E devant ta face aportee,
> Od les virgins puisse regner
> E tun seint nun sen fin loer… (2567–74…25887–90)

(Lord, I entreat you, on behalf of all those who later may have need of my help, and who on account of you will love me so much that they will request your help through me; Lord, grant them good help in their life and in their death and when they have sorrow or distress, that through your grace I may be able to help them… I pray to be delivered to your angels and brought before your face, that I may be able to reign with the virgins and praise your holy name without end.)

Directly following this speech, God himself publicly responds to Catherine, granting her prayer for intercessory identity and publicly confirming her status as the beloved of Christ:

> Parfaite n'ot pas s'oreisun,
> Quant une voiz od un grant sun,
> Ki dez haltes nues eissi,
> Par ices moz li respundi:
> "Venez a mei, amie bele
> Venez, venez, la meie ancele…
> [Li ten sege est al[e]vé
> En la maisun de bonurté]…
> Le dun que m'avez demandé,
> Vus ai de bon voleir granté.
> La recevrai tuz cels en gloire,
> Ki de tei avront fait ci memoire." (2591–608)

(She had not completed her prayer when a voice of great sonorousness, that came from the high clouds, responded to her with these words: "Come to me, fair love, come, come, my handmaiden…your seat is raised in the house of the blessed…the gift that you have asked of me I have granted with good will. I will receive there in glory all those who henceforth make this remembrance of you.")

Clemence's representation of these words from on high echoes the Father's response to Christ's baptism by John the Baptist, further strengthening the parallels between Catherine and Christ and confirming her identity as a legitimate model of sanctity.[33] In each episode of divine sanction, a heavenly speaker publicly confirms the holiness of the subject. Each speech is delivered in direct discourse, the same narrative mode of Catherine's speeches, strengthening the imitative relationship between Catherine and Jesus. They also confirm Catherine's directly preceding self-canonization. Once again, however, a comparison with the Latin source reveals pointed translation choices:

Necdum orationem compleuerat, et ecce uox huiusmodi, de sublimi nube emissa, ad eam redditur: "Veni, dilecta mea, speciosa mea. Ecce tibi beatitudinis ianua aperitur, ecce quietis eterne mansio, tibi parata, aduentum tuum expectat; iam in occursum tuum chorus ille uirgineus sanctorum, exultantibus animis, cum triumphali aduentat corona. Veni ergo, et ne solliciteris de donis que postulas; nam et his qui passionem tuam deuotis mentibus celebrauerint, et qui in periculis et necessitatibus te inuocauer-int, presidia optata et opem celerem de celo promitto."[34]

(But she had not yet completed her prayers, when behold, a voice of this manner, sent from the highest clouds, was rendered to her: "Come, my beloved, my spouse. Behold, the door of blessedness is open to you; behold, the dwelling of eternal rest, prepared for you, awaits your approach; now that chorus of holy virgins, with exulting spirits, draw near your arrival with triumphant crowns. Therefore come, and do not be worried about the gifts you pray for; for to those who will celebrate your passion with devoted mind, and those who will invoke you in danger and need, I promise desired protection and speedy help from heaven.")

Clemence translates the Latin into more erotic, courtly love-language than that of the stately Latin source text; reminiscent of the Song of Songs, Clemence's text suggests that Christ is the specific member of the trinity whose voice is heard ("Venez a mei, amie bele/Venez, venez, la meie ancele").[35] This translation renders the divine endorsement in both religious and courtly terms, characterizing the love relationship with the divine through the courtly language of twelfth-century romance—a trope often used by religious writers such as Bernard of Clairvaux. This parallel between the author of the *Life* and its subject, as participants in a courtly milieu, would not have been lost on an audience of enclosed women, particularly the community at Barking, which was well known to be a center of learning and textual production, in Latin as well as the vernacular.[36]

Besides establishing Catherine as a divinely sanctioned public speaker, the speech gives divine sanction to female self-authorization—the same sort of authorization that Clemence herself performs, albeit with altera-tions, in her framing first-person narrative. At the same time that she invokes the canonically accepted tradition of the virgin martyr, Catherine augments and subtly alters that tradition by establishing her future inter-cessory acts as the channels through which her saintly, intercessory iden-tity will be made public and her legend will be maintained.[37] With this proclamation, Catherine joins a small group of female saints and mar-tyrs whose statements of identity shape their subsequent reception and devotional function. In her framing narrative, Clemence imitates this strategy of identity formation by delivering strikingly similar narrative requests, inviting the audience to engage devotionally with her text. Like Catherine, Clemence evokes hagiographic tradition only to subtly alter it for her own narrative purposes. This shared narrative activity suggests that Clemence viewed herself as participating in a specific narrative tradition in imitation of her saintly female subject, perhaps implying that Clemence viewed herself—a twelfth-century cloistered woman author—as participating in the narrative tradition of legendary holy women.

In addition to editing her Latin source text, Clemence adds original material in a contemporary, first-person narrative voice. An original prologue and epilogue, each between 50 and 100 verse lines, frame Catherine's story with Clemence's personal commentary. Nor does Clemence leave her choice to translate into the vernacular unremarked: in the prologue, she justifies her translation as a fear that Catherine's story would fall out of fashion as it currently exists, which seems surprising given Catherine's well-documented popularity. Although this comment perhaps exaggerates contemporary neglect of Clemence's legend, it allows Clemence to combine several conventional hagiographical tropes to unusual effect: a lament over the worldliness of society joins with the familiar authorial modesty topos, in which Clemence professes to desire only to be of use in the promulgation of Catherine's legend, in order to figure her own authorial contribution to Catherine's legend as a necessary, and at the same time humble, act. In the prologue to the *Life*, Clemence introduces her narrative objectives:

> Ele fud jadis translate
> Sulunc le tens bien ordené;
> Mais ne furent dunc si veisdus
> Les humes, ne si envius
> Cum il sunt al tens ki est ore
> E après nus serrunt uncore.
> Pur ço que li tens est mué
> E des humes la qualité
> Est la rime vil tenue
> Car ele est asquans corrumpue. (35–44)

(It was translated before and well arranged according to the time. But men were not so wily then, nor so ill-natured as they are at the present time, and will still be after us. Because the times and men's quality have changed, the poem is considered low, for it is somewhat defective.)

This addition provides a striking example of Clemence's metacommentary on translation and the hagiographic tradition. While acknowledging previous translations as "well set out," Clemence simultaneously disparages previous hagiographic treatments of Catherine by questioning their continued applicability and reception, finally criticizing them directly as "defective in places." By identifying "times and men's quality" as the reason for a decline in the popularity of Catherine's story (or perhaps, in the *Vulgata* version of her life), Clemence mitigates her unflattering characterization of previous *Lives* even as she critically dismisses them.[38] The mitigation results in her subsequent call to literary action: "pur ço si l'estuet amender/E le tens selunc la gent user" (45–46; because of this it is necessary to amend it, and to become accustomed to the times according to the people). This self-conscious commentary on the necessity of continued literary intervention in Catherine's legend places Clemence within the established category of hagiographic authority: able to comment critically on previous treatments of Catherine's *vita* and to justify her own narrative intervention in an established and flourishing tradition that requires stylistic maintenance and updating in order to continue serving a devotional purpose. If, as Sarah Salih has argued, the purpose of hagiography "was to function as a model of imitation," the logical implication of Clemence's prefatory remarks seems to be that contemporarily inflected accounts of *vitae* and *passionae* might serve as more effective devotional aids than lives with less contemporary resonance.[39]

Moreover, these lines invite the reader to participate in the perpetuation of Catherine's legend through imitative action. The precise form such imitative action might take, I argue, remained to a certain degree flexible. In his discussion of excess in fourteenth-century saints' lives, for example, Richard Kieckhefer notes that "the saints' *admiranda* were evidently meant to arouse more than admiration, more even than wonderment: they were supposed to shock the reader, to provoke in him a moral reform, to suggest that the way toward perfection was a strenuous path that required as much fervor as one could sustain."[40] In much the same way as the fourteenth-century saints' lives that Kieckhefer examines allowed their readers a degree of autonomy in the form of ethical response inspired by the text, Clemence's text enjoined its audience to determine individually the form and limit of imitation and admiration. In this way, Catherine's legend continued to function devotionally, reconfigured and adapted to changing times and customs, just as she claimed to hope that it would.

The *imitatio* relationship between Clemence and Catherine is further highlighted when Catherine's extensive sermonizing and speechmaking is compared to Clemence's introduction of new material, particularly in the prologue and epilogue of the life. While Catherine's evangelism is traditionally seen as an example of her *imitatio Christi*, I argue that Clemence's representation of Catherine's speeches is a formal *imitatio* of Catherine's theological *imitatio*. When Clemence represents Catherine engaged in direct discourse, she represents an instance of *imitatio Christi*; that is, she represents Catherine engaged in public speech in imitation of Christ. However, when Clemence frames Catherine's life with her own contemporary commentary, she enters into the cycle of imitation herself, demonstrating an understanding of hagiography as a devotional process for the writer. As Francois Recanati explains, "When we quote someone else's words, we engage in a form of play-acting: we simulate the person in question by actually making the utterance we're ascribing to her."[41] In this way, the hagiographer who imitates the sacred subject performs an *imitatio* that can be seen as a devotional practice: by imitating Catherine's speech, Clemence inhabits Catherine's role as the speaking figure; and by inhabiting this role, Clemence inhabits Catherine's *imitatio Christi* and engages in virtuous Christian activity. In hagiography, then, *oratio recta* can function as the author's *imitatio Christi*.

Clemence continues her metacommentary on hagiography in the final lines of the prologue, where she insists, "Ne l'aiment pas pur mun orgoil,/ Kar preisie ester n'en voil;/Il sul en deit loenge aveir/De qui sai mun povre saveir" (47–50; I am not correcting it through my pride, for I do not desire to be praised in it. He alone ought to have praise in this work, from whom I have my own poor knowledge). By combining her metacommentary on hagiography with a humble deferral to the one authority higher than the *auctores*—an appeal that simultaneously justifies her translation (a term she uses to refer to her entire intellectual production)—Clemence defines the work of hagiography as devotional and positions herself in relation to Christ as a divinely authorized speaking figure, a position that is a direct imitation of Catherine's position as the mouthpiece of God within her text.[42] Although such imitation is certainly not unique to Clemence's text, the *Life*'s narrative structure, in which Catherine and Clemence parallel each other through acts of speech and writing, suggests a parallel between Catherine (as divinely authorized speaker) and Clemence herself. However, as Clemence's twelfth-century moment of production no longer required the public martyrdom Catherine performs within the *vita*, Clemence performs virtuous and moral action in imitation of Catherine's virtue through writing. Thus, the depiction of virtue functions as the writer's ethical response to the text she narrates.

As a virtuous action prompted by imitative devotion, Clemence's intellectual activity becomes her twelfth-century response to—and imitation of—Catherine's late-antique martyrdom. This imitative relationship creates a parallel association between Catherine's *vita* and Clemence's framing commentary. This imitative relationship functions both structurally and devotionally: by suggesting that Clemence speaks from the same authorized position as her subject, the text maintains a metafocus on the activity of *imitatio Christi* within the text, at the level of both the *vita* and the framing narrative. This continued focus on devotional *imitatio* through speech (Catherine) and writing about speech (Clemence) establishes both oral and written activity as devotional acts of imitation in which the reader might potentially engage.[43] And while such imitative relationships may invite the view that all hagiography functions as a potential process of *imitatio Christi*, Clemence's framing narrative reminds us that only hagiography that deliberately situates itself within a contemporary moment of production, differentiated from the narrated situation, invites such comparative reading. Just as the devotional process of *imitatio* requires the practitioner's intent in order to function as a spiritual practice, so the production and reception of hagiography have the potential to function devotionally only in the context of the author's or reader's *intentional* engagement with the text. In this way, only the reading subject who encounters the text with the intent to imitate the *Life*'s subject or author (just as Clemence parallels her authorial activity with Catherine's speech and Catherine's speech with Christ's) engages with the text in a devotional manner.[44]

The framing of Catherine's imitative speech by Clemence's first-person narrative commentary—commentary that explicitly discusses the issues of speech and writing—acts as a metacommentary on speech and the intent or purpose of recording it. This metacommentary invites the reader to engage with a new theological model of *imitatio*: rather than foreground Catherine through traditional hagiographic tropes of devotion, Clemence closes her *vita* with emphasis on the temporal present and the individual Christian reader. The shift in tone and register enacted by such obvious "imitation" calls attention to the fact that, as Victor Bers put it, the "'outside'—that is, the text within which the *oratio recta* appears—is also a fiction."[45] This metatextual awareness allows the reader to differentiate Clemence's personal commentary from Catherine's narrated *Life*, distinguishing between the model and the imitation of the model. By placing herself in the conclusion of the *vita* after Catherine, Clemence returns the reader to the twelfth-century moment of production and the narrator's own concerns, which are inextricably linked to her production of the hagiographic text. While the text's structure asks the reader to engage in an intellectual imitation of Clemence's multiple discursive frames, the text cannot require the reader to imitate Clemence's authorial role.

Unless Clemence envisioned a reading audience comprising solely like-minded nuns interested in textual production, the likelihood that her audience could literally imitate her authorial activities seems doubtful. As Jocelyn Wogan-Browne has shown, the audience of twelfth-century hagiography could include cloistered religious women or pious lay-women, as well as any women associated with such households in domestic or temporary capacities.[46] Such a varied and mixed potential audience would not have shared similar opportunities for devotional activity or even, we may safely assume, similar inclinations for or abilities of devotion; however, the general consensus that Clemence's audience would have consisted mainly of women readers, both lay and enclosed, from the upper classes or upper-class households suggests that Clemence intended the *Life* for an audience familiar with the type of devotional response the text elicits from its readers. Clemence's text offers the opportunity to fashion personal devotional response in the moments of the text in which Clemence's relationship to the reader shifts from the imitative to the prescriptive. As she concludes her text, Clemence emphasizes the possibility of individual choice by gesturing toward her own relationship with her readers.[47]

In the final lines of the text, Clemence imitates Catherine's concern for the state of her own soul but does not display the same confidence as Catherine. Though she imitates Catherine by invoking the idea of intercession, Clemence nonetheless inverts the intercessory relationship with her readers: she asks the reader to pray for her soul, rather than declaring that she will act as intercessor for others:

> A tuz cels ki cest livre orrunt,
> E ki de bon coer l'entenderunt,
> Pur amur Deu pri e requier,
> Qu'il violent Deu pur mei preier,
> Qu'il m'anme mette en pareis,
> E guart le cors tant cum ert vis,
> Ki regne e vit e regnera
> E est e ert e parmeindra. (2693–700)

> (For the love of God, I pray and entreat all those who will hear this book, and who listen to it with a good heart, that they be willing to pray to God on my behalf, that he may place my soul in paradise and guard my body as long as it will be seen, he who reigns and lives and will reign, and is and was and will endure forever.)

This request for her readers' engagement with her own salvation is a marked contrast to the usual tropes of requested prayer in *vitae*: Paul John Jones notes that when final directives to prayer are included in a *vita*, they usually direct readers to pray to the subject of the life on their own behalf.[48] In addition to producing a *translatio* that continues to guarantee devotion to the sanctified subject of a *vita*, Clemence attempts to guarantee perpetual requests for intercession on her own behalf, directly engaging the contemporary reader. These final lines imagine hagiography's power and influence in the hands of the living reader as well as the dead (but eternally living) intercessor, effectively placing the reader in the position of the beatified subject—the position of intercessor. As Laurie Postlewate puts it, "When [the readers] get to that final prayer that establishes an intercessory relationship, [they] discover that they are engaged in an act of devotion."[49] The audience is thus presented with the choice of praying to Catherine on their own behalf, praying to God or Catherine on behalf of Clemence, or engaging in all of these acts of prayer. This devotional innovation reinforces the rhetorical imitation established through the text's multiple narrative levels and imagines the readers as participants in the author's spiritual well-being, inviting them to be spiritually and devotionally active outside their engagement with the text—in effect, to perform their own *imitatio Christi*, just as Clemence defined her own practice of *imitatio* as the work of authorship. That imitation might take the form of prayer, speech, or authorial production, depending on the social context in which the text was received and the desires and capabilities of the reader. Although Clemence never specifies exactly how such devotion ought to be performed beyond the prayers she requests on her own behalf, the variety of devotional praxes portrayed within the narrative suggests that she considered multiple and varied responses as acceptable reactions to her text.

Rhetorical, stylistic, and narrative innovations have been seen as part of the tradition, and even part of the purpose, of hagiography. Karl Uitti, for example, argues that hagiography functions ritualistically through the perpetual retelling of the saint's life and that "inasmuch as participation in the telling of a saint's life was itself an act of faith, an act of witness, it not only permitted but required constant thematic and stylistic variation in the body of the story."[50] Uitti argues that hagiography's ultimate function is to link the narrator, the subject, and the reader together as a Christian community through shared participation in the memorialization of the Christian saint. This model of memorialization and witnessing depends on common linguistic identity, which texts such as Clemence's carefully evoke through the use of the vernacular, as well as through self-conscious commentary on their status as translations. Uitti argues that Old French hagiography's deliberate mixture of varied tenses and moods within grammatical structures allows the hagiographer to claim more authority than, to use his example, the *oratio recta* of romance tradition, since such a mixture imitates the "realistic" patterns of speech and oral narrative.[51] I argue, however, that exactly the opposite is true: that the self-conscious artifice of *oratio recta* is deliberately deployed by hagiographers in order to draw attention to the identity of their texts as devotional tools.

Deliberate use of *oratio recta* allows hagiographers such as Clemence to claim rhetorical authority but not, as Uitti suggests, in imitation of the romance tradition. Rather, the deployment of *oratio recta* within

vernacular hagiography elicits a reading praxis that accepts the veracity—
and by extension, the authority—of imaginative and hypothetical material within the accepted authority of hagiographic narrative, even when
presented by a self-proclaimed female writer, precisely because it functions as the devotional activity of the author. In order to recognize the
imitative function of the instances of *oratio recta* within the narrative, the
reader must simultaneously remain aware of two different narrative levels:
the contemporary framing narrative and the transhistorical, miraculous
life of Catherine. This dialectic evokes a narrative hermeneutic practice
in which the reader maintains an interpretive focus on two distinct narrative threads as he or she reads, literally imitating Clemence's narrative
position as the translator as well as the imitator of Catherine's life. In
this way, Clemence's use of *oratio recta* allows her to depict the process of
imitatio Christi through her characters while engaging in the devotional
act of *imitatio Christi* herself through writing—thus becoming a model for
contemporary devotional behavior.

Clemence invites her audience to imitate Catherine's and her own
acts of devotion and in particular to express their devotion by praying
for her own soul. The vague and unspecific nature of the form these
requested prayers might take allows—in fact requires—the reader to
develop the form of such responsive prayers individually. In her recent
work on exemplarity in female hagiography, Catherine Sanok has argued
that texts such as Clemence's functioned ethically by "endorsing some
saintly practices literally while carefully transforming others through
figural models of *imitation*."[52] Clemence demonstrates—and advocates—
exactly this type of transformative imitation; whereas the structure of
her narrative allows her to imitate her subject, the final lines invite readers to develop their own personal methods of devotion in imitation of
her emulation of Catherine (and, by extension, Catherine's imitation of
Christ). When Clemence asks her readers to pray for her, a request for
a fairly common devotional activity, that request reiterates the parallel
relationship between devotional subject positions that structure the *Life*.
By responding to Clemence's text as she requests, the reader follows in
the footsteps of the beatified subject—Catherine—through efficacious,
intercessory prayer, thus placing herself in an imitative relationship with
the subject of the *vita*. If the reader undertakes the requested prayer, she
or he essentially performs an *imitatio* of the saintly subject.

The implications of this narrative method are far-reaching. Placing
readers into a position of imitative devotional subjectivity invites them
to imagine themselves as spiritually and theologically efficacious. Jocelyn
Wogan-Browne, for example, argues that "Clemence sees a more instrumental role for the writer, in whom wisdom is even more to be valued

than eloquence. The vernacular composer is a channel for the transformative effects on human wills of what is in all senses (as her saint's debate stresses), the fruit of the Word."[53] The theological complexity for which Wogan-Browne argues can be traced throughout the *Life's* content; but I argue that this complexity is equally present in the *way* in which Clemence achieves this *translatio*. Clemence replaces the traditional *imitatio* of hagiography (from one work to another) with the *imitatio* between author and subject, subject and Christ, and author and reader, thus reimagining hagiography as a devotional practice aimed at individual spiritual development.

Notes

1. For the French source text, I cite Clemence of Barking, *The Life of St. Catherine by Clemence of Barking*, ed. William MacBain, Anglo-Norman Text Society 18 (Oxford: Blackwell, 1964). All subsequent quotations are to line numbers from this edition. All translations are my own. In keeping with the source text, I refer to Catherine by her Anglo-Norman spelling, and I have tried to maintain this spelling throughout this chapter when possible; many of the critics I cite, however, refer to Catherine as "Katherine of Alexandria," in keeping with later Middle English practice. I have maintained this spelling within quotation for accuracy.

2. Robert N. Swanson describes devotion as "the external practices of medieval Christianity...[which] aimed to secure God's favor on earth and achieve communion with Him here and in the hereafter...Numerous devotional practices sought that end, aiming through good works and pious foundations to secure prayers and other rewards to benefit the soul after death." See R. N. Swanson, *Religion and Devotion in Europe, c. 1215–c. 1515* (Cambridge: Cambridge University Press, 1995), 136.

3. Anne C. Bartlett, *Male Authors, Female Readers: Representation and Subjectivity in Middle English Devotional Literature* (Ithaca, NY: Cornell University Press, 1995), 32.

4. Countless critics have summarized the antifeminist tradition and its impact on all aspects of medieval life. More specifically, Alcuin Blamires examines intellectual culture, reminding us of "the general principle of women's exclusion from formal theological—as from legal, and to a lesser extent, medical—study in the period...attribute[d]...to male monopolization of powerful professions, combined with ingrained masculine contempt for female intellect." See Alcuin Blamires, "The Limits of Bible Study for Medieval Women," in vol. 1 of *Women, the Book, and the Godly: Selected Proceedings of the St Hilda's Conference, 1993*, ed. Lesley Smith and Jane H. M. Taylor (Cambridge: Boydell and Brewer, 1995), 1 [1–12].

5. For detailed discussion of gendered roles in medieval literary society, see Maud B. McInerney, *Eloquent Virgins from Thecla to Joan of Arc* (New York: Palgrave Macmillan, 2003), and Jocelyn Wogan-Browne, *Saints' Lives*

and Women's Literary Culture, 1150–1300: Virginity and Its Authorizations (Oxford: Oxford University Press, 2001).

6. Robert L. A. Clark, "Constructing the Female Subject in Late Medieval Devotion," in *Medieval Conduct*, ed. Kathleen Ashley and Robert L. A. Clark (Minneapolis: University of Minnesota Press, 2001), 163 [160–82].

7. Mary J. Carruthers, *The Book of Memory: A Study of Memory in Medieval Culture*, 2nd ed., Cambridge Studies in Medieval Literature 70 (Cambridge: Cambridge University Press, 2008), 195. See also the introduction to this volume for more complete discussion of Carruthers's formulation of memorial ethics.

8. Katherine Lewis, *The Cult of St Katherine of Alexandria in Late Medieval England* (Suffolk, UK: Boydell and Brewer, 2000), 2. Lewis traces the "standardization" of Catherine's legend to the eleventh-century Latin *Vulgata* version, which provided the primary source for Catherine's life in Voragine's *Legenda Aurea*. In addition to the Middle English iterations of Catherine's life traced by Lewis, at least 11 Old French versions proceeded from the *Vulgata* text, one of which is Clemence's. The *Vulgata* version of Catherine's legend is widely regarded as Clemence's source; for further description of Clemence's source and discussion of the manuscript evidence, see MacBain's introduction and the notes in the most recent English translation: Clemence of Barking, "The Life of St. Catherine," in *Virgin Lives and Holy Deaths: Two Exemplary Biographies for Anglo-Norman Women*, trans. and ed. Jocelyn Wogan-Browne and Glyn S. Burgess (London: J. M. Dent, 1996), 3–79. The most current edition of the *Vulgata* text is *Seinte Katerine: Re-Edited from MS Bodley 34 and the Other Manuscripts*, ed. S. R. T. O. d'Ardenee and E. J. Dobson, The Early English Text Society, s.s. 7 (Oxford: Oxford University Press, 1981). For discussion of additional Anglo-Norman redactions, see Paul Meyer, "Légendes hagiographiques en français," *Histoire Littéraire de la France* 33 (1906): 342–44; also E. C. Fawtier-Jones, "Les vies de Sainte Catherine d'Alexandrie en ancien français," *Romania* 56 (1930): 80–104.

9. I borrow this term from Pierre Delooz, who ruminates that "all saints are more or less *constructed* in that, being necessarily saints *for other people*, they are remodeled in the collective representation which is made of them…Some saints are solely *constructed* saints simply because nothing is known about them historically: everything, including their existence, is a product of collective representation." Delooz pointedly references Saint Catherine as an example of a saint "who never was a *real* person. In her case, everything has been *constructed*. Again, the construction has been enormous, and has spanned the centuries, ultimately making her the patron saint both of philosophers and spinsters." See Pierre Delooz, "Towards a Sociological Study of Canonized Sainthood in the Catholic Church," trans. Jane Hodgkin, in *Saints and Their Cults: Studies in Religious Sociology, Folklore, and History*, ed. Stephen Wilson (Cambridge: Cambridge University Press, 1983), 195–196 [189–216].

10. Lewis records that by the later Middle Ages in England, Catherine was considered important enough that her feast day included mandatory mass, whereas the feast days of sister virgin martyrs Lucy, Agatha, and Agnes did not.

11. William MacBain, her first twentieth-century editor, imagined Clemence as innovative but ultimately loyal to the Latin source text: "Whatever Clemence deems worthy of a more thorough treatment, she develops, and what she finds tedious or difficult, she curtails, retaining always the essential idea of the Latin text before her." See MacBain, introduction to Clemence of Barking, *Life of St. Catherine*, xiv. Similarly, M. Dominica Legge cautiously describes the text as "interesting for the curious blend of piety and courtliness, this courtliness striking an odd note in a work of praise to a virgin saint." See M. Dominica Legge, *Anglo-Norman Literature and Its Background* (Oxford: Clarendon Press, 1963), 72. This "curious blend" has since been characterized by Barbara Newman as "la mystique courtoise." See Barbara Newman, *From Virile Woman to WomanChrist: Studies in Medieval Religion and Literature*, Middle Ages Series (Philadelphia: University of Pennsylvania Press, 1995).

12. She points out that Clemence's choice to translate was itself political, since she was probably well versed in Latin; Crane argues that Clemence uses stylistic models of authority in her depiction of Catherine in order to combat patriarchal notions of the vernacular as gendered: "For women who write in England, Latin might have been a plausible vehicle, as it was for Hildegard of Bingen, Heloise, and continental authors of religious poetry in the eleventh and twelfth centuries, but French is their chosen medium, perhaps again because of the elite status of that vernacular as well as cultural pressures associating women with the vernacular rather than Latin. As if resisting those pressures, Clemence of Barking's Life of St Catherine (c.1175) honours a notably learned and disputatious saint." See Susan Crane, "Anglo-Norman Cultures in England, 1066–1460," in *The Cambridge History of Medieval English Literature*, ed. David Wallace (Cambridge: Cambridge University Press, 1999), 44, 46 [35–60]. Duncan Robertson also notes the political aspects of Clemence's translation, arguing that Clemence's choice of the vernacular was connected to her milieu of production: "At Barking, the cultivation of the vernacular was closely related to the 'feminist' mission of the abbey...the task of vernacularization therefore takes on a particular urgency. The lives of Catherine and Edward both convey powerfully the identification of women writers, readers, and patrons with the heroines of legend, under the ultimate patronage of the Virgin Mary. St. Catherine, gifted with eloquence, is the very figure of the female vocation, religious and literary." See Duncan Robertson, "Writing in the Textual Community: Clemence of Barking's Life of Saint Catherine," *French Forum* 21, no.1 (1996): 7 [5–28]. While these arguments about localized politics of production are compelling, I am more concerned with the spiritual and theological implications of Clemence's narrative innovations.

13. Wogan-Browne argues that Clemence's statement of love for her community in the final lines reveals the motivating factor behind her translation: "In the case of the Lives from Barking, the source material is also completely refocused in the light of particular thematic interests and relations with inscribed and future audiences. These are signaled in the prologues, as part of the creation of narratorial stances." See Jocelyn Wogan-Browne, "Wreaths of Thyme: The Female Translator in Anglo-Norman Hagiography," in vol. 4 of *The Medieval Translator*, ed. Roger Ellis and Ruth Evans (Exeter, UK: University of Exeter Press, 1994), 53 [46–65].

14. In this volume, Claire Barbetti's discussion of Hildegard of Bingen's *Scivias* and Helene Scheck's examination of the Carolingian *Karolus Magnus et Leo Papa* both address texts concerned with authorial, rhetorical, and textual difference. Each study examines gender as a category of difference in the representation of both author and subject.

15. This model of authorship has been described by Mary Carruthers as the goal of both writing and reading in the Middle Ages, in which "the complete process of reading does not observe in the same way the basic distinction we make between 'what I read in a book' and 'my experience'…'what I read in a book' *is* 'my experience,' and I make it mine by incorporating it (and we should understand the world 'incorporate' quite literally) in my memory." See Carruthers, *Book of Memory*, 211. Furthermore, as recent work on the idea of the vernacular has shown, in this concept of authorial self-authorization, "authors are mediators of an 'entent' that is situated somewhere between their minds and their texts, whose attempts to express 'entent' are inherently vulnerable. In all these texts, 'entent' fragments: dispersing and disseminating its Latin meanings, acquiring a whole new set of vernacular contexts their authors actively evoke, insisting on the difference, rather than the common ground, between their projects and authoritative Latin texts." See Ruth Evans, Andrew Taylor, Nicholas Watson, and Jocelyn Wogan-Browne, "The Notion of Vernacular Theory," in *The Idea of the Vernacular: An Anthology of Middle English Literary Theory, 1280–1520*, ed. Jocelyn Wogan-Browne, Nicholas Watson, Andrew Taylor, and Ruth Evans (University Park: Pennsylvania State University Press, 1999), 329 [314–330].

16. William MacBain quotes O. Sodergard on the uniquely twelfth-century character of the *vita*, which he describes as possessing "l'expression de sa propre pensée sous la forme de commentaires moraux et de réflexions d'un caractère religieux…elle emploie des expressions et des phrases toutes personnelles en ce sens qu'elles ne se trouvent pas dans le latin." See William MacBain, "The Literary Apprenticeship of Clemence of Barking," *Journal of the Australasian Universities Language and Literature Association* 9 (1958): 10 [3–22]. In this volume, Catherine Keene's chapter examining the hagiographical afterlife of Saint Margaret of Scotland explicates a related process of "saint-construction"; Keene argues that while Margaret was a real historical personage, her posthumous textual

identity reflected the political and religious concerns of her descendants, who appropriated her pious identity and royal status in order to construct a saint with associations of dynastic patronage.

17. Catherine Batt, for example, argues that Clemence uses courtly language to characterize Maxentius, the pagan emperor who persecutes Catherine, and thus to symbolize the danger of espousing *cupiditas* rather than *caritas*. Batt sees Clemence's project as a transformation of worldly courtliness into spiritual devotion—a project that nevertheless uses courtly language to great effect in achieving this transformation. See Catherine Batt, "Clemence of Barking's Transformations of *Courtoisie* in *La Vie de Sainte Catherine d'Alexandrie*," *New Comparison: A Journal of Comparative and General Literary Studies* 12 (1996): 102–23.

18. See Jocelyn Wogan-Browne, "'Clerc U Lai, Muïne U Dame': Women and Anglo-Norman Hagiography in the Twelfth and Thirteenth Centuries," in *Women and Literature in Britain, 1150–1500*, ed. Carol M. Meale (Cambridge: Cambridge University Press, 1993), 67 [61–79].

19. Jacques Le Goff describes the increasing emphasis on individual and subjective spirituality, beginning in the twelfth century and culminating with Lateran IV in the thirteenth century: "Everyone was required to examine his conscience: the soul was thus plumbed to new depths, and introspective practices previously limited to clerics, especially monks, were now extended to laymen. This decision was the culmination of a long evolution; it sanctioned a need." See Jacques Le Goff, *The Invention of Purgatory*, trans. Arthur Goldhammer (Chicago: University of Chicago Press, 1986), 216.

20. Clemence often inserts active verbs of speaking in place of elided or implied verbs in the Latin source; for example, Clemence translates "Cui Dominus" as "fait il" or "Cui rethor" as "'Seignurs,' fait ele." *Seinte Katerine*, 187, *La vie*, l. 1853; *Seinte Katerine*, 45, *La vie*, l. 1139.

21. See Victor Bers, *Speech in Speech: Studies in Incorporated Oratio Recta in Attic Drama and Oratory* (London: Rowman and Littlefield Publishers, 1997).

22. Henrik Specht, "'Ethopoeia' or Impersonation: A Neglected Species of Medieval Characterization," *Chaucer Review* 21, no. 1 (1986): 1–15.

23. Ibid., 1.

24. "Illa adhuc audaciora et maiorum, ut Cicero existimat, laterum, fictiones personarum, quae prosopopoiiai dicuntur: mire namque cum variant orationem tum excitant…His et adversariorum cogitationes velut secum loquentium protrahimus (qui tamen ita demum a fide non abhorrent si ea locutos finxerimus quae cogitasse eos non sit absurdum), et nostros cum aliis sermones et aliorum inter se credibiliter introducimus, et suadendo, obiurgando, querendo, laudando, miserando personas idoneas damus…Quin deducere deos in hoc genere dicendi et inferos excitare concessum est. Vrbes etiam populique vocem accipiunt. Ac sunt quidam qui has demum prosopopoiias dicant in quibus et corpora et verba fingimus: sermones hominum adsimulatos dicere dialogous malunt, quod

Latinorum quidam dixerunt sermocinationem." Quintilian, *Institutio Oratia*, trans. and ed. H. E. Butler, Loeb Classical Library (Cambridge, MA: Harvard University Press, 1980), 9.11, ll. 29–32.

25. Carruthers, *Book of Memory*, 116.

26. Peter Brown describes the martyrs as "the *membra Christi* par excellence...The martyr himself, and later the holy man, is often shown in the pose of the Crucified. This identified him not only with the sufferings of Christ, but also with the unmoved constancy of his election and the certainty of his triumph." See Peter Brown, *The Cult of the Saints: Its Rise and Function in Latin Christianity* (Chicago: University of Chicago Press, 1981), 94.

27. *Seinte Katerine*, 187.

28. For description of devotional practice, see Swanson, *Religion and Devotion*, 156, and Richard Kieckhefer, *Unquiet Souls: Fourteenth-Century Saints and Their Religious Milieu* (Chicago: University of Chicago Press, 1984), 151.

29. Wogan-Browne, *Saints' Lives and Women's Literary Culture*, 225.

30. Reames contends that "the eloquent and theologically learned speeches with which [Catherine] converts the philosophers...might be illustrated at length in retellings for clerics but were usually minimized for lay audiences—especially when it was feared that such audiences might try to imitate her, violating the rules against public preaching by women or laymen. Some retellings for the laity skip most of the dialogue and concentrate on the most entertaining aspects of the story." See Sherry L. Reames, ed., *Middle English Legends of Women Saints*, TEAMS Middle English Text Series (Kalamazoo: Western Michigan University's Medieval Institute Publications, 2003), 170.

31. I turn again to Wogan-Browne for a description of the intended audience of Anglo-Norman hagiography: "Where there is direct evidence for women's association with hagiography's initial production contexts and audiences it tends to be in noble or gentry circles (whether lay or in the largely aristocratic and gentry religious houses characteristic of the period)...contemporary indications of their uses and audiences suggest an interest in them which extended beyond these initial contexts. Some saints' lives occur in clerically produced compilations for lay patrons; others, while in the company of clerical texts, must have been designated for use with lay audiences...Women would have heard and sometimes read saints' lives in religious communities, but would also have heard them as part of the mixed audiences of secular households." See Wogan-Browne, "Clerc U Lai, Muïne U Dame," 62. Critics agree that though Clemence's audience was likely to be female (see D. H. Green, *Women Readers in the Middle Ages* [Cambridge: Cambridge University Press, 2007]), it was less uniform in the social situation of those women, who might hail from a variety of social backgrounds and contexts.

32. For further discussion of textual structures meant to evoke specific reading, meditative, and spiritual praxes, see Ella Johnson's writing on Gertrud of Helfta's *Exercitia spiritualia*, chapter 7 in this volume.

33. Compare God's words from the book of Matthew: "Tunc venit Iesus a
Galilaea in Iordanen ad Iohannem ut baptizaretur ab eo Iohannes autem
prohibebat eum dicens ego a te debeo baptizari et tu venis ad me respon-
dens autem Iesus dixit ei sine modo sic enim decet nos implere omnem
iustitiam tunc dimisit eum baptizatus autem confestim ascendit de aqua et
ecce aperti sunt ei caeli et vidit Spiritum Dei descendentem sicut colum-
bam venientem super se et ecce vox de caelis dicens hic est Filius meus
dilectus in quo mihi conplacui." (Vulg., Matt. 3:13–17; Then Jesus came
from Galilee to the Jordan to John, so that he might be baptized by him.
But John forbade him, saying, "I ought to be baptized by you, and you
come to me?" And Jesus answering said to him, "permit it to be so now;
we ought to do so to fulfill all righteousness." Then he permitted him.
And Jesus, when he was baptized, then ascended out of the water: and,
behold, the heavens were opened to him, and he saw the Spirit of God
descending like a dove, and lighting over him, and behold, a voice from
heaven, saying, "This is my beloved Son, in whom I am well pleased.")

34. *Seinte Katerine*, 203.

35. The phrasing of the Latin source here evokes the Father's more platonic
words in Matthew 3:13–17 (see note 33).

36. For discussion of Barking abbey and its intellectual milieu, see Jocelyn
Wogan-Browne's *Saints' Lives and Women's Literary Culture* and Carol
Meale's *Women and Literature in Britain*.

37. Such subtle authorial intervention in the memorial identities of "holy
women" is explored more fully in Margaret Cotter-Lynch's chapter on Notker's "In Natale Sanctarum Feminarum," chapter 2 in this
collection.

38. Both Batt and Duncan Robertson claim that Clemence's choice of the
vernacular is a direct engagement with courtly literature and the *chanson de geste* tradition. Robertson, for example, claims that the *Life* "creatively translates the Latin militarism into the literary language of the
chanson de geste." See Robertson, "Writing in the Textual Community,"
23. Although I do not dispute the presence of courtly tropes and language
in the *Life*, I disagree with the critical stance that the primary purpose of
the *Life* is a reinterpretation of the courtly register into the Christian.

39. See Sarah Salih, "Introduction: Saints, Cults, and *Lives* in Late Medieval
England," in *A Companion to Middle English Hagiography*, ed. Sarah Salih
(Cambridge: Boydell and Brewer, 2006), 18 [1–23].

40. Kieckhefer, *Unquiet Souls*, 14.

41. Francois Recanati, *Oratio Obliqua, Oratio Recta: An Essay on
Metarepresentation* (Cambridge, MA: MIT Press, 2000), 173.

42. Sarah Salih reminds us that due to the highly imitative nature of hagiography, "the genre is both stereotyped and almost infinitely variable...At
the level of generic convention, this means that sanctity is frequently
established by demonstrating the likeness between the individual life and
the lives of other saints or of Christ. Hagiography is full of conventional
motifs, which can be openly transferred from one saint to another." Salih,

"Introduction," 14. Clemence's narrative persona and characterization of Catherine, which includes so much original and additional commentary, challenges this traditional view.

43. In making this argument, I want to claim a more active role for Clemence and her writing than that of social commentary, powerful as such narratives can be; such arguments are typified by Maud Burnett McInerney's claim that "Clemence's retelling of the Vulgate...works to engage women's sympathies in complex ways by mounting a direct assault on those contemporary social and political constructions that worked to silence women, from the traditionally exclusionary and masculine educational system to the ideals of courtly love." See McInerney, *Eloquent Virgins*, 181. Though I do not deny that such contemporary social critique is undoubtedly part of Clemence's milieu of textual production, such arguments have the unfortunate tendency to unconsciously perpetuate the very exclusion they argue against by limiting women's writing to the spheres of social or domestic—earthly—concerns rather than those of the spiritual, doctrinal, or theological.

44. For further discussion of readers' engagement with texts produced in a female religious context, see Ella Johnson's study of Gertrude of Helfta's *Exercitia spiritualia*, chapter 7 in this collection.

45. Bers, *Speech in Speech*, 226.

46. In a critical move similar to that of Wogan-Browne, D. H. Green proposes an audience for Clemence's hagiography as determined more by class and rank than enclosure (or lack thereof): "Even after the Conquest [Barking] abbey can boast the largest number of books of Latin learning in any women's community...The author of the *Vie d'Édouard* is anonymous, but refers to herself as a nun of Barking who translated the work from Latin, possibly, it has been suggested, for aristocratic ladies interested in French books. Another work, a life of Catherine, has to be added, whose author names herself as Clemence, a nun of Barking, and with an audience presumably of noblewomen with the same interest in the vernacular as those for the *Vie d'Édouard*." See Green, *Women Readers*, 138.

47. The possibility of choice and individual variation within one's personal devotions, though not often emphasized, is not unheard-of within medieval devotional life; as Robert Clark notes, "Devotional programs required complex negotiations from their subjects through which the latter ultimately fashioned their conduct, not just before God but in the world." See Clark, "Constructing the Female Subject," 162.

48. Jones speculates that "the anonymity of the lives of the saints is due to a feeling that a religious should not appear to seek anything but the glory of God, and that it is his duty to labor without thought of himself, effacing himself as far as possible just as did the composers of the thousands of Gregorian Chant Hymns and Sequences." See Paul J. Jones, *Prologue and Epilogue in Old French Lives of Saints Before 1400* (Philadelphia: University of Pennsylvania Press, 1933), 62.

49. Laurie Postlewate, "Vernacular Hagiography and Lay Piety: Two Old French Adaptations of the Life of Saint Margaret of Antioch," in *Saints: Studies in Hagiography,* ed. Sandro Sticca (Binghamton, NY: Medieval and Renaissance Texts and Studies, 1996), 128 [115–130].

50. Karl D. Uitti, *Story, Myth, and Celebration in Old French Narrative Poetry, 1050–1200* (Princeton, NJ: Princeton University Press, 1973), 26.

51. Uitti's argument hinges on the assumption of a shared linguistic identity as the foundation for common literary experience, much as Mary Carruthers argues that quotation works in the medieval commentary tradition: "Adaptive freedom is enabled by complete familiarity with the text, the shared memory of it on the part of both audience and author, and hence a delight both in recognizing the familiar words and the skill with which they have been adapted to a new context." Ibid., 91 and Carruthers, *Book of Memory,* 116.

52. Catherine Sanok, *Her Life Historical: Exemplarity and Female Saints' Lives in Late Medieval England* (Philadelphia: University of Pennsylvania Press, 2007), 21.

53. Wogan-Browne, *Saints' Lives and Women's Literary Culture,* 241.

CHAPTER 6

MEMORY, IDENTITY, AND WOMEN'S
REPRESENTATION IN THE PORTUGUESE
RECEPTION OF *VITAE PATRUM*:
WINNING A NAME

Ana Maria Machado

This chapter focuses on the Portuguese reception of the *Vitae patrum* in order to analyze the long path women had to travel to acquire the dignity of a name, which happened mainly when they were repentant sinners. In their role as a potential or active source of temptation, women would generally be relegated to a secondary role; as such, it would make sense that they had no name. In contrast, when the narrative relates a woman's faults and subsequent conversion and exemplarity, her anonymity is replaced by a name, which is a sign of recognition, as it could be memorized, quoted, or imitated.[1] In a text composed by men, translated by men, and largely concerned with recounting the lives of men, the representation of women obviously echoes male perspectives. This makes the representation of women all the more striking when the text expresses wonder and respect toward those who are admitted to the utmost difficulties of desert life or, more rarely, when monks are subjected to female criticism.

Although the Portuguese reception of the *Vitae patrum* comes nearly ten centuries after the original texts, both Portuguese translations and Latin copies in Portuguese medieval libraries still largely echo the original relationship between genders as well as images of womanliness and female saintliness. However, the text selection and a few apparently intentional omissions in the translation clarify the memory that is being re-created.[2]

After a brief presentation of the desert fathers' literature, I will analyze its reception in Portuguese medieval libraries. Then, by selecting the
most representative texts that in one way or another implicate women,
I will show how laywomen in general and religious women in particular were regarded and whether they correspond to what was traditionally expected of them or if one can find some signs of stereotypes being
rejected. My point is that the radical representation of woman as evil,
potential tempter, and feared object echoes in the hermit's behavior and,
as with prejudice in general, this misogyny also resists the other patterns
inspired in Jesus's inclusive attitude toward women. Nevertheless, the
memory of the repentant sinner as represented in the canonical Gospels
was determinant in the rebuilding of a new gender identity.

In these *corpora*, there are only two types of female saints—the anchoress, who is visited by others who want to learn from her, and the repentant sinner. I will analyze both, but in order to understand why penitent
saints are so famous and venerated, I will first indicate which identity was
linked to them and find out whether this discourse is homogeneous or
if one can find occasional ruptures that, minor though they may be, are
not negligible. The near perfection attained by the anchoress category
appears to be foreign to Portuguese reception. Repentant sinners, on
the contrary, appear to arise slowly from the condemnation they were
exposed to and turned out to be the main attraction of this literature.
Their dramatic transformation and the difficulties and suffering in their
lives inspire a more tolerant Christianity and help to educate the audience
in a more hopeful way.

Even if the dominant image of women in the *Vitae patrum* tends to
emphasize their pernicious nature, as the *Ecclesiasticus* tradition so frequently quoted, the Gospel image of the woman-sinner, whose faith
ensured Jesus's forgiveness, is a major reference in the reimagined representation of the new saint, the repentant sinner. The surprising result
of this composition is the opposite of the stereotype of the evil woman
whom the desert fathers feared so badly. The saints' lives arrive at a point
where an identified penitent woman, humbly regretting her previous
lust, exceeds in sanctity the monks' masculine presumption of perfection
or even the virtues they achieve after a long penitence.

The study of these religious life writings demonstrates very clearly
what Mary Carruthers calls the "memorial" feature of medieval culture,
as one can identify not only a *continuum* of quotations and situations,
common to the public's *thesaurus*, but also a very acute sense of creativity
and imagination.[3] This literature shows a very keen attention to the sayings of the fathers and to the stories they told in order to illustrate their
advice.

The *Vitae patrum*'s own logic rests on memory. It supposes hermits' words are memorized, remembered, and imitated. We should therefore not be surprised by the repetition of the same narrative frames, nor the adapted transference of features of a masculine character to a feminine one. The use of a similar discourse on another character generated a new identity, and it potentiates a new kind of hero. Yet it is not enough to make the expression Desert Mothers as impressive as Desert Fathers.

The spoken word prevails in these *corpora*. Monks or laymen from other places travel kilometers hoping to hear some lesson one can say by heart. So the apothegms, better than any other form, capture the monks' sentences and narratives, composing and creating a long list of brief texts attributed to individual monks (sometimes the same sentence or episode is linked with more than one hermit) or simply assigned to an anonymous one. The possibility of stimulating an ethical response from the authors and the quest for exemplarity from the readers are the main concern of this literature.[4]

In composing texts about religious women, authors build their own space within a tradition that is mostly masculine. These authors invent a new gender expression—feminine—in dialogue with a preexisting memorial arts tradition. The textual representation of feminine identity develops inside an implicit confrontation—by imitation or contrast—with a previous *corpus*. Challenging the attention now focused on women whose appearance or even personality can be confused with men's and even surpass theirs, the texts give these religious women a relevance never previously achieved.

Before going any further, we must understand the context in which *Vitae patrum* came to life. The fourth-century Desert Fathers' movement presented a new ideal of sanctity that was to have great longevity. Isolated from the active world, the new *vir dei* followed the model of the first apostles' lives, made of sharing, charity, and abnegation,[5] and elected the desert as the privileged space, following the memory of two charismatic biblical models: Elijah, the prophet, and Saint John the Baptist, Elijah's New Testament successor. Their journey through the desert inspired emulation, as is shown when they are quoted or recalled in desert literature.[6] Furthermore, the exodus to solitude and the denial of material values also seem to be a reaction against village paganism, a kind of disillusion with the way the post-Constantine clergy were progressing and with a general decrease in religious devotion.[7] However, even though there is no monogenesis, it is hard to distinguish what belongs to the first fathers' motivation from the intentions imputed by the authors that preserved them from sinking into oblivion.[8]

The desert spirituality was oral in its essence,[9] as the label "sayings" in some of its literature still reflects. Memory had an important role in its transmission and in the formation of moral character. In this sense, desert literature is an excellent example of what Mary Carruthers emphasizes as the ethical nature of memory.[10] As Jean-Claude Guy recalls, in the beginning, memorized words were used in practical life with no need to be written; even when the monks began to record them, they had no sense of authorial consciousness: the earlier monks responsible for these compilations regarded themselves as collectors.[11] Thus, desert literature was the result of a pedagogical and spiritual need to communicate a new way of life, and its written record helped others to memorize it, similar to the dissemination of sermons and other materials.[12] As the apothegms were prior to the monastic doctrine, they reflect the way each of the hermits behaved and the way this was retold. The only models they had were the vague experiences of Elijah, Saint John the Baptist, and Jesus in the desert. It was up to them to fill those guidelines with concrete deeds and sayings, according the guidance of scripture with each individual's condition. Within this context, compilations of apothegms supplied the lack of behavior guides, but the monks could not avoid the texts' inherent internal contradictions.

The *mouvance* of the fathers' sayings is registered within the texts.[13] Apothegms were released quite soon from the specific context where they had been uttered to be applied to new circumstances; this way they became permanently free to whomever wanted to use them. This is apparent when the monks, questioned, would refer to sayings previously used by other hermits in analogous situations. This assured a continuum that would eventually lead to hagiography and is a demonstration of what Cheryl Glenn calls text-based literacy.[14]

The earlier collections are likely to be from the fifth century. As Jean-Claude Guy explains, they were not organized at first, as one can see from the Greek collections' prologues, which were intended to make the reading clearer. The different principles of order—alphabetical or systematic—depended on the objectives pursued. The compilations were arranged by author if the hermits were still known so that memorization would be easier and more emotional because the audience would be eager to hear the advice of a certain monk; in contrast, if the name had already been forgotten, the criteria would be the spiritual pedagogy.[15] Composed in Greek by anonymous authors, these texts were soon translated into Latin in order to be read in the West. The texts currently called *Vitae patrum* include not only apothegms that were disparate in nature and dimension[16] but also *vitae* of singular saints.

These *Vitae patrum* were very quickly internationalized through copies and translations, as we can see from the Portuguese medieval monastic libraries. The transmission of this literature seems to be particularly

linked to two activities. The people responsible for the first one are Saint
Martin (b. 518–25, d. ca. 579) and Pascasius of Dume. Saint Martin, the
Suevi's apostle and one of the fathers of the Iberian Church, may have
been influenced by Eastern spirituality during his trip to the Holy Land,
from where he probably brought Greek copies of the two collections
whose translation he was later associated with. As he wanted to teach
these anchorites' way of life to the monks of rural Galicia, he translated
the anchorites' lives into a language the monks understood—a little collection of sayings, *Sententiae patrum Aegyptorum*, not yet under a coherent
doctrinal order. The same saint, also bishop of Braga, asked the monk
Pascasius to translate the biggest codex, known as *Apophtegmata patrum.*[17]
Both titles made their way into Portuguese libraries: in a complete copy
that belonged to the Augustinian Holy Cross Monastery (in Coimbra),
now in the Public and Municipal Library of Porto, MS 753 (fifteenth
century); and in a selection of those apothegms, now in the National
Library of Lisbon, MS Alc. CCLXXXIII/BNL 454, and previously in
the Cistercian Alcobaça Monastery.

Vitae patrum was the global name of the other work that arrived at
medieval Portuguese libraries, this time through the hagiographic compilation gathered by the Hispanic Valerio of Bierzo (b. 623–625, d. 695) a
century later. This ascetic extended the Eastern monastic tradition, organizing in the Hispanic domain an important hagiographic compilation in
which he assembled some lives of Egyptian monks—the *Historia monachorum*, translated by Rufinus (345–411)—and the *Apophthegmata patrum*, in
Pelagius and John's translation (sixth century), along with his own works.
The result is a collection that kept growing as it opened up to the heirs
of Eastern monasticism.[18] Such a compilation confirms the permanent
attraction of the desert's ascetic model. In addition, the long manuscript
tradition of this hagiographic synthesis is symptomatic of the length of
the spiritual paradigm in the late Middle Ages.[19]

For this Valerian collection, there are two important hagiological collections from the Cistercian monastery of Alcobaça—Lisbon, MS XV/
BNL 367, written in twelfth-century French calligraphy, and Lisbon,
MS CCLXXXIII/BNL 454, written in late twelfth-century/early thirteenth-century calligraphy—that, according to M. Díaz y Díaz, probably
attest to copies of different manuscripts.[20] MS 367 is focused on the first
texts in an order quite close to the more complete codex, whereas MS
454, notwithstanding the interpolations, matches the final section of an
earlier codex.

Finally, the manuscript of Brasilia—Brasilia University's Central
Library, MS from UdB Central, Secção de Obras Raras, Cofre (sem
cota),[21] copied between 1376 and 1425—is an important Portuguese

translation manuscript and another extension of the Valerian collection with a content very similar to MS 454.[22]

These are the codices I will be referring to, using modern editions or, in the case of Latin MSS 367 and 454, quoting them from the *Patrologia latina (PL)*, as the main differences are related to the instability of medieval Latin, not the content or the meaning of the texts. Thus all the references will be made to the texts favored by Portuguese medieval reception.

After this global presentation of the *corpora*, I shall focus on the texts in which women were subject to any kind of attention in order to question how their identities are represented and how relevant gender issues may be. The number of women mentioned in the *Vitae patrum*'s medieval Portuguese reception is quite small, especially in terms of Desert Mothers. There is no Syncletica or Theodora, although Sara does survive, and one can still find some anchoresses who are discovered by male hermits. Nevertheless, with those omissions, what prevails is the idea of woman as evil, a potential tempter, and thus as an object to be feared or as a repentant sinner.

In early Christianity, women were gradually removed and feared, and interdicts were invented in order to face heterodox movements. Heresies such as Gnosticism tend to disdain the body, sex, and femininity. In its effort to explain evil, Gnosticism postulates a transcendent God and a minor and ignorant divinity, a demiurge who created the flawed material world. Yet matter and body conserve a divine spark, and from a spiritual point of view, the union of masculine and feminine bodies was considered a way to surmount bodily division and acquire spiritual knowledge. In Anselmo Borges's words, along with deep knowledge, Gnosis also means despising the body and seeking purification of the soul in the search for the spirit. And the feminine, too, was regarded rather negatively, so the image of the woman tends to be virilized for the sake of the primordial androgynous.[23]

These ideas appear to be quite close to what one finds in the *Vitae patrum*, where Gnostic influence is also very clear. Evagrius Ponticus (345–399) presented his *The Praktikos* as a result of his desert experience and his intent to preach the Gnostic lesson.[24] This context cannot be forgotten when reading the Desert Fathers' sayings and hagiographies, and it seems to be one of the factors that caused images of women to deviate from scriptural precedent.

After this introduction, we can read Latin and Portuguese apothegms and hagiographies in order to seek signs of reshaping women from their traditional religious image. In addition, we can examine the meaning of those attempts within the context of the *Vitae patrum*'s Portuguese inheritance. As far as praised religious women are concerned, only a few texts were preserved in Portuguese medieval libraries. Reading them along with hagiographies of female saints, also written by male authors, is very useful for studying women's identity construction. In various ways, the desert literature's reception, mainly the texts' selection, reveals a prevalent tendency to exclude a positive idea of women. However, this segregation sometimes has rather bizarre nuances, and it happens to point out more male frailties than one might expect at first.

In its original language, the generative *Life of Anthony*[25] has no feminine counterpart except for Synkletike, who also chose an ascetic lifestyle in the fourth or fifth century and whose life, written by a Pseudo-Athanasius, has a number of similarities with this source.[26]

Synkletike's *Life* demonstrates the process of adaptation from one hagiography to another and the transference of a male's traits and life experiences to a feminine character. Textual memory has a vital role in the emergence of the identity of the female saint. Further, as Annabelle Parker notes, the communities being built in the desert were considered an affair of men, despite the existence of feminine communities. Therefore, and as expected, there is a big *décalage* between men and women in the ascetic movement. Only three women have their names and sayings recorded in the Greek tradition of the *Vitae patrum*: Synkletike, Sara, and Theodora; Sara is the only one whose experience can be read in Portuguese manuscripts. The idea of women teaching appears to have been obliterated from late medieval memory and excluded from the female ideal of sainthood as recorded in Portugal.[27] In late antiquity, men and women shared the same spiritual ideal of sanctity, even though its demands challenged women and men differently.[28] In the *corpora* under analysis, women had to accomplish this ideal by adopting a masculine look, whereas men were not expected to deny either sex or name. The androgynous appearance and the choice of a masculine name are a sort of a visa to the land of saints. I would argue that in some cases there is a conflation between what Barbara Newman calls the "virile woman" paradigm,[29] which is visible in the names such saints would choose and in the claim of having a man's soul, and the androgynous look, which creates doubt about their gender identity. As previously stated, the emergence of a new identity is accompanied by an intense dialogue between the conflicting and the hybrid, through the texts that inhabited the authors' memories.

Despite its different forms, male dominion is obvious, and monks rarely recognize the supremacy of ascetic and teaching women. Needless to say, the gender of medieval authors influenced the ways they represented others; both male and female characters are gendered in very specific ways, as one can see in Sara's sayings. The presumption of the incapacity of women is well expressed in the monks' purported intention to humiliate a known *amma* to prevent her from feeling proud: "Cave ne extollatur mens tua, et dicas: Ecce solitarii ad me mulierem accedunt" (Take care that your soul be not puffed up, and that you don't say, "Look, some hermits have come to consult me, a woman!").[30] By doing so, they are somehow establishing a parallel between the superior *status* of Sara—first an anchoress, then an *amma*—and the possibility (as happens with many hermits) of committing the sin of pride, which, as discussed later, is never assigned to women, probably because men considered anchoresses to be much further behind on the road to perfection. The idea that, in Catherine M. Mooney's words, "women are embodied physicality in a way that men, more often identified with mind and spirit, are not"[31] also seems to be underlying these monks' remarks. In fact, they expect women to commit fleshly sins, not intellectual ones such as pride, because usually women do not attain that stage, exclusive to men. Through this apothegm, monks regard themselves in a mirror. Looking at Sara through supposedly superior male experiences, they think she needs their advice, but at the same time they are not able to admit that she would not fall into that particular sin, as hermits often did.

Although Sara's speech—"Sexu quidem mulier sum, at non animo" (I am a woman in sex, but not in spirit.)[32]—conveys the expectation of the female's bodily inferiority[33] and the male's supremacy of the soul, the conflation of both in the same *amma* also presupposes the interpreter's recognition of her ability to reach the same goal as men, leading to an equality of merit. This formulation is striking when compared with modern discussions challenging the essentialist notions of gender difference. In a very naive way, the *amma*'s answer may well demonstrate how cultural notions determined the main gender choice: needing to be accepted, this *amma* presents herself as a metaphorical hybrid.[34]

The masculine bodily appearance of an anonymous anchoress, whose identity is discovered only after death, is an extreme demonstration of humility, quite distant from the proud presentation of Sara. Such an example is reduced to an absolutely abstract edifying example. Her only recognition begins after death. Before that, she had no life, for no one knew her true identity. She had no name, no voice, and no actions as a woman. And yet the discovery of such bodies and their burial by the monks turned out to be an important motif in hagiographic compositions, and at times it provided an opportunity to reshape gender relations by facing the problem of the ascetic woman/female supremacy and the way such anchoresses accepted the role of masculinity. Previously, when the abbots Bessarion and Dulas first saw what they perceived to be a silent working brother, they could not have imagined that the androgynous figure was in reality a woman. They only realize it when they approach him hoping to hear his lesson. He is dead. As they are lifting him up, they discover her true identity. Then they are free to revere her and to portray her as a positive role model, for since she is dead, she no longer can tempt them or pose a threat to them.

Although these examples are written by male authors, under a masculine standard, the subconscious admission of the superiority of the woman is relevant within a context of prevailing misogyny. Bessarion states it clearly when he expresses his admiration and must face his own negligence in comparison to women's battles: "Et admiratus est senex, dicens: Ecce quomodo et mulieres colluctantur adversus diabolum in eremo, et nos in civitatibus dehonestamur" (And the old man marvelled, saying, "Behold how women struggle against the devil in the desert, and we in the cities live in dishonour").[35]

These cases very clearly demonstrate how female identity is constructed in permanent conflict with a memory of texts haunted by male heroes. The mental image of the monk conveyed by these associations makes it possible to create a new expression of the female gender, all the more striking because it was developed by its most violent critics—men.

Yet male recognition of edifying images of religious women is not at all common. This is why Katrien Heene argues that "the hagiographers' attitude towards women and femininity is far from ambiguous."[36] The most common type represented in these texts is the feared woman. This feeling stems from the perceived negative features of womanliness, such as the source of lust. Indeed, as I will demonstrate, even devout women and female relatives who wanted to meet a hermit could inspire this perception of danger. Finally, I will analyze a specific kind of saint—the repentant sinner—who once inspired rejection but, after conquering evil, often exceeds even men in sanctity. Although the label of woman tempter covers a variety of paradigms, the percentage of female penitents who really tempt men—the last and most relevant type in terms of the reshaping of an identity—is very low.

If one tries to organize hagiographic representations of women into categories, the most impressive is the simple image or thought of a woman and the fear it provokes. Even as a mental image, women are potentially destabilizing, so it is better to avoid thinking about them, as one can deduce from the downfalls that follow those imaginings. In fact, most of the women tempting the monks are not real but rather thoughts, pictures, or recollections of something they had previously seen or experienced.[37] As we can read in an apothegm, when a certain brother is asked by the hermit if he often talks with women, he answers no, but he confesses the cause of his suffering: "Veteres et novi pictores sunt cogitationes meae, et

commemorationes quaedam, inquietantes me ex similitudine mulierum"
(My temptations come from paintings old and new, memories of mine
which trouble me through pictures of women).[38] Unexpectedly, with a
rather surprisingly practical spirit, the hermit counsels him not to bother
with those remembered images but to look into real life; it is the living he
should be fleeing from, not the dead. The images that haunt and disturb
his mind belong to his past experiences and doubts and, possibly, to what
his own imagination could generate.

Women's presence in the dreams of monks is also pernicious, and, as
Dioscorus says, they simply withdraw from the sacred Mysterious those
"quae accidere per somnia hominibus solent, ver per phantasias mulierum
apparentium" (who as pondered on the image of a woman during the
night...in case any of you has had a dream while entertaining such an
image).[39] According to the monk, condemnation is deserved because
imaginings are a symptom of an evil disposition. This *Life* is highly concerned with the sexual morals of monks, since in the narrative development in Latin versions[40] evil and women are closely related. However,
in the Portuguese translation, there is no apparent allusion to the opposite sex. Those excluded from the Eucharist are still the monks but only
those who have sinned by "sonhos ou per maaos cuydares" (dreams or
bad thoughts).[41] In this rather vague and broad reference, the fault is not
detailed further, and it is no longer focused on women's images. This neu-
tralization is quite common in late medieval vernacular translations, but
this tendency to generalize the sinners has no further consequences, nor
does it release women from the traditional anathema. In the Portuguese
translation, women disappear from monks' dreams, and for once women's
images are not said to lead monks into sin. In such a heavily traditional
context, this is a very nice omission.

From the apprehension shown toward women's images, just described,
to the discussion of hypothetically facing real women, which is the next
step in this analysis, monks are counseled to chain the passion because it
never dies. That is what Abraham taught a monk whom he thought had
destroyed lust and other sins. He acknowledged that if, upon entering
his cell, he saw a woman on his mat, he would fight the temptation to
touch her, which means the passion was alive but imprisoned. The Latin
saying continues with the sins of greed and vanity.[42] Still, in the medieval Portuguese milieu, this apothegm, which is only found in Pascasius's
collection, makes no reference to the woman or to the sin of the flesh,
possibly because of his often notoriously shamefaced spirit.[43] What seems
to be most sordid, dangerous, and licentious is suppressed, as if it would
make him blush or as if words have a performative power and make man
sin. Thus, silence appears to be the better way to avoid those fears.

Fleeing from the woman is such a commonplace in desert literature that the same apothegm is almost verbatim recollected in different
contexts, proving that these commonplaces were deeply embedded in
cultural memory. In writings on religious life, both authors and readers generally favor universal events rather than particular ones, so the
same episode is applied to different contexts, like a thesaurus where one
could get the elements that fit in new works. This is one reason for some
anonymous presences, such as the monks in the *Life of Arsenius*. In the
Latin collection, we find: "Dicebat aliquando Abraham discipulus abbatis
Sisois ad eum: Pater, senuisti, eamus parum juxta mundum. Dicit ei abbas
Sisois: Ubi non est mulier, ibi eamus. Dicit ei discipulus ejus: Eu ubi est
locus non habens mulierem, nisi forte in solitudine? Dicit ei senex: Ergo
in solitudinem me tolle." (Once Abraham, the disciple of Sisois, said to
him, "Abba, you are now old. Let us go into the world for a short time."
Sisois said to him: "Yes, provided that we go where there are no women."
The disciple said, "Where is there a place that is without women except
the desert?" Sisois said, "Then let me stay in the desert.")[44] The recipe for
evading lust is to run away from women, and the best place to accomplish
this is the desert, a place intended to belong exclusively to men.

In his own version, which was composed with *Vita patrum* narratives,
Jacob of Voragine's *Legenda aurea* (also present in Portuguese libraries)
emphasizes the pernicious nature of women, including only what he
recalls from the previous saying—that is, the essence of those hermits'
speeches but not their names.[45] The women's flight and refuge in the
desert, a place they do not habitually frequent, is central. The presence of
this saying in another context a few centuries later confirms the conflu-
ence of different female identities: the traditional, echoed in this life; and
the textual representation of a new image slowly being created by male
authors, which, although incapable of completely subverting the prevailing stereotype, offers at least a fresh perspective on gender.

Meanwhile, women are also mentioned along with worldly people,
which is less compromising only because women are for once not alone;
little boys, also potential sexual temptations, join them: "Non des et
accipias cum sæcularibus hominibus; et non habeas notitiam cum muliere,
nec habeas fiduciam diu cum puero" (Do not give or receive anything
from worldly people. Take no notice of women. Do not remain long in
the company of a boy).[46]

The women monks fear are often abstract references, a generalized and
gendered category, and in that, they are absolutely eliminated from the
desert environment. Nevertheless, as one abbess interprets a monk's decision to turn off the road when he saw her, men prove their weakness and
lack of confidence when they cannot resist the sight of a woman. Very

noticeably, she assumes her woman-as-threat condition and blames him: "Tu si perfectus monachus esses, non respiceres nos sic, ut agnosceres quia feminae eramus" (If you had been a true monk, you would not have looked to see that we are women).[47]

Women were feared because of a stereotypical image that interfered in monks' real life or in their imaginary world. If one now looks for concrete representations of feared women, it is possible to find a few who, although nameless because exemplarity lies with the hermit, nonetheless have an important social status. They are respectable women who desperately want to meet the saints in order to venerate and learn from them, but they hear nothing but refusals from the ascetics, some more brutal than others. In spite of this, sometimes hermits do show some consideration in their own very special way and favor their female visitors with an unforgettable encounter.

John of Lycopolis, for instance, maintained his refusal to meet women, as no male or female visitors had entered his cave for 40 years. On one occasion, the tribune's wife wanted a simple blessing, but John told her husband he would not allow her to visit. When she insisted, the hermit announced to the tribune that he would appear to his wife in a dream. With Saint Paul the apostle as a reference, John imitates his attitude and words for those who have not seen his face in the flesh.[48] To an audience familiar with the biblical text, this means that, like the apostle, John too fights and rejoices with others' faith in Christ, even if he is absent. His statements are remarkably reliable as he continues to rephrase biblical passages, presenting himself as a typological figure of Jesus and Paul, which gives him the authority needed to persuade the tribune's wife. John professes to her the virtues of spirit using Jesus's words to his skeptical audience, showing how useless it is to see him bodily; then, vaguely echoing Paul's words after healing the cripple, he also refuses to be seen as a prophet.[49]

Another example is that of a devout woman, a rich lady from Rome who went to Egypt and, despite Arsenius's refusal to receive visitors, reached the hermit's cell when he was outside. When he arrived, she fell at his feet. Arsenius, angry, told her to look at him, but she did not dare. The saint expressed his indignation by telling her such commonplaces as the desert is not a place for a woman, and although all she wanted was for him to remember her, he replied that that was one thing he would not do. Instead, he said, "Ora Deum ut deleat memoriam tui de corde meo" (I pray God He will blot the memory of you from my heart).[50]

The issue is thus the sensory memory images. The sight of a woman is dangerous; therefore hermits should stay away from them. As the bishop later explains to the lady from Rome when she becomes ill from sorrow: "Nescis quia mulier es, et inimicus per mulieres sanctos viros impugnat?" (Do you not realize that you are a woman, and the enemy uses women to attack holy men?), which does not, however, imply that Arsenius would stop praying for her soul.[51] As Mary Carruthers recalls, according to the medieval neuropsychology of memory, an intellectual activity such as praying, as it deals with abstractions, was considered apart from sensory memory. Thus, one could pray for someone without retaining a memory of them.[52]

These two apothegms show that holy men must not see women, although the opposite is possible without damage; women with faith can have quite a persistent will and, in the name of their faith, will not take no for an answer. This example shows the differing vulnerability of saintly men and devout women. Feminine persistence and combativeness is proportional to men's fear.

The vow to isolate themselves from women can get even more radical when applied to the hermits' own families, as they refuse any contact with the women they are related to by blood. The perceived corrupting influence of women invades even the most chaste of relationships, so there is no doubt about the risks of even the slightest approach.[53] These texts, quite extensive in number, show that when it comes to devout or familiar women, monks admit no exception, and the feminine negative stereotype is quite radically assumed, which creates a hard frontier between genders. One can conclude that holy men cannot tolerate the sight of a woman even if she is their own mother. Such interdictions can also prevent acedia, for seeing relatives could trigger memories of home and the secular world and consequently tempt hermits to leave the desert.

This strong misogyny does not spare even a monk's own mother. In a saying, also included in Jacob of Voragine's *Life of Saint Arsenio*,[54] a brother walking with his elderly mother had to carry her as they crossed a river; in order not to touch her body, he wrapped his hands with his cloak. When she asked for an explanation, his argument was very close to Ecclesiasticus 9:8, a constant presence in these commonplaces: "Corpus mulier ignis est. Et ex eo ipso quo te contingebam, veniebat mihi commemoratio aliarum feminarum in animo" (A woman's body is fire. Simply because I was touching you, the memory of other women might come into my mind).[55] Exercising memory favors the perpetuation of identity stereotypes. As we are acknowledging, although other alternatives may be identified/recognized, the *longue durée* of memory freezes and favors excessive generalizations of the woman's threatened image.

As much as they accuse women of being perverse, perversity seems to lay elsewhere. Not being able to tolerate these women, hermits implicitly recognize how their own evil instincts could be easily awakened. This awareness of vulnerability undercuts their reputation for heroic endurance and self-control and reveals a more human character. From this point of view, the so-called epic narrative of the desert can be rather anti-epic. Instead, monks have to struggle with memories of their previous life in the world and, worst of all, with the threat of the devil, the omnipresent figure that haunts the desert, as a metonymy of the obstacles monks must surmount.

In relation to the tempter's action, its protean masks take advantage of the presumptive power of women to pervert monks.[56] The monk's victory over temptation is the most expected scenario described. In fact, the general rule is that monks do not fall into temptation. In the selection of apothegms under consideration, men—not including the hermits—fall only twice. Women, on the contrary, are actually sinning or sinning and repenting, as we shall see. Even if these women become saints, their different treatment seems to reveal the difficulty male authors have in representing themselves in real lust episodes. Imaginary episodes are the only ones they are allowed to face and that may be represented. All other possibilities are experienced by women, which means that even when they are admired and their supremacy is shown, there is still an enormous discrepancy in the portrayal of men and women.

Besides this gender discrimination, women remain nameless; they are merely devils' masks, abstract concepts haunting hermits' souls but rarely flesh-and-blood women. Women enter the hermits' presence only if they are related to men by blood, devout women who want to venerate them, or real *ammas*. That is, only well-intentioned women interact with ascetic men. Even if monks preach that women do not belong in the desert, as long as the women are good they are allowed to briefly share that place or, in some cases, inhabit it.

If one now adds another class of women who fully earned their legitimate right to live in this space, repentant sinners, this tour will end without meeting an actual bad woman, which is most surprising. With the exception of Abba Patermuthius, of *Historia monachorum*, who had been a thief,[57] and of an episodic adulterous deacon,[58] there are no other male repentant sinners. What's more, there is no man who, having lived a luxurious life, became a hermit thanks to an act of repentance.

Hence, as there are no ex-adulterous men in the desert, it is as if this feature were exclusive to women. In fact, the difference between men and women goes further: women go through penitence seeking salvation, but once their new existence is discovered, their life is over, as if a subsequent life could compromise the sanctity already achieved. Death is a reward, the fastest way to reach heaven, although one wonders why none of them survives. And I do not think that gender conventions can resolve that suspicion. Hypothetically, I could suggest some kind of prejudice based on the fear that they would fall again and become compromised, whereas glorious death was definitely edifying. And of course, once they are dead, these holy women no longer pose a threat to monks and hermits and can be safely venerated.

It is as if the acknowledgment of their own greatness was the only climax male authors could represent for these women. The exemplary female presence in a shared space would signify an excessive rupture from the models memory had preserved. The scarce use of direct speech seems to be another feature of these apothegms, as only a few women have the right to speak: one anchoress, the abbess who almost insults the fleeing monk, and the hermits' devotees and relatives. In Tarsis's *Life*, there is a possible answer for this almost complete silence: their mouths are "dirty" and, as Mary of Egypt would say, no ears could bear their words of depravation. Thinking about the rhetorical use of direct speech, that topos may be associated with the recognition women must have in order to have their voice heard.[59]

There is certainly a very negative image of woman, determined by some Old Testament passages and some Pauline and Augustinian interpretations and then underlined by the polemics on heresies. But the repentant sinners' hagiographies undoubtedly proclaim God's mercy, and as one reads in Pelagia's *Life*, the saints also recall some biblical precepts, such as Matthew 21:31: "Verily I say unto you, that the publicans and the harlots go into the Kingdom of God before you." Jesus could not be clearer about their redemption, and the repentant sinners' lives seem to be a rhetorical method of memory training and of perpetuating the divine message.

Besides this sentence, quoted many times, there is another very impressive Gospel image that seems to be always in the background of these saints' actions: the gestures and attitudes of the woman sinner who went to the Pharisee's house to see Jesus "and stood at His feet behind Him weeping; and began to wash His feet with tears and wiped them with the hair of her head" are constantly reimagined in these lives.[60] Although a hospitality ritual, the novelty of this practice being enacted by a sinner is surpassed by the forgiveness of God because of her love.

In the apothegms considered up until now, potentially or actively lustful women performed a sensual lifestyle opposite to the ascetical one. In order to generate models to be imitated, male authors created a new opportunity for women whose past was a world of lust. The licentious women repented, undertook a long penance, and finally earned a name. Without it they would have no identity, no religious cult, no devotion.

From a narrative perspective, the character development ends in the hagiography. Diverging from the previous apothegms, women now play the leading role. Men are simply the intermediaries and testify to females achieving sanctity. But there is a still more important issue: male characters and male authors assure the women's superiority.

I should say that in the original *Vitae patrum* collections, there are other prostitutes—some without a name such as the one Serapion converts with his prayers[61] and whose plot is very close to that of Thais, and others like Paesia or Mary, niece of Abraham, who reject their saintly lives and fall into prostitution until they are saved and converted by a monk.[62] Yet the Portuguese libraries preserved only two other apothegms of this type.

In the first one, the Egyptian harlot is the sister of a very humble monk whose older brothers order him to go to her and to keep her away from lust. The harlot is a woman who has lost many souls and presents herself with her head uncovered, which, as the Portuguese translation adds, gives men more pleasure. In this apothegm, as in the others quoted but not preserved in Portuguese collections, the woman is quite docile and is immediately persuaded by the monks' arguments, as if she were expecting nothing but an opportunity to change her life. When she sees her brother, she runs to embrace him, but he accuses her and reminds her of the eternal torments. As usual, the repentance is sudden—she begins to tremble, asks if she can still be saved, flings herself onto his feet, and demands to go to the desert. Then, with her head covered, a sign of change and rejection of her former life, and bare feet—as she rejects all temporal things—she crosses the desert, bleeding to death without complaining while suffering her penance. Wondering if she was saved, the monks conclude that she gained some sort of martyrdom and was therefore absolved of all her sins.[63]

The male power is still quite imposing as the monks order the harlot's brother to intervene. He suggests that she be redeemed and guides her. Regardless of her death, this is still the story of a conversion by a monk, although I see it as a sort of a basic framework that gathers a few important features that recur in other lives of repentant sinners, the central one being the woman at the brother's feet, recalling Luke's sinner.[64] It is still a very remote image, but it will gain strength in the other lives. This scene seems to be a sign of identification, a kind of ritual at the beginning of a new life, a frontier between a past of sin and the road to sanctity.

From a narrative perspective, Thaisis's life develops previous apothegms and marks the transition from this genre to the hagiographies. It is a very expressive case since, being a saying, it is included in various collections; it also, however, earned its autonomy as a Life of a saint, appearing side by side with other Lives in hagiographic compilations. In the Portuguese translation, it is called "vida de Tarssis" (Life of Thaisis).[65] In contrast with previous sayings, the paradigm evolves and women begin to gain some power. The narrator depicts Thaisis's beauty and the souls she led astray, differing greatly from the monk's sister apothegm, and men fight and die for her, increasing the damage considerably. The emphasis on evil is greater, which means that the change can be more radical and astonishing. This change starts with the way she replies to Abba Pafuntius when he invites her to sin and asks for a more concealed room. And now it is Thaisis who states the question: "Sse dos homeēs as vergonça aqui te nom veerá nehuū. E sse de Deos has vergonça, nom ha logar hu sse o hom ē ascōda ante os seus olhos" (If you are shy with men, no-one will see you here. And if you are shy with God, there is no place where a man can hide from His eyes). When rewriting a textual model where the monk traditionally led the conversion, a new gender identity is constructed when the woman is assigned a conscious intervention in the conversation, thereby proving her religious knowledge and, further on, her awareness of the damnation of her soul and that of her victims and the consequences it brings. The resemblance to Ephraim's harlot is so obvious that when Jacob of Voragine composes his *Life of Thaisis*, he finishes it with a recollection of that apothegm.[66]

As before, Thaisis's contrition is immediate, and she drops to the *abba*'s feet, asking him for three days to settle her life. She then begins her journey to heaven, showing her former clients the lack of importance of worldly belongings by burning all she had earned with sin. After she has symbolically buried the past, the *abba* takes her to a convent for women, where she is locked in a cell with no connection to the exterior except through a little window through which she can obtain frugal nourishment. As a punishment for her lustful life, her hands, mouth, and eyes are so dirty that she is not even allowed to pray. During the three years she is enclosed, all she asks for is God's mercy.

Such an austere penance receives God's divine reward. When Pafuntius asked *Abba* Anthony to pray in order to know if Thaisis was forgiven, one of Anthony's disciples has a glorious night vision in which three virgins on the way to heaven carry a well-adorned bed. Although the disciples initially think that the dream announces *Abba* Anthony's glorious death, a divine voice tells them that the scene alludes to Thaisis. This unexpected revelation emphasizes the recognition of the penitent's repentance and forgiveness. This knowledge is further crowned with another vision: 15 days later, Pafuntius sees Thaisis's soul ascending to heaven surrounded by angels.

Although Thaisis is recognized by men and there is no moral lesson to infer, her supremacy, the empirical facts, and the divine signs are sufficiently eloquent to express how she exceeds the beliefs of men. Men merely help and bear witness; the rest of the apothegm is focused on Thaisis.

I now enter the hagiographic universe with Saint Pelagia, whose life begins with a fairly detailed portrayal of an actress whose group is filled with young men and equally beautiful maidens. When she passes by the bishops, with no veil covering her head and shoulders and proudly riding her donkey, they turn their faces away as if watching her were a great sin. Nonnus is the only one who cannot stop looking at her. Noticing the difference between his reaction and that of the other bishops, and with guilt in his soul, Nonnus confesses his delight and paradoxically warns them, "Em toda verdade vos digo que esta molher nos ha-de preceder e na presença de Deos e ante a sua catedra ha-de julgar nós e todo nosso sacerdocio e clericia" (whom God shall set in presence of His high and terrible seat, in judgment of ourselves and our episcopate).[67]

The author attributes the words of Jesus to Nonnus, which gives him authority and allows us to easily foresee the end.[68] Besides the narrative sign, one cannot forget how biblical memory applied to new characters helped legitimize behavior patterns. Therefore, if the bishop's prophecy is to be fulfilled, Pelagia will convert herself and earn the announced place. With this expectation, the only thing one cannot know is how she will achieve her glory.

Nonnus reduces the common abyss between the monk and the sinner through his lustful ways; this proximity can also be seen in Saint Mary of Egypt's *Life*, where both Mary and the monk pursue an ascending course. Indeed, Nonnus cries and prays all night because of his negligence, but he also blames the sinful nature of this woman.[69] The next step is an allegorical dream, which also predicts how Saint Pelagia will be: a very dirty black dove flies around until the prayer for the catechumens ends and she turns back after the mass for the faithful. When Nonnus plunges the dove into the holy water, it emerges white as snow, flying upward and vanishing from his sight.

Pelagia's story is retold again and again, through a prophecy and an allegory, which allow us to think its author was surely familiar with the art of increasing the audience's interest while reciting by heart the core of this hagiography. Pelagia's true story and conversion, with all the details it deserves, comes only after these rhethorical strategies. Pelagia was a catechumen who had never gone to church. By the grace of God, she hears Nonnus preaching and she bursts into tears of remorse. In the letter she sends him, she asks to be saved, and as did Thaisis, she proves her knowledge of the Gospel by referring to the way God kept company with sinners, bringing us back to the main episode of Luke's sinner, reimagined in these saints' Lives.

For an answer, Pelagia receives an admission of male frailty never before heard from the hermits: "E porem te rogo...que de todo em todo nom desprezes nem abaixes minha humildade, porque som homem pecador" (But this I surely say to thee, seek not to tempt my weakness, for I am a man that is a sinner).[70] The bishop welcomes her in the presence of others, and they all appreciate her repentance as they had never seen such faith, devotion, and tears. Once again, the scene recalls the Gospel's sinner as Pelagia washes Nonnus's feet with her tears and dries them off with her hair.[71]

On the one hand, there are the penitent admirers, and on the other, Pelagia, who in her confession takes responsibility for the condemnation of many souls and admits to being deceived by the devil, which to some extent mitigates her fault. Her evolution is gradual, and it is not enough to give away all her riches to the poor to reach sanctity and plain recognition; she must go away and undergo reclusion in a distant cell under a disguised identity. Pelagia lays aside her baptismal robe, puts on a tunic and a cloak, and leaves. The way the Portuguese translations and Latin copies tell the story, the assumption is that Nonnus knew where she was so he could comfort holy Romana, who was responsible for her. However, only previous versions told that the tunic and cloak she wore belonged to Nonnus, which explains the completeness of his knowledge.[72]

As I have argued in an article about Pelagia, this detail was too audacious as it mixed both the genders and, above all, the penitent's dress with the one belonging to her converter.[73] Lynda Coon adds that, according to the Old Testament, this violates the purity ritual.[74] Nevertheless, one cannot forget the place masculine disguises have in hagiography. In order to avoid marriage or further temptations, gender change is a sort of visa to women saints, as with Pelagia. She flees to Jerusalem, locks herself in a cell under the name of Pelagius, and time and fasting do the rest: her body changes and she becomes thin and haggard. Meanwhile, Pelagia/Pelagius's holy fame spreads far and wide, and "his" true identity is discovered only after his passing.

The change in name and gender can be read as an allegory for the brutal change sinners must go through in order to attain sanctity. Female supremacy is only achieved through masculine disguise. In contrast, in this context, men do not disguise themselves as women. Even so, one can still identify some declarations of expressed admiration, although these are rather few.

Even if they are not sinners, women must go through the male experience, as did one of *Vitae patrum*'s nuns, whose life is a kind of variant of Pelagia's. Ephrosina's father's decision to marry her off leads her to religious life. Here, the disguise motif becomes more complex. When

Ephrosina goes to the monastery, having previously changed her appearance, she presents herself as an emasculate named Esmarado. When her father complains to the abbot, he tells him to go and talk to the recently arrived monk. As expected, Ephrosina's father does not recognize his daughter because she does not belong to the world. In accordance with canonical outcomes, after 38 years of cell solitude, having lost her beauty to fasting, her true identity is discovered after her death.[75]

Maintaining the disguise motif, now apparent, in the *Life of Saint Mary of Egypt*—which is included in Latin and Portuguese manuscripts along with other desert saints—the androgynous figure impresses the hermit who finds her, and she frightens him because he thinks she is a spirit.[76] In the long version of the *Life*, the only one we have in Portuguese medieval libraries, Zosimas commits the sin of pride by thinking he has achieved perfection. An old man appears to him and tells him that there are struggles greater than his own, so he should leave the monastery and go to another one. After a while, he retreats into the desert hoping to find some father who might instruct his spirit. When he discovers Mary's own penitence and is told of her past, she actually fulfils his goal. The encounter between Zosimas and Mary joins two sinners on the path to their redemption from their former sins, and Mary's supremacy is the answer to Zosimas's expectation. Throughout all this process, the man is God's vehicle to find Mary and to witness her holiness as well as to share her exemplary story.

Mary is viewed through a man's eyes. Zosimas first sees the shadow of a human body and fears it might be a vision of the devil; he makes the sign of the Cross, and when he looks again, he catches a glimpse of a sunburned old human body with white hair falling just below its neck. Overjoyed, he runs toward it, but as he approaches it, Mary calls out his name and presents herself as a woman who is naked, asking him to throw his cloak so she can cover herself and they can talk. In the ensuing conversation, she proves her wisdom by calling him a priest and showing that she knows everything about him, which he interprets as a gift of the Holy Spirit for her good deeds.

Another theme reminiscent of Pelagius's talk with the deacon is Mary's willingness to know about the Christian world. She prays for it by levitating, which terrifies Zosimas, who begs for mercy, thinking again that she is a temptation. When Mary realizes this, she scolds him and tells him that she has been baptized. Finally reassured, he then falls at her feet, recognizing she is a product of God's marvelous works and that such a hidden wisdom and secret treasure should be revealed.

This episode in some ways recalls the idea of seeing women as a source of wisdom, as in Sara's sayings, but in Mary's Life, there has to be an important change for wisdom to be attained (i.e., repentance). Mary has to recall all her past evil doings and narrate them to the monk in the first person, like Pelagia did but in more detail. Her retelling gives the bluntest description of her sensual behavior in leading men astray. Worse than that, she did it for pleasure rather than money, which is a scandalous confession. By recognizing this, she admits her sexual desires and the will to perform them, which gives her a special place on the lust scale.[77]

Mary is aware of her sins, and if she is remembering them, she is also obeying Zosimas's demand, even though she is reluctant to enunciate them because she will pollute the air.[78] In her confession, she presents herself as a vessel of the devil and corresponds exactly to the misogynistic image depicted in gender anathema: when she was 12 years old she went to Alexandria, the land of sin, and for about 17 years was an insatiable instrument of public debauchery. Then she took one more step toward the abyss, joining those who were going to Jerusalem for the Exaltation of the Cross with the sole purpose of getting more lovers. Her depravity was such that she frequently forced miserable youths against their will. This rather sacrilegious mixture of sacred and profane continued when she arrived in Jerusalem, and she went on to seduce both locals and foreigners.

Eventually, when she repeatedly tried to enter the church and saw everybody going in except her, she realized that her inability to enter was due to her sinful behavior and began weeping until she saw the image of Holy Mary, prayed for her help, and promised to renounce the world. This is where her 57-year ascent to redemption begins. Such a dramatic turning from a sinful life to sanctity finally merits the mercy of God. Yet the secret must not be revealed for the time being. When Zosimas returns to visit Mary again the next year, Mary has already passed away. As in Jerome's *Life of Saint Paul* (in many aspects recalled here with a feminine voice, since Mary is the edifying portrait of perfection the monk finds), Zosimas buries her with the aid of two lions, after which he can finally tell his brothers about God's miracle so they may always remember Mary's spiritual superiority.

Mary's victory over Zosimas and the defeat of lust allows her to be the master of the sinful disciple and emphasizes the difficulties and the length of her struggle, but it also assumes an a priori weakness of the body compared with the spirit. This shameful and excessive story, depicted in harsh colors, is only bearable because it is continuously interrupted by Mary's signs and expressions of repentance and by Zosimas's requests that she keep on telling it. The guilty way in which she refers to her past sexual obsession clearly shows her disapproval. Yet one may note how Mary's confession reveals what Clare A. Lees calls an "intimate acquaintance" with problems of the flesh, such as the insatiable increase of desire.[79] Zosimas's admiration reveals how Mary's sexuality is transformed into chastity in a dimension men would have never imagined and, as far as I know, has never been portrayed concerning a male protagonist.

There is a certain moral reserve in addressing these subjects. It seems to be easier to attribute lust to women because men dare not open their imagination any wider than in the extreme case of John of Lycopolis.[80] But this common feature might also be seen as a symptom of silenced pride—the worst vice and origin of all other sins, according to the Bible, Evagrius, and Cassian.

An analysis of men's lustful temptations in general is well beyond the scope of this chapter; I did conclude in an earlier work, however, that lust was the second biggest temptation monks suffered, immediately after the sins of the tongue.[81] In the context of this chapter, it is quite remarkable that when men sin they are associated with pride, whereas sinning women are associated with lust. The control of pride as a spiritual sin is the last step to be achieved on the path to perfection, while the carnal sins of lust and gluttony are considered easier to control. Male hagiographers no doubt associated women with the flesh and men with the spirit, and they portrayed male and female figures facing what they perceived as suitable temptations or tests.

To some extent, the fact that, as with Zosimas, a previously lustful woman defeats a formerly prideful monk might be interpreted as a reminder of the natural fallibility of the human being. One might think male hagiographers would be aware of the dangers they have to face. This literature is edifying for new audiences. Moreover, this writing seems to have a therapeutic intention, for by painting a possible self-portrait, the authors might prevent a terrible fall. Depicting women's superiority might equally be a strategy to control the temptation of pride, which reaffirms the tradition that women are associated with the body, whereas men are more often identified with mind and spirit.[82]

However, one must not forget that these lives have more to do with models than with real life itself. In a rather dualistic world, and above all in desert literature, it was easier for both authors and the public to oppose the masculine ascetic body to the feminine sexual body. These gendered perspectives appear to be a point of departure sometimes questioned by the literary characters themselves. In spite of all this success and honor, one must not delude oneself. However saintly they may be, these glorious women earn their names and status through sin, above all through the destruction of their feminine body. They are also a sign and an example of true Christianity, which gives them a chance to be saved and accepts them so long as they deny or destroy their bodies. Although they have to prove themselves through some form of androgyny or male appearance, only when their true identity is rediscovered are they finally valued for their womanhood. In contrast, when men were discovered under these circumstances, only sanctity was praised. The gender issue was not brought up. Male gender supremacy was a postulate. It need not be disclosed.

Given that what one forgets or omits is as relevant as what one remembers, we must emphasize that the *amma* is absent from the Portuguese reception of *Vitae patrum*. Only one is mentioned, but she neither teaches nor attracts disciples or travelers. One could say that this dignity was not important in the Portuguese medieval context; perhaps it was regarded as bizarre to question the authority of the male clergy. Furthermore, as I have already observed, in spite of the whole misogynistic tradition, evil flesh-and-blood women are absent from these apothegms and hagiographies. Nevertheless, the anathema is still present and in a very obvious form, but it is concerned with prejudices, concepts, or imaginary situations instigated by the devil. This is not at all flattering as the dominant mask is women's bodies. All these presences are anonymous and perform secondary roles. In the meantime, the same can be said about the devotees' and monks' relatives. So the woman's name and leading role is an achievement reserved for repentant female saints. Naming is the only way these saints can be memorized, quoted, and used as models.

If this is the stipulation to access the desert and to ensure future memory, behind this conquest there appears to be a happy marriage between two different textual memories significant in the representation of gender identity. One, exclusive to the *Vitae patrum*, is the motif of the remembered or imagined woman as a location of temptation and measure of the monk's spiritual achievement in the desert. The other is the representation of real women modeled on Luke's repentant woman, marked by inclusion and universal forgiveness. This episode appears to be the turning point that broke the anathema that overshadowed the idea of woman. It seems obvious that apothegms and hagiographies need unpolluted characters, so flesh-and-blood women need to be purified before entering the literary domain. Unlike the single case of the complete fall of an anonymous monk, all women deserve redemption. Needless to say, they must undertake a hard and usually long journey, a change of appearance, and even a change of name. The visible boundaries between past and present signal rupture and rebirth as the androgynous appearance or the male name point to an ideal ruled by men. And yet even if the male/female binary is quite clear, the penitent woman—once again, a remake of Luke's adulterous woman—who has also just acquired a name, needs to readapt her identity to the desert spirituality. Performing bodily denial and acquiring a virile soul, she manages to create a new hybrid identity, which in some measure overshadows the persistent anathema that condemned her for so long.

Notes

1. We must remember that in the Middle Ages, hagiographical readers primarily sought models rather than information. See the discussion of the distinction between utility and accuracy in medieval memory arts in the introduction to this volume.

2. On the significance of selective memory and forgetting, see the introduction to this volume.

3. Mary J. Carruthers, *The Book of Memory: A Study of Memory in Medieval Culture*, 2nd ed., Cambridge Studies in Medieval Literature 70 (Cambridge: Cambridge University Press, 2008), 1–17.

4. These apothegms, which apply to quite a number of hagiographies, claim the same way of reading that Margaret Cotter-Lynch observes regarding Notker's "In Natale Sanctarum Feminarum" in chapter 2 of this volume.

5. Athanasius presents Saint Anthony following the apostles' example. See Athanasius, *Vita di Antonio*, 6th ed., ed. G. J. M. Bartelink, trans. Pietro Citati and Salvatire Lilla (Milan: Fondazione Lorenzo Valla, 1998), 9–11.

6. See, for example, Saint Paul's paradigmatic life, where the beginning of monasticism is discussed in Saint Jerome, *Vita Sancti Pauli Eremitae*, in *Patrologia Latina*, ed. J.-P. Migne, vol. 23, col. 17–28. For the English translation, see http://www.newadvent.org/fathers/3008.htm, or see Saint Onophrius's Life, which has a close intertextual relationship with Saint Paul's life. See the Spanish version of the *Legenda aurea* by Jacob of Voragine (written and revised between 1260–1263 and the early 1290s): *Leyenda de los santos* (Burgos, Spain: Juan de Burgos, 1500; London, British Library, IB 53312), fol. 284r. The Portuguese version is lacunar. See *Flos Sanctorum em linguagẽ portugues* (Lisbon: Herman Campos e Roberto Rebelo, 1513; Lisbon, Biblioteca Nacional, Res. 157 A), fol. 220r–220v (from now on FS 1513).

7. See Norman Russell, trans., *The Lives of the Desert Fathers: The Historia Monachorum in Aegypto* (Kalamazoo, MI: Cistercian Publications, 1980), 18; Duncan Robertson, *The Medieval Saints' Lives: Spiritual Renewal and Old French Literature* (Lexington, KY: French Forum, 1995), 76–78; "Monachisme," in *Dictionnaire d'archéologie chrétienne et de liturgie*, ed. Fernand Cabrol and Henri Leclercq (Paris: Letouzey et Ané, 1934), 11.2.1774–947; Jean Decarreaux, *Les moines et la civilisation* (Paris: Arthaud, 1962); André Vauchez, "O Santo," in *O homem medieval*, ed. Jacques Le Goff (Lisbon: Editorial Presença, 1990), 211–32.

8. See the critical review of *Les apophtegmes des pères: collection systématique: chapitres I–IX*, ed. Jean-Claude Guy, Sources Chrétiennes 387 (Paris: Éditions du Cerf, 1993), 1:13–18.

9. See Benedicta Ward, "Traditions of Spiritual Guidance: Spiritual Direction in the Desert Fathers," in *Signs and Wonders: Saints, Miracles and Prayers from the 4th Century to the 14th* (1992; repr., Aldershot: Ashgate, 2001), 61–70.

10. Carruthers, *Book of Memory*, 198–99.

11. Guy, *Les apophtegmes des pères*, 19–23.

12. Carruthers, *Book of Memory*, 198–99.

13. Paul Zumthor, *Essai de Poétique Médiévale* (Paris: Seuil, 1972), 65–75.

14. Cheryl Glenn, "Popular Literacy in the Middle Ages: *The Book of Margery Kempe*," in *Popular Literacy: Studies in Cultural Practices and Poetics*, ed. John Trimbur, Pittsburgh Series in Composition, Literacy, and Culture (Pittsburgh: University of Pittsburgh Press, 2001), 56–73, quoted by Brad Herzog. See chapter 9 in this volume.

15. Jean-Claude Guy, ed., *Os Padres do deserto* (Lisbon: Editorial Estampa, 1991), 7–18.

16. Guy, *Les apophtegmes des pères*, 13–84. The author identifies five kinds of apophtegmata according to their simplicity, from the basic question and answer to excerpts from earlier texts, collective requests, brief biographic records, and longer narratives, which were probably added later.

17. The only information about Pascasius can be found in the preface of this translation addressed to the "Domino venerabili patri Martino, presbytero et abbati"; the translation was done by Pacasius at Martinus's request. See José Geraldes Freire, *A versão latina por Pascásio de Dume dos "Apophtegmata Patrum,"* 2 vols. (Coimbra, Portugal: Instituto de Estudos Clássicos, 1971), 1:1–2:38.

18. In works such as the *Dialogues* of Pope Gregory the Great (540–604) or the anonymous *Life of the Saints Merida's Fathers* (seventh century), the characters still follow the hermits' model.

19. Renan Frighetto, "O modelo de *vir sanctus* segundo o pensamento de Valério do Bierzo," *Helmantica* 158, nos. 145–46 (1997): 59–79.

20. A. F. de Ataíde e Melo, *Inventário dos códices Alcobacenses*, vol. 5 (Lisbon: Biblioteca Nacional de Lisboa, 1932), 339–41 and 424–26; Freire, *A versão latina por Pascásio de Dume*, 2:80; M. Díaz y Díaz, *Valerio del Bierzo: Su persona: Su obra* (Léon: Centro de Estudios e Investigación "San Isidoro," Caja España de Inversiones, Archivo Histórico Diocesano, 2006), 139–40. From now on, these manuscripts will be cited as MS 367 and MS 454.

21. For a description of this codex, see Arthur L.-F. Askins, Harvey L. Sharrer, Aida F. Dias, Martha E. Schaffer, *Bibliografia de textos antigos galegos e portugueses*, University of California, Berkeley, and Universidade de Lisboa, PhiloBiblon (last modified 2008), http://sunsite.berkeley.edu/Philobiblon/BITAGAP/; A. L.-F. Askins, "The MS *Flos Sanctorum* of the Universidade de Brasília: An Early Reflex in Portuguese of the Hagiographic Compilation of Valerio del Bierzo," in *O amor das letras e das gentes: In Honor of Maria de Lourdes Belchior Pontes*, ed. João Camilo dos Santos and Frederick G. Williams (Santa Barbara: University of California at Santa Barbara's Center for Portuguese Studies, 1995), 39–50; Américo

Venâncio Lopes Machado Filho, Um *"Flos Sanctorum"* do século XIV: *Edições, glossário e estudo lingüístico*, vol. 1 (Salvador: Universidade Federal da Bahia, Instituto de Letras, 2003), xxxiii–xlvi.

22. For instance, as in MS 454, the translation also includes the *Vida dos Santos Padres de Mérida*, a Hispanic compilation authored by a Merida deacon, according to A. Maya Sánchez, between 633 and 638 (*Vitas sanctorum patrum emeretensium* [Turnhout, Belgium: Brepols, 1992]). Its presence in the Valerian compilation allowed the propagation of a genre with some resemblances to Gregory's *Dialogues*, which had been added to the Valerian compilation earlier. Regarding Valerio of Bierzo's reception in Portuguese domains, M. Díaz y Díaz recently proposed the existence of two different phases: the first may be the translation of a separate element of the Valerian collection, which had texts added in the meantime; according to a second hypothesis, also possible, those phases corresponded to two parts of the same manuscript with a different treatment. See *Valerio del Bierzo*, 148–52.

23. Anselmo Borges, preface to Maria Julieta M. Dias and Paulo M. Pinto, *A verdadeira História de Maria Madalena* (Cruz Quebrada, Portugal: Casa das Letras–Editorial Notícias, 2006), 16.

24. Évagre Le Pontique, *Traité pratique ou le moine*, vol. 1, eds. Antoine Guillaumont and Claire Guillaumont (Paris: Cerf, 1971).

25. Robertson, *Medieval Saints' Lives*, 76–127.

26. Annabelle Parker, "'Nothing but Blood Mixed with Phlegm': Desert Mothers' Teachings on the Object of Desire," *Gouden Hoorn: Journal of Byzantium* 5, no. 2 (winter 1997–98), http://www.isidore-of-seville.com /goudenhoorn/52annabelle.html.

27. The tension between women and teaching is a *longue durée* phenomenon. As Brad Herzog recalls, although Margery Kempe reinterpreted Christ's words as affirming a vocal woman's praise (Luke 11:27–28), Paul disapproved of women preaching. Although recent studies have revised the radicality of this Pauline interdiction (Carreira das Neves, *O que é a Bíblia* [Lisbon: Casa das Letras, 2008]), it remains true that in the late Middle Ages, the main tendency was to exclude women from the pulpit, seen as a gendered place (see "Portrait of a Holy Life: Mnemonic Inventiveness in *The Book of Margery Kempe*," chapter 9 in this volume), as happened in the late medieval reception of desert spirituality with the suppression of the *ammas*.

28. As Margaret Cotter-Lynch notes, because of the relative cultural values imposed upon men and women, sainthood is easier for men. See "Mnemonic Sanctity and the Ladder of Reading: Notker's 'In Natale Sanctarum Feminarum,'" chapter 2 in this volume.

29. From Barbara Newman's *From Virile Woman to WomanChrist: Studies in Medieval Religion and Literature*, Middle Ages Series (Philadelphia: University of Pennsylvania Press, 1995), 3.

30. I quote from the PL as it presents a more stable orthography. *Vitae Patrum*, book 6, chapter 10, line 76; in *Patrologia Latina*, ed. J.-P. Migne, vol. 73, col. 876. Hereafter, quotes from the *Vitae Patrum* will be cited by

book, chapter, and line number, with corresponding volume and column numbers in the *Patrologia Latina (PL)* as appropriate; MS 454, fol. 134r; Benedicta Ward, trans., *The Desert Fathers: Sayings of the Early Christian Monks* (London: Penguin Books, 2003), 106; *Apophthegmata Patrum*, in *Patrologia Graeca*, ed. J.-P. Migne, vol. 65, col. 419.

31. Catherine M. Mooney, *Gendered Voices: Medieval Saints and Their Interpreters* (Philadelphia: University of Pennsylvania Press, 1999), 13.

32. *Vitae Patrum* 5:10:76. MS 454, fol. 134r; Ward, *Desert Fathers*, 106; *Apophthegmata Patrum, PG* 65:419.

33. This wonderful synthesis expresses an important theological point. As Ella Johnson puts it, "The 'woman' baptized in Christ should aspire to become 'man' insofar as conventions of gendered behavior are concerned." According to Gertrud of Helfta (1265–1302), these conventions include "quintessentially feminine sensuality, weakness and irrationality," which are "hindrances to the religious life." See "'In mei memoriam facietis': Remembering Ritual and Refiguring 'Woman' in Gertrud the Great of Helfta's *Exercitia spiritualia*," chapter 7 in this volume.

34. Merry E. Wiesner-Hanks, *Gender in History* (2001; repr., Malden, MA: Blackwell, 2005), 1–5.

35. *Vitae Patrum* 6:3:1. MS 454, fol. 149v; Freire, *A versão latina por Pascásio de Dume*, 1.93.10:320–21; Helen Waddell, trans., *The Desert Fathers* (1936; repr., London: Constable and Co., 1994), 179.

36. Katrien Heene, "Hagiography and Gender: A Tentative Case-Study on Thomas of Cantimpré," in *"Scribere sanctorum gesta": Recueil d'études d'hagiographie médiévale offert à Guy Philippart*, ed. Étienne Renard, Michel Trigalet, Xavier Hermand, and Paul Bertrand (Turnhout, Belgium: Brepols, 2005), 111 [109–23].

37. The frequency of those tempting visions reflects the suspicions and discussions that took place from classical authors to late medieval philosophers, as one can read in Steven F. Kruger's book *Dreaming in the Middle Ages* (1992; repr., Cambridge: Cambridge University Press, 2005), quoted by Claire Barbetti in her analysis of the description of spiritual visions in Hildegard's *Scivias* (twelfth century), where she demonstrates how "the Western medieval world was and is an incredibly visual world, immersed in and driven by image." See "Secret Designs/Public Shapes: Ekphrastic Tensions in Hildegard's *Scivias*," chapter 4 in this volume. In desert fathers' literature, in order to avoid misunderstandings, sooner or later the narrator or the monk establishes the nature of the vision.

38. *Vitae Patrum* 5:5:6; *PL* 73:875. MS 454, fol. 125v; Waddell, *Desert Fathers*, 35.

39. Rufinus of Aquileia, *Historia Monachorum Seu Liber De Vitis Patrum*, in *Patrologia Latina*, ed. J.-P. Migne, vol. 21, col. 442. MS 367, fol. 31r; Russell, *Lives of the Desert Fathers*, 105.

40. See also Russell, *Lives of the Desert Fathers*, 135n2, and my "Desocultações da intimidade na *Vida dos Padres do Deserto*," *Romance Philology* 65, no. 1 (Spring 2011): 107–20.

41. *Flos sanctorum* of Brasília (hereafter FS Bras.), 2:5, fol. 18. *Flos Sanctorum em linguagẽ portugues.* Lisbon: Herman Campos e Roberto Rebelo, 1513. Lisbon: Biblioteca Nacional, Res. 157 A.

42. *Vitae Patrum*, 5:10:15; *PL* 73:914–915. Ward, *Desert Fathers*, 91–92.

43. Freire, *A versão latina por Pascásio de Dume*, 1.33.9:219.

44. *Vitae Patrum*, 5:2:13; *PL* 73:859–60. MS 454, fol. 120v; Ward, *Desert Fathers*, 11.

45. In the National Library of Lisbon, there are two codices from the previous Cistercian Alcobaça Monastery: CCXCIX/BNL 40 (end of thirteenth/beginning of fourteenth century) and CCXCVIII/BNL 39 (end of fourteenth century). In Lisbon's National Archive of Torre do Tombo, there is another one, from Livr.ª 180 (fifteenth century). Like the other manuscripts from the BNL, we shall use only MS 39. See MS 39, fol. 313r. (I will take MS 39 as reference, and I will indicate the folio where the passage is located.) Unfortunately, Arsenius's *Life* is translated neither in the Castillian *Leyenda de los santos* nor in the Portuguese *Flos Sanctorum.* See "De sancto Arsenio Abbate," in Jacob of Voragine, *Legenda aurea*, ed. Giovanni Paolo Maggioni, 2nd ed. (Florence: Sismel-Edizioni del Galluzo, 1998), 2:1233.

46. *Vitae Patrum* 5:10:87; *PL* 73:928. MS 454, fol. 135r; Ward, *Desert Fathers*, 111.

47. *Vitae Patrum* 5:4:62; *PL* 73:872. MS 454, fol. 124v; Ward, *Desert Fathers*, 30.

48. Col. 2:1; Rufinus, *Historia Monachorum*, col. 393. MS 367, fol. 3v; Russell, *Lives of the Desert Fathers*, 1.7:53.

49. John 6:63 and Acts 14:15; Rufinus, *Historia Monachorum*, col. 393. MS 367, fols. 3r–3v; Russell, *Lives of the Desert Fathers*, 1.4–9:52–53.

50. *Vitae Patrum* 5:2:7; *PL* 73:859. MS 454, fol. 163r; Ward, *Desert Fathers*, 10.

51. *Vitae Patrum* 5:2:7; *PL* 73:859. MS 454, fol. 163r; Ward, *Desert Fathers*, 10. The entire episode can be read in "De sancto Arsenio Abbate," 2:1233.

52. Carruthers, *Book of Memory*, 62.

53. See, for example, Freire, *A versão latina por Pascásio de Dume*, 1.49.1:255; MS 454, fol. 173v; and Freire, *A versão latina por Pascásio de Dume*, 1.49.2:256; MS 454, fol. 174r; PG 65.3:295–96; Freire, *A versão latina por Pascásio de Dume*, 1.49.3:257; MS 454, fol. 174r; PL 73.5.4.61:872.

54. Jacob of Voragine, *Legenda aurea*, 2.175:1233–34; MS 39, fol. 313r.

55. *Vitae Patrum* 5:4:68; *PL* 73:873. MS 454, fol. 125r; Ward, *Desert Fathers*, 31.

56. Rufinus, *Historia Monachorum*, col. 433. MS 367, fol. 21r and 25v; Russell, *Lives of the Desert Fathers*, 93.

57. Rufinus, *Historia Monachorum*, col. 422. MS 367, fol. 19v; Russell, *Lives of the Desert Fathers*, 82.

58. *Vitae Patrum* 5:5:26. MS 454, fol. 159r; Ward, *Desert Fathers*, 41–42.

59. In a different context, see Barbara Zimbalist's chapter on the voice of Saint Catherine in Clemence of Barking's version of the saint's life. See "Imitating the Imagined: Clemence of Barking's *Life of St. Catherine*," chapter 5 in this volume.

60. Luke 7:38–39.

61. *Apophthegmata Patrum* in *Patrologia Graeca*, ed. J.-P. Migne, vol. 65, col. 413–15.

62. Ibid. col. 217–20 and *Vitae Patrum* book 1; *PL* 73:651–60.

63. FS Bras., 2:183–84, fols. 63r–63v; Freire, *A versão latina por Pascásio de Dume*, 1.57.2:274–75.

64. Luke 7:37–38.

65. Translation made between 1431 and 1436, Lisbon, MS Alc. CCLXVI/ ANTT 2274, fols. 73r–74v; "Vida de Tarsis," ed. Ana Maria Martins, *Revista Lusitana*, n.s., 4 (1982–83): 16–17; *Vitae Patrum* book 1, *PL* 73: 661–62. There is also another version in FS Bras., 2:183–86, fols. 63b–64v, and a copy in Freire, *A versão latina por Pascásio de Dume*, 1.57.4:276–79.

66. Jacob of Voragine, *Legenda aurea*, 2.148:1020; MS 39, fol. 270r.

67. MS 2274, fols. 74v–82v; Birger Munk Olsen, "La *Vida de Santa Pelágia*, une traduction portugaise médiévale et son modèle latin," in *Pélagie la pénitente: Métamorphoses d'une légende*, vol. 2 of *La survie dans les littératures européennes*, ed. Pierre Petitmengin (Paris: Etudes Augustiniennes, 1984), 263 [243–77]; Ward, *Desert Fathers*, 269. There is another version in Lisbon, MS Alc. CCLXX/ANTT 771, fols. 133v–144r, from the second half of the fifteenth century.

68. Matt. 21:31. Furthermore, he exploits the commonplace body-spirit binary developed in Pambo's apothegm in two long paragraphs: an actress makes Pambo cry even though her sins are not specified but rather metonymically implicit in her chosen profession ("mulierem theatriam"); The *abba* self-reproaches because he is not as worried about pleasing God as the actress is devoted to human turpitude. See *Vitae Patrum* book 1, *PL* 73: 663–72. cod. 454, f. 121v.; Freire, *A versão latina por Pascásio de Dume*, 266; Ward, *Desert Fathers*, 14–15.

69. Olsen, "La *Vida de Santa Pelágia*," 264; Ward, *Desert Fathers*, 270.

70. Olsen, "La *Vida de Santa Pelágia*," 268; Ward, *Desert Fathers*, 273.

71. With the various expressions of explicit biblical knowledge, the male hagiographer identifies his saint with biblical antecedents. It is a fairly common rhetorical strategy because it can be recognized by the audience as achieving the saint's legitimacy and authority. The same process with a larger trace and insisting on female models is the focus of Elissa Hansen's study of Julian of Norwich's *A Revelation of Love*. See "Making A Place: *Imitatio Mariae* in Julian of Norwich's Self-Construction," chapter 8 in this volume.

72. *Vitae Patrum* book 1, *PL* 73:669.

73. "Du Carnaval au Carême—corps et renoncement dans l'hagiographie médiévale," in *O Carnaval na Idade Média: Discursos, imagens, realidades*, ed. Carlos F Clamote Carreto (Angra do Heroísmo, Portugal: Instituto Açoriano de Cultura, 2008), 149–66. With the deleted information about who the owner of the cloak was, copies and translations avoided defying gender distinctions or shocking the audience. Although hybridism sometimes appears, questioning binaries was problematic for a long time.

74. Deut. 22:5; Lynda L. Coon, *Sacred Fictions: Holy Women and Hagiography in Late Antiquity* (Philadelphia: University of Pennsylvania Press, 1997), 80.

75. *Vitae Patrum* book 1, *PL* 73: 643–51. Josiah H. Blackmore, ed., "Vidas de Santos de um manuscrito alcobacense—II," in *Revista Lusitana*, n.s., 5 (1984–85): 48–55.

76. MS 2274, fols. 50v–66r; Maria da Conceiçäo Mateus Dias and Clara Maria Teixeira Simöes Duarte, eds., "Vida de Santa Maria Egipcíaca," in Ivo Castro et al., "Vidas de santos de um manuscrito alcobacense (II)," *Revista Lusitana*, n.s., 5 (1984–85): 56–71. There is also another version in MS 771, fols. 119r–135v.

77. Dias and Duarte, "Vida de Santa Maria Egipcíaca," 62; Cristina Maria Matias Sobral, "Santa Maria Egipcíaca em Alcobaça: edição crítica das versões medievais portuguesas da Lenda de Maria Egipcíaca" (PhD diss., Faculdade de Letras da Universidade de Lisboa, 1991), 315; the version edited by Guilhermo Antolin seems to be much closer: "Estudios de códices visigodos: Códice a.II.9. de la Biblioteca del Escorial," *Boletín de la Real Academia de la Historia* 54 (1909): 55–67, 117–119, 294–313.

78. Dias and Duarte, "Vida de Santa Maria Egipcíaca," 316.

79. Clare A. Lees, "Chastity and Charity: Ælfric, Women, and the Female Saints," in *Tradition and Belief: Religious Writing in Late Anglo-Saxon England*, Medieval Cultures 19 (Minneapolis: University of Minnesota Press, 1999), 133–53.

80. Rufinus, *Historia Monachorum*, col. 399. MS 367, fol. 7; MS 454, fols. 118v–119r; FS Bras., 2:127, fol. 44v; Russell, *Lives of the Desert Fathers*, 56–57.

81. Ana M. Machado, "A representação do pecado na hagiografia medieval: Heranças de uma espiritualidade eremítica" (PhD diss., Faculdade de Letras da Universidade de Coimbra, 2006), ch. 4.

82. Mooney, *Gendered Voices*, 6.

CHAPTER 7

"IN MEI MEMORIAM FACIETIS": REMEMBERING RITUAL AND REFIGURING "WOMAN" IN GERTRUD THE GREAT OF HELFTA'S *EXERCITIA SPIRITUALIA*

Ella Johnson

Tropes from the Bible and liturgical rites pepper the seven medita-tions comprising the *Teachings of Spiritual Exercises* (*Documenta spiri-tualium exercitionum* or simply *Exercitia spiritualia*) of Gertrud the Great, the thirteenth-century visionary of the Benedictine-Cistercian abbey of Helfta.[1] With the memory of such ritual activity, Gertrud intends to continually renew her readers' attention to the activity of the grace of God present from baptism up to preparation for death. In this way, Gertrud's *Exercitia* serves as a fine example of the literary historian Mary Carruthers's work on the role of memory in the medieval, rhetorical con-struction of identity.[2]

Certainly, several significant inventive aspects of the *Spiritual Exercises'* ritual language have already been noted. Gertrudian studies have shown, for example, that the *Exercitia* was composed in erudite, medieval Latin prose, almost entirely from a female perspective, using feminine gram-matical endings in the Latin original or replacing masculine nouns with feminine ones.[3] To be sure, these meditations differ from the Psalms and liturgical prayers, which address God from the viewpoint of a male sinner or male devotee. In addition, most of Exercise VII addresses God with feminine pronouns and endings (e.g., Goodness [*bonitas*], Charity [*caritas*], Cherishing-love [*dilectio*], Compassion [*misericordia*], Peace [*pax*], Loving-kindness [*pietas*], Wisdom [*sapientia*], and Truth [*veritas*]).[4] Finally, all seven exercises draw from rituals that constitute a day in the life of a nun so that they may be easily remembered by women religious contemporary to Gertrud (i.e., the sacrament of baptism; the rituals of clothing, consecration, and a profession of a cloistered nun; and the Divine Office).[5] All of these features undoubtedly illustrate that the female gender is implicated in Gertrud's rhetorical use of biblical and liturgical tropes as meditative sites.

This chapter considers Gertrud's artful composition of her *Spiritual Exercises* in the light of Carruthers's work on memory arts. By placing Gertrud's *Exercitia* within the context of Carruthers's research, the chapter isolates an important motif within the text that allows one to understand its rhetorical configurations and gender implications with new precision. The motif ultimately shows how Gertrud's text invokes remembered tropes from the biblical, liturgical, and monastic tradition to stretch accepted conventions of feminine behavior. The study concludes by citing evidence that suggests that these gender implications correspond to strategies found within the writings of contemporary women religious. The chapter, therefore, adds depth and complexity to our understanding of the ways in which female authors contributed to and were influenced by the memorial canon, as well as how they (re)invented and expressed gender.

Remembering Ritual in the *Spiritual Exercises* of Gertrud of Helfta

A cursory reading of Gertrud's *Exercitia* certainly reveals the text as laced with tropes, images, and schemes taken from the Bible, the liturgy, and the monastic tradition. In fact, Gertrud begins the first verse of three of her seven exercises by harking back to Jesus's command to his disciples in the rite of the Last Supper: "Do this in memory of me" (Luke 22:19).[6] In Gertrud's Latin use, *In mei memoriam facietis*, the trope also calls to mind the formula for the consecration of bread and wine in the Roman rite canon of the Mass.[7] When considered in the light of Carruthers's work, furthermore, it becomes clear that this biblical-liturgical trope, in particular, is central to the rhetorical strategy Gertrud employs in the construction of her text.

Indeed, Carruthers points out that, for medieval religious authors, "the routes of the liturgy and the routes of a mind meditating its way through the sites (and 'sights') of Scripture became...their essential conception of Invention, the mind thinking."[8] In addition, "this assumption leads...to the need for 'place,' because remembering is a task of 'finding' and of 'getting from one place to another' in your thinking mind."

Carruthers thus shows that "memory work" was conceived as a "process" or a "journey,"[9] which "takes off from its particular beginning toward its target (*skopos*)," and that "the point 'where' one starts" was understood as "all-important" in the sense that it prescribed and mapped out the entire course of meditation.[10] Therefore, *In mei memoriam facietis* should be understood as the place Gertrud particularly chose to indicate and initiate the way her readers' meditations should proceed.

Placing the *Exercitia* in the context of Carruthers's findings is certainly a helpful way to explore the function of "Do this in memory of me" within Gertrud's text. Though Carruthers does not specifically study the Exercises or this specific trope, she does reveal the rhetorical tradition of several other schemes and images that Gertrud's text employs. To be sure, these tropes relate to and build upon the Exercises' starting point, as they constitute the text's memory store or its structure of memory networks. I focus my comments on how Gertrud intimately braids the Eucharistic connotations of *In mei memoriam facietis* with two other tropes from the monastic tradition: the "remember the future" injunction and the "place of the tabernacle" image. I argue that the way these two tropes generate from the Exercises' liturgical starting point draws a relationship between the Eucharist and the Memory of God (*memoria Dei*) and that this is, in fact, a critical motif within the text. On this basis, I then draw conclusions about how Gertrud conceives the role of the liturgical trope "Do this in memory of me" in the meditative memory work of the *Exercitia*.

Carruthers clearly demonstrates that the "remember the future" injunction, which Gertrud employs, is commonplace in the tradition of monastic writing. It harks back to the theme underlying Augustine's *City of God*. And, Carruthers says, the idiom eventually evolved into the fundamental model for monastic life in the Middle Ages.[11] She explains the regular monastic conceptualization: "Remember Jerusalem...is a call not to preserve but to act—in the present, for the future. The matters memory presents are used to persuade and motivate, to create emotion and stir the will. And the 'accuracy' or 'authenticity' of these memories—their simulation of an actual past—is of far less importance...than their use to motivate the present and to affect the future."[12] Carruthers identifies an important belief implicated in this theory: humans are able to "remember the future" because that by which we comprehend time—*memoria*—allows us to recall things past, contemplate things present, and ponder things future "*through their likeness to past things.*"[13]

Gertrud certainly demonstrates the belief Carruthers pinpoints. Based on the ability of the human faculty of memory to comprehend all time, past, present, and future, Gertrud thinks humans in this life should strive to continually contemplate the next life. To assist with this, she composes the prayer to Christ in Exercise I, which anticipates the future end of the present life: "So that while I am on this pilgrimage set up in body alone, my memory [*memoria*] may always abide in avid thought there where you are, my best share... so that, at the termination of my life... I may come to that most dulcet kernel [*dulcissimam nucem*], where, in the new star of your glorified humanity [*in glorificatae humanitatis*], I may see the very brightest light of your very outstanding divinity."[14]

Indeed, for Gertrud, memory is the capacity, in time, that gives the human person access to past, present, future. Yet, in addition to temporal metaphors, Gertrud also uses spatial ones within this passage to build a tension between the *here*, where the human person is on pilgrimage, and the *there*, where Christ resides *in glorificatae humanitatis*. She does so again, more explicitly, in Exercise VI when she writes, "Then, as if you were somewhat refreshed [*refecta*] by praising your God, your king, who is in the sanctuary, rise up now with heart wide open to delight [*deliciandum*] in God, your lover, throwing into him all the love of your heart so that *here* he may nourish [*enutriat*] you with the blessing of his gentleness and *there* may lead you to the blessing of his plentitude of fruition [*fruitionis*] forever [emphasis in original]."[15]

I suggest that Gertrud's *here/there* spatial metaphors are tied to the conception of the "way" of monastic meditation. As Mary Carruthers has made well known, "The rhetorical concept of *ductus* emphasizes wayfinding by organizing the structure of any composition as a journey through a linked series of stages, each of which has its own characteristic flow..., but which also moves the whole composition along." She says, "For a person following the *ductus*," "modes" such as the here/there metaphors Gertrud uses "act as stages of the way or ways through to the *skopos* or destination."[16] It becomes clear, then, that Gertrud's use of "here" and "there" refers not so much to actual places or spaces as to mental positions, serving both as a habitation for the mind and a direction for meditation.

Likewise, Gertrud teaches that by the recollection of the heavenly banquet, her readers will experience a "foretaste" (*praegustatio/praegustare*) here of the "most dulcet kernel" (*dulcissimam nucem*) they will ultimately taste there.

If the memory of your praise [*laudis memoria*] is so dulcet [*dulcis*] in this misery, what will it be like, my God, when in the splendor of your divinity your glory appears? If the small drops of this foretaste [*praegustationis*] of you are so refreshing [*reficunt*], what will it be like, my holy dulcet [*dulcedo*] one, when you are giving to me copiously? If you console me here by fulfilling my desire with good things [*bonis*], what will it be like, O God of my salvation, when you absorb my spirit in you?[17]

The *there* and *skopos* of this passage refers to the *then* of the world made right—that is, the new heavens and the new earth or heaven. This is beyond the future of this life. Because it is beyond time, it is also beyond the capacity of memory, which can only remember temporal past, present, and future. With Eucharistic imagery, she teaches that the Memory of God (*memoria Dei*) evokes for her readers the experience of the refreshment, delight, nourishment, and fruition found both in the eschatological banquet and in the glorified Christ in the Christian life today.

To be sure, in the previous quoted passages, Gertrud has her exercitants recall the fact that even before the Eschaton, through the Memory of God, as in the Eucharist, the human person is nourished by the foretaste (*praegustationis*) and fruition (*fruitionis*) of the next life. For Gertrud, then, the *memoria Dei*, just as the Eucharist, transcends time.

The connection Gertrud makes between the "remember the future" trope and the Eucharist is also based on her belief that the Memory of God, like the Communion host,[18] includes the presence of Christ, the mediator between divinity and humanity, the *here* and *there* and the *then* and *now*. Gertrud's reasoning is especially evident in Exercise V, when she prescribes a meditation on Christ's presence in the Eucharist that reverses the biblical Alpha and Omega (from Rev. 1:8)[19]: "Lo, your face, which the most beautiful dawn of divinity illuminates, is pleasant and comely. Miraculously your cheeks blush [*rubet*] with *omega* and *alpha*. Very bright eternity burns inextinguishably in your eyes. There God's salvation glows as red [*rutilat*] for me as a lamp. There radiant charity sports merrily with luminous truth...Honey and milk drip down from your mouth to me."[20] Noteworthy here is that "rose-colored" (*rosa, rosues*) is used throughout Gertrud's writings as the symbolic color for Christ's human-divine nature.[21] Therefore, in this passage, when she describes Christ's cheeks as flushed and his eyes as glowing red, she is implying that the already/not yet dichotomy is overcome in the Memory of God, as in the Eucharist, because of the humanity-divinity union in the Christ made fully present there. So Gertrud situates her readers' minds between their own future and past in the glorified Christ, the *omega* and *alpha*, because, in this way, they encounter the presence of Christ through the *memoria Dei* today.

To be sure, the way Gertrud uses the "remember the future" idiom in the construction of her text demonstrates her desire to associate the Memory of God with the Eucharist. In fact, in several instances, Gertrud composes a single verse that employs both the idiom and her liturgical starting point, "Do this in memory of me." For instance, in Exercise I, Gertrud tells readers to celebrate the memory (*memoriam*) of their baptism so they might be in the state of grace in the future, at the end of their lives. "Be zealous... in celebrating the memory of your baptism," she says, in order to remember the future, "to be in the condition, at the end of your life, of presenting to the Lord the spotless garment of your baptismal innocence and the whole and undefiled seal of your Christian faith."[22] The rhetorical strategy recurs in Exercise VI. There, Gertrud employs both tropes to motivate her readers in the present by instructing them to celebrate the memory of their future, celestial home: "Celebrate the memory of that radiant praise with which you will be jubilant to the Lord for eternity," she says, "when you will be satisfied fully by the presence of the Lord; and your soul will be filled with the glory of the Lord."[23] So, in an effort to stir her readers further toward their heavenly aim, Gertrud combines the traditional monastic idiom "remember the future" with the liturgical trope "Do this in memory of me." She therefore makes clear to her readers that the Memory of God, like the consecratory formula, (re-) creates a channel through which the human person may directly encounter and experience Christ, the mediator between the *then* and *now*.

The relationship Gertrud constructs between the Eucharist and *memoria Dei* is further illustrated by her use of another particularly rich monastic trope, the "place of the Tabernacle." Carruthers shows how, in its medieval, rhetorical use, this trope, too, connotes the transcendence of time. It brings together the future, the present, and the past by simultaneously conjuring up images of the Heavenly Citadel, the Eucharistic tabernacle, and Ezekiel's Temple.[24] Indeed, Gertrud stands in line with the monastic tradition in this regard. She uses the Heavenly City/ tabernacle/temple trope to arrange and link up the future and past in the minds and lives of her readers in the present. Two prayers from Exercise VI illustrate her creative use of the monastic schema. She first evokes the image of the past tabernacle: "May that wonderful tabernacle [*tabernaculum*] (Ps. 41:5; 42–43:4) of your glory, which alone has ministered to you worthily as a holy dwelling-place and through which you can best make amends for me to yourself for the due measure of praise and glory that I owe you, be jubilant to you."[25] Then she brings to mind an image of the Heavenly City: "My soul... groaning because I am delayed by my sojourn, mentally follows you into the sanctuary [*sancta*] where you yourself, my king and my God, abide in the substance of my flesh. Oh, how blessed are those who dwell in your house."[26] It becomes evident, then, that Gertrud understands the *memoria Dei* to entail a Eucharistic kind of union with Christ, physically manifest in the past tabernacle of the Covenant, in the present tabernacle of the Eucharist, and in the future Heavenly City. In rhetorical terms, the reader will know this happy collation of the images of the Heavenly City, tabernacle, and temple by the experience of the *templum Dei* of 1 Corinthians 3, that *templum* that is inside each person.

Therefore, Gertrud adds the image of the heart to the Heavenly City/tabernacle/temple trope. Noteworthy is that she does so in terms reminiscent of John Cassian's counsel to "build in your heart the sacred tabernacle of spiritual knowledge" [*si scientiae spiritalis sacrum in corde uestro uultis tabernaculum praeparare*].[27] For example, in the *Legatus*, she describes both God's deified heart and her own heart as a tabernacle or ark of divine presence and truth and as a sign of the Ark of the Covenant. On one occasion, she reports to Christ,

> Your most compliant sweetness kindly promised…"Don't complain! Come and receive the official confirmation of my covenant [*pacti*] with you." I saw you open up as if with both hands that ark [*arcam*] of divine constancy and infallible truth [*divinae fidelitatis atque infallibilis veritatis*], that is, your deified Heart [*deificatum Cor*]. I saw you commanding me…to place my right hand within it. Then you shut the opening up, with my hand caught inside it, saying "There! I promise to maintain in their integrity the gifts I have conferred on you."[28]

In addition, she reflects, "For although I wavered mentally and enjoyed certain dangerous pleasures, when I returned to my heart [*cor*]—after hours and even after days, alas, and after weeks, I fear to my great sorrow—I always found you there."[29] Based on her experience, Gertrud believes that the presence of God—found in the Ark of the Covenant, the Heavenly City, and the Eucharist—may also be found within the human heart. One only has to be attentive to it.[30]

One can now identify how Gertrud conceives the role of the liturgical trope "Do this in memory of me" in meditative memory work. The liturgical trope provides a Eucharistic framework and map for the entire meditative text. As Carruthers's research shows, this framework is undoubtedly supported by other idioms and images commonly found within ancient and medieval meditative texts. Gertrud's use of such tropes from the rhetorical tradition forms a locational structure for her readers, which centers on one main idea: the relationship between the memory of God and the Eucharist. For Gertrud, the formula "Do this in memory of me" concludes the consecration of the host in the liturgy of the Eucharist. It is a channel that allows the human person to transcend time through an encounter with the mediator between the then and now, the already and not yet. Indeed, the biblical command to repeat "*in mei memoriam facietis*" itself connotes the transcendence of time. As the philosopher Catherine Pickstock observes, "It is a present imperative, a recall that is anticipated, a detour not by the past but by the future, when after is before, and before is after, and where isolating an homogenous thread of time becomes a delicate task."[31] It is fitting, then, for Gertrud to designate "*in mei memoriam facietis*" as the starting point for her *Exercitia*, which intends to continually renew people's attention to the activity of the grace of God present from baptism up to preparation for death. Her text instructs persons in the Memory of God, which for Gertrud (re-)creates or (re)invents a channel for the human person to transcend time and to directly encounter Christ in the here and now, the mediator between the *then* and *now*, the human and the divine.

These conclusions thus illustrate Carruthers's demonstration of how ancient and medieval authors of meditative texts sought to construct a memory inventory (*inventio*) from which to invent (*inventio*) new identities for its readers.[32] In the case of the *Exercitia*, "*in mei memoriam facietis*" operates to constantly (re)invent a new, more fulsome Christian identity for its readers. The memory inventory of Gertrud's text shows the meditative path by which human persons may be transformed into Christ through transcending time in Christ, the divine mediator.

These conclusions also have implications for interpreting the female perspective of the *Exercitia*. It is appropriate now to ask how the female gender figures into Gertrud's intention to construct a memory inventory from which to invent new identities. What is the role of the female perspective in the *Exercises'* instructions for the *memoria Dei*? What happens to gender when time is transcended? What is the place of the female gender in the Christian identity the *Exercitia* invents for its readers?

The Gender Implications of Gertrud's Use of the Memorial Canon in Her *Exercitia*

Understanding Gertrud's sense of the memorial canon and her rhetorical use of the formula as a meditative starting point certainly casts new light on the way gender is implicated in the *Spiritual Exercises'* ritual language. As mentioned earlier, all seven Exercises, whether Gertrud composes prayers to God or addresses her readers, are written from the feminine perspective. This is seen most frequently when her prayers use explicitly feminine grammatical endings. For example: "That in the violence of living love I may become your prisoner [*captiva*] for all time."[33] At other times, her instructions insert appropriate feminine nouns. For instance, the reader is told to envision herself as the "prodigal daughter" (*prodiga filia*)[34] or as the "adopted daughter" (*filiam adoptasti*).[35]

However, there are two places where Gertrud shifts to the masculine gender to have the reader speak about herself as "man." Faced with this puzzle, the English translator of the *Exercitia*, Gertrud Lewis, interprets the change in gender perspective as abrupt and inadvertent. The interpretation is based on the fact that the nuns in the choir at Helfta used masculine nouns and pronouns to refer to themselves when they chanted the Divine Office. So, for Lewis, "These two passages let us appreciate all the more Gertrud's conscious effort throughout to maintain the feminine perspective." Indeed, she understands Gertrud's shifts to the masculine gender as simply momentary "relapses into this generally adopted male *persona*."[36]

In contrast to Lewis, I argue that Gertrud's shifts from the feminine to the masculine gender are far from inadvertent. Rather, they are important features of her meticulously constructed text. As we saw earlier, Gertrud took great pains to build a memory store for her readers, one that turns upon the idea that the *memoria Dei*, like the Eucharist, transcends time and entails an encounter with Christ, the mediator between the *then* and *now*, humanity and divinity. When Gertrud's momentary shift from the female to the male perspective is comparatively analyzed in the light of this motif, it becomes clear that the shift is an important linguistic tool employed by Gertrud within the locational structure of her text. She uses the tool to express the gendered identity she invents in her instructions on the Memory of God.

In this discussion, it is first important to note that Gertrud did not envision her *Exercitia* to be read only by women. As her biographer testified in the *Legatus*, Gertrud intended the "examples of spiritual exercises" (*documenta spiritualium extercitationum*) primarily for the women of the Helfta community but also for "all those who wished to read them."[37] Given that Gertrud could foresee men as well as women practicing her Exercises, she would have anticipated the fact that both male and female readers would adopt the female persona maintained throughout most of the seven Exercises. Therefore, it is correct to read the female perspective of the *Exercitia* as a female persona that Gertrud invents rather than as a gender-specification of the audience that Gertrud intends to address. For this reason, we can explore the kind of female identity Gertrud expresses and invents in her text. Undoubtedly, questions regarding accepted conventions of feminine behavior acquire particular relevance in the context of Gertrud's life. As the social historian Caroline Walker Bynum has argued, the fact that Gertrud was raised in the established female community at Helfta, and lived there most of her life, freed her from male theories about women's inferiority and her internalization of them.[38] Therefore, in this exploration of the gendered identity Gertrud's text invents, we shall consider whether or not the female persona stretches or challenges the behaviors and traits typically associated with the female gender.

To be sure, the influence of ancient ideas about gender regularly appears in a variety of writings of Gertrud's day, in works of theological, philosophical, and even scientific nature. As much recent scholarship has revealed, medieval works commonly demonstrate an asymmetrical evaluation of "man" and "woman" as soul/body, humanity/divinity, rational/irrational, and virility/weakness.[39] Indeed, Gertrud's *Exercitia* also engages with this binary. Several of the prayers Gertrud composes from the female perspective discuss the need to renounce feminine sensuality, weakness, and sinfulness in order to gain masculine virility and rationality. Ultimately, this is the path Gertrud charts out toward a divinized identity. For instance, Exercise V, written in female voice, prescribes a prayer to God in language replete with masculine, military imagery. In this way, according to Gertrud, the "fragile sex" makes progress toward union with Christ.

> Ah! O queen of queens, charity [*reginarum regina charitas*], make [me], for the sake of your glory, bound to you by oath in the new warfare of cherishing you [*in nova tuae dilectionis militia*] . . . Gird my thigh with the sword of your Spirit [*gladio spiritus tui*], most mighty [*potentissime*] one, and make me put on virility in my mind [*mente virum*] so that in all virtue I may act manly and energetically [*viriliter agam et strenue*]; and inseparably with you, I may persevere, well strengthened [*bene solidata*] in you, with an unconquerable mind [*invincibili mente*].[40]

Herein, Gertrud undeniably demonstrates the influence of traditional gender binaries. She describes the change in identity required for the "fragile sex" to attain divine union as such: conventionally defined feminine sensuality and weakness must be replaced with conventionally defined masculine virility and rationality. To be sure, the fact that the prayer is composed in female voice—in rational, virile language—shows that the performance of the Exercise already effects the transformation into the kind of female persona who achieves divine union. This idea coheres with the locational structure of the *Exercitia*, which emphasizes the idea that the *memoria Dei* transcends time and entails a transformative encounter with Christ, the mediator between the already/not yet dichotomy. Gertrud believes, then, that the Memory of God allows women to transcend the cultural conventions of gendered behavior.

Care must be taken at this point. In considering the female persona Gertrud's Memory of God invents, one must distinguish between the body and the behavior conventionally associated with it. It is not that the *memoria Dei* transforms the female gender so that "woman" becomes "man"—in body or soul. Rather, the memory of God challenges the conventions of gendered behavior so that "woman" may behave as a "man," virile and strong. Put differently, union with the divine mediator, according to Gertrud, does not require the annihilation of the female body or gender but rather requires the transcendence of restrictive prescriptions for female behavior.

To be sure, Gertrud is clear that femininity ipso facto is not wholly excluded from divinity. The point is illustrated in two ways in the same prayer from Exercise V. First, Gertrud personifies as feminine the way for women to possess traits conventionally defined as masculine and divine. She writes that the "queen of queens, charity" (*reginarum regina charitas*) enables "woman" to become "well strengthened [*bene solidata*]...with an unconquerable mind [*invincibili mente*]."[41] Second, Gertrud describes as female the "woman" made strong in Christ. As Gertrud Lewis and Jack Lewis note, "Given the context of repetitions of 'virility' in the prayer, Gertrud seems to intend a pun on *bene solidata*. Instead of 'well strengthened,' the phrase could be translated as 'the female/woman soldier' (from *solidatus* which means 'soldier, mercenary')."[42]

Furthermore, in the conclusion of the prayer, Gertrud envisions the annihilation of conventionally defined "feminine" traits in "woman" to lead to a female, "bridal" kind of divine union. She writes,

> May all my vigor [*vires*] become so appropriated to your charity and my senses so founded and firm [*sensus mei in te fundati et firmati*] in you that, while of the fragile sex [*sexu fragili*], I may, by virtue of a rational soul and virile mind [*animi menteque virili pertingam*], attain to that kind of love which leads to the bridal-couch [*thalamum cubiculi*] of the interior bed-chamber of perfect union with you. Now, O love, hold and possess me as your own, for already I no longer have—if not in you—either spirit or soul. Amen.[43]

When Gertrud composes the climactic conclusion of this prayer to God, "I no longer have—if not in you—either spirit or soul," the kind of soul (and body) that Gertrud envisions for a woman transformed or even (re) invented, in the *memoria Dei*, is still a woman. But the woman is no longer limited by conventionally defined feminine sensuality and weakness in her Godward progress.

Even when Gertrud has her reader pray from the female perspective for death of self, later in Exercise V, death refers to female-specific

hindrances (*impedimenta*) to the religious life, such as the archetypal feminine temptation to sin (*tentamenta*)—not the female gender per se.

> O Wisdom [*sapienta*], most outstanding virtue of divine majesty, if only
> your efficacy prevailed over me, an unworthy *woman* [emphasis added]. If
> only, with the breath of your mouth, you were to blow upon and anni-
> hilate in me, small as I am, all hindrances to your will and gracious pur-
> pose, that through you I might conquer all temptations [*tentamenta*], and
> through you overcome all hindrances [*impedimenta*], that in greatness of
> love, dying to myself, I might live in you.[44]

Here again, exercitants petition in female voice to a feminine personification of divine virtue for assistance in their transformation into the kind
of female persona who achieves divine union. Indeed, as the prayer concludes, exercitants call out to "Wisdom [*sapienta*],...through you I might
conquer all temptations [*tentamenta*], and through you overcome all hindrances [*impedimenta*], that in greatness of love, dying to myself, I might
live in you." According to Gertrud, the encounter with the mysteries
of Christ's Incarnation, Crucifixion, and Resurrection in the Memory
of God allows "woman" to die to the restrictions of her conventionally
defined feminine sinfulness and live a new life of virtue in *Sapientia*.

It is now proper to consider the place in the *Exercitia* where Gertrud
shifts the gender perspective of prayers she prescribes to God. This occurs
in the seventh and final exercise, an "Exercise of Making Amends for
Sins and of Preparing for Death."[45] In the context of this meditation on
the theme of death, and the passages considered already, it seems right
to understand Gertrud's momentary shift from the female to the male
perspective as a linguistic tool to call for the final, absolute death of typically restrictive feminine behaviors. Indeed, the female persona Gertrud
invents momentarily adopts a male persona, in a prayer for self-death:

> O my Peace [*Pax*], most dulcet Jesus, how long will you be silent? How
> long will you be secretive? How long will you say nothing? Ah, rather
> speak for me now, saying a word in charity: I will redeem him [*eum*].
> Surely, you are the refuge of all those who are miserable [*miserum*]. You
> pass by no one without a greeting. You have never left unreconciled any-
> one who has taken refuge in you. Ah, do not pass me by without charity,
> miserable [*miserum*] and hopeless [*desperatum*] as I am.[46]

One will note, here, that while praying in the voice of man, the exer-
citant no longer renounces conventionally defined female traits (e.g.,
sensuality, weakness, irrationality). This, I contend, is because the very
act of adopting a male persona already signifies the total annihilation of

female-specific hindrances (*impedimenta*) to the religious life. As I noted earlier, in my consideration of Exercise V, Gertrud uses the language of her prayers to illustrate that the performance of the Memory of God *already* effects the transformation into the *not yet* identity, required for divine union. This, of course, is due to her belief that the Memory of God entails the encounter with Christ, the mediator between the already/not yet dichotomy. Here, in Exercise VII, the momentary shift in gender perspectives especially makes the encounter with the mediator between the already/not yet dichotomy clear. The restrictive conventions of feminine behavior have been annihilated *already* in the female persona so much so that she may adopt a male persona. According to Gertrud, the Memory of God assists in this kind of annihilation required for women to progress toward divine union.

Yet here in Exercise VII, Gertrud is again clear that the *memoria Dei* does not lead women to a male divinized identity. Gertrud quickly shifts back into composing prayers from the feminine perspective because she wants her readers to step back into the female persona her text invents. Indeed, the male persona Gertrud has her readers adopt is "miserable [*miserum*] and hopeless [*desperatum*]." And he cries out to the feminine personification of divine peace (*Pax*) for a redeemed identity: "O my Peace [*Pax*]…speak for me now, saying a word in charity: I will redeem him [*eum*]." From here until the conclusion of the Exercises, readers resume with female voice their prayers for a religiously integrated identity.

There is, then, nothing inadvertent about the way Gertrud's pen lapses into the male perspective. Gertrud uses the momentary shift from the female to the male perspective as a linguistic tool to make a theological point clear. The "woman" baptized in Christ should aspire to become "man" insofar as conventions of gendered behavior are concerned. This is because, according to Gertrud, quintessentially feminine sensuality, weakness, and irrationality are hindrances to the religious life, whereas quintessentially masculine traits of virility and rationality are aids. Critical for Gertrud here is the fact that the *memoria Dei* transcends time and entails a transformative encounter with Christ, the mediator between the already/not yet dichotomy. For the encounter with the divine mediator in the Memory of God allows women on their journey toward divine union to *already* transcend the cultural conventions of gendered behavior. Yet, for Gertrud, even when the "feminine" traits of "woman" have been annihilated in Christ so much so that she may speak as "man," "woman" has *not yet* achieved her full religiously integrated character. Freedom from restrictive prescriptions for gendered behavior simply allows women *already*, while in the female body, to make the same progress allowed for men toward life in Christ.

Conclusion

Recognition of Gertrud's rhetorical strategy, in view of Carruthers's work, thus provides a hermeneutical key to the way gender is implicated in the ritual language of the *Exercitia*. Indeed, we have seen that interrelation of the tropes Gertrud appropriates from the biblical, liturgical, and monastic tradition isolate a critical motif within the text: the idea that the *memoria Dei*, like the Eucharist, transcends time. This motif, supported by the *auctoritas* of traditional institutions within the text's memory inventory, is the springboard for the new identity Gertrud invents: the female persona, liberated from accepted standards of female behavior. Therefore, the way Gertrud composes her meditative text refigures women's religious identities and possibilities.

The *Exercises*' implications for women also raise the question as to the degree to which Gertrud's text innovates her own way or builds upon previous iterations, making room for feminine piety and authority. Indeed, recent scholarship has revealed that medieval women used various gender strategies differently, though deeply rooted in structures of Christian thought, to furnish alternatives to mainstream femininity. Carolyn Walker Bynum and others following her have pointed to the way that medieval women writers—such as the nuns Catherine of Siena, Catherine of Genoa, and Beatrice of Nazareth as well as the beguines Hadewijch of Brabant, Marguerite Porete, Beatrice of Nazareth, and Mechthild of Magdeburg—claimed the ancient association of the female with the flesh as the means by which women achieve sanctification, aligning themselves with the humanity of Christ.[47]

Literary historian Barbara Newman has named this kind of gender strategy the "womanChrist" model. This is because, according to Newman, the model claims the "possibility that woman, qua woman, could imitate Christ with particularly feminine inflections and thus achieve a high-ranking religious status in the realm of the spirit."[48] Newman distinguishes this gender strategy from a previous one, the "virile woman" model, found in patristic and Desert Fathers' writing.[49] This *virago* ideal, as Ana Maria Machado's chapter makes clear, calls women to learn to live by the traits associated with man and thereby claims the potential for Christian women to surpass their brothers in holiness.

Newman illustrates the transition "from virile woman to woman-Christ" in her book-length study of the gender ideals appropriated in female religious life writing from the early twelfth century to the early sixteenth century. For example, Newman points out how the accomplished female author Heloise rejected the Neoplatonic conventions of feminine behavior and embraced the masculine ideal of the philosopher.

Yet Heloise did not use the virile woman model to account for her alternative behavior. Rather, Newman shows how Heloise forged a way to embrace the ascetic ideal through language of "disinterested passion" for Abelard as well as "absolute self-surrender" to him.[50] Indeed, Newman demonstrates how Hildegard of Bingen, writing in the twelfth century, also ignored the "virile woman topos." Rather than claiming virility, as Newman points out, Hildegard accounted for her gender by exploiting the "womanChrist" model in an intriguing, original way. "Instead of seeing herself as masculine she developed a paradoxical self-image combining two different versions of the feminine: 'the weak woman' (whom God had chosen to shame strong men) and the exalted virgin … embodied in the Virgin Mary and each individual virgin, but also in diverse instantiations of the cosmic Ecclesia, the feminine Virtues, the divine figures of Wisdom and Charity."[51] To be sure, Claire Barbetti further illuminates how Hildegard made a space of religious authority for her "beatitudinally 'meek'" female voice through ekphrasis, by subtly shifting the inherited meaning of the male-dominated public world to the place where one can hear the voice of God speak. In addition, Elissa Hansen's chapter shows how Julian of Norwich rhetorically fashioned an authoritative space for recluses, without directly challenging ecclesiastical hierarchy, by prescribing the memory and imitation of the Virgin Mary.

Thus, the tradition of female religious life writing testifies that Gertrud is not alone in reimagining deeply rooted institutions in the structure of Christian thought to extend women's religious possibilities. While retaining an impeccably orthodox piety, Gertrud, like so many women religious authors, claimed a female religious identity and ranking equal to, if not above, that of men.[52]

Certainly, in several instances, Gertrud's gender strategy corresponds with and complicates previous ways of reinventing female identities and behaviors. In fact, it seems that the female persona in Gertrud's *Exercitia* builds upon the kind of gender-specific religious path for women claimed by the "womanChrist" model.[53] Like Hildegard's "exalted virgin," for example, Gertrud's female identity embodies the feminine virtues. Unlike the writings of several women religious and beguines, such as Hadewijch, though, the constitutive moments of Gertrud's rhetorical strategy, singled out for comment in this chapter, do not particularly emphasize the alignment of female flesh with the humanity of Christ. Of course Gertrud does not reject the ancient association of the female with the flesh. But, as we have seen, she is more concerned with challenging the *behaviors* prescribed by the archetypal gender binaries. Gertrud requires women to renounce not the feminine flesh but rather the conventionally defined feminine traits of irrationality and weakness. And she wants women to aspire to behavior typically associated with men, for example, rationality and virility. By embracing "masculine" ideals in this way, Gertrud's gender strategy corresponds to that of Heloise. Unlike Heloise, however, Gertrud does not use philosophical ideals to validate the way her female persona stretches accepted conventions of feminine behavior. Indeed, Gertrud turns to images, tropes, and schemes from the Bible, liturgy, and the monastic tradition.

Drawing on the tradition of women's religious life writing, Gertrud refashions accepted female behaviors and identities in the structure of Christian thought. By interrelating key tropes from liturgical and meditative tradition, Gertrud crafts the idea that the *memoria Dei* transcends time, just as does the Eucharist. And it is from this idea, with the *auctoritas* of the Christian tradition behind it, that Gertrud (re)invents female identity and behavior. Gertrud's text, therefore, may be understood as the fruit of an evangelical impulse to provide a vivid call to everyone, men or women, to remember God without ceasing. Since accepted conventions of the feminine stymie women's ability to make Godward progress in Gertrud's view, her *Exercises* forge a female-specific way to the Memory of God, which entails the rejection of restrictive gender prescriptions for behavior. Ultimately, Gertrud painstakingly constructs her *Exercitia* to invent a new way of being female, precisely through the way she calls women to be Christians first.

Notes

1. Much scholarship has noted the liturgical quality of Gertrud's writings. See Hilda Graef, "From Other Lands: St. Gertrude, Mystical Flowering of the Liturgy," *Orate Fratres* 20 (1945–46): 171–74; Jean Leclercq, "Liturgy and Mental Prayer in the Life of Saint Gertrude," *Sponsa Regis* 32, no. 1 (September 1960): 1–5; Maria Teresa Porcile Santiso, "Saint Gertrude and the Liturgy," *Liturgy* 26, no. 3 (1992): 53–84; Cypriano Vagaggini, "The Example of a Mystic: St. Gertrude and Liturgical Spirituality," in Vagaggini, *Theological Dimensions of the Liturgy: A General Treatise on the Theology of the Liturgy*, trans. Leonard J. Doyle and W. A. Jurgens (Collegeville, MN: Liturgical Press, 1976), 740–803.

2. Indeed, the English translators of the *Exercitia* say that Gertrud's "exquisite style and accomplished use of rhetoric cannot be mistaken for that of anyone else." Gertrud Jaron Lewis, "Introduction," in *Gertrud the Great of Helfta: Spiritual Exercises*, trans. Gertrud J. Lewis and Jack Lewis (Kalamazoo, MI: Cistercian Publications, 1989), 5 [1–18]. For Carruthers's work on the rhetorical construction of identity, see the introduction to this volume. In general, see Mary J. Carruthers, *The Craft of Thought: Meditation, Rhetoric, and the Making of Images, 400–1200*, Cambridge Studies in Medieval

Literature 34 (Cambridge: Cambridge University Press, 2000). See also Carruthers's related work in Mary J. Carruthers, *The Book of Memory: A Study of Memory in Medieval Culture*, 2nd ed., Cambridge Studies in Medieval Literature 70 (Cambridge: Cambridge University Press, 2008); Mary Carruthers and Jan M. Ziolkowski, eds., *The Medieval Craft of Memory: An Anthology of Texts and Pictures* (Philadelphia: University of Pennsylvania Press, 2002).

3. Lewis, "Introduction," 6–9.

4. Ibid., 7.

5. Gertrud parenthetically remarks that readers outside of the religious state of life should make the appropriation to their own life circumstances. St. Gertrud the Great of Helfta, *Œuvres spirituelles I: Les exercices*, trans. and ed. Jacques Hourlier and Albert Schmitt, *Sources Chrétiennes* 127 (Paris: Les Éditions du Cerf, 1967), 3.21, p. 94.

6. Ibid., 1.5, 2.1, 6.6.

7. On the medieval history of the consecratory formula, see Francis J. Wengier, *The Eucharist-Sacrifice* (Milwaukee, WI: Bruce Publishing Co., 1955), 173–85.

8. Carruthers, *Craft of Thought*, 61.

9. Ibid., 23.

10. Ibid., 116.

11. Ibid., 66–69.

12. Ibid., 67.

13. Ibid., 69 (my emphasis). Carruthers illustrates this idea with the work of Boncaompagno da Signa, a rhetoric professor in 1235 at Bologna.

14. Gertrud the Great of Helfta, *Spiritual Exercises*, trans. Gertrud J. Lewis and Jack Lewis (Kalamazoo, MI: Cistercian Publications, 1989), 41; *Les exercices* 1.205, p. 74: "Ut in hac peregrinatione solo corpore constituta, cogitatione avida, ibi mea semper versetur memoria, ubi tu es pars mea optima, ut in termino vitae meae...perveniam ad illam dulcissimam nucem, ubi in glorificatae humanitatis tuae novo sidere, videam tuae praestantissimae divinitatis praeclarissimam lucem." In another place, in the same Exercise, Gertrud similarly writes, "O most dulcet guest of my soul, my Jesus very close to my heart, let your pleasant embodiment be for me today the remission of all my sins...so that, while I am on this pilgrimage set up in body alone, my memory may always abide in avid thought where you are, my best share." Gertrud the Great of Helfta, *Spiritual Exercises*, 204–5; *Les exercices* 1.189–90, 204–5, pp. 72, 74: "O animae meae hospes dulcissime, Iesu mi praecordialissime, tua suavis incorporatio sit mihi hodie omnium peccatorum meorum remissio...ut in hac peregrinatione solo corpore constituta, cogitatione avida, ibi mea simper versetur memoria, ubi tu es pars mea optima."

15. Gertrud the Great of Helfta, *Spiritual Exercises*, 111; *Les exercices* 6.490–95, p. 236: "Tunc quasi aliqualiter refecta laude dei tui, regis tui, qui est in sancto iam dilatato corde assurge ad deliciandum in deo amatore tuo, iactans in eum omnem amorem cordis tui, ut ipse enutriat te hic

in benedictionibus suae dulcedinis, et ibi perducat te ad benedictionem plenitudinis suae perpetuae fruitionis."

16. Carruthers, *Book of Memory*, 73, 80–81.

17. Gertrud the Great of Helfta, *Spiritual Exercises*, 111; *Les exercices* 6.500–505, p. 236: "Si sic dulcis est in hac miseria tuae laudis memoria, quid erit, deus meus, cum in splendore divinitatis tuae apparuerit gloria tua? Si sic reficiunt tuae praegustationis stillicidia, quid erit, o dulcedo sancta, cum dabitur mihi tui copia? Si consolatio tua replet hic in bonis desiderium meum, quid erit quum in te, o deus salutis meae, absorbueris spiritum meum?"

18. Indeed, only about 50 years prior to Gertrud's birth, the Fourth Lateran Council (1215) officially used the term "transubstantiation" for the first time to define the physical presence of Christ in the Eucharist. "One indeed is the universal Church of the faithful, outside which no one at all is saved, in which the priest himself is the sacrifice, Jesus Christ, whose body and blood are truly contained in the sacrament of the altar under the species of bread and wine; the bread (changed) into his body by the divine power of transubstantiation, and the wine into the blood [*transsubstantiatis pane in corpus et in sanguinem potestate diuina*], so that to accomplish the mystery of unity we ourselves receive from his (nature) what he himself received from ours." Quoted in Michael O'Carroll, *Corpus Christi: An Encyclopedia of the Eucharist* (Wilmington, DE: Michael Glazier Books, 1988), 196.

19. See Gertrud the Great of Helfta, *Spiritual Exercises*, 75n21.

20. Ibid., 75; *Les exercices* 5.69–73, p. 162: "In genis tuis mirabiliter rubet Omega et Alpha. In oculis tuis inextinguibiliter ardet praelara aeternitas. Ibi salutare dei mihi rutilat ut lampas. Ibi luminosae veritati iucunde alludit speciosa charitas... Mel et lac stillat mihi tuo ex ore."

21. See Gertrud the Great of Helfta, *Spiritual Exercises*, 30n56.

22. Ibid., 21; *Les exercices* 1.1, p. 56: "Ut in fine vitae tuae immaculatam baptismalis innocrentiae tunicam, et fidei christianae sigillum integrum et illaesum domino valeas praesentare... Memoriam baptismi celebrare."

23. Gertrud the Great of Helfta, *Spiritual Exercises*, 93; *Les exercices* 6.1, pp. 5–8, 200: "Celebrabis memoriam illius speciosae laudis, in qua in aeternum iubilabis domino, quando satiaberis dei praesentia et gloria domini implebitur anima tua."

24. For more on this theme generally in medieval monastic rhetoric, see Carruthers, *Craft of Thought*, 269–71 and, generally, all of ch. 5.

25. Gertrud the Great of Helfta, *Spiritual Exercises*, 109; *Les exercices* 6.451–54, p. 232: "Iubilet tibi hoc admirabile tabernaculum gloriae tuae, quod solum tibi ministravit digne sancta inhabitatione, per quod tu tibimetipsi optime potes supplere pro me modum laudis et gloriae, quae tibi debetur ex me."

26. Gertrud the Great of Helfta, *Spiritual Exercises*, 97; *Les exercices* 6.105–7, p. 208: "Spiritus mei... gemens pro mora incolaus mei, mente sequitur te in sancta, ubi tu ipse, rex meus et deus meus, manes cum meae carnis substantia. O quam beati qui habitant in domo tua."

27. Quoted in Carruthers, *Craft of Thought*, 270.

28. Gertrud the Great of Helfta, *The Herald of God's Loving Kindness, Books One and Two*, trans. Alexandra Barratt (Kalamazoo, MI: Cistercian Publications, 1991), 155; St. Gertrud the Great of Helfta, *Œuvres spirituelles, Le héraut, livres I–II*, 2.20.14, trans. Pierre Doyère (Paris: Les Editions du Cerf, 1968), 113: "Tua tractabilissima suavitas…promisit, dicens: 'Ne haec causeris accede et suscipe pacti mei firmamentum.' Et statim parvitas mea conspexit te quasi utrisque minibus expandere arcam illam divinae fidelitatis atque infallibilis veritatis, scilicet deificatum Cor tuum…dextram meam imponere, et sic apertuaram contrhens manyu mea inclusa dixisti: 'Ecce dona tibi collat me tibi illibata servaturm promitto.'"

29. Gertrud the Great of Helfta, *Herald*, 106; *Le héraut* 2.3.3, p. 238: "Ego enim licet mente vagarer, in quantumvis lubricis delectarer, cum post horas et heu! Post dies, et ut proh dolor! Timeo, post hebdomadas, rediens ad cor meum simper in idipsum inveni." See also *Le héraut* 2.1.2. Indeed, Gertrud testifies that only on one occasion, as the result of a worldly conversation, could she not feel the presence of God when she evoked the *memoria Dei*. See *Le héraut* 2.3.3, 2.23.2–3.

30. To stress the importance of such attentiveness to the presence of God within the human heart, Gertrud even relates the heart to the Eucharistic banquet. She praises God in another passage from the *Legatus*: "Hail, my salvation and the light of my soul! May all that is encompassed by the path of heaven, the circle of the earth and the deep abyss give you thanks for the extraordinary grace with which you led my soul to experience and ponder the innermost recesses of my heart…You endowed me with a clearer light of knowledge of you…I do not remember…having ever enjoyed such fulfillment except on the days when you invited me to taste the delights of your royal table." Gertrud the Great of Helfta, *Herald*, 103–4; *Le héraut* 2.2.1–2, p. 234: "Ave, salus mea et illuminatio animae meae, grates tibi referat quidquid coeli ambitu, terrarium circuitu profundoque abyssi complectitur, pro inusitata illa gratia qua introduxisti animam meam ad cognoscenda et consideranda interiora cordis mei…Donabas enim me ex tunc clariore luce congitionis tuae…Non recordor me fruitionem talium habuisse extra dies illos in quibus me ad delicias regalis mensae tuae vocabas."

31. Catherine Pickstock, *After Writing: On the Liturgical Consummation of Philosophy* (Oxford: Blackwell Publishers, 1998), 223.

32. Carruthers, *Craft of Thought*, 3–5. For discussion of this concept, see the introduction to this volume.

33. Gertrud the Great of Helfta, *Spiritual Exercises*, 124; *Les exercices* 7.65, p. 262: "Ut in vivi amoris violentia fiam tua perpetua captiva."

34. Gertrud the Great of Helfta, *Spiritual Exercises*, 63; *Les exercices* 4.184, p. 126.

35. Gertrud the Great of Helfta, *Spiritual Exercises*, 91; *Les exercices* 5.510, p. 196.

36. Lewis, "Introduction," 5–6. Emphasis in the original.

37. Gertrud the Great of Helfta, *Herald*, 39; *Le héraut* 1.1.2, p. 35. The biographer goes on to say in the next section of the same chapter that Gertrud counseled several women within the Helfta community and a large number of outsiders. *Le héraut* 1.1.3.

38. Caroline Walker Bynum, "Women Mystics in the Thirteenth Century: The Case of the Nuns of Helfta," in *Jesus as Mother: Studies in the Spirituality of the High Middle Ages* (Berkeley: University of California Press, 1982), 252–53 [170–262].

39. On this association in medieval theories of science and medicine, see Vern L. Bullough, "Medieval, Medical and Scientific Views of Women," *Viator* 4 (1973): 485–501; Joan Cadden, *Meanings of Sex Difference in the Middle Ages: Medicine, Science, and Culture*, Cambridge History of Medicine (Cambridge: Cambridge University Press, 1993); Danielle Jacquart and Claude Alexandre Thomasset, *Sexuality and Medicine in the Middle Ages* (Princeton, NJ: Princeton University Press, 1988). On the theory within medieval theology and religious writing, see Caroline Walker Bynum, "...And Women His Humanity: Female Imagery in the Religious Writing of the Later Middle Ages," in *Gender and Religion: On the Complexity of Symbols*, ed. Caroline Walker Bynum, Steven Harrell, and Paula Richman (Boston: Beacon Press, 1986), 280 [257–89].

40. Gertrud the Great of Helfta, *Spiritual Exercises*, 87, with slight emendations; *Les exercices* 5.384–400, p. 186: "Eia o reginarum regina charitas, fac pro tua Gloria tecum coniurare in nova tuae dilectionis militia...Tu gladio spiritus tui femur meum accinge potentissime, et fac me mente virum induere, ut in omni virtute viriliter agam et strenue, et in te bene solidata tecum inseparabiliter perseverem invincibili mente."

41. See previous note.

42. Gertrud the Great of Helfta, *Spiritual Exercises*, 87n81.

43. Ibid., 87; *Les exercices* 5.384–400, p. 186: "Omnes meae vires sic fiant appropriatae tuae charitati, et sensus mei in te fundati et firmati, ut in sexu fragili, virtute animi menteque virili pertingam ad hoc genus amoris, quod perducit ad thalamum cubiculi interioris tuae perfectae unionis. Nunc o amor, tene et habe me tibi in propriam, quia iam ultra nisi in te nec spiritum habeo, nec animam. Amen."

44. Gertrud the Great of Helfta, *Spiritual Exercises*, 130; *Les exercices* 7.232–38, p. 274: "O sapientia, divinae maiestatis virtus praestantissima, utinam in me indigna tua praevaleat efficacia. Utinam in me tantilla spiritu oris tui exsuffles et adnihiles omnia impedimenta tuae voluntatis et beneplaciti, ut per te vincam omnia tentamenta, per te superem omnia impedimenta, ut in amoris magnitudine mihi moriens vivam in te."

45. Gertrud the Great of Helfta, *Spiritual Exercises*, 122n1.

46. Ibid., 127; Gertrude d'Helfta, *Les exercices* 7.52–158, pp. 268, 270: "O pax mea Iesu dulcissime, quosque siles? Quousque dissimulas? Quousque taces? Eia vel nunc pro me loquere, verbum in charitate dicens: Ego redimam eum. Tu qui es omnium miserorum refugium. Tu neminem

praeteris insalutatem. Tu nunquam aliquem ad te confugietum dismisisti irreconciliatum. Eia ne pertranseas sine charitate me miserum et desparatum."

47. Caroline Walker Bynum, *Fragmentation and Redemption: Essays on Gender and the Human Body in Medieval Religion* (New York: Zone Books, 1991). See also Laurie Finke, *Feminist Theory, Women's Writing*, Reading Women Writing (Ithaca, NY: Cornell University Press, 1992); Linda Lomperis and Sarah Stanbury, eds., *Feminist Approaches to the Body in Medieval Literature*, New Cultural Studies. (Philadelphia: University of Pennsylvania Press, 1993); Ulrike Wiethaus, *Maps of Flesh and Light: The Religious Experience of Medieval Women Mystics*, 1st ed. (Syracuse, NY: Syracuse University Press, 1993); Grace Jantzen, *Power, Gender, and Christian Mysticism* (Cambridge: Cambridge University Press, 1995); Barbara Newman, *From Virile Woman to WomanChrist: Studies in Medieval Religion and Literature*, Middle Ages Series (Philadelphia: University of Pennsylvania Press, 1995); Ingrid Bennewitz and Ingrid Kasten, eds., *Genderdiskurse und Körperbilder im Mittelatler: eine Bilanzierung nach Butler und Laquer* (Muenster: LIT Verlag, 2002); Sarah Kay and Miri Rubin, eds., *Framing Medieval Bodies* (Manchester: Manchester University Press, 1996).

48. Newman, *From Virile Woman*, 3.

49. Ibid.

50. Ibid., 9.

51. Ibid., 16–17. Noteworthy, too, is the rhetorical strategy to which Newman calls attention in the writings of three literary beguines: Hadewijch, Mechthild of Magdeburg, and Marguerite Poréte. She shows how they joined the traditional monastic discourse of bridal mysticism with the dominant secular and courtly discourse of love, resulting in what Newman calls *la mystique courtoise*. As a result, this *mystique courtoise* literature, Newman says, reinvented the gendered identities of both God and God's lover. "Male and female, self and other, abjection and exaltation," Newman shows are part of the beguine writers' linguistic game of identity. Newman, *From Virile Woman*, 12–13.

52. For Gertrud's confident sense of self and her own femininity, see Bynum, *Jesus as Mother*, 196–209. Indeed, in the *Legatus* the Helfta nuns say that Gertrud "composed many prayers...and many other examples of spiritual exercises, in a style so fitting that it was impossible for any authority [*nulli magistrorum*] to find fault with it...which was founded on such honeyed texts from holy Scripture that no one, theologian [*theologorum*] or believer, could scorn it. This must be ascribed, there can be not dispute, to the gift of spiritual grace." Gertrud the Great of Helfta, *Herald*, 39; Gertrude d'Helfta, *Le héraut* 1.1.2, p. 122: "Composuit etiam plures orationes...et alia multa ædificatoria documenta spiritualiam exercititationum, stylo tam decenti quod nulli magiostrorum refutare...illius tamque mellitus sacrae Scripturae eloquiis condita, quod nullum theologorum sive devotorum decet ea fastidire. Unde sine omni contraditione attribuendum est dono spiritualis gratiae."

53. As I have argued elsewhere, Gertrud's writings affirm the possibility that woman, qua woman, could attain a particularly direct body-soul union with Christ in Eucharistic communion and thereby participate in and represent Christ's body here on earth. See Ella Johnson, "Bodily Language in the Spiritual Exercises of Gertrud the Great of Helfta," *Magistra* 14, no. 1 (2008): 79–107.

CHAPTER 8

MAKING A PLACE: *IMITATIO MARIAE* IN JULIAN
OF NORWICH'S SELF-CONSTRUCTION

Elissa Hansen

The long version of Julian of Norwich's *A Revelation of Love* merges
Julian's goals of reaching God and reaching others by acting as an
intermediary device to help others reach God.[1] Negotiating between her
desire to annihilate the self and the personal attention that her textual
practice and role as an anchoress garnered, Julian's self-characterization
offers her audience a way to think of her that deflects admiration and
gratitude for her teaching to its proper recipient—God—but that also
positions the anchoress and her message for continued popular appeal.
Julian constructs herself as an intermediary for the community she
addresses, a tool authorized to guide and participate in her audience's
devotional practice and conception of divinity. In *A Revelation of Love*,
the visionary contemplative is unworthy of adoration in herself, yet she
remains integral to the religious climate of Norwich.

This chapter contends that to encourage such an understanding of
Julian's role, *A Revelation* structures Julian's memories of her showings
around what Mary Carruthers has termed "publicly held commonplaces"
about Marian qualities, especially Mary's maternal intercession, and about
female visionary experience.[2] By aligning contemplative practice and the
gift of revelation with teachings about the Virgin Mary, Christendom's
intercessor par excellence, *A Revelation* establishes Julian as a legitimate
authority on humanity's relationship with God.[3] The potential for clerical criticism of a writing woman, present throughout the Middle Ages,
was exacerbated by Julian's subject matter—her God-given revelations—
requiring her to reconcile her visionary experience with the institutional

authority of the church.[4] By embracing the *imitatio Mariae* (or imitation of Mary) trope, Julian foregrounds similarities between the visionary recluse and the mother of Christ, especially in terms of their contributions to the Christian community. The anchoress thus activates readers' "strategic memory networks" surrounding Mary.[5] As Barbara Zimbalist also demonstrates in this volume, such "imitative rhetorical strategies play a crucial part in the construction of narrative identity."[6] To follow this thread in Julian's text, I briefly sketch some contemporary trends in English spirituality and illustrate their creation of demand for a Marian mediatrix. I then examine the passages in *A Revelation of Love* that involve Mary, suggesting that Julian's identification with the Virgin shapes her subjectivity and self-characterization in a manner that establishes her relevance without threatening clerical primacy. I conclude by considering Julian's Marian imagery in conjunction with earlier writings by several well-known holy women, as well as with hagiographical representations of these women.

Julian's account of her revelations operates as a devotional tool for both lay and religious audiences, mediating their understanding of God. All Christians relied on their priests for communion, absolution, and advice on godly living. But at times, believers sought out supplementary avenues to God, such as pilgrimages to saints' shrines, readings from personal devotional texts such as the primer, or conferences with local anchorites. Julian's revelation and vow of reclusion gave her the personal authority and institutional authorization to advise and to pray on behalf of such petitioners. This function might have particularly appealed to people embracing new expressions of piety that not all clergy accepted as orthodox—think, for example, of Margery Kempe. Julian's vernacular narrative and interpretation of her revelatory experience provide her audience with another accessible way to meditate on God's love, bridging between the mundane and the divine. Her text thus functions as a material realization of the links between God and man that her narrative explicates.

Julian's self-construction creates a place for her and her text as mediators in this milieu, but it also upholds traditional ecclesiastical authority by foregrounding Julian's dissimilarity to the clergy while repeatedly referencing her theological alignment with church doctrine.[7] A spiritual adviser and intercessor of Julian's nature would have proved especially attractive in fourteenth-century England because of a persistent gap between the idea and reality of pastoral care. "The clergy was removed further and further from the lifestyle of the laity and from certain kinds of contact with women and family," the very people for whom they were to intercede with God.[8] However, although Julian did not preach from a pulpit, her vernacular textual production could have threatened clerics anxious about competition for the community's spiritual reliance as well as economic support.[9] The church's concerns about female integrity made the possibility of such an encroachment particularly problematic. As Claire Sahlin notes, "Widespread scientific and theological assumptions about women's intellectual weakness, spiritual instability, and vulnerability to delusion brought great suspicion on female prophets" and visionaries.[10] Interacting with these tensions in the ecclesiastical sphere, Julian's Marian self-modeling discourages a reading of her text in which the visionary contemplative occupies a position of dominance over, or even parity with, the clergy because of her direct access to God. Instead, it insinuates that while priests serve a purpose more central to community spirituality than that of anchorites, each vocation should recognize the other's importance to their fellow Christians. Julian situates herself in the fourteenth-century lay religious movement by providing clerical mediation with an addendum, which the text structures by aligning Julian with Mary. The clergy, in contrast, are identified with Christ, reinforcing their self-conception and their social and spiritual standing; their authority is no less compatible with Julian's than Christ's is with Mary's.

Julian's imitation of Mary offers her audience a familiar framework in which to consider Julian's role. The idea of Mary as the ultimate intercessor, privileged by her unique relationship with the Godhead, took hold in the high and late Middle Ages as the affective piety movement burgeoned.[11] This theological trend held that while not concurrently divine and human like Christ, Mary stood out for her sympathy to human frailty and her willingness to mediate between repentant sinner and God. Hilda Graef suggests that Mary became more accessible as an intercessor over time; she traces a shift in literary and artistic representations of the Virgin from deified, conquering queen of heaven to human mother at the Nativity and at the cross.[12] Bernard of Clairvaux describes Mary as a "*mediatrix*," an "aqueduct" through which Christ came to earth, characterizing Christian life in the phrase, "We seek grace, and we seek it through Mary."[13] Ambrose assigns Mary the same intercessory role and adds that her *Magnificat* is a prophetic utterance stemming from her infusion with the Holy Spirit during Christ's conception. "We find hardly anyone," he writes, "to have prophesied more fruitfully than the mother of the Lord."[14] Julian, though not given the keys to heaven like the clergy, prays for individuals and the city in order to facilitate forgiveness, and her *Revelation* helps Christians to negotiate God's and the church's expectations, making both author and text vital to the Christian community.[15] In addition, Julian's female body enables her to mimic certain aspects of Mary's reproductive and revelatory functions. Though only priests can transubstantiate the Eucharist, Julian claims the ability to incarnate the word of God, providing a conduit for his message to reach believers and for them to access his mercy and love.

I begin my discussion of Julian's Marian performativity by exploring the revelations, or showings, involving the Virgin with an eye toward Julian's appropriation of Mary's piety and connection to God. I follow with an explication of Julian's initial prayer for three gifts and the ways in which it guides the audience's conception of the anchoress as a Marian intermediary. I then consider passages in which Julian solidifies her orthodox stance that as Christ's glory surpasses that of Mary, who is blessed above all other women, the clergy has greater understanding and authority than a female revelator, though she serves a unique function in Christian society. Throughout my analysis, I propose that while Julian does at times employ the *imitatio Christi* trope as a distinguishing feature of the contemplative's inner life, she adds to it the *imitatio Mariae* that, as commentators such as Carolyn Walker Bynum have argued, many female visionaries reject.[16]

During her revelations, Julian sees three visions of Mary that have convinced her of the Virgin's special importance to her as a visionary recluse by the time she composes her long version. In Julian's first revelation, a childlike Mary receives the Word at the Annunciation.[17] In the eighth revelation, Julian sees Mary's "compassion" at the Crucifixion.[18] In the 11th, Mary appears apotheosized, "as she is now in lykynge, worschyppe and joy."[19] Perhaps because Julian is convinced that Mary's prominence in her showings sanctions a comparison of the two women's roles, *A Revelation of Love* employs parallels that legitimize Julian's position as an intermediary in the Virgin's fashion.

Both women experience direct revelation from God, and they incorporate his word (or Word) in order to transmit it to the faithful. Mary does so by giving birth in two ways: physically, to Christ at the Nativity, and also spiritually, to the church at the Crucifixion. The physical illness that surrounds Julian's revelatory experience mirrors these birthing acts, and her desire to see the Crucifixion through Mary's eyes strengthens the connection between the two women. Finally, Julian casts herself as a motherly intercessor for parishioners, speaking to them not as a disciplinarian but as a comforter. Julian notes that God shows her Mary as an "exsample" of the love he feels for all Christians and that Mary is the only thing God shows her "in specialle...and her he shewed thre tymes."[20] By "in specialle," Julian seems to mean "particularly for her"; every other aspect of her visions, she emphasizes, is pertinent to Christians in general.[21] Julian's establishment of a textual and spiritual relationship between herself and Mary, then, arises naturally from her visions' emphasis on the Virgin's especial relevance to Julian.

Nicholas Watson and Jacqueline Jenkins have already observed that Julian's account of her first vision of Mary, at the Annunciation, parallels the anchoress's description of her own reaction to her first revelation, only eight lines earlier.[22] I would add that this alignment sets the tone for future comparisons of the two women's intermediary functions. "Full greatly was I astonned," Julian recounts, "for wonder and marvayle that I had, that he that is so reverent and so dreadful will be so homely with a sinful creature liveing in this wretched flesh."[23] Soon afterward, she sees Mary "marvayling with great reverence that he would be borne of her that was a simple creature of his making. For this was her marvayling: that he that was her maker would be borne of her that was made."[24] The repetition here fosters a connection between the two women's humble attitudes toward God and their reactions to his call. Both women's reverent marveling is also accompanied by an utterance. Julian, reacting to her showing of Christ's blood, exclaims, "'Benedicite dominus!'…with a mighty voice."[25] Mary responds "full meekely to Gabriel: 'Lo me here, Gods handmaiden.'"[26]

The third time that Julian sees Mary, she receives a vision not of the Virgin's body but of her soul.[27] The "vertuse of her blissed soule," Julian writes, are "her truth, her wisdom, [and] her cherite."[28] Truth, wisdom, and charity appear in patristic and contemplative works as specifically contemplative graces, providing a link between Mary's soul and Julian's vocation.[29] Julian furthers this connection by emphasizing each woman's humility and emotional connection to God with the phrase "reverent dread." Mary's "beholding of God fulfilled her of reverent drede. And with this she sawe herselfe so litille and so lowe, so simple and so poor in regard of her God, that this reverent drede fulfilled her of mekness." For this meekness, God rewards her with "grace and…alle maner of vertues, and [she] overpasseth alle creatours."[30] Foregrounding the similarity of her own humble response when confronted with God's greatness, Julian uses the term "reverent dread" three times. She also casts Mary as the mimetic model for this response: by perceiving the distinctive qualities of the Virgin's soul, the anchoress can "leern to know myself, and reverently drede my God."[31]

However, Julian avoids sounding prideful about this learning by implying that her revelatory experience is not an end but a means to grow closer to God, allowing that "for the shewing I am not good but if I love God the better."[32] Moving from descriptions of her personal experience and piety to recommendations for her audience, Julian emphasizes that all Christians must likewise adopt this attitude of reverent dread and enjoy the increased confidence in God that it affords: "Desyr we than of oure lorde God to drede him reverently and to love him mekly and to trust in him mightly. For when we drede him reverently and love him mekly, oure trust is never in vain."[33] Indeed, their salvation depends on it, since "wele I wot, oure lorde shewd me no soules but thoe that dred him."[34] Mary's piety informs Julian's devotion by providing a framework in which to imagine her response to God, but it also "encourage[s] and promote[s] similarly productive spiritual activity in others."[35] In this way, Julian puts herself on a plane with her evenchristen, thereby avoiding the accusation that her modesty topos is indeed just a convention, while Mary's and Julian's responses to the visionary texts God shows them mediate both the reading practice and devotional practice of the audience. Holding up these two women as examples of reading that dispose Julian's evenchristen to adopt a humble and receptive attitude toward *A Revelation*, Julian's account advances the model of devotional practice that the showings have taught her, one characterized by reverent dread.

The bond that Julian creates between herself and Mary is also attested in the prayer for three gifts with which her long version begins. As a girl, she writes, she "desired before thre giftes by the grace of God. The first was mind of the passion. The secund was bodily sicknes. The thurde was to have of Godes gifte thre woundes."[36] When the younger Julian prayed for "mynd of the passion," she wished she could have been at the Crucifixion but not, as the *imitatio Christi* convention might lead readers to expect, on the cross with Christ. Instead, she envisioned herself "with Mary Magdaleyne and with other that were Christus lovers, that I might have seen bodily the passion that our lord suffered for me, that I might have suffered with him *as other did that loved him*. And therfore I desired a bodely sight, wherin I might have more knowinge of the bodily paines of our sauior, *and of the compassion of our lady, and of all his true lovers that were living that time and saw his paines*."[37] Julian sought "knowinge" of Christ's pain, but she points out that his pain is also Mary's and the disciples'. She finally states that her wish was to "have be one of them and have suffered with them," further conflating the individual experiences of Christ, mother, and followers.[38] Her perspective in this passage is not that of the body on the cross but of a spectator: she wanted to see the Crucifixion "bodely" while participating in its emotional impact, as contemporary theology recognized Mary as having done.[39] This passage implies that Julian had envisioned herself in a Marian role since before the revelations.

Second, Julian recalls, she asked for a "sicknes...so hard as to the death...myselfe wening that I should die...for I would have no maner of comforte of fleshly ne erthely life."[40] As a woman set for the religious life who (as far as we know) did not have children, Julian may have sought this "bodely sicknes" as an experiential parallel not to Christ's suffering but to Mary's pain at the foot of the cross. Her account of her illness reflects

aspects of a woman's ordeal in a birthing chamber: the room seems dark
to her, even though it is daytime; her body feels "dead from the middes
downward"; and the short version tells us that her mother was present.[41]
It is during Julian's infirmity that she "births" her revelations, reinforcing
her physical likeness to Mary.[42] Though medieval exegetes seem to agree
that Mary did not suffer during Christ's birth, some, including Rupert of
Deutz and Saint Bonaventure, write of her agony at the Crucifixion in
terms of labor.[43] Rupert argues that Mary gave birth not only to Christ
but to the church through him and that only during the Crucifixion was
this motherhood fully realized. In his commentary on the book of John,
he suggests that at the cross, Mary

> is truly a woman, and truly a mother, and at this hour, she has the true
> pains of her childbirth. Certainly this woman did not have this pain, like
> the anguish in which other mothers have given birth, when the infant was
> born to her; but now she suffers, is tormented, and has sorrow, because
> her hour has come...In the Passion of her only begotten son, the Blessed
> Virgin gave birth to the salvation of us all; to be sure, she is the mother
> of us all.[44]

Julian closely echoes this perspective: "Oure lady is oure moder, in
whome we be all beclosed and of her borne in Crist. For she that is
moder of oure savioure is mother of all that ben saved in our saviour."[45]
Contemporary art as well as text reinforced the idea that Mary's swoon
at the cross was not only the result of her compassion for Christ's physical
pain, but also a marker of her own physical strain in bringing the Word
into the world and in redeeming believers.[46] In conjunction with her revelations, Julian's mimesis of aspects of the birthing act legitimizes her and
her text as Marian tools for those seeking salvation: through her suffering, her receipt of divine knowledge, and her account of both, Christians
may conceptualize and reach God in new ways.

Julian's third request of God for "thre woundes" included "the wound
of very contrition, the wound of kind compassion, and the wound of wil-
full longing to God."[47] The idea of compassion as a wound links Julian's
suffering to Mary's, recalling Simeon's prophecy that a sword will pierce
the Virgin's soul "so that out of many hearts thoughts may be revealed"
(Luke 2:35).[48] That the anchoress suffers, and that she identifies her suffering with Mary's, is clear in her eighth revelation, where she witnesses
the Crucifixion:

> Here felt I sothfastly that I loved Crist so much above myselfe that ther was
> no paine that might be suffered like to that sorow that I had to see him

in paine. Here I saw in parte the compassion of our lady, Saint Mary. For Crist and she was so oned in love that the gretnes of her love was cause of the mekillehede [greatness] of her paine... For so mekille as she loved him more then alle other, her paine passed alle other.[49]

Both women suffer in ways that defy description, that can only be communicated through a positive comparison with lesser pain. This parallel suggests that God may use Julian's compassionate suffering as he did Mary's: to encourage Christians' self-reflection and continued remembrance of their purpose and identity in Christ.[50] This benefit is itself a product of Mary's wound, which has prepared hearts such as Julian's to receive revelations; Julian is Mary's inheritor by virtue of her visionary activity even before she communicates her understanding to others.

The fact that Julian does communicate her showings, when considered alongside her requests for physical and psychological suffering similar to Mary's, indicates Julian's sense of responsibility to her evenchristen as mediatrix. Rather than focusing solely on her own union with God, she devotes "fifteen yere after" her showings "and mor" to crystallizing their "mening" for human salvation.[51] By presenting God as empty of blame for our "customeabl[e]" sin, her text frees its readers from overwhelming guilt for the unavoidable trespasses of daily life, advancing a perception of the Lord as merciful instead of judgmental: "I understode that the lorde behelde the servant with pitte and not with blame, for this passing life asketh not to live alle without blame and sinne."[52] As Mary intercedes with her son to forgive these sins, then, *A Revelation* creates God as already disposed toward forgiveness, performing a similar role to Mary's in constructing belief in God's acceptance. Bernard considered Mary a "tool" for thinking about love, and Julian writes in order to provide such an instrument for her audience.[53] *A Revelation of Love*, coupled with her anchoritic lifestyle, constitutes the lifelong realization of this goal—as far as it lies in her hands. As she writes in her final chapter, "This boke is begonne by Goddes gifte and his grace, but it is not yet performed, as to my sight."[54] The external measure comes later, as her audience is moved to imaginatively identify with Julian's revelatory process and as her showings and interpretations inform their devotional practice. Her visionary experience and her record of it, if they propel others closer to God, constitute a successful performance by both anchoress and text as Marian intermediaries.

Julian's *imitatio Mariae* shapes and buttresses her desire to comfort, advise, and pray on behalf of her evenchristen. Meditating on these aspects of anchoress life in her sixth chapter, she attempts to articulate her position on the use of intermediaries as a "custome of our prayer."[55]

The result reveals her hesitation to assign herself too much authority as an intercessor, but it finally casts mediation in a favorable light and places Mary in a central role. Two perspectives on the issue enter Julian's mind "in the same tyme."[56] Since she claims to have received them concurrently, she could have placed them in either order and remained faithful to the experiential reality, but she treats the more negative one first and the positive second. By including this discussion toward the beginning of *A Revelation* and by situating the positive reading of mediation as the immediate antecedent to the remainder of her text, Julian inflects her audience's understanding of the remaining 79 chapters. Her first point is not an argument against using intermediaries but rather a caution that they should not constitute believers' exclusive method of access to God. Julian writes, "It is more worship to God, and more very delite, that we faithfully pray to himselfe of his goodness...then if we made all the meanes that hart may thinke. For if we make all these meanes, it is to litle and not ful worshippe to God."[57] In working out the purpose of mediation in a general sense, this passage also suggests to clerical readers that Julian does not envision herself as the community's main pathway to God but rather emphasizes her limitations as a provider of spiritual succor.

Having perhaps released some of the tensions regarding the intermediary's primacy on the road to redemption, the anchoress follows this passage with an extensive argument in favor of intercession, drawing the audience's focus away from any doubts she initially raises about its usefulness: "God of his goodnes hath ordained meanes to helpe us full faire and fele. Of which the chiefe and principal meane is the blessed kinde that he toke of the maiden, with all the meanes that gone before and come after, which belong to our redemption and to our endles salvation."[58] The hierarchy setting the incarnated Christ above Mary is unquestionable here, but Mary remains prominent in the discussion: "We pray him [Christ] for his sweete mothers love that him bare: and all the helpe that we have of her, it is of his goodnes."[59] Mary's role in clothing Christ in the "blessed kinde" of humanity that enables mankind's redemption couples with her reverent dread for God to enable her intercession for the faithful. That reverent dread is the "grounde" through which she was "fulfilled of grace" that sets her closer to God than anyone else; she "overpasseth alle creatours" in "alle maner of vertues."[60] Other, implicitly lesser intercessors include the Cross, the saints, and the "company of heaven."[61] In the chapter's third paragraph, following the argument against relying solely on mediation and the discussion of Christ and Mary as "meanes," Julian concludes that "it pleaseth him [God] that we seke him and worshippe him by meanes" but that we keep in mind that only through God's "goodnes" is this technique effective.[62]

Julian thus organizes her composition in a manner that maximizes its endorsement of the visionary recluse as mediatrix while maintaining a humble tenor. She first appears to shy away from overprivileging mediatory prayer, but then she re-establishes God's advocacy of it. The chapter reminds readers that Christ is "the chiefe and principal meane," suggesting that the clergy who follow in his footsteps remain the community's primary conduit to salvation. In addition, though, it casts Mary as a key intercessor early in the text, a characterization that reverberates in each instance of Julian's *imitatio Mariae* and encourages the audience to assign Julian an intermediary function along with other Marian attributes.

Julian bolsters her self-construction as a mediator in several instances, emphasizing her direct connection to God and her vocation as a comforter and adviser. When she has her first showing, a vision of blood trickling down Jesus's face, she "conceived truly and mightly that it was himselfe that shewed it me, without any meane."[63] The idea that people leading the contemplative life receive unmediated access to God appears frequently in contemporary texts. *The Cloud of Unknowing* devotes a chapter to the issue, including this passage:

> Right as the meditations of them that continually work in this grace and in this work rise suddenly without any means, right so do their prayers. I mean of their special prayers, not of those prayers that be ordained of Holy Church [e.g., mass]…But their special prayers rise evermore suddenly unto God, without any means or any premeditation in special coming before, or going therewith.[64]

As a contemplative and a revelator, Julian communicates with God directly, and he with her. But crucially for her reception as an intercessor, Julian states that she anticipates her revelations may affect her audience's relationship with God more than her own: "In as much as ye love God the better, it [the showing] is more to you than to me."[65] *A Revelation of Love* imparts the message Julian has received so that its reader may be "truly taught and mightily comforted, if him nedeth comfort," acting as a conduit for grace from God to Christian, as does the Virgin.[66] Although the church, of course, intercedes for sinners as well, I read Julian's text as distinguishing between priestly mediation and her own, especially in her association of the church with Christ and in the priesthood's direct authority to forgive.

While establishing her authority as a visionary and an intercessor by linking her function with Mary's, Julian consistently avoids undermining the primacy of the clerical role to Christian salvation. To do so, the anchoress articulates a hierarchical relationship between Christ and

Mary and an allegorical relationship between Christ and the institutional church. Whereas Mary is "more then all that God made beneth her in worthines and in fullhead," reflecting the truth, wisdom, and love of the Trinity more purely than other mortals can, she is eclipsed by her incarnated son: "Above her is nothing that is made but the blessed manhood of Christ, as to my sight."[67] Similarly, though God graces Julian with exceptional visions and understanding of his nature, she expresses no claim to overshadow her ecclesiastical superiors. This propriety is evident in her explicit conflation of the Church and Christ in chapters 60 and 61, where she admonishes her audience to "mekly and mightly be fastened and oned to oure moder holy church, that is Crist Jhesu."[68] Immediately following this identification, she invokes the cleric's confessional function while talking about Christ's capacity to forgive: "For the flode of mercy that is his deerworthy blode and precious water is plentuous to make us fair and clene. The blessed woundes of oure saviour be open and enjoye to hele us. The swet, gracious handes of oure moder be redy and diligent about us. For he, in alle this werking, useth the very office of a kinde nurse, that hath not elles to done but to entende about the salvation of her childe."[69] The phrase "handes of oure moder" is the antecedent of "he," Christ, but the proximate naming of the "holy church" as "oure moder" and the inclusion of "precious water" along with "deerworthy blode" calls to mind the clergy's participation in spiritual cleansing through baptism and the Eucharist and their claim of authority derived directly from Christ. Julian strengthens this connection by quoting Christ: "I it am that holy church precheth the and techeth the . . . All the helth and the life of sacramentes, alle the vertu and the grace of my worde, alle the goodnesse that is ordained in holy church to the, I it am."[70] Priests administering the sacraments and reading the Bible directly communicate Christ to the community; his power to forgive and to preach is realized through them.

Though Julian also claims the authority to teach through her text, she recalls incidents that could only serve to place clerical understanding above her own. In chapter 66, for example, she describes her lapse in faith and the reassurance she receives from an insightful "religious person," probably a friar or a canon.[71] When this man comes to ask Julian how she fares, she tells us, "I saide I had raved to day," discounting her visions as illness-induced hallucinations.[72] When she describes her vision of the bleeding crucifix to him, "the person that I spake to waxed all sad and merveyled."[73] Although Julian experiences the vision of the bleeding crucifix and believes while in its throes that it came from God, the priest is better intellectually equipped to realize the episode's significance; his overall grasp of the holy exceeds hers here, since she lapses from belief to questioning. The words she uses to describe herself

reinforce the hierarchical distinction illustrated by the priest's discernment and belief in the face of her doubt. She speaks of "my febilnes,
wretchednes, and blindnes"; calls herself "baren and...drye," "a wrech,"
and a "fole"; says she was "sore ashamed and astoned for my rechele-
snesse"; and labels her dismissal of the showings as ravings "a gret sinne
and a gret unkindnesse."[74]

In casting her period of disbelief in this light (notably with the label
"baren"), Julian subordinates herself to the biblical picture of the woman
she imitates: Mary, though confused and troubled at the Annunciation
(Luke 1:29), is not recorded as questioning the validity of Gabriel's prophecy.[75] Just as the clergy cannot realistically live up to the Christlike standard that Christian tradition sets for them, then, Julian falls short of her
Marian goal.[76] Both parties are fallible, but they succeed in proportion to
one another, with Julian occupying a lower place in the spiritual community's hierarchy. Two generations later, as Brad Herzog notes, Margery
Kempe employs a similar *imitatio sancti* trope to contrary effect, reordering instead of re-establishing this hierarchy and its boundaries as she
hails a lay community of Christians seeking ecclesiastical reform.[77] Both
Julian and Margery's performances of holy women's attributes invoke the
"memory networks" that key stakeholders, clerical and lay, bring to their
texts, imagining their own reception by gauging their audiences' recall of
stories about Mary and Saints Katherine and Margaret.[78] These counter-
examples suggest the continuous perception of *imitatio* as a powerful tool
for women's literary self-rendering and authorization and for community
formation in late-medieval Norfolk.

But the successful deployment of *imitatio* can be hindered by ambiguity as to whom the writer is imitating. The text's assignation of Marian
characteristics to Julian deflects accusations of self-aggrandizement in a
text that characterizes God *as* a mother, forestalling the interpretation
that Julian aligns herself with the maternal aspect of God rather than
with Mary. Such a reading might constitute a challenge to ecclesiastical authority, depending on how clerics understood her construction
of God's motherhood and fatherhood. As Nicholas Watson has argued,
Julian's division between God's motherly and fatherly attributes actually
assigns greater authority to God as father: whereas the motherly aspect
of God is a compassionate intercessor, the fatherly aspect is strict and just
to perform the work of salvation.[79] For Julian, God the mother is tied
to sensuality rather than substance (which is God the father's domain)
and cannot compare to the "grethede" of that more complete aspect.[80]
This hierarchical distinction reinforces the anchorite's self-positioning
vis-à-vis the clergy. But although the idea of God's different attributes
was orthodox, the suggestion of ranking them could still trouble both

religious and lay readers. Some audiences might thus perceive an association with God's motherhood as setting Julian-as-mediatrix on a par
with the clergy who perform the regulatory "saving work" of the father
on earth. This possibility becomes more incriminating when one considers that earlier writers such as Bernard of Clairvaux do not limit the
motherhood analogy to God but also compare "Jesus, Moses, Peter, Paul,
prelates in general, [and] abbots in general" with the nursing mother.[81] For Bernard, these male figures' outpouring "of affectivity or of
instruction"—and, in Jesus's case, of blood—mimics the breasts' outpouring of milk to the thirsty child.[82] Julian's audience could certainly
read Julian's revelation, her writing, and her advice to parishioners as
parallels to such giving of nourishment. Her emphasis on *imitatio Mariae*
becomes essential, then, to deflect an interpretation aligning her with
God as a mother, which could invite censorship and accusations of presumption to an inappropriate level of authority. Julian's identification
with Mary, whom Christians recognize to be fully human, forestalls the
possibility that the anchoress claims a parallel to divinity as well as to
Mary's intercessory ability.

     To conclude this study, I hope to initiate a discussion about contem-
porary influences on Julian's self-construction as an intermediary. For my
part, I wish to align Julian's Marian model of visionary experience with
an understanding of female piety that informed male perspectives, both
popular and religious, on visionary women in the thirteenth, fourteenth,
and fifteenth centuries: namely, that these women qua women were
uniquely situated to imitate Mary's mediatory function, which is ancillary
to Christ's salvific role. Many such women relied on "their own access to
the other world" through visions and paramystical activity, whereas men
in the religious life foregrounded Marian mediation as a means of access-
ing God.[83] However, male hagiographers' characterization of female
piety elided the connections to biblical masculine authorities present in
these women's writings, including their imitation of Christ, by aligning them instead with Mary and other female models. After her death,
Clare of Assisi (not a visionary but a holy woman) underwent a textual
metamorphosis from an imitator of Christ like Saint Francis (the focus
of her own writings) to an imitator of Mary secondary to Saint Francis
(according to ecclesiastical and hagiographical narratives).[84] One can
trace a similar transformation in the reception history of female visionaries. Saint Birgitta of Sweden's *Revelations* link her with male prophets,
as do Hildegard of Bingen's writings, and Elisabeth of Schönau seems
to have understood her prophetic vocation as foreign to her identity as
a woman.[85] However, Birgitta's and Hildegard's posthumous devotees
and male hagiographers imagined the holy women as following in the

footsteps of "feminine role models" such as Leah, Rachel, Deborah, and the bride in the Song of Songs.[86] Elisabeth's brother Ekbert legitimizes Elisabeth's prophetic activity by linking her to "Hulda, Deborah, Judith, Jael, and others like them," and he further foregrounds her femaleness by defensively arguing that the flawed nature of contemporary pastoral leadership necessitates God pouring his spirit into an "unworthy vessel of divine revelation."[87] Since Mary's *Magnificat* suggests that she considers herself undeserving of the Word, marveling that God has "regarded the humility of his handmaid," we can read the Annunciation story as a source for hagiographical descriptions of visionary women as unworthy vessels, informing the association of female revelation with Mary and with revelatory experiences by other women.[88]

Julian's *imitatio Mariae* may indicate that ecclesiastical narratives of holy and visionary women interpellated Julian as a visionary, shaping her experience of the divine according to a received understanding of appropriate contemplative models. Julian perpetuates this gendered yoking by conceptualizing her revelations as closely tied to her Marian qualities. As I have attempted to demonstrate, Julian's Marian self-fashioning works to claim her a niche role in the Christian community's religious practices, as she sanctions, guides, and participates in its use of intermediaries. The heuristic on which this literary strategy relies is a matrix of conceptions about Mary and about female visionary experience within Julian's cultural environment. Julian's Marian visions and performativity engage her audience to recall similar stories they have heard about Birgitta of Sweden, Elisabeth of Schönau, Clare of Assisi, and Hildegard of Bingen, situating the anchoress within a tradition of holy women whose interpreters associated them with gender-appropriate biblical antecedents.[89] Perhaps the hagiographical reworkings even increased the popularity of some saints' lives by aligning them with contemporary trends in piety. These same texts that provide the norms on which Julian's text draws may have informed and shaped her revelatory experiences and her interpretation of them, infusing them with a Marian flavor, in addition to encouraging Julian to communicate her showings.[90]

Certainly, *imitatio Mariae* is part of visionary self-fashioning before and during Julian's lifetime. The representational strategies in Saint Birgitta's *Revelations* further illuminate the benefits of a Marian persona to contemplative women imagining their relationship to clerical authority.[91] Claire Waters observes that *Revelations* aligns Birgitta's body and heart with Mary's, allowing the visionary "to enter the lineage of authority at a point that, while recognizably authoritative, is nonetheless still quite distinct from the clerical hierarchy. She reworks that hierarchy by insisting on the familiar, personal qualities of inspiration and instruction."[92]

Similarly, Julian's Marian performativity responds to and interacts with anxieties surrounding the production of ecclesiastically sanctioned texts. It allays concerns that she is crossing vocational boundaries to challenge clerical primacy in teaching and preaching, as her Marian imagery simultaneously emphasizes her humanity and accessibility, distinguishing her from the often-divinized and intimidating clergy, and authorizes her intercessory function and transmission of the Word. In addition, Birgitta's identification with Mary casts Birgitta as an intermediary, contributing to the matrix of Marian theology on which Julian's *imitatio Mariae* relies for its reception.[93] More broadly, throughout the Middle Ages, writers representing holy women activated memory networks surrounding Mary in order to defuse potential readings of such women as transgressing clearly established (yet troublingly malleable) boundaries.[94]

Julian's long version of *A Revelation of Love* foregrounds Mary as a model instead of focusing exclusively on Christ's humanity and thereby aligning Julian with him, as do many contemplative writings of the high and late Middle Ages. By means of this device, *A Revelation of Love* avoids setting Julian on par with the clergy, who derive their authority in large part through their association with Christ as shepherd. Integrating the familiar idea of Mary's maternal intercession into Julian's account of her visionary experience and interpretive skill, the text claims Julian's privileged connection with God and unique intermediary function in a manner easily accessible to many audiences. The clergy's inability to perform such a function for their flock creates a space in the social and ecclesiastical order to which Julian's *imitatio Mariae* responds, providing a locus for her self-construction as an intercessor for the people of Norwich. It is no wonder, considering this element of her text and her identity, that she is often remembered as Mother Julian.[95]

Notes

1. All quotations from *A Revelation of Love* come from Julian of Norwich, *The Writings of Julian of Norwich: "A Vision Showed to a Devout Woman" and "A Revelation of Love,"* ed. Nicholas Watson and Jacqueline Jenkins (University Park: Pennsylvania State University Press, 2005), and are cited by chapter and line number. Watson and Jenkins's edition uses the Paris manuscript as its base (Bibliotheque Nationale MS Fonds Anglais 40), emending for "texture" and nuance from the Sloane and Amherst manuscripts (British Library MS Sloane 2499 and British Library MS Additional 37790). Their detailed and convincing rationale for this "hybrid" text appears on pp. 24–43. Quotations from Julian's short text, *A Vision Showed to a Devout Woman*, come from the same volume and are cited by chapter and line number.

Exactly when Julian began and finished writing her long version remains contested. Edmund Colledge and James Walsh hypothesize that she began it in 1388 and completed it by 1393. Julian of Norwich, *A Book of Showings to the Anchoress Julian of Norwich*, ed. Colledge and Walsh, 2 vols., Studies and Texts 35 (Toronto: Pontifical Institute of Mediaeval Studies, 1978), 1:19. Nicholas Watson argues for 1393 as the start date, placing the text's completion between 1413 and 1415, in "The Composition of Julian of Norwich's *Revelation of Love*," *Speculum* 68, no. 3 (1993): 678 [637–83]. Lynn Staley sets the completion date at 1399 in "Julian of Norwich and the Crisis of Authority," in *The Powers of the Holy: Religion, Politics, and Gender in Late Medieval English Culture*, ed. David Aers and Lynn Staley (University Park: Pennsylvania State University Press, 1996), 126 [107–78].

2. Mary J. Carruthers, *The Book of Memory: A Study of Memory in Medieval Culture*, 2nd ed., Cambridge Studies in Medieval Literature 70 (Cambridge: Cambridge University Press, 2008), 183. Scholarship thus far has treated the Marian visions as tangential to Julian's central message of God's love in various forms, especially her representation of God as mother. Liz Herbert McAvoy reads Julian's Marian visions as an exploration of motherhood that leads naturally into her development of Christ as mother: "As a mirror image of his own mother's suffering and transcendence of it, Christ's salvific labouring on the cross becomes the process by which he gives birth to redemption for humanity. Thus, Christ is already being absorbed into a hermeneutic of divine motherhood" (*Authority and the Female Body in the Writings of Julian of Norwich and Margery Kempe* [Cambridge: D. S. Brewer, 2004], 79). This analysis upholds the hierarchy that Elizabeth Ann Robertson has recognized in devotional writing for women, which sees female experience as a stepping stone to a higher, masculine, rational way of knowing while eliding the anchorite's identification with Mary herself (*Early English Devotional Prose and the Female Audience* [Knoxville: University of Tennessee Press, 1990], 193). Nicholas Watson and Carmel Davis have both contended that Julian's description of a multifaceted God rehabilitates women as members of the Christian community and sets up a synecdoche in which the feminine can stand for humanity as a whole. For Watson's argument, see "'Yf Wommen Be Double Naturelly': Remaking 'Woman' in Julian of Norwich's *Revelation of Love*," *Exemplaria* 8, no. 1 (1996): 1–34. Carmel Bendon Davis also briefly ties Julian's Marian visions into her imagery of God as mother. She argues that the "motherhood allusion" speaks to "the enclosure of humanity in God, of God in our souls, and of Christ in our humanity" (*Mysticism and Space: Spatiality in the Works of Richard Rolle, "The Cloud of Unknowing" Author, and Julian of Norwich* [Washington, DC: Catholic University of America, 2008], 243). Mary, having physically borne Christ, reinforces this chiasmus of enclosure— God in humanity and humanity in God—by appearing as "a creature of God's making who would be instrumental in the making of God"

(244)

(244). I attempt here not to divorce the Marian imagery from the context of Julian's meditation on God's love, which unquestionably inflects it, but rather to foreground some implications for Julian's self-perception and presentation that the anchorite's recurring identification with Mary suggests.

3. I use the words *revelation* and *vision* synonymously to refer to "an experience (not necessarily solely visual) which is thought not to originate with the recipient but to mediate directly between that person and some transcendent reality" (Watson, "Composition," 643n16). The term *contemplation* here describes the practice of meditation and prayer directed at achieving union with God, not specifically at receiving a revelation. Many vowed religious dedicated themselves to lives of contemplation without experiencing visions like Julian's. I use the term *religious* as a noun and adjective denoting career religious (clergy, monastics, and contemplatives), as opposed to the laity.

4. "The church" here denotes the Roman Catholic Church, established in England during the late antique period.

5. Introduction to this volume.

6. Barbara Zimbalist, "Imitating the Imagined: Clemence of Barking's *Life of St. Catherine*," chapter 5 in this volume.

7. Twenty-five apologia to this effect appear in Julian's long text, such as, "But in all thing I believe as holy church precheth and techeth. For the faith of holy church, which I had beforehand understonde—and, as I hope, by the grace of God willefully kept in use and custome—stode continually in my sighte, willing and meaning never to receive onything that might be contrary therto" (*Revelation* 9.2, pp. 21–25); for a list that compares these apologia in the short and long versions, see Elisabeth Hansen's master's thesis, "A Vision of Her Place: Julian of Norwich and the Contemplative's Role in the Christian Community" (University of Wyoming, 2007), 71–87.

8. Caroline Walker Bynum, *Jesus as Mother: Studies in the Spirituality of the High Middle Ages* (Berkeley: University of California Press, 1982), 11; see also Claire Waters, *Angels and Earthly Creatures: Preaching, Performance, and Gender in the Later Middle Ages* (Philadelphia: University of Pennsylvania Press, 2004), 3.

9. See Staley, "Crisis of Authority," 125–26.

10. Claire Sahlin, "Gender and Prophetic Authority in Birgitta of Sweden's *Revelations*," in *Gender and Text in the Later Middle Ages*, ed. Jane Chance (Gainesville: University Press of Florida, 1996), 70 [69–95].

11. A vast literature exists on this topic. See, for example, Laurelle LeVert, "'Crucifye hem, Crucifye hem': The Subject and Affective Response in Middle English Passion Narratives," *Essays in Medieval Studies* 14 (1997): 73–90; Alastair Minnis, "Affection and Imagination in *The Cloud of Unknowing* and Hilton's *Scale of Perfection*," *Traditio* 39 (1983): 323–66; and Carolyn Walker Bynum, *Holy Feast and Holy Fast: The Religious Significance of Food to Medieval Women* (Berkeley: University of California, 1987). The

trend toward affective piety encouraged increasing numbers of woman visionaries who, like Julian, had to frame and communicate their visions in ways acceptable to the church. The doctrine of *discretio spirituum*, discernment of spirits, informed the church's testing of such visionaries. See Rosalynn Voaden, *God's Words, Women's Voices: The Discernment of Spirits in the Writing of Late-Medieval Women Visionaries* (Woodbridge, UK: Boydell and Brewer, 1999), and Nancy Caciola, *Discerning Spirits: Divine and Demonic Possession in the Middle Ages* (Ithaca, NY: Cornell University Press, 2003).

12. Hilda Graef, *Mary: A History of Doctrine and Devotion*, 2 vols. (New York: Sheed and Ward, 1963), 1:210–64.

13. The appellation *mediatrix* appears, for example, in Bernard's prayer to the Virgin in his sermon *De verbis Isaiae ad Achaz*: "Domina nostra, mediatrix nostra, advocata nostra, tuo Filio nos reconcilia, tuo Filio nos commenda, tuo nos Filio repraesenta" (St. Bernard of Clairvaux, *De adventu Domine*, in *Patrologia latina*, edited by J.-P. Migne, vol. 183 [Paris: Migne, 1844–45], 723 [703–17] [hereafter *PL*]; all Latin translations are my own). In his sermon *De aquaeductu*, Bernard writes that Christ "descendit per aquaeductum vena illa coelestis." He asks, "Quid nos alia concupiscimus, fratres? Quaeramus gratiam, et per Mariam quaeramus" (St. Bernard of Clairvaux, *In navitate B. V. Mariae*, in *PL* 183:1013, 1015 [1012–19]). Christ, to Bernard, is also a mediator but one who might seem inaccessible and intimidating to believers (Catherine M. Mooney, "*Imitatio Christi* or *Imitatio Mariae*? Clare of Assisi and Her Interpreters," in *Gendered Voices: Medieval Saints and Their Interpreters*, ed. Catherine M. Mooney [Philadelphia: University of Pennsylvania Press, 1999], 69 [52–77]).

14. "Nec facile ullam prophetasse uberius quam matrem Domini reperimus." Ambrosius Mediolanensis, *Expositio evangelii secundum Lucam*, in *PL* 15:1293 [1260–544].

15. The claim of clerical power to absolve and condemn derives from Matthew 16:19, where Jesus tells Peter, "I will give to thee the keys of the kingdom of heaven. And whatsoever thou shalt bind upon earth, it shall be bound also in heaven: and whatsoever thou shalt loose upon earth, it shall be loosed also in heaven" ("tibi dabo claves regni caelorum et quodcumque ligaveris super terram erit ligatum in caelis et quodcumque solveris super terram erit solutum in caelis"). According to the doctrine of apostolic succession, the first pope was Peter's successor, and he received the power to bind and loose along with his mandate. Subsequent popes and ordained clergy inherited this same authority. All biblical quotations are from the *Douay-Rheims Bible* (Rockford, IL: Tan Books, 1989).

16. Bynum, *Jesus as Mother*, especially 162 and 173. For additional examples, see Sharon Elkins, "Gertrude the Great and the Virgin Mary," *Church History* 66, no. 4 (1997): 720–34.

17. *Revelation* 4.

18. *Revelation* 18.1, p. 1.

19. *Revelation* 25.1, p. 34.

20. *Revelation* 25.2, pp. 26, 31–32.

21. In *Revelation* 8.1, p. 24, for example, Julian expresses her wish to communicate her vision to "mine evenchristen, that they might alle see and know the same that I sawe, for I wolde that it were comfort to them. For alle this sight was shewde *in generalle*" (my emphasis). See also *Revelation* 79.2, pp. 1–8. For an analysis of Mary's function as a model not specifically for Julian but for every Christian, see Marion Glassoe, *English Medieval Mystics: Games of Faith* (London: Longman, 1993), 221. Glassoe asserts, "Mary projects the pattern of transfiguration possible for all men to 'worshippe and ioye' in Christ whose glory is ineffably the completion of all partiality" (221).

22. See Watson and Jenkins's notes to citations in this paragraph.

23. *Revelation* 4.2, pp. 14–16.

24. Ibid., pp. 28–31.

25. Ibid., pp. 13–14.

26. Ibid., pp. 32–33.

27. Julian strictly distinguishes between bodily and spiritual sights, likely because of contemplative tradition's distrust of revelations received via the senses, especially the eyes.

28. *Revelation* 25.2, pp. 16–17.

29. See, for example, Thomas Aquinas, *Summa theologica*, trans. Fathers of the English Dominican Province, 3 vols. (New York: Benziger Bros., 1947–48), vol. 1, articles 2–4; John Cassian, *John Cassian: The Conferences*, trans. Boniface Ramsey (New York: Paulist Press, 1997), ch. 8 and 17; and *The Cloud of Unknowing*, ed. Patrick J. Gallacher, TEAMS Middle English Texts (Kalamazoo: Western Michigan University's Medieval Institute Publications, 1997), ch. 24.

30. *Revelation* 7.2, pp. 5–8. The formulation "reverent drede," and variants of it, appears 15 times in *A Revelation of Love*, and Julian sees it as a theme throughout her entire "matter" (*Revelation* 76.1).

31. *Revelation* 25.1, p. 17; for Julian's other descriptions of her "reverent drede," see also *Revelation* 8.1, p. 20, and 83.1, p. 7.

32. *Revelation* 9.1, p. 1. In her passages describing the Virgin's connection to God, Julian focus on Mary's emotional response, marking an implicit contrast with the clergy's more intellectual link to heaven.

33. *Revelation* 74.2, pp. 41–43; for Julian's encouragement of "reverent drede" in her audience, see also *Revelation* 74.2, pp. 26–27; 65.2, pp. 7–8, 25–26; and 75.2, pp. 35–36.

34. *Revelation* 76.2, pp. 2–3.

35. Zimbalist, "Imitating the Imagined," chapter 5 in this volume. Clemence of Barking's *Life of St. Catherine*, written nearly 200 years earlier, allowed Clemence "to perform an imitation of Christ while simultaneously providing a model for further imitation on the part of her readers," operating in a manner similar to these passages of Julian's *Revelation*.

36. *Revelation* 2.2, pp. 3–4.

37. Ibid., pp. 7–12 (emphasis added).

38. Ibid., pp. 12–13.

39. Henry Suso's *Horologium Sapientiae*, for example, describes Mary's sorrow at the Cross in the final chapter of book one, entitled "A singular commendation of the Blessed Virgin and of her inestimable grief, which she had at the passion of the Son" (Commendatio singularis beatae virginis et de dolore eius inaestimabili, quem habuit in passione Filii"). See Henry Suso, *Heinrich Seuses Horologium Sapientiae: Erste Kritische Ausgabe unter Benützung der Vorarbeiten von Dominikus Planzer OP*, ed. Pius Künzle (Freiburg, Germany: Universitätsverlag, 1977), 1.16.

40. *Revelation* 2.2, pp. 18–21.

41. *Revelation* 3.1, p. 24; 3.2, pp. 14–15; *Vision* 10.2, pp. 26–28.

42. The anchorhold itself also recalls the womb, where Julian's interpretations of the revelations gestate and from which her writings issue. Living in such a space may have given Julian greater affinity for Mary after her initial revelations, during which she does not seem to have been enclosed, and contributed to her *imitatio Mariae*. For a helpful Freudian and Kristevan analysis of this idea, see Nancy Coiner, "The 'Homely' and the Heimliche: The Hidden, Doubled Self in Julian of Norwich's Showings," *Exemplaria* 5, no. 2 (1993): 305–23.

43. Amy Neff, "The Pain of *Compassio*: Mary's Labor at the Foot of the Cross," *Art Bulletin* 80, no. 2 (1998): 255 [254–73].

44. "Quid autem dico similem, cum vere sit mulier, et vere mater, et veros habeat in illa hora partus sui dolores? Non enim habuit haec mulier hanc poenam, ut in dolore pareret sicut caeterae matres, quando infans sibi natus est; sed nunc dolet, cruciatur, et tristitiam habet, quia venit hora ejus…In passione unigeniti omnium nostrum salutem beata Virgo peperit, plane omnium nostrum mater est" (Rupertus Tuitiensis, *Commentaria in Joannem, PL* 169:90–348 [Paris: 1844–45], 789–90). I referred to Amy Neff's translation while making my own ("Pain of *Compassio*," 256).

45. *Revelation* 57.2, pp. 40–42.

46. Neff, "Pain of *Compassio*."

47. *Revelation* 2.2, pp. 34–35.

48. "Et tuam ipsius animam pertransiet gladius ut revelentur ex multis cordibus cogitationes."

49. *Revelation* 17.2, pp. 50–52; 18.2, pp. 1–3, 5–6.

50. Rachel Fulton, *From Judgment to Passion: Devotion to Christ and the Virgin Mary, 800–1200* (New York: Columbia University Press, 2002), 199.

51. *Revelation* 86.12, p. 379.

52. *Revelation* 82.2, pp. 8–9.

53. Fulton, *Judgment to Passion*, 308.

54. *Revelation* 86.2, pp. 1–2.

55. *Revelation* 6.1, p. 2.

56. Ibid., p. 9.

57. *Revelation* 6.2, pp. 4–8.

58. Ibid., pp. 19–22.

59. Ibid., pp. 12–13.

60. *Revelation* 7.1, p. 8. Julian uses cataphatic language to describe how Christians' divine attributes reflect those of the Trinity: "For God is endlesse sovereyne truth, endlesse sovereyne wisdom, endlesse sovereyne love unmade. And mans soule is a creature in God, which hath the same propertes made" (*Revelation* 44.2, pp. 9–11).

61. *Revelation* 6.1, p. 16.

62. Ibid., pp. 22–24.

63. *Revelation* 4.2, pp. 6–8.

64. *The Cloud of Unknowing*, ch. 37.

65. *Revelation* 9.1, p. 1.

66. Ibid., p. 16.

67. *Revelation* 4.2, pp. 33–35.

68. *Revelation* 61.2, pp. 51–52.

69. Ibid., pp. 52–57.

70. *Revelation* 60.2, pp. 29–31

71. *Revelation* 66.2, p. 12; p. 334.

72. Ibid., pp. 12–13.

73. Ibid., pp. 14–15.

74. Ibid., pp. 4, 9–10, 22, 15, 23. Although Julian wants to confess her shameful response to the revelations, she draws a comparison between herself and her priest that convinces her he will not believe she had a vision, even though the "religious person" just did: "I waxed full gretly ashamed, and wolde have bene shriven. But I coulde telle it to no prest. For I thought: 'How shulde a preste believe me? I beleved not oure lorde God'" (ibid., pp. 18–20). Here, as surely in other places, the text undermines Julian's hierarchical presentation of herself vis-à-vis the clergy.

75. "Quae cum vidisset turbata est in sermone eius et cogitabat qualis esset ista salutatio."

76. On clerical experiences of and responses to tension between the preacher's human nature and his idealized, "angelic" role, see Waters, *Angels and Earthly Creatures*.

77. Brad Herzog, "Portrait of a Holy Life: Mnemonic Inventiveness in *The Book of Margery Kempe*," chapter 9 in this volume.

78. Ibid.

79. Watson, "Wommen," 27.

80. *Revelation* 75.1, p. 35.

81. Bynum, *Jesus as Mother*, 11. In "Jesus as Mother and Abbot as Mother: Some Themes in Twelfth-Century Cistercian Writing," Bynum warns against reading these images as "feminine" in their original Cistercian context. The twelfth-century monastic devotion to God's maternal attributes focused less on suffering and more on "breasts and nurturing, the womb, conception, and union as incorporation" (*Harvard Theological Review* 70, nos. 3–4 (1977): 258 [257–84]). Julian's use of the God-as-mother analogy

might hint at her inheritance of authority from such theological giants as
Bernard and Aelred of Rievaulx.

82. This metaphor relies on the "medieval medical theory [that] breast milk
is processed blood" (Bynum, *Jesus as Mother*, 132).

83. Mooney, "*Imitatio Christi*," 69.

84. Mooney traces Clare's posthumous reception history beginning with
her process of canonization in 1255, demonstrating the disconnect
between the *imitatio Christi* evident in Clare's own writings and the *imitatio Mariae* that later characterizations impose on her ("*Imitatio Christi*,"
esp. 71).

85. On Birgitta, see Sahlin, "Gender and Prophetic Authority," 75. On
Hildegard, see Barbara Newman, "Hildegard and Her Hagiographers,"
in *Gendered Voices: Medieval Saints and Their Interpreters*, ed. Catherine M.
Mooney (Philadelphia: University of Pennsylvania Press, 1999), 16–34.
On Elisabeth, see Anne L. Clark, "Holy Woman or Unworthy Vessel?
The Representations of Elisabeth of Schönau," in Mooney, *Gendered
Voices*, 40–42 [35–51].

86. Newman, "Hildegard," 25.

87. Clark, "Holy Woman," 40.

88. Luke 1:48.

89. In *The Book of Memory*, Mary Carruthers explores the operation of
such "publicly held commonplaces" in memorial florilegium (182–83).
These collections of rhetorical texts reinforce ethical principles by
"occasionaliz[ing] a norm," as Julian's text provides a concrete site for
popular ideas of Mary and of revelation to interact (181). This approach
contrasts with that of traditional exegesis, which holds specifics (or acci-
dentals) forth as timeless and universal rather than identifying discrete
realizations of overarching concepts.

90. Julian's *imitatio Mariae* may also have encouraged subsequent efforts to
construct devotional texts for women by using women as models. The
early fifteenth-century meditative handbook *Speculum devotorum*, for
example, reworks Henry Suso's "male-centered text" *Horologium sapientiae* for a specifically "female spirituality," largely through its emphasis on
Mary as "a model whose behaviour the reader is encouraged to emulate"
(Rebecca Selman, "Spirituality and Sex Change: *Horologium sapientiae*
and *Speculum devotorum*," in *Writing Religious Women: Female Spiritual and
Textual Practice in Late Medieval England*, ed. Denis Renevey and Christiana
Whitehead (Toronto: University of Toronto Press, 2000), 65 [63–80]).
Crucially, though, Julian interprets her own revelations; for this practice's
implications for authority, see Staley, "Crisis of Authority."

91. Analysis of Birgitta's Marian tropes is constrained, however, by the textual mediation of her male confessors. Whereas Julian's writings are the
product of her own musings on her experiences (though inescapably
inflected by her surroundings), Birgitta's *Revelations* represent "a collaborative effort to convey what they [Birgitta and her confessors] believed
to be the divine word—the word of God—conveyed through Birgitta."

Claire L. Sahlin, *Birgitta of Sweden and the Voice of Prophecy* (Rochester, NY: Bogdell, 2002), 33.

92. Waters, *Angels and Earthly Creatures*, 138.

93. See Sahlin, *Birgitta of Sweden*, ch. 3, esp. 80–82. My connection of Julian's self-representation to Birgitta's *imitatio Mariae* counters Sahlin's assertion that "the predominant posthumous image of Birgitta's devotion to Mary overshadowed the prophetic authority she derived through her identification with Mary's maternity and thereby restrained rather than encouraged any similar impulses to find empowerment by emulating Mary's role as the vessel of divine revelation" (107).

94. Margaret Cotter-Lynch demonstrates, for example, that Notker of Saint Gall deproblematizes Perpetua's gender identity for a monastic readership by constructing the saint in Marian terms. "Mnemonic Sanctity and the Ladder of Reading: Notker's "In Natale Sanctarum Feminarum," chapter 2 in this volume.

95. For this appellation, popular in modern Catholicism, see, for example, *The Columbia Encyclopedia*, 6th ed., s.v. "Juliana of Norwich," accessed May 5, 2008, http://www.infoplease.com/ce6/people/A0826735.html, and Geoffrey Curtis, "Mother Julian of Norwich: Two Kinds of Marriage," *Mystics Quarterly* 8 (1982): 62–71.

CHAPTER 9

PORTRAIT OF A HOLY LIFE: MNEMONIC
INVENTIVENESS IN *THE BOOK OF
MARGERY KEMPE*

Brad Herzog

> *Narration is a form of spatial strategy. A storyteller creates new boundaries in old spaces, or builds skywalks between existing spaces, or razes buildings to create new frontiers.*[1]

After waiting 20 years to compose her book, Margery Kempe—in the 1430s—dictated the account of her life to two scribes, one of whom helped her revise. Even though Kempe claims to be illiterate, she mines her rich memory stores to frame, structure, and authorize her account. To do so, she draws on tropes, figures, *exempla*, character types, plot lines, and settings from biblical accounts, saints' lives, and virgin martyr legends. Even though she was unschooled, she avidly listened to public sermons and the private instructions of her amanuensis, who read and interpreted many religious texts for her, texts whose modes and messages she recorded in her prolific memory. Drawing on the work of Mary Carruthers, accounts of Christ's passion, and virgin martyr tales, I examine Kempe's use of memory arts in the invention and arrangement of her heresy trial accounts.

In *The Craft of Thought*, Carruthers identifies medieval memory arts not as techniques for rote memorization but as creative, imaginative resources for rhetorical invention. As we note in the introduction, Carruthers argues that medieval thinkers regarded memory both as a structured archive allowing for convenient image recollection and retrieval and as a dynamic associational network or construction machine for creatively combining and recombining images for endless varieties of compositions.[2] Since each individual fashioned a unique memory network reflecting and shaping his or her own character, memory networks involved a personal moral or ethical dimension. Yet since each network's constituent foundations, associations, and contents derived in part from cultural commonplaces, memory networks also included political or civic dimensions.[3] Ultimately, interpreting words, actions, or events within the contexts of certain memory networks informs one's identity and situates one within a community or culture.

Shared memory networks can be deployed in politically and culturally powerful ways. Groups or individuals can crowd out selected memories, block competing memories, or overlay and co-opt rival memory networks. As Carruthers illustrates in *The Craft of Thought*, societies often reinforced dominance over competing traditions, religions, or ideologies by preserving remembered traces of their rivals and by co-opting them within strategic memory networks. This constituted a more effective strategy than trying to erase or forget all traces of the competing tradition.[4]

In this chapter, I will explore how Margery Kempe employed memory arts in composing her book, overlaying the account of her heresy trials with virgin martyr legends and Christ's passion. In doing so, she co-opts her persecutors in a strategic narrative that validates her spiritual vocation. Through her use of memory arts, moreover, Kempe engrafts her account with tropes, figures, character types, plot lines, settings, dialogue, and conflicts from the Bible and martyrologies as a way of imitating Christ's passion and the passions of virgin martyrs. This imitation authorizes her in redefining the limits of the public acts permitted her as a woman. In addition, like virgin martyrs who attracted communities of converts and later cult followings through their radical opposition to pagan authorities, Kempe—through her critiques of inadequate clergy and her claims of personal access to the divine—invokes and anticipates a reform-minded community. By drawing on remembered commonplaces from martyrologies, Kempe ultimately encourages reform-minded audiences to place her in the company of defiant holy women—and, within the context of her book's memory networks, to read themselves as her "converts" in opposing her "corrupt" adversaries.

Examining medieval memory arts and composition processes, Cheryl Glenn contends that "Margery composes her book as cyclical and associational...Using her memory as a conceptual filter for image formation and recollection...she orders her impressive, self-contained vignettes so that they render the whole message."[5] Moreover, "her tellings represent the intertextual compositions of medieval popular literacy, the easy commingling of autobiography, hagiography, social history, scripture, and Franciscan practices for the edification and pleasure of her intended audience."[6] These textual and oral traces mingle in her memory. Tapping these mnemonic resources, Kempe inventively infuses them into the account of her life, imaginatively reshaping and authorizing her account.

Examining Kempe's use of memory in her composing process, Naoe Kukita Yoshikawa argues that the study of medieval memory arts illuminates the structure and composition of Kempe's book. According to Yoshikawa, "Recent study on the mnemonic technique and practice of meditation in medieval monastic education claims that the monastic traditions of memory became part of general culture in the thirteenth, fourteenth, and later centuries."[7] More than likely, Kempe would have learned about "the technique of *divisiones* and *compositio* and that of ordering the material by participating in the various forms of Church liturgy...But Kempe seems to be most influenced by the Franciscans' imaginative meditation elaborated in [Giovanni de Cauli's] *Meditationes vitae Christi*, which was available to her both in Latin and in Nicholas Love's abridged translation in English, the *Mirror of the Blessed Life of Jesus Christ*."[8] Since "alle Þo Þinges Þat Jesus dide, bene not written in Þe Gospelle," Love asserts, the *Mirror* employs "ymaginacions of cristes life" to stir "symple soules to Þe loue of god & desire of heuenly Þinges."[9] This style of contemplative devotion, Carruthers affirms, "is also an inventive act, a 'construction'" of memory.[10]

Drawing on the texts of medieval religious authorities, Carruthers argues that medieval religious communities employed memory arts in their devotional practices to invent, imagine, compose, and imitate. Yoshikawa affirms that the liturgy, the Franciscans, and texts such as the *Mirror* transmitted memory arts—including imitative devotional practices—to lay audiences, so both religious and lay audiences had access to these arts and practices. In the twelfth century, Barbara Zimbalist notes, Clemence of Barking engaged in imitative devotion by imitating Catherine and Christ through her process of creating a vernacular hagiography of Saint Catherine. As Zimbalist affirms, "The hagiographer who imitates the sacred subject performs an *imitatio* that can be seen as devotional practice: by imitating Catherine's speech, Clemence inhabits Catherine's role as the speaking figure; and by inhabiting this role, Clemence inhabits Catherine's *imitatio Christi* and engages in virtuous Christian activity."[11] Citing Anne Clark Bartlett, Zimbalist asserts that "*imitatio*—the fashioning and reconstruction of the self in accordance with the multiple models provided by the holy family, male and female saints, aristocratic ideals, and an assortment of textualized personages"— served as the main purpose of "devotional discourse."[12]

Like Clemence, Julian of Norwich practices imitative devotion, for she engages in *imitatio Mariae*. By requesting a "bodily" sight of Christ's passion, asserts Elissa Hansen, Julian asks to experience the crucifixion the way that Mary and the disciples experienced it. Julian also requests three wounds. These wounds link "Julian's suffering to Mary's"—a suffering that Simeon prophesied would be like a sword piercing the virgin's soul.[13] Finally, Julian describes her near-death experience in a way that recalls the pangs of giving birth, pangs—Saint Boneventure maintains—that the virgin felt at the crucifixion because she was giving birth to the church through Christ's passion.[14] Like Julian, Margery Kempe also shows her devotion through imitation. Using the resources of her memory inventories, Kempe imitates the lives of Christ and the virgin martyrs.

Kempe may have heard legends of virgin martyrs from sermons based on Mirk's *Festial* or the *South English Legendary*.[15] Their lives also are recounted in Jacobus de Voragine's *Legenda aurea*, and their images frequently appeared "on the rood screens of East Anglia."[16] The anonymous "Stanzaic Life of Katherine" probably was composed during the thirteenth century, in part as an answer to the popularity of secular romances.[17] According to Yoshikawa, "The saints in [Kempe's] meditation seem to be rooted in the Sarum liturgy and in popular hagiography," and she may have viewed "scenes from the lives of saints illustrated in Books of Hours."[18] In addition, one of Kempe's contemporaries—Osbern Bokenham—wrote the *Lyvys of Seyntys or Legendys of Hooly Wummen*."[19] Since virgin martyr legends were an inescapable part of the milieu of medieval England, Kempe must have heard about them since childhood.[20] Engrafting tropes, figures, plots, and images from the legends of Saint Margaret, Saint Katherine, and other virgin martyrs, Kempe establishes her ethos as a holy woman and redefines the limits of women's public religious acts. To these ends, Kempe skillfully employs the trope of the virgin martyr confounding her oppressors.

In *The Book of Margery Kempe*—as in the tales of Katherine and Margaret—the antagonists treat the heroine as a threat, augment their rage exponentially at her defiance, and suffer some form of divine retribution for their unjust acts. One reason for the perceived threat and the antagonists' increase in rage is the divine gift of speech, wisdom, and irrefutable truth granted to each heroine. Maxence summons the 50 wisest and most knowledgeable men in his kingdom to debate Katherine,[21] to convince her to give up her faith, and to persuade her to worship the pagan gods. After each one presents his arguments, Katherine overpowers them all with her divinely inspired wisdom and convinces them to convert to Christianity. Salih compares Katherine's victory to Kempe's, for Kempe defends herself and maintains her orthodoxy in spite of the many learned

clergymen arrayed against her in her heresy trials (97–98).[22] Impressed by
her success, many in York rejoice "in our Lord who had given her…wit
and wisdom to answer so many learned men without villany or blame"
(95). Even the lawyers wonder at her. "We have gone to school many
years," they acknowledge. "Yet we are not sufficient to answer as you do"
(100). Kempe, of course, gives credit to the Holy Ghost (100).

Kempe's interrogation at Cawood reveals some of her most powerful reasoning and rhetoric. Enjoined by the archbishop not to teach in
his diocese, Kempe flatly refuses his ban, declaring that she never will
cease speaking of God as long as she lives. Ingeniously adapting a gospel
account to sanction her public voice, Kempe asserts that "God almighty
forbids not, sir, that we shall speak of him," for "when the woman had
heard our Lord preach, she came before him with a loud voice and said
'Blessed be the womb that bore you and the teats that gave you suck.'
Then our Lord said again to her, 'Forsooth so are they blessed that hear
the word of God and keep it.' And therefore, sir, I think that the gospel
gives me leave to speak of God" (93). Seizing on Kempe's exegesis of
the gospel, one of the clerks claims that she has a devil and cites Saint
Paul's injunction against women preaching. Responding, Kempe avers,
"I preach not, sir, I go in no pulpit. I use but communication and good
words, and that will I do while I live" (93). Ingeniously, Kempe creatively
reinterprets remembered scriptures. In Luke's gospel, Christ's reply to
the woman praising his mother doesn't explicitly validate her outspoken-
ness.[23] Rather, he pronounces those "blessed" who keep God's word.[24]
Like her application of remembered commonplaces from virgin martyr
legends, Kempe's reinterpretation of biblical passages validates her acts of
evangelizing as appropriate to the role of a holy woman.

Besides creatively adapting Christ's words to sanction her own out-
spokenness, Kempe also redefines preaching so narrowly that she opens
up an immense scope for her own religious utterances. In her research,
Roxanne Mountford identifies the pulpit as a highly contested, gendered
public space. By forfeiting her claim to the pulpit, Kempe appears to be
yielding to the male clergy. In reality, given the constraints of her day,
she does something quite remarkable: she transforms the public sphere,
redefining the exclusive domain of the male clergy as the narrow space
behind the pulpit and reclaiming for herself every other public space.[25]
Moreover, even though she "comes in no pulpit," she publicly employs
remembered preaching genres—"scriptural exegesis," pious "exempla," "sermon vocatives," quotes from preachers, quotes from scripture,
"reproofs" for sin, and "admonitions" to repentance[26]—before large lay
and religious congregations gathered in churches for her heresy trials. A
shrewd rhetorical move, Kempe's claim that she does not preach actually

enables her to preach without reprisals.[27] As Mountford asserts, "The preacher's narrative rearranges sacred space, removing barriers to form an enlarged 'here,' setting barriers to a new 'there.'"[28] Ironically, the clergy who wish to silence her unwittingly provide her with the audience, occasion, and setting for her best preaching. Finally, the piercing cries manifest through her gift of tears saturate even the exclusive male space behind the pulpit, disrupting male discourse with her overdetermined, undecidable female body—a body that issues tears because of her memorative contemplations of Christ's passion. Through her creative memory work, Margery Kempe transforms the public sphere for women and invokes the authority of virgin martyrs without imitating their self-destructive ideology. Drawing on commonplaces from martyrologies, moreover, Kempe portrays herself turning the tables on her powerful adversaries.

Kempe also employs memory arts through imitative devotional arts. With a suffering body characteristic of *imitatio Christi*—and irrepressible tears characteristic of *imitatio Mariae*—Margery Kempe disrupts established religious spaces, hierarchies, and discourses. The codified, institutionalized Latin of the mass left little room for personal voice or expression. The hierarchy of cultural and architectural spaces separating clergy from congregation allowed scant opportunity for the exercise of lay authority. The weight of vestments and priesthoods, the imbalance in education and literacy, the force of symbols and ceremony all made it unlikely that a laywoman could wield power in the church. Yet, in her book, Kempe does just that.

Issuing from her body, Kempe's cries—like an aural Holy Ghost—permeate every corner of the church, piercing even immaculate, masculine spaces. Disrupting sermons and her own heresy trials, Kempe's tears authorize her by evoking in her audience memories of other tearful holy women such as Mary of Oignies—and the weeping women at the crucifixion, the Virgin Mary, and Mary Magdalene. Resisting contemporary authority, Kempe's thrashing, suffering body imitates and reminds audiences of Christ's passion. The immediacy of Christ's passion to her soul trumps the taboos of social etiquette. Reproving Kempe for disrupting a church service, a priest states, "Damsel, Jesus is dead long since." In reply, Kempe affirms, "Sir, his death is as fresh to me as if he had died this same day, and so I think it ought to be to you and to all Christian people. We ought ever to have mind of his kindness and ever think of the doleful death that he died for us" (109). While church services and proceedings reaffirm institutional identity, Kempe's crying disrupts the authorities' program, redirecting cultural memory networks and confronting her audience with an immediate awareness and memory of divine suffering.

Ultimately, Kempe's crying, *passio*, and *imitatio Christi* disrupt the established community, opening the possibility—however remote—of forg-
ing a new one.

What community might Kempe fashion? How does she reconfigure
cultural commonplaces—or *res memoribiles*—in ways that could unify an
alternative community? For its patterns of community formation, Kempe's
book draws on memorable precedents, especially those of Christ's life.
Christ's body—pierced, lacerated, bloodied, and crucified—reconstitutes
itself through the resurrection, albeit with traces of its wounds, the return
of the sublated term in the new synthesis of body and soul, an indelible
reminder of his sacrifice, an enduring link with humanity, and a channel
to salvation.

Even though Christ's executioners did not sever his body parts, Christ's
body—like Osiris's flesh—symbolically suffers sacramental fragmentation and restoration. According to the doctrine of transubstantiation, the
water and wine of communion transform into Christ's flesh and blood
before entering the partakers' bodies.[29] Christ's redemptive power not
only reconstitutes his and others' private bodies through the resurrection
but also incorporates them into a larger body, the public communal body
of the church. In Paul's words, "The cup of blessing which we bless, is it
not the communion of the blood of Christ? The bread which we break, is
it not the communion of the body of Christ? For we being many are one
bread, and one body; for we are all partakers of that one bread."[30] The
"one bread," of course, is Christ, the head of the church, the new body of
believers, for as Paul affirms, "he is the head of the body, the church."[31]
Emphasizing the unity of members in this body, Paul asserts, "Now ye
are the body of Christ, and members in particular."[32] Suffering martyrdom, Christ reconstitutes his own body and the bodies of humanity.
Moreover, disseminating his body sacramentally, Christ reincorporates
it—and its partakers—into his communal body, the church. Invoking
culturally constructed memories of Christ's passion, communion serves
as a basis of identification for congregation members, uniting them in
Christ's body politic, a community with new possibilities, motives, and
symbolic resources.

Functioning as imitations of Christ's passion, virgin martyrs' passions
shape communities in- and outside the text in ways that serve as precedents for the account of Kempe's life. Like the blood and body of Christ
disseminated in communion, the actions, relics, and intercessory prayers
of virgin martyrs serve as shared memorial commonplaces and bases of
identification for religious communities. Margaret Cotter-Lynch identifies similar community-shaping functions in Notker of Saint Gall's hymn
"In Natale Sanctarum Feminarum." According to Cotter-Lynch, the

hymn invokes "images" associated with the account of Saint Perpetua, a third-century martyr whose legend contributed to the memory inventories of Notker's contemporaries. Pointing to these shared memories, Cotter-Lynch affirms, Notker's hymn shapes audience members' "individual and communal identities." Ultimately, "the memorial structure that Notker provides...is also an institutional structure within which individuals place themselves as members of a community," a placement that shapes their identities. In the end, "remembering within a given pattern can be constitutive of community membership" and of one's identity.[33]

Illustrating the connection among memory, identity, and community, Mary Carruthers recounts the way that Libanus—a member of Antioch's ruling class in the mid-fourth century—greeted "the legal advisers" of the new governor. "How did Odysseus rule when king of Ithaca?" Libanus queried. "Gently as a father," the advisers replied, thereby identifying themselves as members of Libanus's class and culture. Because of their "common store of *res memorabiles*" and educational background, Libanus, the legal advisers, and other men of their class shared not only a "means of communication" but also "a web of community or commonality."[34] In this case, lines from the *Odyssey* represent a cultural heritage that serves as a common ground for members of a privileged class. Similarly, a man convicted of a capital crime in England could escape the noose in favor of a more merciful death—such as beheading—if he could "read or recite a verse from the Bible, thus proving himself to be a member of the clerical class." By remembering a biblical verse (dubbed the "neck verse"), convicts could establish a "common ground" with members of "an educated class, who were immune from hanging by legal custom."[35]

Like Libanus, the governor's advisers, and savvy convicts, Margery Kempe uses her own and her audience's memory inventories to establish her identity and to place herself and her audience within certain communities.[36] Given their familiarity with the legends of virgin martyrs such as Katherine and Margaret, Kempe's audiences would have recognized the influence of hagiographic stock characters such as courageous maidens, wicked judges, and humble converts; common plot devices such as theological debates, cruel punishments, and supernatural interventions; and tropes such as defending one's virtue, out-debating one's opponents, praying for one's spiritual posterity, and defying authorities. By tapping her own and her audience's memories of virgin martyr tales, Kempe places herself within a community of defiant holy women—and places her accusers in the company of corrupt, worldly, and coercive judges.[37] Moreover, she provides a way for lay audiences to support her, for she invokes memory networks that encourage them to identify themselves as her "converts,"[38] opposing the "corrupt" authorities who afflict her. Besides identifying with Kempe because of her background as a lay-woman, lay audiences—who had suffered from some of the excesses and abuses of religious authorities—would have sympathized easily with the plight of a laywoman persecuted by religious officials.

Serving as precedents for Kempe, Katherine and Margaret invoke audiences of sympathetic onlookers. Describing the way that many responded to Margaret's torment, John Lydgate writes, "Thei that stode beside/Ful sore wepten of compassyoun."[39] When Olibrius had Margaret burned with brands and cast into boiling water, "The folkes alle, that stonden enviroun/Of doolful pite, that saw this aventure,/Gan wepe and pleyne, and of compassyoun/Merveyled sore a tendre creature/Sustene myght suche tourment and endure."[40] Like the sorrowful witnesses of Margaret's passion, those present at Saint Agatha's death weep: "[There] was mani a soriman & mani a weeping [eye]."[41] Katherine, too, inspires the pity of onlookers. Like the women who weep at Christ's crucifix-ion, women weep at Katherine's execution.[42] According to the "Stanzaic Life of Katherine," "Wyves fele and maydenys bothe/Folewyd here of that cyte/Makyng sorewe and wepynge harde/For that maydyn fayr and free."[43] Invoking these commonplaces—which would have been familiar to her audience—Kempe recounts how "women wept sorely" for her when they heard the "good tales" that she told from her prison window in Beverly after the Duke of Bedford's men arrested her on suspicion of Lollardy (96). Just as onlookers pitied Christ and the virgin martyrs, the women of Beverly wept for Kempe, lamenting, "Alas, woman, why shall you be burnt?" (96). By drawing these parallels and constructing these memory networks, Kempe encourages her audience to place her in the company of virgin martyrs.

Kempe—like Christ and prominent virgin martyrs—also faces reproof from audiences of critics. Criticizing and taunting Christ, the chief priests, scribes, and elders challenge him to "come down from the cross." "He saved others," they mock; "himself he cannot save."[44] Margaret also faces remonstrating spectators. Bleeding profusely from her lacerated flesh, Margaret hears onlookers urge her to halt her suffering by giving up her faith. "Have mercye on thiselfe and on thi bodyes welfare," they admonish. Unshakeable, Margaret retorts, "A, ye wreched counselloures, why rede ye me soo?...Alle is to me grete joye that ye wene is woo."[45] Responding to audiences of sympathizers and critics, both Margaret and Katherine affirm that they are willing to suffer pain and death for Christ since he suffered so much more for them.[46]

In a scene reminiscent of virgin martyrs' legends, Margery Kempe—under arrest and traveling toward Beverly to face heresy charges—hears the local inhabitants exclaim, "Damsel, forsake this life that you have, and go spin and card as other women do, and suffer not so much shame and so much woe" (96). Replying, Kempe asserts, "I suffer not so much sorrow as I would do for our Lord's love, for I suffer but sharp words, and our merciful Lord Christ Jesus...suffered hard strokes, bitter scourgings, and shameful death at the last for me and for all mankind" (96). Here, Kempe sounds like a virgin martyr who affirms her willingness to suffer for Christ's love—and who resists the crowd's temptation to escape danger by abandoning what she believes to be her holy vocation and calling.

Kempe's book evinces other similarities to virgin martyr legends. Just as the *vitae* of virgin martyrs credit them with the founding of convert communities, so Kempe's book portrays laypeople who rally around her as a supportive community during her heresy trials. Remarkably, Katherine's and Margaret's converts become martyrs themselves and thus—in the eschatology of virgin martyr legends—elect members of God's transcendent, heavenly community. After angels rescue Margaret from a vessel of boiling water, thousands of people convert to Christianity. Promptly, they suffer beheading by Olibrius's order.[47] In some versions, Margaret influences even the executioner to convert, whereupon he collapses in death after beheading her, a parallel to the crucified thief who acknowledges Christ's divinity.[48] Margaret also forgives her executioner,[49] just as Christ forgives his. Kempe's book recalls this trope of forgiving one's enemies, for she forgives the mayor of Leicester, who falsely accuses her (85).

Like Margaret, Katherine converts many. Katherine's success reaches comic proportions as more and more of the pagan emperor Maxence's subjects defy him and declare their faith in Katherine's Christian God. Initially smug, Maxence summons the 50 wisest scholars of his realm, trusting that they will confound her. To his astonishment and dismay, Katherine not only overpowers their arguments but converts them as well. Apoplectic with rage, Maxence orders the scholars' execution on the pyre. Maxence's queen and chief knight Porphurye convert to Christianity when they witness angels ministering to Katherine in prison and listen to her counsel.[50] These bold betrayals push Maxence to the edge of his sanity, especially when Porphurye's knights decide to convert. Incandescent with anger, Maxence straightway orders the beheading of Katherine and her converts.[51] In the legend, of course, these martyrs join God's community of elect. Describing this ideal community to Porphurye, Katherine says, "Ther is non in that ryche empere/That hungyr has, cold, ne threste;/Drede ne wraththe is ther non there,/But love and lykyng, joye and reste."[52] Although Kempe does not convert a community of martyrs, she does win the support of many laypeople at her heresy trials, a process of potential community formation that I will examine in detail further on.

Similar to Katherine's and Margaret's *vitae*, Kempe's book portrays the influence of miraculous events on her audience. When the mayor of Leicester imprisons Kempe and her pilgrim companions, severe lightning storms strike the area, frightening the people. "Then there befell great thunders and lightnings and many rains," recounts the book, "so that the people thought it was for vengeance of the said creature" (87). This violent storm recalls the thunder[53] and earthquake[54] accompanying Margaret's angelic rescue from scalding water, phenomena that in turn recall the earthquake and darkness at Christ's death.[55] Even Saint Agatha, condemned to death by fire, has her sentence temporarily commuted by an earthquake that slays the judges who condemned her.[56] These elemental interventions function as memorable precedents for Kempe's life and book. By evoking memories of virgin martyrs' legends, Kempe invites readers to identify her as a holy woman confronting unjust persecutors.

Kempe's book also imitates other events in the life of Christ and the lives of virgin martyrs. Just as Katherine impresses the scholars with her divine eloquence—and just as Christ, as a young boy, amazes the doctors in the temple—so Kempe impresses the laypeople at her heresy trials with her inspired speech. Kempe—like Katherine and Christ—also enrages the authorities with her inspired words. During her second meeting with the archbishop of York, the infuriated steward and clergy exclaim, "Lord [Archbishop], we pray you let her go hence at this time, and, if ever she comes again, we shall burn her ourselves" (99). Imaginatively adapting remembered events from the lives of virgin martyrs and Christ, Kempe authorizes her own life.

In contrast to the virgin martyrs and Christ, of course, Kempe does not suffer martyrdom. Nor does she create communities of martyrs. Skillfully transforming virgin martyr tales in her book's memory networks, Kempe broadens the repertoire of roles and life stories for holy women. According to the book, Christ comforts Kempe before her heresy trial in Beverly, saying, "Daughter, it is more pleasing unto me that you suffer despites and scorns, shames and reproofs, wrongs and troubles than if your head were smote off three times a day every day for seven years" (97). Setting aside the self-aggrandizement of Kempe's persona and the question of why beheadings might please Kempe's Lord, one can see the book validating Kempe's life in terms reminiscent of virgin martyrs' *vitae*, for beheadings are a common fate in such *vitae*.[57] Through Christ's words, Kempe one-ups the virgin martyrs without suffering their grisly fate. Furthermore, Christ's words link Kempe's persecution with the virgin martyrs' passion, an imitation of Christ's passion.[58] For Barbara Zimbalist, moreover, even the act of writing a hagiography can substitute for martyrdom as a Christian labor or devotional exercise validating a holy life.[59] Kempe makes just such a substitution by writing a hagiography—an autohagiography[60] through which she remembers, shows devotion to, and imaginatively imitates the virgin martyrs and Christ.[61] Moreover, by directing the critical force of her *imitatio* and memory work toward church representatives and practices—rather than pagan institutions and ideologies—Kempe creates a basis of identification for a reformist community.

Providing a precedent for Kempe, hagiographers often encourage communities outside the text to venerate the hagiographies' subjects. Imitating Christ's intercessory prayer, Margaret—in her own intercessory prayer—prays that all who read, hear, or remember her passion will receive joy, honor, and mercy for their souls.[62] Furthermore, she prays that the women in labor who invoke her may have their wombs opened and their children born healthy. Finally, the author or scribe of Margaret's "Stanzaic Life" promises healing for the sick who visit Margaret's tomb.[63]

Katherine—like Margaret—invokes blessings on those who read, hear, or remember her passion. She asks that the Lord grant them grace and answer their prayers in times of need or at the brink of death.[64] Sherry Reames states that aristocratic women regarded her as an advocate because of her royal lineage. Nuns esteemed her because she devoted herself as a chaste bride of Christ. Since she confounded 50 scholars in a debate, university students and preachers admired her. She interceded for "women with evil husbands"—and for "nursing mothers (because milk flowed from her neck when she was beheaded)."[65] Because of the hooked wheels created as instruments for torturing her, she ironically "became the patron saint of wheelwrights, millers, and other craftsmen who worked with wheels."[66] Furthermore, the author of Katherine's "Stanzaic Life" claims that angels transported Katherine's inanimate body to Mount Sinai, where it was interred in a monastery's tomb that subsequently exuded oil. According to medieval traditions, this oil had the power to heal the sick.[67]

Like Christ, saints such as Margaret and Katherine served as bases for identification. Saints' relics and tales—like the emblems of Christ's blood and body—were disseminated among cult followings, uniting people with certain needs, circumstances, or motives. The Mount Sinai monastery, for example, sold Katherine's oil to sick pilgrims[68]—and parchment scrolls containing Margaret's tale sometimes were fastened about the abdomens of women in labor.[69] The tales and relics of saints served as symbolic resources that helped unite and define communities such as monasteries, religious orders, congregations, and trade guilds.

By disseminating Kempe's memory networks, Kempe's book also offers a basis of identification for a certain type of community, a lay community with access to religious power. During Kempe's heresy trials, a lay community rallies in her support, sometimes in defiance of secular and religious authorities. When the mayor of Leicester orders Kempe to prison, the jailer's man secures permission to place her under house arrest in his home. In doing so, he protects her chastity, which would have been at risk had she been placed in prison with the male inmates (82). Summoning Kempe to appear before the archbishop of York at Cawood, a judge in York commands that she be imprisoned while she awaits her trial. Defying the judge, "the secular people answered for her and said she should not go into prison, for they would themselves be surety for her and go to the Archbishop with her" (90). Perhaps intimidated by the number of laypeople, "the clerks said no more to her at that time, for they rose up and went wherever they would and let her go where she would" (90). Conducting Kempe seven miles to appear before the archbishop of York, a good man and his wife face criticism from a cleric, who remarks, "Sir, why have you and your wife brought this woman hither? She shall steal away from you, and then shall you have shame of her" (91). Defending Kempe, the good man retorts, "I dare well say she will abide and be at her answering with good will" (91). Finally, when Kempe vindicates herself at her trials, the laypeople rejoice with her. In Leicester, for example, "many good folk...[came] to welcome her, thanking God who had preserved her and given her the victory of her enemies" (86). And in Cawood, she "was received by many people and by full worthy clerks, who delighted in our Lord who had given her, not lettered, wit and wisdom to answer so many learned men without villainy or blame" (95). By drawing on remembered commonplaces from martyrologies, Kempe ultimately encourages reform-minded audiences to place her in the company of defiant holy women—and, within the context of her book's memory networks, to read themselves as her "converts" in opposing her "corrupt" adversaries.[70]

Kempe's criticisms of the clergy seem to be one of the reasons why she wins the support of laypeople. In her trial at Cawood, Kempe tells an *exemplum* in which a priest, lost in a wood, seeks shelter for the night in a garden graced by a blossoming pear tree.[71] Suddenly, a bear approaches, devours the pear blossoms, and defecates in the priest's presence (93). Upon meeting an elderly pilgrim the following day, the priest relates his disturbing encounter. Interpreting the experience, the pilgrim reveals that the pear blossoms represent the priest's commendable acts—such as "saying [his] service and administering the sacraments"—whereas the bear's act of consuming and expelling blossoms represents the priest's shameful behavior (94). The priest's disgraceful acts include performing his services and administering the sacrament without devotion, lacking "contrition" for his sin, "buying and selling," "giving [himself] to gluttony and excess, to lust of [the] body through lechery and uncleanness," and breaking God's commandments "through swearing, lying, detraction, and backbiting" (94). When one of the clerics at Cawood objects to the *exemplum*, protesting that it "smites [him] to the heart," Kempe retorts, in the words of a preacher whom she admires, that those who express displeasure with a sermon are guilty of the vices it condemns (94). Even though Kempe clearly is orthodox in her beliefs regarding the sacrament, she nonetheless—like the Lollards—criticizes corrupt priests and clerics for their misbehavior. Elsewhere in her book, Kempe criticizes the bishop of Worcestor's men for their vanity in wearing fine clothes (80)—and she even reproves the archbishop of York for being a "wicked man" (92).

Imaginatively employing memory arts, Kempe overlays her account with virgin martyr legends, authorizing her life as holy woman—and co-opting her opponents within her narrative by casting them in the role of the martyrs' pagan accusers.[72] From their perspective, her accusers no doubt view themselves as holding the line against heresy. Like the hagiographies of Katherine and Margaret, however, Kempe's book portrays her accusers as angry and unjust, shows Kempe winning over the spectators at her heresy trials, and recounts how Kempe refuted her opponents through divinely inspired eloquence. Emphasizing what is at stake in conflicts over accounts and memory networks like these, Mary Carruthers writes, "Where two or more competing patterns exist in one site, only one will be seen: the others, though they may remain potentially visible, will be blocked or absorbed by the overlay."[73] Such memory work characterizes Kempe's account, for she blocks or crowds the clergy's perspective, appropriating the clergy for her own purposes by overlaying their actions with those of the martyr's pagan persecutors. In doing so, she directs toward church representatives and practices the critiques regarding corruption and injustice reserved for pagan rulers in the virgin martyr legends.[74]

Apart from criticizing the clergy, Kempe asserts—in her book's account—that she receives divine inspiration and power directly. In spite of the concerns of religious authorities, Kempe succeeds in convincing them that God has instructed her to wear white clothing. Disobeying her confessor Robert Spryngolde, Kempe follows God's command to accompany her daughter-in-law to Danzig (165). Defying the archbishop of York's prohibitions, she asserts her privilege and duty to speak of God, even in public (93). Through her strategic defiance of authorities, Kempe echoes the lives of virgin martyrs. Yet in contrast to the virgin martyrs, she challenges not pagan rulers but Catholic Church authorities. In doing so, she composes a book and an ethos that echo some concerns of Lollards and later Protestant reformers.

Fearing that Kempe represents a threat like that of Lollard heretics, the clerics at Cawood warn the archbishop, saying, "we will not suffer her to dwell among us, for the people have great faith in her dalliance, and perhaps she might pervert some of them" (92). In a time of intense Lollard persecution, the clergy's tendency to identify Kempe with Lollard heretics is not surprising. Moreover, the clergy may not be far wrong. William Sawtrey, a convicted Lollard who burned on a pyre in Smithfield in 1401, had been "the parish priest of Kempe's home church, St Margaret's in King's Lynn," a man whom Kempe may have known.[75] When Kempe was a young woman, guilt and fear from an unconfessed sin drove her mad for eight months.[76] Charity Scott Stokes speculates that Kempe's unconfessed sin might have been associated with Lollard heresy.[77] If Kempe was a Lollard, she might have found Lollardy attractive because it "allowed women outlets for religious activity that were not to be found in the established church."[78] Lollards contended that women could be "learners, readers and expounders of the gospel."[79] Arguing that women should not be "excluded from the Christian priesthood," the Lollard Walter Brut asserted that women could perform even priestly functions such as baptizing, performing extreme unction, and administering communion. Kempe might have found especially appealing Brut's "defence of women preachers."[80]

Lollard or not, Margery Kempe still faced questions concerning her orthodoxy. Doubting Kempe's orthodoxy, the Steward of Leicester tested her to see whether she understood Latin (83), for layfolk who knew Latin were assumed to be Lollards. When Kempe—dressed in her white clothes—first encountered the archbishop of York, he enquired whether she was a "maiden." In response to her statement that she was "a wife," the archbishop ordered her to be "fettered" as a "false heretic" (91) because of her perceived deviance—as a married woman—in wearing white clothes, associated with chaste holy women and celibate members of cloistered religious communities. Moreover, his household called her a "lollard" and "heretic," swearing that "she should be burnt" (91). The two men who arrested Kempe in Hessle even accused her falsely of being the "daughter" of the notorious Lollard Lord Cobham (Sir John Oldcastle), who allegedly sent her "to bear letters about the country" (97). Of course, we have no solid evidence that Kempe was a Lollard. In

fact, her recitation of the Articles of Faith at her heresy trials is so orthodox that it stymies her accusers.[81] Still, far from relying exclusively on
church hierarchies and authorities, Kempe criticizes corrupt clerics and
claims direct access to divine inspiration and power.

Like certain characters in Kempe's book, Beverly Boyd, Karma
Lochrie, and Lynn Staley associate some of Kempe's words, views, and
behaviors with those characteristic of Lollards. Beverly Boyd asserts that
Kempe "made herself unique" by resisting her "proper [estate] in life." By
violating "the medieval, feudal concept of order," Boyd affirms, Kempe
risked being condemned as a Lollard.[82] Beyond that, Lynn Staley contends that Kempe—whom she characterizes as a fictional persona—actually shares some Lollard concerns and attitudes. Ultimately, the author of
The Book of Margery Kempe "uses Margery in a way that evinces her sen-
sitivity to the whole range of issues that had accrued around the Lollard
heresy and that suggests her sympathies for what might loosely be called
Lollard views."[83]

Similar to Staley, Karma Lochrie maintains that Kempe—by asserting her right to speak—defies "prescriptions against woman's speech
in scriptural and patristic writing" and "runs dangerously close to the
boundaries of Lollard heresy in fifteenth-century England."[84] Although
Lollards did not explicitly promote women as preachers, they nonetheless
asserted—in the words of the Lollard Hawisia Moone—that "every man
and every woman beyng in good lyf oute of synne is as good prest and
hath [as] much poar of God in al thynges as ony prest ordred, be he pope
or bishop."[85] Furthermore, the Lollards in Leicester contended that "any
layman can preach and teach the gospel anywhere."[86] Of course, Kempe
stops short of this broad statement. Nevertheless, her qualifying statements and distinctions regarding preaching differ from Lollard views less
in substance than in semantics.

Affirming a connection between the Protestant Reformation, affective piety like Kempe's, and the Lollards' egalitarianism and critiques of
inadequate clergy,[87] Caroline Walker Bynum argues that female piety
shaped lay piety, even extending to the Reformation. "In the fourteenth century," Bynum contends, "women's mysticism was repeatedly
criticized and sometimes persecuted." By the fifteenth century, though,
female piety had become mainstream lay piety, for "a highly emotional,
sentimental, frantically active yet mystical piety was characteristic of
many layfolk in Europe" and included "laywomen, beguines, nuns, and
tertiaries of the Low Countries, the Rhineland, and Italy."[88] Although
leaders of the Reformation in the sixteenth century reacted against the
emotional displays, charismatic performances, and excessive asceticism
of late medieval female piety, they nonetheless championed the service

ethic and egalitarianism characteristic of that piety. In their view, every Christian should serve others—and each Christian could approach God in a direct, personal way. In a sense, "the piety of Europe on the eve of the Reformation was, in Reinhard Bedix's general description of historical process, the 'style of life of a distinct status group' (women) that eventually became 'the dominant orientation' of Christianity."[89]

By imaginatively imitating remembered tropes, events, and language from the lives of Christ and virgin martyrs, Kempe persuasively promotes some of the values and critiques shared by Lollards while resisting her opponents' efforts to silence and discredit her by defining her as a Lollard. She does not seek the martyr's self-destructive pathway to transcendence. Nor does she bring martyrdom on her supporters. Imitating the virgin martyrs helps her claim authority and make institutional critiques—but toward ends different from those of the virgin martyrs, who mainly condemn pagan idolatry.

By disseminating the resources of her memory networks through her book, Kempe creates a common ground for unifying a community of reform-minded laypeople. Drawing on commonplaces to structure a unique memory network, Kempe redirects toward church representatives the critiques meant for unjust pagan rulers in the original virgin martyr tales that she imitates. In doing so, she invites lay members of her audience to place themselves within her memory networks, identifying themselves as her "converts" in opposing corrupt clergy.

A pious laywoman, Kempe represents the values of her class—and anticipates those of the Reformation. A former businesswoman from a town of merchants who value commerce and exchange, Kempe values the privilege of exchanging religious words and texts without excessive restrictions imposed by authorities. A member of a growing and powerful class of guilds and merchants, Kempe shares their resourcefulness in circumventing and subverting feudal hierarchies. She also shares their tendency to critique inadequate or hypocritical church authorities. Instead of Latin, she uses her native English to admonish, rebut, reprove, uplift, and evangelize. Representing the growing mobility and independence of her class, Kempe asserts her freedom to travel where she will and to redefine her religious vocation and identity in spite of pressure from church authorities to conform to institutionally sanctioned norms. Following the *via positiva*, she helps the needy and cares for the sick. A practitioner of female affective piety and an imitator of virgin martyrs, she demonstrates confidence in her ability to approach God in a direct, personal way—a way that does not always require the mediation of institutional hierarchies or authorities. No wonder so many laypeople support her, defend her, and celebrate her victories during her heresy trials. In recounting her public religious dramas, Kempe employs strategic memory networks in her book, networks that transgress and rearrange boundaries, anticipating and invoking a community of believers who freely exchange and personally approach the Word.

Notes

1. Roxanne Mountford, *The Gendered Pulpit: Preaching in American Protestant Spaces*, ed. Cheryl Glenn and Shirley Wilson Logan, Studies in Rhetorics and Feminisms (Carbondale: Southern Illinois University Press, 2003), 96.

2. Mary J. Carruthers, *The Craft of Thought: Meditation, Rhetoric, and the Making of Images, 400–1200*, Cambridge Studies in Medieval Literature 34 (Cambridge: Cambridge University Press, 2000), 11–14, 16, 22–23.

3. Ibid., 19–21.

4. Ibid., 54–57.

5. Cheryl Glenn, "Popular Literacy in the Middle Ages: *The Book of Margery Kempe*," in *Popular Literacy: Studies in Cultural Practices and Poetics*, ed. John Trimbur, Pittsburgh Series in Composition, Literacy, and Culture (Pittsburgh: University of Pittsburgh Press, 2001), 69 [56–73].

6. Ibid., 69.

7. Naoe K. Yoshikawa, *Margery Kempe's Meditations: The Context of Medieval Devotional Literature, Liturgy and Iconography* (Cardiff: University of Wales Press, 2007), 5.

8. Ibid., 6.

9. Nicholas Love, *The Mirror of the Blessed Life of Jesus Christ: A Reading Text by Nicholas Love*, ed. Michael G. Sargent (Exeter: University of Exeter Press, 2004), 10–11. "As Love informs his reader," Denis Renevey asserts, "imagination plays an important role in this hermeneutic process. Neither is that role limited to the writing process. Rather, Love exhorts his readers to engage affectively with his material in order to become active in filling in the affective gaps left blank by his text and the gospel accounts." Denis Renevey, "Margery's Performing Body: The Translation of Late Medieval Discursive Religious Practices," in *Writing Religious Women: Female Spiritual and Textual Practices in Late Medieval England*, ed. Denis Renevey and Christiana Whitehead (Toronto: University of Toronto Press, 2000), 203.

10. Carruthers, *Craft of Thought*, 23.

11. Barbara Zimbalist, "Imitating the Imagined: Clemence of Barking's *Life of St. Catherine*," chapter 5 in this volume.

12. Ibid.

13. Elissa Hansen, "Making A Place: *Imitatio Mariae* in Julian of Norwich's Self-Construction," chapter 8 in this volume.

14. Ibid.

15. Sarah Salih, *Versions of Virginity in Late Medieval England* (Cambridge: D. S. Brewer, 2001), 195, 197.

16. Naoe K. Yoshikawa, "Veneration of Virgin Martyrs in Margery Kempe's Meditation: Influence of the Sarum Liturgy and Hagiography," in Renevey and Whitehead, *Writing Religious Women*, 18.

17. Sherry L. Reames, ed., *Middle English Legends of Women Saints*, TEAMS Middle English Text Series (Kalamazoo: Western Michigan University's Medieval Institute Publications, 2003), 170.

18. Yoshikawa, "Veneration of Virgin Martyrs," 178, 180.

19. Ibid., 181.

20. Salih, *Versions of Virginity*, 195.

21. Sherry L. Reames, "Stanzaic Life of Katherine," in *Middle English Legends*, 180 [175–209].

22. Margery Kempe, *The Book of Margery Kempe: A New Translation, Contexts, Criticism*, trans. and ed. Lynn Staley (New York: Norton, 2001). All references are to this edition of Kempe's book.

23. As Karma Lochrie notes, Kempe "seems to assume that Christ's response to the woman authorizes her to speak about him." However, she "blatantly ignores his instruction that people should only *hear* and *keep* the word of God" (emphasis in original). Karma Lochrie, *Margery Kempe and Translations of the Flesh* (Philadelphia: University of Pennsylvania Press, 1991), 466.

24. Luke 11:27–28.

25. Emphasizing the effectiveness of this rhetorical move, Genelle Gertz-Robinson writes, "By defining preaching as the occupation of a pulpit…Kempe reserves for herself the possibility of preaching in other public settings." Genelle Gertz-Robinson, "Stepping into the Pulpit? Women's Preaching in *The Book of Margery Kempe* and *The Examinations of Anne Askew*," in *Voices in Dialogue: Reading Women in the Middle Ages*, ed. Linda Olson and Kathryn Kerby-Fulton (Notre Dame, IN: University of Notre Dame Press, 2005), 459.

Identifying a precedent for Kempe's rhetorical strategy, Karma Lochrie refers to a popular fifteenth-century treatise called *Speculum Christiani* in which the author makes the following distinctions between teaching and preaching: "Preaching occurs in a place where there is a summoning together or following of people on holy days in churches or other special places and times ordained thereto. And it belongs to them who are thereto ordained, who have jurisdiction and authority, and to no one else. Teaching means that each body may inform and teach his brother in every place and at a suitable time, as he sees it necessary. For this is a spiritual almsdeed, to which every man who possesses cunning is bound." Lochrie, *Margery Kempe*, 111.

26. Gertz-Robinson, "Stepping into the Pulpit," 465–68.

27. Ibid., 460, 466.

28. Mountford, *Gendered Pulpit*, 96.

29. Describing this belief, Carolyn Walker Bynum writes, "The eucharistic host, fragmented by human teeth and digestive processes" nonetheless transubstantiates so that "every minute crumb" constitutes "the whole

body of Christ." This sacramental dissemination of Christ's flesh within
mortals' flesh is God's "guarantee" to humankind of "wholeness." Carolyn
Walker Bynum, *Fragmentation and Redemption: Essays on Gender and the
Human Body in Medieval Religion* (New York: Zone Books, 1991), 12.

30. 1 Cor. 10:16–17.
31. Col. 1:18.
32. 1 Cor. 12:27.
33. Margaret Cotter-Lynch, "Mnemonic Sanctity and the Ladder of Reading:
    Notker's 'In Natale Sanctarum Feminarum,'" chapter 2 in this volume.
34. Carruthers, *Craft of Thought*, 44.
35. Ibid.
36. Explaining how Kempe situates herself within her community's sacred
    contexts, Naoe Kukita Yoshikawa writes that Kempe's act of "kneeling
    before the eucharist on the altar signifies more than a physical posture she
    assumes in the church. Traditionally, the eucharist—the Body of Christ—is
    identified with the church, thereby reinforcing an idea of Christian com-
    munity as unity in the faith. As Lynn Staley argues, Margery seems con-
    sciously to locate herself at 'the focal point of the community of the Body
    of Christ.'" Yoshikawa, *Margery Kempe's Meditations*, 132.
37. Employing these commonplaces from virgin martyr legends, Kempe con-
    structs a persona that is public, not just private. As Sarah Salih asserts,
    Kempe enacts "her martyrdom in social space rather than engaging in pri-
    vate penitential practices," thereby placing "sanctity and identity in soci-
    ety." In doing so, she "recognises the cultural production of sanctity and
    foregrounds the formation of identity." Salih, *Versions of Virginity*, 213.
38. Asserting that Kempe's *Book* "positions all its readers as Margery's dis-
    ciples," Sarah Salih writes, "The *Book*, as a hagiography, presents a holy
    woman as an example to its readers." Ultimately, "Margery's example of
    contrition and compunction provokes others to emulate her; her saintly
    practices are imitable. The *Book* aims to perform a similar function for
    those who do not have the advantage of a personal acquaintance with
    Margery, using the written version of her as an example of God's mercy."
    Salih, *Versions of Virginity*, 175–76.
39. John Lydgate, "The Lyfe of Seynt Margarete," in Reames, *Middle English
    Legends*, 154 [147–62].
40. Ibid., 159.
41. Charlotte D'Evelyn and Anna J. Mill, ed., *The South English Legendary*,
    EETS (London: Oxford University Press, 1956), 58.
42. Providing a precedent for the portrayal of women weeping at Katherine's
    execution, women weep at Christ's crucifixion. Responding to their
    cries, "Jesus tells them instead to weep for themselves and their children."
    Reames, "Stanzaic Life of Katherine," 205nn679–82.
43. Ibid., 196.
44. Matt. 27:42.
45. Reames, "Stanzaic Life of Margaret," in *Middle English Legends*, 119–20
    [115–27].

46. Reames, "Stanzaic Life of Margaret," 120; "Stanzaic Life of Katherine," 188.

47. Reames, "Stanzaic Life of Margaret," 125.

48. "In many versions of the Margaret legend," Sherry Reames notes, "the executioner Malchus, converted by Margaret's prayer and the answering voice from heaven, falls dead at her side after striking the fatal blow." This echoes the crucified thief who professes faith in Christ and who dies with the hope of paradise. Reames, "Stanzaic Life of Margaret," 135nn328–34.

49. Ibid., 127.

50. Reames, "Stanzaic Life of Katherine," 170, 180–82, 184–86.

51. Ibid., 170, 191–94.

52. Reames, "Stanzaic Life of Katherine," 186.

53. Reames, "Stanzaic Life of Margaret," 125.

54. Lydgate, "Lyfe of Seynt Margarete," 159.

55. Matt. 27:45, 27:51.

56. D'Evelyn and Mill, *South English Legendary*, 57.

57. As Sarah Salih affirms, "Martyrdom by decapitation is a near-compulsory element of virgin martyr legends." Salih, *Versions of Virginity*, 199.

58. Here, Kempe follows established conventions in medieval hagiography. As the age of martyrdom ended, early medieval hagiographers portrayed asceticism in terms reminiscent of martyrdom. Jo Ann McNamara examines the identification of ascetic cloistered and enclosed women with martyrs. Jo Ann McNamara, *Sainted Women of the Dark Ages* (Durham, NC: Duke University Press, 1992), 13.

   The Desert Fathers may serve as a precedent here, for as Ana Maria Machado notes, they replaced martyrdom with asceticism as a sign of holiness. Ana Maria Machado, "Memory, Identity, and Women's Representation in the Portuguese Reception of Vitae Patrum: Winning a Name," chapter 6 in this volume.

59. Zimbalist, "Imitating the Imagined," chapter 5 in this volume.

60. Richard Kieckhefer coined the term "autohagiography" in his discussion of Kempe's book. Richard Kieckhefer, *Unquiet Souls: Fourteenth-Century Saints and Their Religious Milieu* (Chicago: University of Chicago Press, 1984), 6.

61. Associating the blood shed during Christ's passion with the tears shed during her heresy trials and elsewhere, Kempe prays for "all the tears that may increase my love for you…Good Lord, spare no more the eyes in my head than you did the blood in your body which you shed plenteously for sinful man's soul." Kempe, *Book of Margery Kempe*, Book 2, 181.

62. In her own intercessory prayer—a parallel to Christ's and the virgins'—Kempe invokes the Lord, saying, "For all those that believe and trust or shall believe and trust in my prayers into the world's end, such grace as they desire, ghostly or bodily, to the profit of their souls, I pray you, Lord, grant them for the multitude of your mercy." Ibid., 184.

63. Reames, "Stanzaic Life of Margaret," 126–27.

64. Reames, "Stanzaic Life of Katherine," 197.
65. Ibid., 170.
66. Ibid.
67. Ibid., 169, 198–99.
68. Ibid., 169.
69. Reames, "Stanzaic Life of Margaret," 111.
70. During her heresy trials, Kempe enjoys remarkable success in winning the support of lay audiences. Throughout her pilgrimages and crying episodes, by contrast, many laypeople revile her and some religious authorities support and defend her. Clearly, audiences' reactions to Kempe are not monolithic. The spectacle of her imitation of virgin martyrs appeals to reform-minded lay audiences, whereas the forms of saintly and Christlike imitation dominating other parts of her book require that contemporary lay audiences scorn and persecute her (just as many persecuted Christ and the apostles). Each of these styles of *imitatio* has its roots in devotional and contemplative exercises associated with memory arts and affective piety. Each has a way of identifying Kempe as a holy woman, yet different acts of *imitatio* appeal to different audiences. Consequently, the book is not as unified as a modern reader might expect. Ultimately, the nimble and resourceful forensic orator of the heresy trials does not square with the self-absorbed, chatty, and maudlin persona presented elsewhere in the book. The fact that the book performs different modes of *imitatio* accounts for this apparent inconsistency.
71. Lynn Staley also interprets this exemplum, although she focuses on how it functions within the narrative to set up a "confrontation between Margery and Henry Bowet, the actively anti-Lollard Archbishop of York." Lynn Staley, *Margery Kempe's Dissenting Fictions* (University Park: Pennsylvania State University Press, 1994), 6–7.
72. Whether or not Kempe's book is fictional, Salih affirms, this reading still "holds." Even "if the *Book* is fictional here…its author has made the imaginative leap of identifying the pagan persecutors of legend with the authorities of her own day, and the critique is no less effective." Salih, *Versions of Virginity*, 199.
73. Carruthers, *Craft of Thought*, 57.
74. Lynn Staley argues that Kempe uses "Margery's life as a means of scrutinizing not only the foundations of English society but also the nature of ecclesiastical and political authority," developing "what was nascent in the traditions of sacred biography she would have inherited from Latin and Continental models." Staley, *Margery Kempe's Dissenting Fictions*, 37.
75. Mary Morse, "'Take and Bren Hir': Lollardy as Conversion Motif in *The Book of Margery Kempe*," *Mystics Quarterly* 29, nos. 1–2 (March–June 2003): 29.
76. Kempe, *Book of Margery Kempe*, Book 1, 6.
77. Charity S. Stokes, "Margery Kempe: Her Life and the Early History of Her Book," *Mystics Quarterly* 25, nos. 1–2 (March–June 1999): 25.

78. Margaret Aston, *Lollards and Reformers: Images and Literacy in Late Medieval Religion* (London: Hambledon, 1984), 50.

79. Ibid., 50.

80. Ibid., 52–53, 55.

81. According to Beverly Boyd, "The examination as [Kempe] reports it was aimed at Wyclif's teaching on the nature of the Eucharist and its relationship to the virtue of the consecrating priest." Beverly Boyd, "Wyclif, Joan of Arc, and Margery Kempe," *Mystics Quarterly* 12, no. 3 (1986): 114–115.

82. Ibid., 117.

83. Staley, *Margery Kempe's Dissenting Fictions*, 125.

84. Lochrie, *Margery Kempe*, 107.

85. Ibid., 108.

86. Ibid.

87. Even though Lollardy and the Reformation were distinct, Lollards and leaders of the Reformation shared similar concerns regarding inadequate clergy and access to the divine. Figures important to the Reformation even tried to establish Lollards as their religious forebears. Aston, *Lollards and Reformers*, 219–20.

88. Bynum, *Fragmentation and Redemption*, 77–78.

89. Ibid., 78.

MASTER BIBLIOGRAPHY

Aelred of Rievaulx. "Eulogium Davidis ab Ailredo." In *Vitae Antiquae Sanctorum qui Habitaverunt in ea parte Britanniae nunc vicata Scotia vel in ejus insulis*, edited by Johannes Pinkerton, 437–56. London: Johannis Nichols, 1789.

———. *Aelred of Rievaulx: The Historical Works*. Translated by Jane Patricia Freeland. Edited by Marsha L. Dutton. Kalamazoo, MI: Cistercian Publications, 2005.

Alcuin. *De ratione animae*. In "Alcuin, *De ratione animae*: A Text with Introduction, Critical Apparatus, and Translation," edited and translated by James Curry. PhD diss., Cornell, 1966.

———. *Epistolae*. Edited by Ernst Dümmler. MGH. Epistolae 4, Epistolae Karolini Aevi 2. 1895. Reprint, Munich: MGH, 1994.

Amat, Jacqueline, ed. *Passion de Perpétue et de Félicité suivi des Actes*. Vol. 417, Sources Chrétiennes. Paris: Éditions du Cerf, 1996.

Ambrose of Milan, St. *Expositio evangelii secundum Lucam*. In *Patrologia latina*, edited by J.-P. Migne. Vol. 15. Paris: Migne, 1844–45.

Anderson, A. O., and M. O. Anderson, eds. *Chronicle of Melrose from the Cottonian Manuscript, Faustina B. IX in the British Museum*. London: Percy Lund Humphries and Co., 1936.

———. *Early Sources of Scottish History, A.D. 500 to 1286*. 2 vols. 1922. Reprint, Stamford, Lincolnshire, UK: Paul Watkins, 1990.

Angilbert. "To Charlemagne and His Entourage." In *Poetry of the Carolingian Renaissance*, edited and translated by Peter Godman, 114–15. Norman: University of Oklahoma Press, 1985.

Antolin, Guilhermo. "Estudios de códices visigodos: Códice a.II.9. de la Biblioteca del Escorial." *Boletín de la Real Academia de la Historia* 54 (1909): 55–67, 117–19, 294–313.

Apophthegmata Patrum, in *Patrologia Graeca*, edited by J.-P. Migne. vol. 65. Paris: Migne, 1864.

Aquinas, St. Thomas. *Summa theologica*. Translated by Fathers of the English Dominican Province. 3 vols. New York: Benziger Bros., 1947–48.

———. *Summa theologica*. 2nd ed. Translated by Father Laurence Shapcote of the Fathers of the English Dominican Province. Great Books of the Western World, vols. 17–18. Chicago: Encyclopædia Britannica, 1990.

Askins, A. L.-F. "The MS *Flos Sanctorum* of the Universidade de Brasília: An Early Reflex in Portuguese of the Hagiographic Compilation of Valerio del Bierzo." In *O amor das letras e das gentes: In Honor of Maria de Lourdes Belchior Pontes*, edited by João Camilo dos Santos and Frederick G. Williams, 39–50. Santa Barbara: University of California at Santa Barbara's Center for Portuguese Studies, 1995.

Askins, Arthur L.-F., Harvey L. Sharrer, Aida F. Dias, and Martha E. Schaffer. *Bibliografia de textos antigos galegos e portugueses*. University of California, Berkeley, and Universidade de Lisboa. PhiloBiblon. Last modified 2008. http://sunsite.berkeley.edu/Philobiblon/BITAGAP/.

Aston, Margaret. *Lollards and Reformers: Images and Literacy in Late Medieval Religion*. London: Hambledon, 1984.

Athanasius, St. *Vita di Antonio*. 6th ed. Edited by G. J. M. Bartelink. Translated by Pietro Citati and Salvatire Lilla. Milan: Fondazione Lorenzo Valla, 1998.

Barrow, G. W. S. "The Kings of Scotland and Durham." In Rollason, Harvey, and Prestwich, *Anglo-Norman Durham*, 311–23.

———. *Kingship and Unity: Scotland 1000–1306*. 1981. Reprint, Toronto and Buffalo, NY: University of Toronto Press, 1998.

———. "Margaret [St Margaret] (d. 1093)." In *Oxford Dictionary of National Biography*. Oxford University Press, 2004–. Online edition May 2011. Accessed July 22, 2011. http://www.oxforddnb.com.proxy.libraries.smu .edu/view/article/18044.

Bartlett, Anne C. *Male Authors, Female Readers: Representation and Subjectivity in Middle English Devotional Literature*. Ithaca, NY: Cornell University Press, 1995.

Bartlett, Robert. "Cults of Irish, Scottish and Welsh Saints." In *Britain and Ireland 900–1300: Insular Responses to Medieval European Change*, edited by Brendan Smith, 67–86. Cambridge: Cambridge University Press, 1999.

———. *The Hanged Man: A Story of Miracle, Memory, and Colonialism in the Middle Ages*. Princeton, NJ: Princeton University Press, 2004.

———, ed. and trans. *The Miracles of St Æbbe of Coldingham and St Margaret of Scotland*. Oxford: Clarendon Press, 2003.

Batt, Catherine. "Clemence of Barking's Transformations of *Courtoisie* in *La Vie de Sainte Catherine d'Alexandrie*." *New Comparison: A Journal of Comparative and General Literary Studies* 12 (1996): 102–23.

Bede, the Venerable. *Ecclesiastical History of the English People*. Edited by Bertram Colgrave and R. A. B. Mynors. Oxford: Clarendon Press, 1969.

———. *Vita S. Cuthberti*. In *Two Lives of Saint Cuthbert*, edited by Bertram Colgrave, 142–306. Cambridge: Cambridge University Press, 1940.

Benedict, St., and David Oswald Hunter Blair. *The Rule of St. Benedict*. Fort Augustus, Scotland: Abbey Press, 1906.

Benko, Stephen. "Virgil's Fourth Eclogue in Christian Interpretation." *Aufstieg und Niedergang der römischen Welt*, 2nd ser., 31, no. 1 (1980): 646–705.

Bennewitz, Ingrid, and Ingrid Kasten, eds. *Genderdiskurse und Körperbilder im Mittelatler: eine Bilanzierung nach Butler und Laquer*. Muenster: LIT, 2002.

Bernard of Clairvaux, St. *De adventu Domine*. In *Patrologia latina*, edited by J.-P. Migne. Vol. 183. Paris: Migne, 1844–45.

———. *In navitate B. V. Mariae*. In *Patrologia latina*, edited by J.-P. Migne. Vol. 183. Paris: Migne, 1844–45.

Bers, Victor. *Speech in Speech: Studies in Incorporated Oratio Recta in Attic Drama and Oratory.* London: Rowman and Littlefield Publishers, 1997.

Biblia Sacra Vulgata. Edited by R. Gryson, B. Fischer, H. I. Frede, H. F. D. Sparks, and W. Thiele. Peabody, MA: Hendrickson Publishers, 2006.

Bischoff, Bernhard. "The Court Library of Charlemagne." In *Manuscripts and Libraries in the Age of Charlemagne,* translated and edited by Michael Gorman, 56–75. Cambridge: Cambridge University Press, 1994.

———. "Die Kölner Nonnenhandschriften und das Skriptorium von Chelles." In *Mittelalterliche Studien: Ausgewählte Aufsätze zur Schriftkunde und Literaturgeschichte,* 1:16–34. Stuttgart: Anton Hiersemann, 1966.

Bitel, Lisa. "'In Visu Noctis': Dreams in European Hagiography and Histories, 450–900." *History of Religions* 31, no. 1 (August 1991): 39–59.

Blackmore, Josiah H., ed. "Vidas de Santos de um manuscrito alcobacense—II." *Revista Lusitana,* n.s., 5 (1984–85): 48–55.

Blamires, Alcuin. "The Limits of Bible Study for Medieval Women." In vol. 1 of *Women, the Book, and the Godly: Selected Proceedings of the St Hilda's Conference, 1993,* edited by Lesley Smith and Jane H. M. Taylor, 1–12. Cambridge: Boydell and Brewer, 1995.

Boyd, Beverly. "Wyclif, Joan of Arc, and Margery Kempe." *Mystics Quarterly* 12, no. 3 (1986): 112–18.

Bray, Dorothy Ann. "Heroic Tradition in the Lives of the Early Irish Saints: A Study in Hagio-Biographical Patterning." *Proceedings of the First North American Congress of Celtic Studies; Held at Ottawa from 36th–30th March, 1986* (1988): 261–71.

Bremmer, Jan N., and Marco Formisano, eds. *Perpetua's Passions: Multidisciplinary Approaches to the Passio Perpetuae et Felicitatis.* New York: Oxford University Press, 2012.

Broun, Dauvit. *The Irish Identity of the Kingdom of the Scots.* Woodbridge, UK: Boydell Press, 1999.

———. *Scottish Independence and the Idea of Britain from the Picts to Alexander III.* Edinburgh: Edinburgh University Press, 2007.

Brown, Peter. *The Cult of the Saints: Its Rise and Function in Latin Christianity.* Chicago: University of Chicago Press, 1981.

Bullough, Vern L. "Medieval, Medical and Scientific Views of Women." *Viator* 4 (1973): 485–501.

Bynum, Caroline Walker. "... And Women His Humanity: Female Imagery in the Religious Writing of the Later Middle Ages." In *Gender and Religion: On the Complexity of Symbols,* edited by Caroline Walker Bynum, Steven Harrell, and Paula Richman, 257–89. Boston: Beacon Press, 1986.

———. *Fragmentation and Redemption: Essays on Gender and the Human Body in Medieval Religion.* New York: Zone Books, 1991.

———. *Holy Feast and Holy Fast: The Religious Significance of Food to Medieval Women.* Berkeley: University of California, 1987.

———. "Jesus as Mother and Abbot as Mother: Some Themes in Twelfth-Century Cistercian Writing." *Harvard Theological Review* 70, nos. 3–4 (1977): 257–84.

————. *Jesus as Mother: Studies in the Spirituality of the High Middle Ages*. Berkeley: University of California Press, 1982.

Cabrol, Fernand, and Henri Leclercq, eds. *Dictionnaire d'archéologie chrétienne et de liturgie*. Paris: Letouzey et Ané, 1934.

Caciola, Nancy. *Discerning Spirits: Divine and Demonic Possession in the Middle Ages*. Ithaca, NY: Cornell University Press, 2003.

Cadden, Joan. *Meanings of Sex Difference in the Middle Ages: Medicine, Science, and Culture*. Cambridge History of Medicine. Cambridge: Cambridge University Press, 1993.

Carruthers, Mary J. *The Book of Memory: A Study of Memory in Medieval Culture*. 2nd ed. Cambridge Studies in Medieval Literature 70. Cambridge: Cambridge University Press, 2008.

————. *The Craft of Thought: Meditation, Rhetoric, and the Making of Images, 400–1200*. Cambridge Studies in Medieval Literature 34. Cambridge: Cambridge University Press, 2000.

Carruthers, Mary, and Jan M. Ziolkowski, eds. *The Medieval Craft of Memory: An Anthology of Texts and Pictures*. Philadelphia: University of Pennsylvania Press, 2002.

Cassian, John. *John Cassian: The Conferences*. Translated by Boniface Ramsey. New York: Paulist Press, 1997.

Clancy, T. O., ed. *The Triumph Tree: Scotland's Earliest Poetry AD 550–1350*. Translated by Gilbert Márkus. Edinburgh: Canongate Books, 1998.

Clark, Anne L. "Holy Woman or Unworthy Vessel? The Representations of Elisabeth of Schönau." In *Gendered Voices: Medieval Saints and Their Interpreters*, edited by Catherine M. Mooney, 35–51. Philadelphia: University of Pennsylvania Press, 1999.

Clark, Robert L. A. "Constructing the Female Subject in Late Medieval Devotion." In *Medieval Conduct*, edited by Kathleen Ashley and Robert L. A. Clark, 160–82. Minneapolis: University of Minnesota Press, 2001.

Clemence of Barking. "The Life of St. Catherine." In *Virgin Lives and Holy Deaths: Two Exemplary Biographies for Anglo-Norman Women*, translated and edited by Jocelyn Wogan-Browne and Glyn S. Burgess, 3–79. London: J. M. Dent, 1996.

————. *The Life of St. Catherine by Clemence of Barking*. Edited by William MacBain. Anglo-Norman Text Society 18. Oxford: Blackwell, 1964.

The Cloud of Unknowing. Edited by Patrick J. Gallacher. TEAMS Middle English Texts. Kalamazoo: Western Michigan University's Medieval Institute Publications, 1997.

Coiner, Nancy. "The 'Homely' and the Heimliche: The Hidden, Doubled Self in Julian of Norwich's Showings." *Exemplaria* 5, no. 2 (1993): 305–23.

Colecção com várias vidas de santos. Lisbon: AN/TT, Livª nº 771 (olim alcob. CCLXX), 171 fls.

Colecção com várias vidas de santos. Lisbon: AN/TT, Livª nº 2274 (olim alcob. CCLXVI), 160 fls.

Colecção de vidas de santos. Lisbon: Biblioteca Nacional, Alc. 367 (olim XV), 163 fls.

Colecção hagiológica. Lisbon: Biblioteca Nacional, Alc. 454 (olim CCLXXXIII), 186 fls.

Coleman, Janet. *Ancient and Medieval Memories: Studies in the Reconstruction of the Past.* Cambridge: Cambridge University Press, 1992.

Colgrave, Bertram, ed. *The Life of Bishop Wilfrid by Eddius Stephanus.* Cambridge: Cambridge University Press, 1927.

———. *Vita S. Cuthberti auctore anonymo.* In *Two Lives of Saint Cuthbert*, edited by Bertram Colgrave, 60–139. Cambridge: Cambridge University Press, 1940.

Collis, Louise. *Memoirs of a Medieval Woman: The Life and Times of Margery Kempe.* 1964. Reprint, New York: Colophon-Harper, 1983.

The Columbia Encyclopedia. 6th ed., s.v. "Juliana of Norwich." Accessed May 5, 2008. http://www.infoplease.com/ce6/people/A0826735.html.

Contreni, John. "The Carolingian Renaissance: Education and Literary Culture." In vol. 2 of *The New Cambridge Medieval History*, edited by Rosamond McKitterick, 709–57. Cambridge: Cambridge University Press, 1995.

Coon, Lynda L. *Sacred Fictions: Holy Women and Hagiography in Late Antiquity.* Philadelphia: University of Pennsylvania Press, 1997.

Cotton Tiberius D.iii. Fos. 179v–186r. British Library, London.

Cotton Tiberius E.i. Part II. Fos. 11v–13v. British Library, London.

Crane, Susan. "Anglo-Norman Cultures in England, 1066–1460." In *The Cambridge History of Medieval English Literature*, edited by David Wallace, 35–60. Cambridge: Cambridge University Press, 1999.

Crawford, Barbara. "Norse Earls and Scottish Bishops in Caithness: A Clash of Cultures." In *The Viking Age in Orkney, Caithness and the North Atlantic: Select Papers from the Eleventh Viking Congress, Thurso and Kirkwall, 22 August–1 September 1989*, edited by Colleen E. Batey, Judith Jesch, and Christopher D. Morris, 129–47. Edinburgh: Edinburgh University Press for Centre for Continuing Education, University of Aberdeen and Department of Archaeology, University of Glasgow, 1993.

Crocker, Richard L. *The Early Medieval Sequence.* Berkeley: University of California Press, 1977.

———. *Studies in Medieval Music Theory and the Early Sequence.* Brookfield, VT: Variorum, 1997.

Cross, J. E. "The Influence of Irish Texts and Traditions on the Old English Martyrology." *Proceedings of the Royal Irish Academy* 91, section C (1981): 173–92.

Cubitt, Catherine. "Memory and Narrative in the Cult of Early Anglo-Saxon Saints." In *The Uses of the Past in the Early Middle Ages*, edited by Yitzhak Hen and Matthew Innes, 29–66. Cambridge: Cambridge University Press, 2000.

———. "Monastic Memory and Identity in Early Anglo-Saxon England." In *Social Identity in Early Medieval Britain*, edited by William O. Frazer and Andrew Tyrell, 253–76. New York: Leicester University Press, 2000.

Curtis, Geoffrey. "Mother Julian of Norwich: Two Kinds of Marriage." *Mystics Quarterly* 8 (1982): 62–71.

Curtius, Ernst R. *European Literature and the Latin Middle Ages.* 3rd ed. Translated by Willard R. Trask. Bolligen Series 36. Princeton, NJ: Princeton University Press, 1990.

Dalton, Paul. "Scottish Influence on Durham 1066–1214." In Rollason, Harvey, and Prestwich, *Anglo-Norman Durham*, 340–52.

Daniel, Walter. *The Life of Aelred of Rievaulx and the Letter to Maurice*. Edited and translated by F. M. Powicke, introduction by Marsha L. Dutton. Kalamazoo, MI: Cistercian Publications, 1994.

Davis, Carmel Bendon. *Mysticism and Space: Spatiality in the Works of Richard Rolle, "The Cloud of Unknowing" Author, and Julian of Norwich*. Washington, DC: Catholic University of America, 2008.

Decarreaux, Jean. *Les moines et la civilisation*. Paris: Arthaud, 1962.

Delooz, Pierre. "Towards a Sociological Study of Canonized Sainthood in the Catholic Church." Translated by Jane Hodgkin. In *Saints and Their Cults: Studies in Religious Sociology, Folklore, and History*, edited by Stephen Wilson, 189–216. Cambridge: Cambridge University Press, 1983.

Despres, Denise L. "Franciscan Spirituality: Vision and the Authority of Scripture." PhD diss., Indiana University, 1985.

―――. "The Meditative Art of Scriptural Interpolation in *The Book of Margery Kempe*." *Downside Review* 106 (October 1988): 253–63.

D'Evelyn, Charlotte, and Anna J. Mill, eds. *The South English Legendary*. EETS. London: Oxford University Press, 1956.

Dias, Maria da Conceição Mateus, and Clara Maria Teixeira Simões Duarte, eds. "Vida de Santa Maria Egipcíaca." In Ivo Castro et al., "Vidas de santos de um manuscrito alcobacense (II)." *Revista Lusitana*, n.s., 5 (1984–85), 56–71.

Dias, Maria Julieta M., and Paulo M. Pinto. *A verdadeira História de Maria Madalena*. Cruz Quebrada, Portugal: Casa das Letras–Editorial Notícias, 2006.

Díaz y Díaz, M. *Valerio del Bierzo: Su persona: Su obra*. Léon: Centro de Estudios e Investigación "San Isidoro," Caja España de Inversiones, Archivo Histórico Diocesano, 2006.

Dinshaw, Carolyn. *Chaucer's Sexual Poetics*. Madison: University of Wisconsin Press: 1989.

Dodds, M. H. "The Little Book of the Birth of St Cuthbert." *Archaeologia Aeliana*, 4th ser., 6 (1929): 52–94.

Donaldson, Gordon, ed. *Scottish Historical Documents*. New York: Barnes and Noble, 1970.

Dowden, John. *The Bishops of Scotland*. Edited by Dr. J. Maitland Thomson. Glasgow: J. MacLehose, 1912.

Doyère, Pierre. "Gertrude the Great." In *New Catholic Encyclopedia*, 450–451. New York: McGraw-Hill, 1967–79.

Dronke, Peter. *Abelard and Heloise in Medieval Testimonies*. Glasgow: University of Glasgow Press, 1976.

―――. *Women Writers of the Middle Ages: A Critical Study of Texts from Perpetua to Marguerite Porete*. Cambridge: Cambridge University Press, 1984.

Duncan, A. A. M. *Scotland: The Making of the Kingdom*. Vol. 1 of *The Edinburgh History of Scotland*. 1975. Reprint, Edinburgh: Mercat Press, 2000.

―――. "Yes, the Earliest Scottish Charters." *Scottish Historical Review* 78 (1999): 1–35.

Einhard. *Einhardi Vita Karoli Magni.* Edited by O. Holder-Egger. MGH. Scriptores rerum Germanicarum in usum scholarum 25. Hanover, Germany: Hahn, 1911.

———. "Life of Charlemagne." In *Two Lives of Charlemagne,* translated and edited by David Ganz, 15–44. New York: Penguin, 2008.

Eisler, Riane. *The Chalice and the Blade.* San Francisco: Harper, 1987.

Elkins, Sharon. "Gertrude the Great and the Virgin Mary." *Church History* 66, no. 4 (1997): 720–34.

Elliott, Dyan. *Proving Woman: Female Spirituality and Inquisitional Culture in the Later Middle Ages.* Princeton, NJ: Princeton University Press, 2004.

Erler, Mary, and Maryanne Kowaleski, eds. *Women and Power in the Middle Ages.* Athens: University of Georgia Press, 1988.

Évagre Le Pontique. *Traité pratique ou le moine.* Vol. 1. Edited by Antoine Guillaumont and Claire Guillaumont. Paris: Cerf, 1971.

Evans, Ruth, Andrew Taylor, Nicholas Watson, and Jocelyn Wogan-Browne. "The Notion of Vernacular Theory." In *The Idea of the Vernacular: An Anthology of Middle English Literary Theory, 1280–1520,* edited by Jocelyn Wogan-Browne, Nicholas Watson, Andrew Taylor, and Ruth Evans, 314–330. University Park: Pennsylvania State University Press, 1999.

Fairfax 6. Fos. 164r–173v. Bodleian Library, Oxford.

Farmer, Sharon. "Persuasive Voices: Clerical Images of Medieval Wives." *Speculum* 6, nos. 1–3 (1986): 517–43.

Fawtier-Jones, E. C. "Les Vies de sainte Catherine d'Alexandrie en ancien français." *Romania* 56 (1930): 80–104.

Filho, Américo Venâncio Lopes Machado. *Um "Flos Sanctorum" do século XIV: Edições, glossário e estudo lingüístico.* Vol. 1. Salvador: Universidade Federal da Bahia, Instituto de Letras, 2003.

Finke, Laurie. *Feminist Theory, Women's Writing.* Reading Women Writing. Ithaca, NY: Cornell University Press, 1992.

Finucane, Ronald C. *Miracles and Pilgrims: Popular Beliefs in Medieval England.* 1977. Reprint, New York: St. Martin's Press, 1995.

———. "The Posthumous Miracles of Godric of Finchale." *Transactions of the Architectural and Archaeological Society of Durham and Northumberland* 3 (1975): 47–50.

Flos Sanctorum em linguagẽ portugues. Lisbon: Herman Campos e Roberto Rebelo, 1513. Lisbon: Biblioteca Nacional, Res. 157 A.

Folz, Robert. *Les saintes reines du moyen âge en occident, VIe–VIIIe siècles.* Brussels: Société des Bollandistes, 1992.

Forbes, A. P., ed. *The Lives of St Ninian and St Kentigern.* The Historians of Scotland 5. Edinburgh: Edmundston and Douglas, 1874.

Forbes-Leith, W., ed. *The Gospel Book of St Margaret: A Facsimile.* Edinburgh, 1896.

Foreville, Raymonde. "Les 'Miracula S. Thomae Cantuariensis.'" In *Actes du 97e Congrès national des sociétés savantes, Nantes, 1972, section de philolgie et d'histoire jusqu'à 1610,* 443–68. Paris: Bibliothèque Nationale, 1979.

Foster, Tara. "Clemence of Barking: Reshaping the Legend of Saint Catherine of Alexandria." *Women's Writing* 12, no. 1 (2005): 13–27.

Frantzen, Allen J. *The Literature of Penance in Anglo-Saxon England.* New Brunswick, NJ: Rutgers University Press, 1983.

Freire, José Geraldes. *A versão latina por Pascásio de Dume dos "Apophtegmata Patrum."* 2 vols. Coimbra, Portugal: Instituto de Estudos Clássicos, 1971.

Frighetto, Renan. "O modelo de *vir sanctus* segundo o pensamento de Valério do Bierzo." *Helmantica* 158, nos. 145–46 (1997): 59–79.

Fulton, Rachel. *From Judgment to Passion: Devotion to Christ and the Virgin Mary, 800–1200.* New York: Columbia University Press, 2002.

Gameson, Richard. "The Gospels of Margaret of Scotland and the Literacy of an Eleventh-Century Queen." In *Women and the Book: Assessing the Visual Evidence,* edited by Jane H. M. Taylor and Lesley Smith, 148–71. Toronto: University of Toronto Press, 1999.

Gardiner, Dorothy. *English Girlhood at School: A Study of Women's Education through Twelve Centuries.* London: Oxford University Press, 1929.

Geary, Patrick J. *Furta Sacra: Theft of Relics in the Middle Ages.* Rev. ed. Princeton, NJ: Princeton University Press, 1991.

———. *Phantoms of Remembrance: Memory and Oblivion at the End of the First Millennium.* Princeton, NJ: Princeton University Press, 1994.

"Gertrude d'Helfta." In *Dictionnaire de spiritualité, ascétique et mystique, doctrine et histoire,* 5:331–339. Paris: Beauchesne, 1937.

Gertrud the Great of Helfta, St. *The Herald of God's Loving Kindness, Books One and Two.* Translated by Alexandra Barratt. Kalamazoo, MI: Cistercian Publications, 1991.

———. *Œuvres spirituelles I: Les exercices.* Translated and edited by Jacques Hourlier and Albert Schmitt. Sources Chrétiennes 127. Paris: Les Éditions du Cerf, 1967.

———. *Œuvres spirituelles, Le héraut, livres I–II,* 2.20.14. Translated by Pierre Doyère. Paris: Les Éditions du Cerf, 1968.

———. *Spiritual Exercises.* Translated by Gertrud Jaron Lewis and Jack Lewis. Kalamazoo, MI: Cistercian Publications, 1989.

Gertz-Robinson, Genelle. "Stepping into the Pulpit? Women's Preaching in *The Book of Margery Kempe* and *The Examinations of Anne Askew.*" In *Voices in Dialogue: Reading Women in the Middle Ages,* edited by Linda Olson and Kathryn Kerby-Fulton, 459–482. Notre Dame, IN: University of Notre Dame Press, 2005.

Gies, Frances, and Joseph Gies. *Women in the Middle Ages.* New York: Perennial-Harper, 1978.

Gilson, Etienne. *Heloise and Abelard.* Translated by L. K. Stook. Ann Arbor: University of Michigan Press, 1960.

Glassoe, Marion. *English Medieval Mystics: Games of Faith.* London: Longman, 1993.

Glenn, Cheryl. "Author, Audience, and Autobiography: Rhetorical Technique in *The Book of Margery Kempe.*" *College English* 53 (September 1992): 540–53.

———. "Medieval Literacy outside the Academy: Popular Practice and Individual Technique." *College Composition and Communication* 44 (December 1993): 497–508.

————. "Popular Literacy in the Middle Ages: *The Book of Margery Kempe*." In *Popular Literacy: Studies in Cultural Practices and Poetics*, edited by John Trimbur, 56–73. Pittsburgh Series in Composition, Literacy, and Culture. Pittsburgh: University of Pittsburgh Press, 2001.

————. "Re-examining *The Book of Margery Kempe*: A Rhetoric of Autobiography." In *Reclaiming Rhetorica*, edited by Andrea Lunsford, 53–72. Pittsburgh: University of Pittsburgh Press, 1995.

————. *Rhetoric Retold: Regendering the Tradition from Antiquity through the Renaissance*. Carbondale: Southern Illinois University Press, 1997.

Godman, Peter. "The Poetic Hunt." In *Charlemagne's Heir: New Perspectives on the Reign of Louis the Pious (814–840)*, edited by Peter Godman and Roger Collins, 565–89. Oxford: Clarendon Press, 1990.

————, ed. *Poetry of the Carolingian Renaissance*. Norman: University of Oklahoma Press, 1985.

Goodich, Michael. *Miracles and Wonders: The Development of the Concept of Miracle, 1150–1350*. Burlington, VT: Ashgate Publishing, 2007.

————. "The Politics of Canonization in the Thirteenth Century: Lay and Mendicant Saints." In *Saints and Their Cults*, edited by Stephen Wilson, 169–87. Cambridge: Cambridge University Press, 1983.

————. *Vita Perfecta: The Ideal of Sainthood in the Thirteenth Century*. Stuttgart: A. Hiersemann, 1982.

The Gospel Book of Queen Margaret. MS. Lat. Liturgy. Fol. 5. Bodleian Library, Oxford.

Graef, Hilda. "From Other Lands: St. Gertrude, Mystical Flowering of the Liturgy." *Orate Fratres* 20 (1945–46): 171–74.

————. "Liturgy and Mental Prayer in the Life of Saint Gertrude." *Sponsa Regis* 32, no. 1 (September 1960): 1–5.

————. *Mary: A History of Doctrine and Devotion*. 2 vols. New York: Sheed and Ward, 1963.

————. "Méditation et célébration: A propos du mémorial de sainte Gertrude." In *La liturgie et les paradoxes Chrétiens*, edited by Jean LeClercq. Lex Orandi 36. Paris, 1963.

Grant, Alexander. "The Province of Ross and the Kingdom of Alba." In *Alba: Celtic Scotland in the Middle Ages*, edited by E. J. Cowan and R. A. McDonald, 88–126. 2000. Reprint, Edinburgh: John Donald, 2005.

Green, D. H. *Women Readers in the Middle Ages*. Cambridge: Cambridge University Press, 2007.

Green, Roger P. H. "Moduin's 'Eclogues' and the 'Paderborn Epic.'" *Mittellateinisches Jahrbuch* 16 (1981): 43–53.

Gregory the Great, St. *Dialogues*. Edited by Adalbert de Vogüé. Sources Chrétiennes 251, 260, 265. Paris: Les Éditions du Cerf, 1978–80.

Grosjean, P. "The Alleged Irish Origin of St Cuthbert." In *The Relics of Saint Cuthbert*, edited by C. F. Battiscombe, 144–54. Oxford: Printed for the Dean and Chapter of Durham Cathedral at the University Press, 1956.

Grotans, Anna A. *Reading in Medieval St. Gall*. Cambridge Studies in Palaeography and Codicology 13. Cambridge: Cambridge University Press, 2006.

Guy, Jean-Claude, ed. *Les apophtegmes des pères: collection systématique: chapitres I–IX.* 3 vols. Sources Chrétiennes 387. Paris: Éditions du Cerf, 1993.

———, ed. *Os Padres do deserto.* Lisbon: Editorial Estampa, 1991.

Hagstrum, Jean. *The Sister Arts: The Tradition of Literary Pictorialism and English Poetry from Dryden to Gray.* Chicago: University of Chicago Press, 1987.

Hansen, Elisabeth. "A Vision of Her Place: Julian of Norwich and the Contemplative's Role in the Christian Community." Master's thesis, University of Wyoming, 2007.

Heene, Katrien. "Hagiography and Gender: A Tentative Case-Study on Thomas of Cantimpré." In *"Scribere sanctorum gesta": Recueil d'études d'hagiographie médiévale offert à Guy Philippart,* edited by Étienne Renard, Michel Trigalet, Xavier Hermand, and Paul Bertrand, 109–23. Turnhout, Belgium: Brepols, 2005.

Heinrich, Sister Mary Pia. *The Canonesses and Education in the Early Middle Ages.* PhD diss., Catholic University of America, 1924.

Hennessy, William M., and Bartholomew MacCarthy, eds. *Annals of Ulster.* Dublin: Printed for H. M. Stationery Office by A. Thom and Co., 1887–1901.

Hen, Yitzhak. "The Annals of Metz and the Merovingian Past." In *The Uses of the Past in the Early Middle Ages,* edited by Yitzhak Hen and Matthew Innes, 175–90. Cambridge: Cambridge University Press, 2000.

Hildegard of Bingen. *Causae et curae.* Edited by Paulus Kaiser. Leipzig: Teubner, 1903.

———. *Scivias.* Translated by Columba Hart and Jane Bishop. The Classics of Western Spirituality. New York: Paulist Press, 1990.

Hirschfield, Jane, ed. *Women in Praise of the Sacred: 43 Centuries of Spiritual Poetry by Women.* New York: HarperPerennial, 1995.

Hollander, John. "The Poetics of Ekphrasis." *Word & Image* 4 (1988): 209–19.

Hughes, Kathleen. "Some Aspects of Irish Influence on Early English Private Prayer." *Studia Celtica* 5 (1970): 48–61.

Huyskens, A. *Der sogenannte Libellus de dictis quattor ancillarum s. Elisabeth confectus.* Munich and Kempten, Germany: Kempten Kösel, 1911.

———. "Die Schriften über die heilige Elisabeth von Thüringen." In vol. 3 of *Die Wundergeschichten des Caesarius von Heisterbach,* edited by Alfons Hilka, 329–90. Bonn: Hanstein, 1937.

———. *Quellenstudien zur Geschichte der hl. Elisabeth Landgräfin von Thüringen.* Marburg, Germany: N. G. Elwert, 1908.

Ireland, Colin. "Penance and Prayer in Water: An Irish Practice in Northumbrian Hagiography." *Cambrian Medieval Celtic Studies* 34 (1997): 51–66.

Isidore of Seville. *Sententiae.* In *Patrologia latina,* edited by J.-P. Migne. Vol. 83. Paris: Migne, 1844–45.

Jacquart, Danielle, and Claude Alexandre Thomasset. *Sexuality and Medicine in the Middle Ages.* Princeton, NJ: Princeton University Press, 1988.

Jager, Eric. *The Book of the Heart.* Chicago: University of Chicago Press, 2000.

Jantzen, Grace. *Power, Gender, and Christian Mysticism.* Cambridge: Cambridge University Press, 1995.

Jerome, St. *The Life of Paulus the First Hermit.* Translated by W. H. Fremantle, G. Lewis, and W. G. Martley. Nicene and Post-Nicene Fathers, 2nd Series, vol. 6. Edited by Philip Schaff and Henry Wace. Buffalo, NY: Christian Literature Publishing Co., 1893. http://www.newadvent.org/fathers/3008.htm.

Jocelin of Furness. *Vita S. Waldevi.* Edited by Guilelmus Cuperus. In *Acta Sanctorum.* vol. 1 for August, 248–76. Brussels and Antwerp: Societé des Bollandistes, 1733.

John of Fordun. *Johannis de Fordun Chronica Gentis Scotorum.* Edited by William F. Skene. Edinburgh: Edmonston and Douglas, 1871. Translated as *John of Fordun's Chronicle of the Scottish Nation (1872).* Translated by Felix J. H. Skene. Edited by William F. Skene. Edinburgh: Edmonston and Douglas, 1872.

John of Salisbury. *Policraticus.* Edited by Clemens C. I. Webb. Oxford: Clarendon Press, 1909.

Johnson, Ella. "Bodily Language in the Spiritual Exercises of Gertrud the Great of Helfta." *Magistra* 14, no. 1 (2008): 79–107.

Jones, Paul J. *Prologue and Epilogue in Old French Lives of Saints Before 1400.* Philadelphia: University of Pennsylvania Press, 1933.

Julian of Norwich. *A Book of Showings to the Anchoress Julian of Norwich.* Edited by Edmund Colledge and James Walsh. 2 vols. Studies and Texts 35. Toronto: Pontifical Institute of Mediaeval Studies, 1978.

———. *The Writings of Julian of Norwich: "A Vision Showed to a Devout Woman" and "A Revelation of Love."* Edited by Nicholas Watson and Jacqueline Jenkins. University Park: Pennsylvania State University Press, 2005.

Jungmann, Josef. *The Mass of the Roman Rite: Its Origins and Development (Missarum Sollemnia).* Translated by F. A. Brunner. 2 vols. New York: Benzinger, 1951, 1955.

Karolus Magnus et Leo Papa. Edited by Ernst Dümmler. MGH Poetae Latini Aevi Carolini 1. 1881. Reprint, Zurich: Weidmann, 1964.

Kay, Sarah, and Miri Rubin, eds. *Framing Medieval Bodies.* Manchester: Manchester University Press, 1996.

Keene, Catherine. *Saint Margaret, Queen of the Scots: Her Life and Memory.* PhD diss., Central European University, 2011.

Kempe, Margery. *The Book of Margery Kempe.* Edited by Sanford Brown Meech and Hope Emily Allen. Early English Text Society. London: Oxford University Press, 1940.

———. *The Book of Margery Kempe.* Edited by W. Butler-Bowden. London: Oxford University Press, 1940.

———. *The Book of Margery Kempe: A New Translation, Contexts, Criticism.* Translated and edited by Lynn Staley. New York: Norton, 2001.

Kętrzyński, Wojciech, ed. *Vita sancti Stanislai cracoviensis episcopi (Vita maior) auctore fratre Vincentio OFP.* In *Monumenta Poloniae Historica,* edited by Wojciech Kętrzyński, 4:319–438. Lviv, Ukraine: Nakładem Academii Umiejętności w Krakowie, 1884.

Kieckhefer, Richard. "Convention and Conversion: Patterns in Late Medieval Piety." *Church History* 67, no. 1 (1998): 32–51.

Kieckhefer, Richard. *Unquiet Souls: Fourteenth-Century Saints and Their Religious Milieu*. Chicago: University of Chicago Press, 1984.

King, Sallie B. "Two Epistemological Models for the Interpretation of Mysticism." *Journal of the American Academy of Religion* 56, no. 2 (1988): 257–79.

Klaniczay, Gábor. "Dreams and Visions in Medieval Miracle Accounts." In *The "Vision Thing": Studying Divine Intervention*, edited by William A. Christian Jr. and Gábor Klaniczay, 37–64. Budapest: Collegium Budapest Workshop Series 18, 2009.

———. *Holy Rulers and Blessed Princesses: Dynastic Cults in Medieval Central Europe*. Translated by Éva Pálmai. Cambridge: Cambridge University Press, 2002.

———. "Proving Sanctity in the Canonization Process (Saint Elizabeth and Saint Margaret of Hungary)." In *Procès de Canonisation au Moyen Âge: Aspects juridiques et religieux—Medieval Canonization Processes: Legal and Religious Aspects*, edited by Gábor Klaniczay, 117–48. Collection de L'École française de Rome 340. Rome: École française de Rome, 2004.

Kleinberg, Aviad M. *Prophets in Their Own Country: Living Saints and the Making of Sainthood in the Later Middle Ages*. Chicago: Chicago University Press, 1992.

Krieger, Murray. *Ekphrasis: The Illusion of the Natural Sign*. Baltimore: Johns Hopkins University Press, 1992.

Kruger, Steven F. *Dreaming in the Middle Ages*. 1992. Reprint, Cambridge: Cambridge University Press, 2005.

Lapidge, Michael. *Anglo-Latin Literature, 600–899*. 2 vols. London: Hambledon Press, 1996.

Laporte, Jean-Pierre. *Le tresor des saints de Chelles*. Chelles, France: Societe archeologique et historique de Chelles, 1988.

Lawrie, Archibald C. *Early Scottish Charters prior to 1153*. Glasgow: James MacLehose and Sons, 1905.

Law, Vivien. *Grammar and Grammarians in the Early Middle Ages*. Longman Linguistics Library. New York: Longman, 1997.

Leclercq, Jean. "Liturgy and Mental Prayer in the Life of Saint Gertrude." *Sponsa Regis* 32, no. 1 (September 1960): 1–5.

Lees, Clare A. *Tradition and Belief: Religious Writing in Late Anglo-Saxon England*. Medieval Cultures 19. Minneapolis: University of Minnesota Press, 1999.

Legge, M. Dominica. *Anglo-Norman Literature and Its Background*. Oxford: Clarendon Press, 1963.

Le Goff, Jacques. *The Invention of Purgatory*. Translated by Arthur Goldhammer. Chicago: University of Chicago Press, 1986.

LeVert, Laurelle. "'Crucifye hem, Crucifye hem': The Subject and Affective Response in Middle English Passion Narratives." *Essays in Medieval Studies* 14 (1997): 73–90.

Lewis, Gertrud Jaron. "Introduction." In *Gertrud the Great of Helfta: Spiritual Exercises*, translated by Gertrud J. Lewis and Jack Lewis, 1–18. Kalamazoo, MI: Cistercian Publications, 1989.

Lewis, Katherine. *The Cult of St Katherine of Alexandria in Late Medieval England*. Suffolk, UK: Boydell and Brewer, 2000.

Leyenda de los santos. Burgos, Spain: Juan de Burgos, 1500. London: British Library; IB 53312.

Limberis, Visiliki. *Divine Heiress: The Virgin Mary and the Creation of Christian Constantinople*. New York: Routledge, 1994.

Lochrie, Karma. *Margery Kempe and Translations of the Flesh*. Philadelphia: University of Pennsylvania Press, 1991.

Lomperis, Linda, and Sarah Stanbury, eds. *Feminist Approaches to the Body in Medieval Literature*. New Cultural Studies. Philadelphia: University of Pennsylvania Press, 1993.

Love, Nicholas. *The Mirror of the Blessed Life of Jesus Christ: A Reading Text by Nicholas Love*. Edited by Michael G. Sargent. Exeter: University of Exeter Press, 2004.

MacBain, William. "The Literary Apprenticeship of Clemence of Barking." *Journal of the Australasian Universities Language and Literature Association* 9 (1958): 3–22.

Machado, Ana M. "Desocultações da intimidade na *Vida dos Padres do Deserto*." *Romance Philology* 65, no. 1 (Spring 2011): 107–20.

———. "Du Carnaval au Carême—corps et renoncement dans l'hagiographie médiévale." In *O Carnaval na Idade Média: Discursos, imagens, realidades*, edited by Carlos F Clamote Carreto, 149–66. Angra do Heroísmo, Portugal: Instituto Açoriano de Cultura, 2008.

———. "A representação do pecado na hagiografia medieval: Heranças de uma espiritualidade eremítica." PhD diss., Faculdade de Letras da Universidade de Coimbra, 2006.

Maya Sánchez, A. *Vitas sanctorum patrum emeretensium*. Turnhout, Belgium: Brepols, 1992.

McAvoy, Liz H. *Authority and the Female Body in the Writings of Julian of Norwich and Margery Kempe*. Cambridge, UK: D. S. Brewer, 2004.

McDonald, R. Andrew. *Kingdom of the Isles: Scotland's Western Seaboard c. 1100–c. 1336*. 1997. Reprint, Edinburgh: John Donald, 2008.

———. *Outlaws of Medieval Scotland: Challenges to the Canmore Kings, 1058–1266*. Phantassie, East Linton, Scotland: Tuckwell Press, 2003.

McFadden, George. "The Life of Waldef and Its Author, Jocelin of Furness." *Innes Review* 6 (1955): 5–13.

McInerney, Maud B. *Eloquent Virgins from Thecla to Joan of Arc*. New York: Palgrave Macmillan, 2003.

McKitterick, Rosamond. *Books, Scribes and Learning in the Frankish Kingdoms, 6th–9th Centuries*. Aldershot, UK: Ashgate, 1994.

———. *History and Memory in the Carolingian World*. Cambridge: Cambridge University Press, 2004.

———. "Nuns' Scriptoria in England and Francia in the Eighth Century." *Francia* 19 (1992): 1–35.

McNamara, Jo Ann. *Sainted Women of the Dark Ages*. Durham, NC: Duke University Press, 1992.

Melo, A. F. de Ataíde e. *Inventário dos códices Alcobacenses*. Vol. 5. Lisbon: Biblioteca Nacional de Lisboa, 1932.

Metcalfe, W. M., ed. *Pinkerton's Lives of the Scottish Saints.* 2 vols. Paisley, UK: Alexander Gardner, 1889.

Meyer, Kuno, ed. "Echtra Nerai." *Revue celtique* 10 (1889): 212–28.

Meyer, Paul. "Légendes hagiographiques en français." *Histoire Littéraire de la France* 33 (1906): 342–44.

Minnis, Alastair. "Affection and Imagination in *The Cloud of Unknowing* and Hilton's *Scale of Perfection.*" *Traditio* 39 (1983): 323–66.

Mitchell, Allan. *Ethics and Exemplary Narrative in Chaucer and Gower.* New York: Palgrave Macmillan, 2009.

Mitchell, W. J. T. *Picture Theory: Essays on Visual and Verbal Representation.* Chicago: University of Chicago Press, 1994.

Molinari, P. *Julian of Norwich, the Teachings of the Fourteenth-Century Mystic.* London: Chapman, 1985.

Mooney, Catherine M. *Gendered Voices: Medieval Saints and Their Interpreters.* Philadelphia: University of Pennsylvania Press, 1999.

———. "*Imitatio Christi* or *Imitatio Mariae*? Clare of Assisi and Her Interpreters." In *Gendered Voices: Medieval Saints and Their Interpreters*, edited by Catherine M. Mooney, 52–77. Philadelphia: University of Pennsylvania Press, 1999.

Morse, Mary. "'Take and Bren Hir': Lollardy as Conversion Motif in *The Book of Margery Kempe.*" *Mystics Quarterly* 29, nos. 1–2 (March–June 2003): 24–44.

Mountford, Roxanne. *The Gendered Pulpit: Preaching in American Protestant Spaces.* Edited by Cheryl Glenn and Shirley Wilson Logan. Studies in Rhetorics and Feminisms. Carbondale: Southern Illinois University Press, 2003.

MS II 2097. Fos. 1r–17v. Biblioteca del Palacio Real, Madrid.

Musurillo, Herbert. *The Acts of the Christian Martyrs.* Oxford Early Christian Texts. Oxford: Clarendon Press, 1972.

Nagy, Joseph Falaky. "Close Encounters of the Traditional Kind in Medieval Irish Literature." In *Celtic Folklore and Christianity*, edited by Patrick Ford, 129–49. Santa Barbara, CA: McNally and Loftin, 1983.

Neff, Amy. "The Pain of *Compassio*: Mary's Labor at the Foot of the Cross." *Art Bulletin* 80, no. 2 (1998): 254–73.

Nelson, Janet. *Courts, Elites, and Gendered Power in the Early Middle Ages.* Aldershot, UK: Ashgate, 2007.

———. *The Frankish World, 750–900.* London: Hambledon, 1996.

———. "Perceptions du Pouvoir chez les Historiennes du Haut Moyen Âge." In *Les Femmes au Moyen Âge*, edited by M. Rouche, 77–87. Maubeuge, France: Maulde et Renou-Sambre, 1990.

———. "Women at the Court of Charlemagne: A Case of Monstrous Regiment?" In *Medieval Queenship*, edited by John Carmi Parsons, 43–61. London: St. Martin's, 1993.

Neves, Carreira das. *O que é a Bíblia.* Lisbon: Casa das Letras, 2008.

Newman, Barbara. *From Virile Woman to WomanChrist: Studies in Medieval Religion and Literature.* Middle Ages Series. Philadelphia: University of Pennsylvania Press, 1995.

———. *God and the Goddesses: Vision, Poetry, and Belief in the Middle Ages.* Philadelphia: University of Pennsylvania Press, 2003.

————. "Hildegard and Her Hagiographers." In *Gendered Voices: Medieval Saints and Their Interpreters*, edited by Catherine M. Mooney, 16–34. Philadelphia: University of Pennsylvania Press, 1999.

————. "Poet: '*Where the Living Majesty Utters Mysteries.*'" In *Voice of the Living Light: Hildegard of Bingen and Her World*, edited by Barbara Newman, 176–92. Berkeley: University of California Press, 1998.

————. "What Did It Mean to Say 'I Saw'? The Clash between Theory and Practice in Medieval Visionary Culture." *Speculum* 80, no. 1 (January 2005): 1–43.

O'Carroll, Michael. *Corpus Christi: An Encyclopedia of the Eucharist.* Wilmington, DE: Michael Glazier Books, 1988.

Olsen, Birger Munk. "La *Vida de Santa Pelágia*, une traduction portugaise médiévale et son modèle latin." In *Pélagie la pénitente: Métamorphoses d'une légende*, vol. 2 of *La survie dans les littératures européennes*, edited by Pierre Petitmengin, 243–77. Paris: Etudes Augustiniennes, 1984.

Onians, John. *Bearers of Meaning: The Classical Orders in Antiquity, the Middle Ages, and the Renaissance.* Princeton, NJ: Princeton University Press, 1988.

Ouspensky, Leonid, and Vladimir Lossky. *The Meaning of Icons.* Translated by G. E. H. Palmer and E. Kadloubovsky. New York: St. Vladimir's Seminary Press, 1989.

Paciocco, Roberto. *Canonizzazioni e culto dei santi nella christianitas (1198–1302).* Assisi: Porziuncola, 2006.

Pálsson, Hermann, and Paul Edwards, trans. *Orkneyinga Saga: The History of the Earls of Orkney.* New York: Penguin, 1981.

Parker, Annabelle. "'Nothing but Blood Mixed with Phlegm': Desert Mothers' Teachings on the Object of Desire." *Gouden Hoorn: Journal of Byzantium* 5, no. 2 (Winter 1997–98), http://www.isidore-of-seville.com /goudenhoorn/52annabelle.html.

Paschasius Radbertus. "The Life of Saint Adalhard." In *Charlemagne's Cousins: Contemporary Lives of Adalard and Wala*, translated by Allen Cabaniss, 25–82. Syracuse, NY: Syracuse University Press, 1967.

————. *Vita Sancti Adalhardi.* MGH. SS 2, edited by George H. Pertz, 524–32. Hanover, Germany: Hahn, 1829.

Pertz, G. H., ed. *Annales regni Francorum (741–829) qui dicuntur Annales Laurissenses maiores et Einhardi.* Revised by Friedrich Kurze. SRG 6. Hanover, Germany: Hahn, 1895.

Petroff, Elizabeth Alvilda. *Medieval Women's Visionary Literature.* New York: Oxford University Press, 1986.

Pickstock, Catherine. *After Writing: On the Liturgical Consummation of Philosophy.* Oxford: Blackwell Publishers, 1998.

Porcile Santiso, Maria Teresa. "Saint Gertrude and the Liturgy." *Liturgy* 26, no. 3 (1992): 53–84.

Postlewate, Laurie. "Vernacular Hagiography and Lay Piety: Two Old French Adaptations of the Life of Saint Margaret of Antioch." In *Saints: Studies in Hagiography*, edited by Sandro Sticca, 115–30. Binghamton, NY: Medieval and Renaissance Texts and Studies, 1996.

Quintilian. *Institutio oratoria*. Translated and edited by H. E. Butler. Loeb Classical Library. Cambridge, MA: Harvard University Press, 1980.

Raine, James, ed. *Libellus de Ortu Sancti Cuthberti*. Miscellanea Biographica. Surtees Society 8. London and Edinburgh, 1838.

Ratkowitsch, Christina. *Karolus Magnus—alter Aeneas, alter Martinus, alter Iustinus: Zu Intention und Datierung des "Aachener Karlsepos."* Vienna: Verlag der Österreichischen Akademie der Wissenschaften, 1997.

Reames, Sherry L., ed. *Middle English Legends of Women Saints*. TEAMS Middle English Text Series. Kalamazoo: Western Michigan University's Medieval Institute Publications, 2003.

Recanati, Francois. *Oratio Obliqua, Oratio Recta: An Essay on Metarepresentation*. Cambridge, MA: MIT Press, 2000.

Reginald of Durham. *Libellus de Vita et Miraculis S. Godrici, Heremitae de Finchale*. Edited by J. Stevenson. Miscellanea Biographica. Surtees Society, vol. 20. London, 1847.

Renevey, Denis. "Margery's Performing Body: The Translation of Late Medieval Discursive Religious Practices." In *Writing Religious Women: Female Spiritual and Textual Practices in Late Medieval England*, edited by Denis Renevey and Christiana Whitehead, 197–216. Toronto: University of Toronto Press, 2000.

Ritchie, R. L. Græme. *The Normans in Scotland*. Edinburgh: Edinburgh University Press, 1954.

Robertson, Duncan. *The Medieval Saints' Lives: Spiritual Renewal and Old French Literature*. Lexington, KY: French Forum, 1995.

———. "Writing in the Textual Community: Clemence of Barking's Life of Saint Catherine." *French Forum* 21, no. 1 (1996): 5–28.

Robertson, Elizabeth Ann. *Early English Devotional Prose and the Female Audience*. Knoxville: University of Tennessee Press, 1990.

Robinson, J. C., and J. B. Sheppard, eds. *Materials for the History of Thomas Becket, Archbishop of Canterbury*. 7 volumes. London: Longman, 1875–85.

Rollason, David, and Lynda Rollason, eds. *The Durham "Liber Vitae": London, British Library, MS Cotton Domitian A.VII*. 3 vols. London: British Library, 2007.

Rollason, David, Margaret Harvey, and Michael Prestwich, eds. *Anglo-Norman Durham, 1093–1193*. Woodbridge, UK: Boydell Press, 1994.

Rufinus of Aquileia. *Historia Monachorum*. In *Patrologia latina*, edited by J.-P. Migne. Vol. 21. Paris: Migne, 1844–45.

Rupert of Deutz. *Commentaria in Joannem*. In *Patrologia latina*, edited by J.-P. Migne. Vol. 169. Paris: Migne, 1844–45.

Rushforth, Rebecca. *St Margaret's Gospel Book: The Favourite Book of an Eleventh-Century Queen of Scots*. Oxford: Bodleian Library, University of Oxford, 2007.

Russell, Norman, trans. *The Lives of the Desert Fathers: The Historia Monachorum in Aegypto*. Kalamazoo, MI: Cistercian Publications, 1980.

Sahlin, Claire L. *Birgitta of Sweden and the Voice of Prophecy*. Rochester, NY: Bogdell, 2002.

———. "Gender and Prophetic Authority in Birgitta of Sweden's *Revelations*." In *Gender and Text in the Later Middle Ages*, edited by Jane Chance, 69–95. Gainesville: University Press of Florida, 1996.

Salih, Sarah. "Introduction: Saints, Cults, and *Lives* in Late Medieval England." In *A Companion to Middle English Hagiography*, edited by Sarah Salih, 1–23. Cambridge: Boydell and Brewer, 2006.

———. *Versions of Virginity in Late Medieval England.* Cambridge: D. S. Brewer, 2001.

Salisbury, Joyce E. *Perpetua's Passion: The Death and Memory of a Young Roman Woman.* New York: Routledge, 1997.

Sanok, Catherine. *Her Life Historical: Exemplarity and Female Saints' Lives in Late Medieval England.* Philadelphia: University of Pennsylvania Press, 2007.

Schaller, Dieter. "Das Aachener Epos für Karl den Kaiser." *Frühmittelalterliche Studien* 10 (1976): 134–68.

Scharer, Anton. "Charlemagne's Daughters." In *Early Medieval Studies in Memory of Patrick Wormald*, edited by Stephen Baxter, Catherine E. Karkov, Janet L. Nelson, and David Pelteret, 269–82. Farnham, UK: Ashgate, 2009.

Scheck, Helene. *Reform and Resistance: Formations of Female Subjectivity in Early Medieval Ecclesiastical Culture.* Albany, NY: SUNY Press, 2008.

Schiller, Isabella, Dorothea Weber, and Clemens Weidmann. "Sechs Neue Augustinuspredigten Teil 1 Mit Edition Dreier Sermones." *Weiner Studien* 121 (2008): 227–84.

Schönborn, Christoph. *God's Human Face: The Christ-Icon.* Translated by Lothar Krauth. San Francisco: Ignatius Press, 1994.

Seinte Katerine: Re-Edited from MS Bodley 34 and the Other Manuscripts. Edited by S. R. T. O. d'Ardenne and E. J. Dobson. The Early English Text Society, s.s.7. Oxford: Oxford University Press, 1981.

Selman, Rebecca. "Spirituality and Sex Change: *Horologium sapientiae* and *Speculum devotorum*." In *Writing Religious Women: Female Spiritual and Textual Practice in Late Medieval England*, edited by Denis Renevey and Christiania Whitehead, 63–80. Toronto: University of Toronto Press, 2000.

Sharpe, Richard. "Were the Irish Annals Known to a Twelfth-Century Northumbrian Writer?" *Peritia* 2 (1983): 137–39.

Shaw, Francis, ed. *The Dream of Óengus: "Aislinge Óenguso."* Dublin: Browne and Nolan, 1934.

Sheingorn, Pamela, trans. *The Book of Sainte Foy.* Philadelphia: University of Pennsylvania Press, 1995.

Shewring, W. H. *The Passion of Ss. Perpetua and Felicity Mm; a New Edition and Translation of the Latin Text Together with the Sermons of S. Augustine upon These Saints.* London: Sheed and Ward, 1931.

Sigal, Pierre-André. *L'homme et le miracle dans La France médiévale, XIe–XIIe siècle.* Paris: Editions du Cerf, 1985.

Sobral, Cristina Maria Matias. "Santa Maria Egipcíaca em Alcobaça: edição crítica das versões medievais portuguesas da Lenda de Maria Egipcíaca." PhD diss., Faculdade de Letras da Universidade de Lisboa, 1991.

Specht, Henrik. "'Ethopoeia' or Impersonation: A Neglected Species of Medieval Characterization." *Chaucer Review* 21, no. 1 (1986): 1–15.

Staley, Lynn. "Julian of Norwich and the Crisis of Authority." In *The Powers of the Holy: Religion, Politics, and Gender in Late Medieval English Culture*, edited by David Aers and Lynn Staley, 107–78. University Park: Pennsylvania State University Press, 1996.

———. *Margery Kempe's Dissenting Fictions.* University Park: Pennsylvania State University Press, 1994.

Steiner, Wendy. *The Colors of Rhetoric: Problems in the Relation between Modern Literature and Painting.* Chicago: University of Chicago Press, 1982.

Stella, Francesco. "Autore e attribuzioni del 'Karolus Magnus et Leo Papa.'" In *Am Vorabend der Kaiser Krönung: Das Epos "Karolus Magnus et Leo Papa" und der Papstbesuch in Paderborn 799*, edited by Peter Godman et al., 19–33. Berlin: Akademie Verlag, 2002.

Stokes, Charity S. "Margery Kempe: Her Life and the Early History of Her Book." *Mystics Quarterly* 25, nos. 1–2 (March–June 1999): 9–67.

Suso, Henry. *Heinrich Seuses Horologium Sapientiae: Erste Kritische Ausgabe unter Benützung der Vorarbeiten von Dominikus Planzer OP.* Edited by Pius Künzle. Freiburg, Germany: Universitätsverlag, 1977.

Swanson, R. N. *Religion and Devotion in Europe, c. 1215–c. 1515.* Cambridge: Cambridge University Press, 1995.

Symeon of Durham. *Historia Regum.* In *Symeonis monachi Opera Omnia*, edited by Thomas Arnold, 2:3–283. Rolls Series. London, 1882–5.

Taylor, Alice. "Historical Writing in Twelfth- and Thirteenth-Century Scotland: The Dunfermline Compilation." *Historical Research* 83, no. 220 (May 2010): 228–52.

Thornton, Sarah. *Seven Days in the Art World.* New York: W. W. Norton, 2008.

Tiago de Voragine. *Flores seu legendae sanctorum.* Lisbon: Biblioteca Nacional, Alc. 39 (olim ccxcVIII), 358 fls.

Turgot of Durham. *Life of St. Margaret.* In *Acta Sanctorum*, vol. 1 for June 10. Brussels and Antwerp: Societé des Bollandistes, 1966.

———. "The Life of Saint Margaret, Queen of Scotland." In *Ancient Lives of Scottish Saints, Part Two*, translated by W. M. Metcalfe, 297–421. Felinfach, UK: Llanerch Publishers, 1998.

Uitti, Karl D. *Story, Myth, and Celebration in Old French Narrative Poetry, 1050–1200.* Princeton, NJ: Princeton University Press, 1973.

Vagaggini, Cypriano. "The Example of a Mystic: St. Gertrude and Liturgical Spirituality." In *Theological Dimensions of the Liturgy: A General Treatise on the Theology of the Liturgy*, translated by Leonard J. Doyle and W. A. Jurgens, 740–803. Collegeville, MN: Liturgical Press, 1976.

Van Houts, Elizabeth. *Memory and Gender in Medieval Europe 900–1200.* Toronto: University of Toronto Press, 1999.

Vauchez, André. "O Santo." In *O homem medieval*, edited by Jacques Le Goff, 211–32. Lisbon: Editorial Presença, 1990.

———. *La sainteté en occident aux derniers siècles du moyen âge d'après les procès de canonisation et les documents hagiographiques.* Rome: École française de Rome; Paris: Diffusion de Boccard, 1981. Translated as *Sainthood in the Later Middle Ages*, by Jean Birrell. Cambridge: Cambridge University Press, 1997.

"Vida de Tarsis." Edited by Ana Maria Martins. *Revista Lusitana*, n.s., 4 (1982–83): 16–17.

Voaden, Rosalynn. *God's Words, Women's Voices: The Discernment of Spirits in the Writing of Late-Medieval Women Visionaries.* Woodbridge, UK: Boydell and Brewer, 1999.

Voragine, Jacob of. *The Golden Legend: Readings on the Saints,* vol. 2. Translated by William Granger Ryan. Princeton, NJ: Princeton University Press, 1993.

———. *Legenda aurea.* 2nd ed. 2 vols. Edited by Giovanni Paolo Maggioni. Florence: Sismel-Edizioni del Galluzo, 1998.

Waddell, Helen, trans. *The Desert Fathers.* 1936. Reprint, London: Constable and Co., 1994.

Wall, Valerie. "Malcolm III and the Cathedral." In Rollason, Harvey, and Prestwich, *Anglo-Norman Durham,* 325–37.

Ward, Benedicta, trans. *The Desert Fathers: Sayings of the Early Christian Monks.* London: Penguin Books, 2003.

Ward, Benedicta. *Miracles and the Medieval Mind: Theory, Record and Event 1000–1215.* Rev. ed. Philadelphia: University of Pennsylvania Press, 1987.

———. "Traditions of Spiritual Guidance: Spiritual Direction in the Desert Fathers." In *Signs and Wonders: Saints, Miracles and Prayers from the 4th Century to the 14th,* 61–70. 1992. Reprint, Aldershot: Ashgate, 2001.

Waters, Claire. *Angels and Earthly Creatures: Preaching, Performance, and Gender in the Later Middle Ages.* Philadelphia: University of Pennsylvania Press, 2004.

Watson, Nicholas. "The Composition of Julian of Norwich's *Revelation of Love.*" *Speculum* 68, no. 3 (1993): 637–83.

———. "Translation and Self-Canonization in Richard Rolle's *Melos Amoris.*" In *The Medieval Translator: The Theory and Practice of Translation in the Middle Ages,* edited by Roger Ellis, 167–80. Cambridge: D. S. Brewer, 1989.

———. "'Yf Wommen Be Double Naturelly': Remaking 'Woman' in Julian of Norwich's *Revelation of Love.*" *Exemplaria* 8, no. 1 (1996): 1–34.

Watt, D. E. R., et al., eds. and trans. *Scotichronicon by Walter Bower in Latin and English.* 9 vols. Aberdeen and Edinburgh: Aberdeen University Press, 1989–98.

Weissman, Hope P. "Margery Kempe in Jerusalem: *Hysteria compassio* in the Late Middle Ages." In *Acts of Interpretation: The Text in Its Contexts, 700–1600: Essays on Medieval and Renaissance Literature,* edited by Mary J. Carruthers and Elizabeth D. Kirk, 201–17. Norman, OK: Pilgrim, 1982.

Wengier, Francis J. *The Eucharist-Sacrifice.* Milwaukee, WI: Bruce Publishing Co., 1955.

Werner, Karl Ferdinand. "Die Nachkommen Karls des Grossen." In *Karl der Grosse: Lebenswerk und Nachleben,* vol. 4, edited by Wolfgang Braunfels, 403–79. Dusseldorf: Verlag Schwann, 1967.

Whitelock, Dorothy, David C. Douglas, and Susie I. Tucker, eds. *The Anglo-Saxon Chronicle, A Revised Edition.* New Brunswick, NJ: Rutgers University Press, 1961.

Wiesner-Hanks, Merry E., ed. *Gender in History.* 2001. Reprint, Malden, MA: Blackwell, 2005.

Wiethaus, Ulrike. *Maps of Flesh and Light: The Religious Experience of Medieval Women Mystics.* 1st ed. Syracuse, NY: Syracuse University Press, 1993.

Wilson, Katharina M., ed. *Medieval Women Writers*. Athens: University of Georgia Press, 1984.

Witkowska, Aleksandra. "Miracula malopolskie Z XIII i XIV wieku: Studium zrodloznavcze" [Miracles of lesser Poland in the thirteenth and fourteenth centuries: A study of the sources]. *Roczniki Humanistyczne* 2 (1971): 29–161.

Wogan-Browne, Jocelyn. "'Clerc U Lai, Muïne U Dame': Women and Anglo-Norman Hagiography in the Twelfth and Thirteenth Centuries." In *Women and Literature in Britain, 1150–1500*, edited by Carol M. Meale, 61–79. Cambridge: Cambridge University Press, 1993.

———. *Saint's Lives and Women's Literary Culture, 1150–1300: Virginity and Its Authorizations*. Oxford: Oxford University Press, 2001.

———. "Wreaths of Thyme: The Female Translator in Anglo-Norman Hagiography." In vol. 4 of *The Medieval Translator*, edited by Roger Ellis and Ruth Evans, 46–65. Exeter, UK: University of Exeter Press, 1994.

Wright, Charles D. *The Irish Tradition in Old English Literature*. Cambridge: Cambridge University Press, 1993.

Yacobi, Tamar. "The Ekphrastic Model: Forms and Functions." In *Pictures into Words: Theoretical and Descriptive Approaches to Ekphrasis*, edited by Valerie Robillard and Els Jongeneels, 21–34. Amsterdam: VU University Press, 1998.

Yates, Frances A. *The Art of Memory*. Chicago: University of Chicago Press, 1966.

Yoshikawa, Naoe K. *Margery Kempe's Meditations: The Context of Medieval Devotional Literature, Liturgy and Iconography*. Cardiff: University of Wales Press, 2007.

———. "Veneration of Virgin Martyrs in Margery Kempe's Meditation: Influence of the Sarum Liturgy and Hagiography." In *Writing Religious Women: Female Spiritual and Textual Practices in Late Medieval England*, edited by Denis Renevey and Christinia Whitehead, 177–96. Toronto: University of Toronto Press, 2000.

Zumthor, Paul. *Essai de Poétique Médiévale*. Paris: Seuil, 1972.

INDEX